Bob Algozzine   Ann P. Daunic   Stephen W. Smith

Preventing
Problem
Behaviors

Schoolwide Programs
and Classroom Practices

T0064958

Skyhorse Publishing

Skyhorse Publishing books may be purchased in bulk at special discounts for sales promotion, corporate gifts, fund-raising, or educational purposes. Special editions can also be created to specifications. For details, contact the Special Sales Department, Skyhorse Publishing, 307 West 36th Street, 11th Floor, New York, NY 10018 or info@skyhorsepublishing.com.

Skyhorse® and Skyhorse Publishing® are registered trademarks of Skyhorse Publishing, Inc.®, a Delaware corporation.

Visit our website at www.skyhorsepublishing.com.

10 9 8 7 6 5 4 3 2 1

Library of Congress Cataloging-in-Publication Data is available on file.

Cover design by Karine Hovsepian

Print ISBN: 978-1-63220-563-6
Ebook ISBN: 978-1-63220-979-5

Printed in the United States of America

Contents

In memory of a cherished colleague and dear friend, Pam Kay.

Acknowledgments

W e gratefully acknowledge the contributions of the following individuals:

Melody Aldrich, English Teacher
Florence High School
Florence, AZ

Renee Bernhardt, Special Education Facilitator
Cherokee County School District
Canton, GA

DaShonera E. Griffin, Assistant Professor of Exceptional Education
School of Education
Clark Atlanta University
Atlanta, GA

Michael Humphrey, Assistant Professor
Department of Special Education and Early Childhood Studies
Boise State University
Boise, ID

Jane Hunn, Middle-Level Science Teacher
Tippecanoe Valley Middle School
Akron, IN

Erin Jones, Special Education Teacher
Tea Area Elementary School
Tea, SD

Sally Koczan, Science Teacher
Meramec Elementary School
Clayton, MO

Alison Martins, Special Education Teacher
Seven Hills Charter Public School
Worcester, MA

Gregory A. O'Connell, Facilitator/Assistant Principal
Cedar Rapids Community Schools/Grant Wood Elementary School
Cedar Rapids, IA

Cathy Patterson, Elementary Learning Specialist
Walnut Valley Unified School District
Walnut, CA

Laura Peterson, Special Education Teacher
Center School
Nashoba Regional School District
Stow, MA

Diane P. Smith, School Counselor
Port Allegany, PA

Deborah D. Therriault, Special Education Teacher POHI/EI
Clarkston Community Schools
Clarkston, MI

Marta Turner, Staff Development Coordinator
Northwest Regional Education Service District
Hillsboro, OR

About the Authors

Bob Algozzine is a Professor in the Department of Educational Leadership at the University of North Carolina and Project Codirector of the U.S. Department of Education-supported Behavior and Reading Improvement Center. With 25 years of research experience and extensive firsthand knowledge of teaching students classified as seriously emotionally disturbed, Algozzine is a uniquely qualified staff developer, conference speaker, and teacher of behavior management and effective teaching courses. He is active in special education practice as a partner and collaborator with professionals in the Charlotte-Mecklenburg schools in North Carolina and as an editor of several journals focused on special education. Algozzine has written more than 250 manuscripts on special education topics, including many books and textbooks on how to manage emotional and social behavior problems.

Ann P. Daunic is an Associate Scholar in the Department of Special Education, School Psychology, and Early Childhood Studies at the University of Florida. For the past 12 years, she has directed applied research projects focused on the prevention of problem behaviors through school- and classroom-based interventions, including conflict resolution, peer mediation, and instruction in social problem solving. Her interest in preventive interventions for students at risk for school failure reflects an academic background in psychology and her experience as a college counselor for economically and educationally disadvantaged students from the New York City metropolitan area. She has also served as a private high school administrator and guidance counselor, collaborating with teachers and parents to address the social and instructional needs of students with behavioral and academic difficulties. She is currently Director of the Prevention Research Project, a four-year study funded by the Institute of Education Sciences to evaluate the efficacy of a social problem-solving curriculum for fourth- and fifth-grade students. Associated research interests include merging social-emotional and academic learning and the role of social cognition in the self-regulation of emotions and behavior.

 **Stephen W. Smith** is a Professor in the Department of Special Education at the University of Florida (UF). Prior to receiving his PhD in Special Education from the University of Kansas, he was a teacher of special education students for eight years. Dr. Smith teaches graduate courses in the area of emotional and behavioral disorders and research in special education at UF and has conducted multiple federally funded investigations of effective behavior management techniques, including the study of social conflict and the effects of schoolwide peer mediation programs. As the Principal Investigator of a large-scale prevention science research grant funded by the U.S. Department of Education, Institute of Education Sciences (IES), Dr. Smith is investigating the effects of a universal cognitive-behavioral intervention in the form of a social problem-solving curriculum to reduce student aggression and chronic classroom disruption. He has presented his findings and recommendations at numerous state, regional, national, and international professional conferences. While at UF, Dr. Smith has received three teaching awards and a University Research Award, and he has served twice as a UF Research Foundation Professor. He is a member of the IES Social and Behavioral Education Scientific Research Review Panel and is a member of the Executive Board of the Division for Research, Council for Exceptional Children.

About the Contributors

Kate Algozzine is currently working as a consultant with the National Center for Research on Early Childhood Education (NCRECE) Professional Development Study. She recently was a Research Associate and Coordinator of School-Wide Behavior Intervention for the Behavior and Reading Improvement Center at the University of North Carolina at Charlotte. She has been a general education and special education classroom teacher and college instructor for more than 30 years in public and private schools and universities in Florida and North Carolina. Educational materials that she has published are used in teacher preparation courses around the country. She has been a featured speaker at local, state, national, and international professional conferences and is widely recognized as an expert on effective Schoolwide Behavior Intervention.

Jeffrey P. Bakken, PhD, is Professor and Chair of the Department of Special Education at Illinois State University. He has a bachelor's degree in Elementary Education from the University of Wisconsin—LaCrosse and graduate degrees in the area of Special Education—Learning Disabilities from Purdue University. Dr. Bakken is a teacher, consultant, and scholar. His specific areas of interest include transition, teacher effectiveness, assessment, learning strategies, and technology. He has written more than 80 academic publications, including a book, journal articles, chapters, monographs, reports, and proceedings; and he has made over 190 presentations at local, state, regional, national, and international levels. Dr. Bakken has received the College of Education and the University Research Initiative Award, the College of Education Outstanding College Researcher Award, the College of Education Outstanding College Teacher Award, and the Outstanding University Teacher Award from Illinois State University. Additionally, he is on the editorial boards of many scholarly publications, including *Multicultural Learning and Teaching* and *Remedial and Special Education*. Recently, he was chosen as the Newsletter Editor for the Council on Children with Behavioral Disorders. Through his work, he has committed himself toward improving teachers' knowledge and techniques, as well as services for students with exceptionalities and their families.

Rob Bartolotta is a doctoral candidate in the University of Maryland's Department of Special Education. Previous to his doctoral work, he taught in various restrictive settings, including a residential treatment center, a regional alternative educational program, and a juvenile detention facility. These experiences have contributed to his research interest in support programs for at-risk students and interventions designed to facilitate their reintegration into less restrictive settings.

Douglas Cheney, PhD, is Professor of Special Education at the University of Washington—Seattle (UW), where he teaches courses in classroom and behavior management, functional behavioral assessment, and social skills instruction. He has 35 years' experience in special education and currently directs the UW's master's program with a specialization in emotional or behavioral disabilities (EBD). He also was Codirector of UW's doctoral training program in Positive Behavioral Support (PBS) from 2000 to 2005. He is currently the Principal Investigator at Washington's Behavior Research Center on Evidenced-Based Practices (federally funded) and codirects Washington's Positive Behavior Support Network. The network provides training and evaluation to Washington schools implementing PBS.

Dr. Cheney is Coeditor of *The Journal of Emotional and Behavioral Disorders*, an Associate Editor for *Intervention in the School and Clinic*, and a Consulting Editor for *Behavioral Disorders and Beyond Behavior*. He cochaired Washington's Statewide Task Force on Behavioral Disorders from 1997 to 1999, which provided a blueprint for the state's Positive Behavior Support Network, and he is a Past President (1998–1999) of the International Council for Children with Behavioral Disorders. He was Director of the Institute on Emotional Disturbance at Keene State College, New Hampshire, from 1992 to 1997, where he evaluated model programs for students with emotional disturbance. Dr. Cheney presents his research findings frequently at national conferences and in publications and has had published numerous articles and chapters on Positive Behavioral Support for students with EBD and school and family collaboration.

Rob Horner is the Alumni-Knight Endowed Professor of Special Education at the University of Oregon, where he directs the Educational and Community Supports research unit. He received his undergraduate degree in Psychology from Stanford University, his master's in Experimental Psychology from Washington State University, and his PhD in Special Education from the University of Oregon. Dr. Horner's research has focused on developing evidence-based interventions that result in socially significant changes for people with and without disabilities. As Codirector with Dr. George Sugai of the OSEP Technical Assistance Center on Positive Behavioral Interventions and Supports, Dr. Horner coordinates research and technical assistance activities with multiple partners across the nation. During the past 20 years, he has worked directly with schools and school administrators in the development of approaches for implementing schoolwide systems of Positive Behavior Support. He has been the editor of the *Journal of the Association for Persons with Severe Handicaps*, coeditor of the *Journal of Positive Behavior Interventions*, and associate editor for the *Journal of Applied Behavior Analysis* and the *American Journal on Mental Retardation*. In recognition of his achievements, Dr. Horner has received multiple awards, among them the SABA Public Service Behavior Analysis Award (2006), the AAMR Education Award (2002), the TASH Positive Approaches Award (2000), and the APA Fred Keller Educational Research Award (1996).

Kelly Jewell, MEd, is a doctoral student in Special Education at the University of Washington—Seattle (UW), where she is focusing her studies on prevention research for students with behavioral problems, as well as interventions for students with emotional and/or behavioral disorders. She completed her master's degree at the University of Illinois in Emotional/Behavioral Disorders as a Behavior Specialist. While at the University of Illinois, she completed an internship with Illinois's Positive Behavior Interventions and Supports Network.

Ms. Jewell taught public school for two years, with one of those years in the Chicago Public Schools. Her classroom experience included teaching high school students with autism. Ms. Jewell is currently Vice President of the Association of Positive Behavior Supports student network. She has presented at conferences focused on Positive Behavioral Supports for students at risk or with emotional or behavioral disabilities.

Hazel Jones is an Associate Professor in the Department of Special Education, School Psychology, and Early Childhood Studies at the University of Florida, where she teaches in the Unified Early Childhood Program. Her work in the area of families and collaboration includes coauthoring *Interactive Teaming: Enhancing Programs for Students With Special Needs* (4th edition) and coediting two monographs for the Council for Exceptional Children, Division of Early Childhood. These are *Young Exceptional Children Monograph No. 5: Family-Based Practices* and *Young Exceptional Children Monograph No 6: Interdisciplinary Teams.*

Debra Kamps is a Senior Scientist with the Schiefelbusch Institute for Life Span Studies at the University of Kansas, Associate Director of Juniper Gardens Children's Project, and Director of the recently established Kansas Center for Autism Research and Training. She has appointments in the Departments of Applied Behavioral Science and Special Education. Dr. Kamps has been a classroom teacher and consultant in the area of autism, behavior disorders, and school-based interventions for 30 years. Research and professional interests include peer networks, social skills, and behavioral interventions for children with autism and school-based academic, social, and behavioral interventions, including classwide peer tutoring and classwide group contingency programs for children at risk and with behavioral disorders. Research has included longitudinal studies of prevention intervention for young children and multitiered interventions, including Schoolwide Positive Behavior Support and small-group intensive reading instruction in elementary schools. She and collaborators recently completed a five-year longitudinal, randomized trial for the Center for Early Intervention in Reading and Behavior, a multisite national project.

Peter E. Leone is a Professor in the Department of Special Education at the University of Maryland, where he trains teachers and conducts research in the area of behavior disorders. During his professional career, he has taught adolescents with behavioral disorders, monitored education programs in juvenile and adult corrections, and studied marginalized youth. A primary focus of his scholarship and related activities is academic competence and entitlement of adjudicated individuals with disabilities. His current research interests include studying school-based referrals to police and juvenile courts and the school life histories of incarcerated youth.

Ya-yu Lo, PhD, is an Assistant Professor in the Department of Special Education and Child Development at the University of North Carolina at Charlotte. Dr. Lo's research interests include social skill instruction, Positive Behavior Interventions and Supports, effective academic instruction, challenging behavior, and behavioral disorders. Her current research project, Peers as Social Skills Instruction Trainers (PASSIT), funded by the Spencer Foundation, aims to quantify the effects of a peer-directed, multimedia-integrated social skills instruction program in which students at risk for behavioral disorders serve as peer trainers. Dr. Lo has coauthored 21 in-press or published articles, books, and book chapters and has made over 50 professional presentations at the national/international, state/regional, or local/community levels. She received the Council for Exceptional Children Division for Research Early Career Publication Award in 2008 and was a recipient of the 2007 North Carolina Association for Research in Education Distinguished Paper Award. She is currently the Managing Editor of *The Journal of Special Education* and the President-Elect of the North Carolina Association for Behavior Analysis.

Tina McClanahan has worked for the Charlotte-Mecklenburg Schools (CMS) in North Carolina since her graduation from West Virginia State College. During her time with CMS, she has held the positions of classroom teacher, literacy teacher, Reading Recovery teacher, and K–2 Literacy Facilitator, and she is currently a PreK Literacy Facilitator. She also worked for the University of North Carolina at Charlotte' s Behavior and Reading Improvement Center as a Center Support Coordinator. She received National Board status in 2001 as an Early Childhood Generalist. She resides in Matthews, North Carolina, with her husband and two daughters.

Festus E. Obiakor, PhD, is a Professor in the Department of Exceptional Education at the University of Wisconsin—Milwaukee. He is one of the leading scholars in the fields of general and special education—he is the author of more than 150 publications, including books and journal articles. In his works, he is interested in reducing the traditional misidentification, misassessment, miscatgorization, misplacement, and misintruction of studnts who come from culturally and linguistically diverse backgrounds. In addition, he advocates a Comprehensive Support Model that takes advantage of the collaborative spirits of students, families, schools, community members, and government agencies in solving behavioral problems.

Robert F. Putnam, PhD, BCBA, is Senior Vice President of School Consultation at the May Institute and was on the faculty of the Harvard Medical School. He also serves as Director of Consultation at the National Autism Center. Dr. Putnam oversees one of eight national collaboration sites in conjunction with the University of Oregon and the University of Connecticut, comprising the National Technical Assistance Center for Positive Behavior Interventions and Supports funded by the Office of Special Education Programs, U.S. Department of Education. Dr. Putnam received his PhD from Boston College and currently serves on the faculty of Northeastern University. His research interests are in the use of function-based interventions to improve prosocial skills, behavioral support strategies for individuals with autism spectrum disorder, as well as Schoolwide Behavior Support Interventions. He has published extensively and presents regularly at national, regional, and local conferences on these topics.

Cynthia Simpson, PhD, has more than 16 years of experience in the public and private sector as a preschool teacher, special education teacher, elementary teacher, educational diagnostician, and administrator. She received her graduate degree from Texas A&M University. She is currently an Associate Professor and Special Education Program Coordinator in the College of Education at Sam Houston State University, where she teaches courses in cognitive assessment and special education. Dr. Simpson maintains an active role in the field of special education as an educational consultant in the areas of assessment and inclusive practices. Her professional responsibilities include serving on the National Council for Accreditation of Teacher Education/National Association for the Education of Young Children Review Panel, as well as holding the position of State Advisor to the Texas Educational Diagnostician Association. She also represents college teachers as the Vice President of Legislative Affairs for Texas Association of College Teachers. Cynthia has numerous publications to her credit, including books, articles, and training materials, and is a featured speaker at the international, national, and state level. Cynthia was recently awarded the 2008 Susan Phillips Gorin Award, the highest honor that can be bestowed on a professional member of the Council for Exceptional Children by its student membership. Her honors also include the 2007 Katheryn Varner Award (awarded by the Texas Council for Exceptional Children) and the 2009 Wilma Jo Bush Award.

George Sugai is Professor and Carole J. Neag Endowed Chair in the Neag School of Education at the University of Connecticut. His research and practice interests include Schoolwide Positive Behavior Support, emotional and behavioral disorders, applied behavior analysis, organizational management, and classroom and behavior management. He has been a classroom teacher, program director, personnel preparer, and applied researcher.

Introduction

Changing the Lives of Students With Problems

Current prevention science offers opportunities to address problems effectively with interventions at different levels of intensity and support. If a student is not making adequate progress, decision-making teams should consider whether the interventions were implemented with fidelity. If not, additional support should be provided or intervention plans revised to match better the context of the classroom and the teacher's ability to respond effectively. While these efforts offer great promise, "it is untrue and misleading to claim that we currently have a necessary and sufficient knowledge base to guide the[ir] implementation . . . across all grades, for all academic [and behavior] skills, in all content areas, for all children and youth" (Fuchs & Deshler, 2007, p. 134).

The prevention practices described in our book are based on the premise that early response to problems can lead to better outcomes for students. These efforts should be built into the school's general education program, and they should be accessible to all students. They address four areas: Foundations, Intervention, Collaboration, and Evaluation (see Table 0.1).

Table 0.1 Evidence-Based Prevention Practices		
Area	**Practice**	**Chapter**
Foundations	Preschool Behavior Support	2
	Schoolwide Positive Behavior Support	3
Intervention	Cognitive-Behavior Interventions in School Settings	4
	Social Skills Instruction and Generalization Strategies	5
	Conflict Resolution, Peer Mediation, and Bullying Prevention	6
	Classroom Interventions and Individual Behavior Plans	7
Collaboration	Effective Home-School Partnerships	8
	Community and Interagency Partnerships	9
	Culturally Responsive Teaching	10
Evaluation	Monitoring Student Progress and Evaluating Prevention Practices	11
	Building and Sustaining Effective Prevention Practices	12

Broad, general approaches to prevention are described in two chapters. First, we review why teaching social skills to children in preschool programs is important, describe critical social skills that support the success of young children in school, identify and describe effective practices for teaching social skills to young children, and review examples of evidence-based approaches for teaching social skills to young children. In Chapter 3, we describe effective practices for implementing Schoolwide Positive Behavior Support and review evidence of effectiveness of Schoolwide Positive Behavior Support programs.

We address more specific interventions in four chapters. In Chapter 4, we provide a context for using promising cognitive-behavioral interventions (CBIs) to address problem behaviors in school settings, describe a theoretical framework for CBI, review research studies on selected school-based CBIs designed to prevent or reduce maladaptive behaviors, and discuss the research to practice issues relevant to implementing CBIs successfully in schools. In Chapter 5, we review why small-group social skill instruction is important, describe characteristics of small-group social skill instruction programs, identify and describe effective small-group social skill instruction programs and practices, describe critical features that support the implementation and effective use of small-group social skill instruction, and review evidence of effectiveness of small-group social skill instruction. Chapter 6 illustrates why conflict resolution, peer mediation, and bully-proofing are important in preventive classroom efforts. We describe the characteristics of conflict resolution, peer mediation, and bully-proofing programs; identify and describe effective programs and practices; describe critical features that support implementation and use of such programs; and review evidence of the effectiveness of these programs. In Chapter 7, we review why using individual behavior plans is important, describe characteristics of individual behavior plans, identify and describe critical features that support the implementation and effective use of individual behavior plans, and review evidence of the effectiveness of using individual behavior plans to prevent problem behaviors.

We address collaboration in three chapters. In Chapter 8, we review why home-school partnerships are important, describe characteristics of home-school partnerships, identify and describe effective home-school partnership programs and practices, describe critical features that support implementation and effective use of home-school partnership programs, and review evidence of their effectiveness. In Chapter 9, we focus on why community partnerships are important, describe their characteristics, identify and describe effective community partnership programs and practices, describe critical features that support implementation and effective use of these programs, and review evidence of their effectiveness. In Chapter 10, we review why culturally responsive teaching is important, describe characteristics of culturally responsive teaching, identify and describe effective culturally responsive teaching practices, describe critical features that support the implementation and effective use of culturally responsive teaching, and review the evidence of such programs effectiveness.

In the climate of accountability that drives best practices, continuous evaluation is essential for all efforts to promote interventions designed to prevent problems in school. In Chapter 11, we review why monitoring progress and evaluating prevention programs is important, describe characteristics of progress monitoring practices, identify and describe effective progress monitoring practices, describe critical features of effective evaluations, and review the evidence of effectiveness of progress monitoring and efforts to evaluate prevention practices. After discussing evaluation, we review what is known about building and sustaining programs that prevent problem behaviors in Chapter 12, focusing on summarizing, integrating, and reconsidering critical features of programs and practices for preventing problem behaviors.

1

Prevention Science and Practice

In this chapter, we

- provide a context for current prevention practices,
- describe and discuss links between response-to-intervention and prevention practices, and
- provide an overview of information in our book.

School personnel face daily and continuous challenges in their efforts to establish and maintain safe and orderly classroom environments where teachers can teach and students can learn. Prevention practices are preferred to other behavior management approaches because of their potential to reduce the development of new, and the severity of current, school-related problems. A well-crafted approach to prevention improves the efficiency and effectiveness of school, classroom, and individual instructional and support systems. Programs grounded in prevention science also have broad usefulness for counselors and other professionals.

WHAT WE KNOW ABOUT PREVENTION PRACTICE

Students who exhibit problem behavior are a growing concern for school and community safety, generating a continuing need for primary-, secondary-, and tertiary-level interventions (Cheney, Flower, & Templeton, 2008; Gresham, MacMillan, & Bocian, 1996; Hage et al., 2007; Kamps, Kravitz, Stolze, & Swaggart, 1999; Nelson, 1996; Romano & Netland, 2008; Rose & Gallup, 2007; Vanderstay, 2006). Challenging behavior also has a profound impact on the lives of the individuals exhibiting it. For example, it has long been known and continually demonstrated that children and young adults with behavior problems are more likely than their peers to enter special education and/or the juvenile justice system (Kamps & Tankersley, 1996; Kauffman & Landrum, 2009; Nelson, Sprague, Jolivette, Smith, & Tobin, 2009; Vanderstay, 2006; Wehby, Symons, & Hollo, 1997; Ysseldyke, Algozzine, & Thurlow, 2000). In recent years, interest in maintaining discipline and order has become more focused as a result of the concern of some school professionals about the growing numbers of students with behavior problems in general education classrooms and the increasing student diversity common in America's schools (Kauffman & Landrum).

Best practices in prevention are based on the

> scientific assumption that human behavior, while affected by a complex mix of biological, societal, and learning factors, can change as a function of certain actions performed by others in a supportive, caregiving role for people of all cultures, ages, and levels of competence. (Dunlap, Sailor, Horner, & Sugai, 2009, p. 4)

The logic of prevention and its importance for children is straightforward: It is difficult to learn when you are spending more time in discipline-related interactions than in those related to learning academic content (Miles & Stipek, 2006). The significance for teachers is reflected in the belief that "behavior problems may make it difficult for practitioners to provide effective instruction" (Sutherland, Lewis-Palmer, Stichter, & Morgan, 2008, p. 223).

The body of work directly and more distantly related to preventing problem behaviors is large and reflects a variety of perspectives. Contemporary behavior and classroom management interventions represent a broad spectrum of methods, ranging from student-centered approaches to teacher- and community-centered practices (Kauffman & Landrum, 2009). The majority of these programs focus on reducing problem behaviors while improving social-cognitive skills, peer relations, and academic skills of individual students, and many are beginning to focus on proactive, schoolwide implementations (Algozzine & Algozzine, 2009). Though not always in favor (see Cowen, 1997), programs and practices designed to prevent social behavior problems are now widely recognized as essential in improving results for all children (see Dunlap et al., 2009; Durlak, 2003; Durlak & Wells, 1997a, 1997b; Hage et al., 2007; Kamps et al., 1999; Kratochwill, 2007; Resse, 2007; Romano & Netland, 2008; Vera & Reese, 2000).

Unfortunately, many children with behavioral issues are typically identified after their problems have reached serious levels—too late to receive the full benefit of preventive interventions. This is a discouraging situation, since a substantial and compelling body of research focuses on how to assess, identify, and help children at risk for behavioral problems. For instance, research indicates that these children

- can be assessed and identified early with relative ease and accuracy.
- often fall behind because they do not receive appropriate interventions earlier.
- can make tremendous gains when provided with effective services during early childhood.
- may need individually tailored interventions because one approach may not fit all children.
- are at high risk for academic failure, exhibiting more severe discipline problems, and dropping out of school unless effective interventions are implemented.

As school administrators and other professionals face daily challenges in efforts to establish and maintain safe and orderly classroom environments, a well-crafted approach to prevention improves their efficiency and effectiveness. In this regard, efforts to improve general learning conditions revolve around preventing inappropriate behaviors and teaching more appropriate replacements. For example, Nelson, Crabtree, Marchand-Martella, and Martella (1998) argued that "students will behave according to social norms if [teachers] take the trouble to teach those students those norms and supervise them in a consistent way" (p. 4). They proposed a model that emphasized direct interventions within and across all school settings, ensuring that disruptive behavior did not occur or become entrenched (i.e., *preventative* focus) or was corrected (i.e., *remedial* focus). They argued that different types of students (i.e., typical, at-risk, target) need different types of preventive interventions according to the nature of their problems. In this context, school-wide (Tier I) interventions (e.g., effective teaching, schoolwide discipline) are most appropriate for students who are not at risk for problems. Targeted (Tier II) interventions (e.g., conflict resolution, anger management) are most appropriate for students at risk of developing disruptive behavior problems. Intensive, comprehensive (Tier III) interventions (e.g., community-based service linkages, school and community partnerships) are most appropriate for students exhibiting persistent disruptive behavior patterns.

Preventing and reducing behavior problems is not the responsibility of any one group or individual. Administrators need assistance identifying, implementing, and supporting effective interventions. Teachers need help teaching behavior and academics, and students need to be taught appropriate social, behavioral, and academic norms. Parents need assistance participating as partners in making schools safer and more positive places to send their children. Thus, preventing and reducing behavior problems requires a coordinated plan. Kamps and Tankersley (1996) delimited the following key features about the prevention of behavior problems:

- Prevention means early intervention; the most effective and efficient treatment begins with young children.
- Prevention involves parents as key interventionists; family variables are closely related to progress and problems in development.
- Prevention involves cross-setting, multiple, and proactive interventions; school interventions are critical to overall, effective treatment.
- Prevention involves administrators, teachers, peers, and others; cohesive treatment opportunities for success are maximized when key people are included in treatment.
- Prevention involves self-management; maintenance and generalization are expected within natural environments.
- Prevention involves collaboration among families, schools, and service providers; improving behavior is not the sole responsibility of any one caregiver.

Successful prevention programs are theory driven, socially and culturally relevant, and delivered across multiple contexts (e.g., individual, family, school, community) connected within systems of care. The scientific knowledge base that informs prevention practice has grown in recent years and suggests that best practice involves providing multiple levels of intervention services, including

primary prevention interventions aimed at promoting protective factors for widespread or universal populations, secondary prevention interventions focused on enhancing protective factors for selected populations that are indicated to be at risk or suffering, and tertiary preventive interventions targeted at limiting dysfunction for populations who have chronic disorders. (Hage et al., 2007, p. 522)

Evidence from outcome evaluations indicates that most "prevention programs . . . significantly reduced problems and significantly increased competencies, and affected functioning in multiple adjustment domains" (Durlak & Wells, 1997a, p. 137).

It is clearly understood that schools need practical, proven methods for improving academic behavior. They also need practical, proven methods for improving social behavior and providing behavior support if children are to achieve adequately in school. Prevention science and practice both indicate that it is difficult for teachers to teach and children to learn when problem behaviors interfere with instruction. This is the logic underlying "response-to-intervention" efforts designed to improve academic outcomes and reduce the numbers of children eligible for and placed in special education programs.

WHAT WE KNOW ABOUT RESPONSE TO INTERVENTION

Response to Intervention (RTI) "integrates high quality teaching and assessment methods in a systematic way so that students who are not successful when presented with one set of instructional methods can be given the chance to succeed with the use of other practices" (Brown-Chidsey & Steege, 2005, p. 3). RTI is based on the critical but simple concept that "quality instruction must be in place for *all* before it can be said that *some* have [special problems]" (Sailor, Doolittle, Bradley, & Danielson, 2009, p. 734). RTI has emerged as the new way to think about both identification and prevention for the "most vulnerable, *academically* [emphasis added] unresponsive children" in schools and school districts (Fuchs & Deshler, 2007, p. 131). According to Bradley, Danielson, and Doolittle (2007), the popularity of RTI is partly grounded in the promise that "teachers no longer would have to wait for students to fail before the students could receive services" (p. 8) and partly in the pledge of change at the first indication of unresponsiveness to classroom implementations of scientifically based interventions. Those who promise potential payoff from RTI see it coming from early identification of and strong preventive intervention for academic problems.

RTI is "a multitier *prevention* [emphasis added] model that has at least three tiers" (Bradley et al., 2007, p. 9). In this context, a "tier" refers to intervention provided in response to increasing needs of students. A three-tier prevention model is aimed at catching students early—*before* they fall significantly behind—and providing the supports they need throughout their early years of schooling (Vaughn, 2003). Regular benchmark assessments and progress monitoring are prominent in RTI and reflect the importance of using screening measures and cut points proactively to identify students experiencing continuing difficulties for different tiers of intervention and support (Bradley et al., 2007; Case, Speece, & Molloy, 2003; Fletcher et al., 2002; Fuchs, 2003; Fuchs & Deshler, 2007; Gresham, 2005; Kamps & Tankersley, 1996; Vaughn).

What Is Tier I Intervention?

Primary (Tier I) interventions are designed to address the majority of students' instructional needs. Schools using RTI assume that students who are in need of additional support have received high-quality instruction that has been successful with a majority of their peers. To identify and meet the educational needs of students requiring additional support, therefore, the classroom environment itself must be addressed. As part of any prevention program, school professionals must continually look at classroom-level data to determine the overall health of the instructional setting. Classrooms where the number of students experiencing difficulties is consistently high require analysis and attention. Administrators and support teams are expected to work with those classroom teachers to pinpoint the areas in which they are most in need of professional development. Only after high-quality instruction has been provided at both the schoolwide and classroom levels can school professionals conclude that a student needs additional services.

What Is Tier II Intervention?

Once a student has been identified as needing additional support, RTI directs the use of evidence-based interventions that are easy to administer to small groups of students and require limited time and staff involvement. Secondary (Tier II) intervention is for students for whom Tier I instruction has been insufficient (i.e., students who fall behind on benchmarks skills and require additional intervention to achieve expectations). Thus, Tier II consists of small-group supplemental instruction. Although there are many instructional procedures with promise for Tier II, "widespread uncertainty" exists about what "scientifically validated" instruction means within RTI (Fuchs & Deshler, 2007, p. 131). Therefore, at the district and school levels, professionals are encouraged to monitor closely the implementation and outcomes of Tier II programs, because if implemented poorly, their efforts will not be likely to produce desired impacts. When students fail to profit from high-quality implementation of Tier II interventions, RTI proponents direct that additional support be provided.

What Is Tier III Intervention?

Tertiary (Tier III) intervention is specifically designed and customized instruction that is extended beyond the time allocated for Tier I and II programming. Prior to selecting any intervention tier, a school team should meet to conduct a more in-depth analysis of a student's progress monitoring data, which at this point would include all of the information examined at Tiers I and II, as well as the fidelity of and the student's response to the previous interventions. The classroom teacher(s) should have a significant role at this level of the problem-solving process, as more in-depth information is collected through one-on-one consultation. At Tier III, access to an array of assessment information is essential for effective team decision making. At this tier, more intensive progress-monitoring techniques should be applied.

Building the Plane as We Fly It

The good news is that there are many ways to use RTI to prevent learning and behavior problems. The bad news is that there are many ways to use RTI to prevent behavior and learning problems. The truth is, the manual describing best practices for constructing a RTI system remains unwritten, and precise explanations for when and how students move within and between the tiers are not easy to find in the vast emerging literature on this promising practice.

In the broadest sense, elementary, middle, and high schools implementing RTI use universal screening and benchmark assessments to provide initial information on which students need additional targeted (Tier II) or intensive (Tier III) support. Professionals in one school may decide that students scoring below the 25th percentile on reading progress-monitoring tests require additional attention to prevent further learning problems, while at another school, the "critical" score for initiating RTI may be higher or lower. Similarly, differentiated instruction and attention may be provided to a student receiving two office discipline referrals (ODRs) in a week in one school, while in another, the criterion may be two ODRs in a month.

For example, at an elementary school in California, grade-level teams meet every two weeks to review student assessment data, design interventions, identify students in need of supplemental support, and place students in appropriate individualized interventions. At the middle school in the same district, the counseling staff works with groups of teachers periodically to review instructional programs and students' responses to them and identify areas of concern in core subject areas. Every three weeks, students with overall grades below 75% are targeted for additional support. Under all these conditions, school professionals monitor the quality of teaching and fidelity of program implementation and provide focused staff development when necessary to maximize instructional time (Buffum, Mattos, & Weber, 2009).

WHAT WE KNOW ABOUT BEHAVIOR AND ACHIEVEMENT

Researchers in psychology, sociology, public health, and education have long posited a connection between academic achievement and social behavior. Interest in this relationship has gained strength with the current focus on prevention, especially for students at risk of experiencing acute and chronic school failure. The large body of work directly and more remotely related to the conjoining of academic performance and other behavior falls into the general categories of illustrative, comparative, and predictive studies. Descriptions of achievement and the behavior characteristics of different groups and summaries of extant literature, usually presented in book chapters, exemplify the *illustrative* body of knowledge. Generally, this work shows that groups experiencing achievement problems also experience behavior problems (achievement and behavior are related). In *comparative* work, researchers describe the behavior and achievement problems for different groups of students. Generally, this work shows that some groups exhibit more behavior problems and lower achievement than other groups do. Finally, *predictive* studies provide descriptions of covariance and functional relationships between academics and behavior. Generally, this work shows that the relationship between behavior and academic competence/proficiency scores is statistically significant, albeit often weak.

With regard to the link between academic achievement and social behavior, Gerald Patterson, as early as 1976, suggested that some students are both a "victim and architect" (p. 268) in a system that works in one of at least three ways:

1. The child's response may serve as a stimulus, which sets the occasion for an immediate repetition of the same response.

2. Famil member may provide specific consequences that serve to maintain a coercive response once it has been initiated.

3. In extended interactions, the behavior of the child and the family member may create *mutual*, or bilateral, effects, both of which maintain ongoing coercive behaviors. (p. 272)

Patterson's (1976) perspective speaks for the importance of focusing on prevention when addressing problems of children. Problem behavior reduces academic engagement, and reduced academic engagement leads to reduced academic achievement. Children who engage in problem behavior maintained by peer or adult attention appear to benefit most from interventions that focus primarily on social variables. Children who engage in problem behavior maintained by escape from curricular demands appear to benefit best when the intervention includes curricular revision (changes in the content or delivering of instruction).

Despite knowledge that systematic academic instruction and support improves achievement, some children fail to profit from the educational menu of experiences provided in America's schools. It has also been demonstrated that systematic *behavior* instruction and support improves behavior and that establishing reading and behavior skills *early* (in elementary school) is predictive of later success in school. The trick at the school level is determining whether systematic instruction is happening in all areas of academic achievement and social behavior and, if not, ensuring that it does. The trick at the individual level, for a child who is failing to benefit from intensive attention to improve achievement in academics and behavior, is identifying the antecedents and consequences of failure and manipulating changes that will enable the child to benefit from the high-quality instruction. Empirical evidence indicates that doing less leads to academic failure. The strategy, therefore, is comprehensive:

- Provide high-quality academic and behavior instruction for all children and regularly verify that both are happening with intensity and treatment fidelity. The best medicine in the world will not be effective unless a patient takes it according to directions. There is evidence that universal, schoolwide academic and behavior support systems reduce academic and behavioral challenges, but more research is needed to convince educators to invest in evidence-based prevention.
- Provide focused and direct instruction in natural classrooms and groups, verify fidelity of implementation, and continuously monitor progress when frequent and direct measurements suggest that academic and social problems exist. The promise of Response to Intervention as salvation for the rising numbers of children requiring special education and the failure of prior practices to solve the problem is grounded in the belief that change can and will happen and make a difference, but research is needed to convince educators that the promise can be a reality.
- Continuously monitor progress and make appropriate adaptations as needed. Effective teaching is iterative and recurring, with every behavior of a learner serving as a basis for supportive or corrective action designed to continue the learning cycle.

In the end, what is known about the relationship between achievement and behavior is prescriptive: the education community needs to examine the effects of implementing high-quality instruction on achievement *and* behavior, and ignoring either outcome will be counterproductive.

An Illustration From Practice

The mission of Mortimer Elementary School is to achieve academic excellence in positive, nurturing, culturally rich learning environments for 725 students in kindergarten through fifth grade. The children at the school come from diverse backgrounds, including 59 percent African-American, 2 percent Asian, 21 percent Hispanic, 2 percent multiracial, 1 percent Native American, and 15 percent White families. Seventy-seven percent of the students are on free or reduced lunch. With support from the local university, administrators, teachers, and other professionals adopted a three-tiered model of reading and behavior instruction to help meet the needs of the students at their school.

To enhance the strong primary level of reading instruction provided by implementing an evidence-based core-reading program, literacy facilitators provided kindergarten and first-grade teachers with mini-lessons and additional practice activities (see Algozzine, Marr, McClanahan, & Barnes, 2008) for use with students needing additional instruction during daily 30-minute independent work times included in the district-mandated literacy block. Additionally, a peer-coaching fluency-building program (see Marr & Dugan, 2007) was implemented to support oral reading in second-grade classrooms.

Administrators, teachers, and other professionals at Mortimer also taught behavior relentlessly by promoting similar attitudes toward instruction of academics and behavior, reinforcing school and class rules and expectations with high levels of praise and prompting, using a consistent correction procedure unified across personnel to address inappropriate behavior, and adopting mutually supportive roles (see White, Algozzine, Audette, Marr, & Ellis, 2001). Within the schoolwide behavior model, threats to safety were addressed with a correction procedure that resulted in an immediate office referral, but minor disruptions were handled with classroom-based practices. Strategic (or secondary) and intensive (or tertiary) support was provided using evidence-based small-group social skills interventions and functional behavior assessments so that students who were not successful when provided with schoolwide instructional methods were given a chance to succeed with the use of other practices (see Algozzine, Cooke, et al., 2008).

REFERENCES

Algozzine, B., & Algozzine, K. (2009). Facilitating academic achievement through Schoolwide Positive Behavior Support. In W. Sailor, G. Dunlap, G. Sugai, & R. Horner (Eds.), *Handbook of Positive Behavior Support* (pp. 521–550). New York: Springer.

Algozzine, B., Cooke, N., White, R. Helf, S., Algozzine, K., & McClanahan, T. (2008). The North Carolina Reading and Behavior Center's K–3 prevention model: Eastside Elementary School case study. In C. R. Greenwood, T. R. Kratochwill, & M. Clements (Eds.), *Schoolwide prevention models: Lessons learned in elementary schools* (pp. 173–214). New York: Guilford.

Algozzine, B., Marr, M. B., McClanahan, T., & Barnes, E. (2008). *Strategies and lessons for improving basic early literacy skills.* Thousand Oaks, CA: Corwin.

Bradley, R., Danielson, L., & Doolittle, J. (2007). Responsiveness to intervention: 1997 to 2007. *Teaching Exceptional Children, 39*(5), 8–12.

Brown-Chidsey, R., & Steege, M. W. (2005). *Response to Intervention: Principles and strategies for effective practice.* New York: Guilford.

Buffum, A., Mattos, M., & Weber, C. (2009). *Pyramid response to intervention.* Bloomington, IN: Solution Tree.

Case, L. P., Speece, D. L., & Molloy, D. E. (2003). The validity of a Response-to-Intervention paradigm to identify reading disabilities: A longitudinal analysis of individual differences and contextual factors. *School Psychology Review, 32,* 557–582.

Cheney, D., Flower, A., & Templeton, T. (2008). Applying Response to Intervention metrics in the social domain for students at risk of developing emotional or behavioral disorders. *The Journal of Special Education, 42,* 108–126.

Cowen, E. (1997). The coming of age of primary prevention: Comments on Durlak and Well's analysis. *American Journal of Community Psychology, 25,* 153–167.

Dunlap, G., Sailor, W., Horner, R. H., & Sugai, G. (2009). Overview and history of Positive Behavior Support. In W. Sailor, G. Dunlap, G. Sugai, & R. Horner (Eds.), *Handbook of Positive Behavior Support* (pp. 3–16). New York: Springer.

Durlak, J. (2003). Effective prevention and health promotion programming. In T. P. Gullotta & M. Bloom (Eds.), *Encyclopedia of primary prevention and health promotion* (pp. 61–69). New York: Kluwer.

Durlak, J. A., & Wells, A. M. (1997a). Primary prevention mental health programs for children and adolescents: A meta-analytic review. *American Journal of Community Psychology, 25,* 115–152.

Durlak, J. A., & Wells, A. M. (1997b). Primary prevention mental health programs: The future is exciting. *American Journal of Community Psychology, 25,* 233–243.

Fletcher, J. M., Foorman, B. R., Boudousquie, A., Barnes, M. A., Schatschneider, C., & Francis, D. J. (2002). Assessment of reading and learning disabilities: A research-based intervention oriented approach. *Journal of School Psychology, 40,* 27–63.

Fuchs, L. (2003). Assessing intervention responsiveness: Conceptual and technical issues. *Learning Disabilities Research and Practice, 18,* 172–186.

Fuchs, D., & Deshler, D. D. (2007). What we need to know about responsiveness to intervention (and shouldn't be afraid to ask). *Learning Disabilities Research & Practice, 22,* 129–136.

Gresham, F. M. (2005). Response to Intervention: An alternative means of identifying students as emotionally disturbed. *Education and Treatment of Children, 28,* 328–344.

Gresham, F. M., MacMillan, D. L., & Bocian, K. (1996). "Behavioral earthquakes": Low frequency, salient behavioral events that differentiate students at risk for behavioral disorders. *Behavioral Disorders, 21,* 277–292.

Hage, S. M., Romano, J. L., Conyne, R. K., Kenny, M., Matthews, C., Schwartz, J. P., et al. (2007). Best practice guidelines on prevention practice, research, training, and social advocacy for psychologists. *The Counseling Psychologist, 35,* 493–566.

Kamps, D., Kravits, T., Stolze, J., & Swaggart, B. (1999). Prevention strategies for at-risk students and students with EBD in urban elementary schools. *Journal of Emotional and Behavioral Disorders, 7,* 178–188.

Kamps, D. M., & Tankersley, M. (1996). Prevention of behavioral and conduct disorders: Trends and research issues. *Behavioral Disorders, 21*(1), 41–48.

Kauffman, J. M., & Landrum, T. J. (2009). *Characteristics of emotional and behavioral disorders of children and youth.* Upper Saddle River, NJ: Prentice Hall.

Kratochwill, T. R. (2007). Preparing psychologists for evidence-based school practice: Lessons learned and challenges ahead. *American Psychologist, 62,* 829–843.

Marr, M. B., & Dugan, K. K. (2007). Using partners to build fluency. *Preventing School Failure, 51*(2), 52–55.

Miles, S. B., & Stipek, D. (2006). Contemporaneous and longitudinal associations between social behavior and literacy achievement in a sample of low-income elementary school children. *Child Development, 77,* 103–117.

Nelson, C.M., Sprague, J. R., Jolivette, K., Smith, C. R., & Tobin, T. J. (2009). Positive Behavior Support in alternative education, community-based mental health, and juvenile justice settings. In W. Sailor, G. Dunlap, G. Sugai, & R. Horner (Eds.), *Handbook of Positive Behavior Support* (pp. 465–496). New York: Springer.

Nelson, J. R. (1996). Designing schools to meet the needs of students who exhibit disruptive behavior. *Journal of Emotional and Behavioral Disorders, 4,* 147–161.

Nelson, J. R., Crabtree, M., Marchand-Martella, N., & Martella, R. (1998). Teaching behavior in the whole school. *Teaching Exceptional Children, 30*(4), 4–9.

Patterson, G. R. (1976). The aggressive child: Victim and architect of a coercive system. In E. J. Mash, L. A. Hamerlynck, & L. C. Handy (Eds.), *Behavior modification and families* (pp. 267–316). New York: Brunner/Mazel.

Reese, L. E. (2007). Beyond rhetoric: The ABCs of effective prevention practice, science, and policy. *The Counseling Psychologist, 35,* 576–585.

Romano, J. L., & Netland, J. D. (2008). The application of the theory of reasoned action and planned behavior to prevention science in counseling psychology. *The Counseling Psychologist, 36,* 777–806.

Rose, L. C., & Gallup, A. M. (2007). The 39th Annual Phi Delta Kappa/Gallup poll of the public's attitudes toward the public schools. *Phi Delta Kappan, 89,* 33–48.

Sailor, W., Doolittle, J., Bradley, R., & Danielson, L. (2009). Response to Intervention and Positive Behavior Support. In W. Sailor, G. Dunlap, G. Sugai, & R. Horner (Eds.), *Handbook of Positive Behavior Support* (pp. 729–753). New York: Springer.

Sutherland, K. S., Lewis-Palmer, T., Stichter, J., & Morgan, P. L. (2008). Examining the influence of teacher behavior and classroom context on the behavioral and academic outcomes for students with emotional or behavioral disorders. *The Journal of Special Education, 41,* 223–233.

Vanderstaay, S. L. (2006). Learning from longitudinal research in criminology and the health sciences. *Reading Research Quarterly, 41,* 328–350.

Vaughn, S. (2003, December). *How many tiers are needed for Response to Intervention to achieve acceptable prevention outcomes?* Paper presented at the National Research Center on Learning Disabilities Responsiveness-to-Intervention Symposium, Kansas City, MO.

Vera, E. M., & Reese. L. E. (2000). Preventive interventions with school-age youth. In S. D. Brown & R. W. Lent (Eds.), *Handbook of counseling psychology* (pp. 411–434). New York: John Wiley.

Wehby, J. H., Symons, F. J., & Hollo, A. (1997). Promote appropriate assessment. *Journal of Emotional and Behavioral Disorders, 5,* 45–54.

White, R., Algozzine, B., Audette, R., Marr, M. B., & Ellis, E. D., Jr. (2001). Unified discipline: A school-wide approach for managing problem behavior. *Intervention in School and Clinic, 37*(1), 3–8.

Ysseldyke, J. E., Algozzine, B., & Thurlow, M. L. (2000). *Critical issues in special education.* Boston: Houghton Mifflin.

2

Preschool Behavior Support

In this chapter, we

- review why helping teachers to teach social skills to young children is important,
- identify and describe effective practices for teaching social skills to young children,
- describe characteristics of Schoolwide Positive Behavior Support systems,
- describe critical social skills that support the success of young children, and
- provide a perspective on and an illustration from the practice of teaching social skills to young children.

Two pieces of federal legislation—the No Child Left Behind Act of 2001 (NCLB) and the Education Sciences Reform Act of 2002—put forth the idea that education should be an evidence-based field in which information exists to support adoption and sustained use of best teaching practices (see Fuchs & Deshler, 2007; Kratochwill & Shernoff, 2004; Merrell & Buchanan, 2006; National Research Council, 2005). This belief applies to all children, including those in preschool, and to learning social as well as academic skills and to prevention as well as intervention practices (Jolivette, Gallagher, Morrier, & Lambert, 2008).

Children learn inappropriate behavior the same way they learn appropriate behavior. In the words of the legendary song by Richard Rodgers and Oscar Hammerstein II in the 1949 play *South Pacific*, they've "got to be carefully taught." As teachers, we are responsible for teaching children all that they need to be successful in school. In a book titled *How to Be an Effective Teacher*, Harry and Rosemary Wong (1998) shared three characteristics the "successful teacher must know and practice" to be effective:

- The effective teacher has positive expectations for student success.
- The effective teacher is an extremely good classroom manager.
- The effective teacher knows how to design lessons that help students reach mastery (p. vii).

13

IMPORTANCE OF TEACHING SOCIAL SKILLS IN PRESCHOOL

Current educational practice and policy focus heavily on academic achievement. Performance on high-stakes tests is used as a benchmark for quality in school, district, state, and national comparisons. Of course, academic success is only one element of learning in preschool and other educational programs. As Knitzer (2002) pointed out, key findings from research illustrate that policy makers and practitioners should invest in improving the social and emotional skills of young children for the following reasons:

- The earliest years set the stage for lifetime emotional skills, competencies, and problems.
- Many young children are not developing the emotional skills that they will need to succeed in school and be productive members of society.
- Achieving the national policy goal of school readiness for all children requires paying more strategic attention to early social, emotional, and behavioral challenges as well as cognitive and physical development. (p. 3)

Evidence from early childhood programs, such as Head Start, illustrates that becoming more effective at dealing with emotional and social behavioral issues is among educators top needs for training and technical assistance (Buscemi, Bennett, Thomas, & Deluca, 1995; Huffman, Mehlinger, & Kerivan, 2000; Peth-Pierce, 2000; Shonkoff & Phillips, 2000). Furthermore, most teachers agree that "readiness to learn" and "teachability" are "marked" by abilities to exhibit and sustain positive social behaviors (Rimm-Kaufman, Pianta, & Cox, 2000). Table 2.1 summarizes appropriate and problem behavior of young children.

Table 2.1 Categories and Descriptors of Appropriate and Problem Behavior of Young Children	
Category	Descriptors
Content	• Interacting with toys, materials, or others without frowning, showing fear or sadness, crying, or whining; observing others; face showing interest or even smiling
Discontent • Crying • Fussy • Silent distress • Verbal distress • Clinging	• Audibly crying with tears; loud, intense sounds accompanied by mucous from the child's nose • Whining or making noises that seem to communicate unhappiness; tears not present. May appear to be asking for attention. • Frowning, scowling, or looking as if about to cry; appearing fearful, anxious, or sulking • Saying things that indicate distress or unhappiness • Holding onto an adult staff member (e.g., grabbing and holding onto the leg of an adult); clinging to the adult while being held (holding on more tightly than when relaxed, burying head in adult's shoulder to avoid eye contact)
Problem Behavior • Aggression • Destruction • Noncompliance • Social withdrawal/ isolation • Territorial infringement	• Hitting, kicking, biting, pushing others (peers or adults), or verbally threatening others • Throwing, kicking, breaking, and banging toys/materials in ways other than their prescribed use, with the intent to destroy or with the inferred intent of anger • Not following an adult request and displaying defiant behaviors verbally or nonverbally • Not being in close proximity to others, not interacting with others or with toys, or appearing to be avoiding or moving away from others • Taking another child's toys or materials or getting in another child's space

Raver and Knitzer (2002) have integrated and summarized important evidenced-based findings establishing the value and importance of emotional and social skills as follows:

- Young children without developmentally appropriate emotional and social competencies participate less in the classroom and are less accepted by classmates and teachers. Also, teachers provide them with less instruction and positive feedback. They like school less and learn less.
- Social-emotional competence (i.e., successful, independent interactions with peers and positive, regulated emotions) of young children predicts their academic performance in first grade, even when controlling for their cognitive skills and family backgrounds.
- Young children and their caregivers need appropriate interventions that will prevent more serious behavior issues, repair problematic relationships, and help them develop emotional and social skills they need to succeed in school.

In general, social and emotional factors, including positive interactions with teachers, positive representations of self derived from attachment relationships, emotion knowledge, emotion regulatory abilities, social skills, and nonrejected peer status, often uniquely predict school outcomes, even when other pertinent variables, such as earlier academic success, are taken into account (Carlton, 1999; Colvin & Fernandez, 2000; Howes & Smith, 1995; Izard et al., 2001; Jacobsen & Hofmann, 1997; O'Neil, Welsh, Parke, Wang, & Strand, 1997; Pianta, 1997; Pianta, Steinberg, & Rollins, 1995; Shields et al., 2001).

The clearest picture from recent developmental psychological literature is that children with poor social skills are more likely to have difficulties with peer relationships and thus, indirectly, with school adjustment (Buhs & Ladd, 2001; Hernandez, 2003; Keane & Calkins, 2004; Kupersmidt, Coie, & Dodge. 1990; Newcomb, Bukowski, & Pattee, 1993; Vitaro, Gagnon, & Tremblay, 1990; Warden & Mackinnon, 2003). Children with low social skills and poor peer relationships are at increased risk of eventually dropping out of school (Kupersmidt et al.; Masten & Coatsworth, 1998). Normandeau and Guay (1998) also found that kindergartners' prosocial behavior predicted their first-grade cognitive self-control (defined as the ability to plan, evaluate, and self-regulate one's problem-solving activities and attention), which then predicted first-grade achievement. Prevention and intervention programming results also have shown improvements in social skills to be associated with overall school adjustment and success (Bierman & Greenberg, 1996; Jolivette et al., 2008).

In identifying critical social skills for school success of young children, some educational researchers have focused directly on the skills of attending, listening, working cooperatively with others, and following directions (Brigman, Lane, Switzer, Lane, & Lawrence, 1999; Brigman & Webb, 2003). Wooster and Carson (1982) correlated these skills specifically with later school achievement. Further, kindergarten screening of cooperation and self-control figured prominently in predicting first-grade academic success. Social skill subscales play significant roles in predicting promotion and retention after first grade (Agostin & Bain, 1997). As well, educational researchers have discovered that parents' and teachers' beliefs about the indirect advantages of social skills suggest that

if children can interact meaningfully with each other and adults, follow simple rules and directions, and demonstrate some degree of independence in the classroom . . . teachers could teach them the other academic skills and knowledge they would need to be successful in school. (Wesley & Buysse, 2003, p. 357)

An important reason children develop different behavior patterns in school may also rest in the type of critical feedback they receive. Kamins and Dweck (1999) demonstrated that children show more helpless behavior after person praise or criticism (e.g., criticizing attributes of the child) than after process praise or criticism (e.g., focus on effort and behavior). It is not known whether children from disadvantaged backgrounds receive more or less process-oriented feedback than do middle-class children, but research shows that they receive significantly fewer affirmations and significantly more negative remarks from caregivers than children from middle-class backgrounds, which may relate to motivation patterns (Hart & Risley, 1995).

As Knitzer (2002) pointed out, "for most young children, early experiences—sensitive, responsive parents, stable child care situations, and generally supportive emotional experiences—provide the kind of nurturing and stimulation that enables them to develop age-appropriate emotional and cognitive competencies" (p. 3). Also, many young children do not come to school with fully developed behavioral skills and are then at risk for poor cognitive, academic, and social outcomes. Knowledge of appropriate goals, interventions, and strategies is fundamental to helping teachers build effective practices for teaching social skills to young children (see Tables 2.2 and 2.3 for examples). Success also depends on effective partnerships among teachers, families, and other professionals to identify inappropriate behaviors that trigger and maintain problems followed by the development and implementation of interventions that teach and support appropriate behavior.

Table 2.2	Examples of Evidence-Based Interventions Applied to Preschool Students' Behavior Problems	
Student Behavior (Research Support)	**Intervention**	**Example**
Compliance (Ardoin, Martens, Wolfe,1999; Austin & Agar, 2005; Davis & Reichle, 1996; Killu, Sainato, Davis, Ospelt, & Paul, 1998)	"Behavioral momentum" or high-probability command sequences (HPCS) involve the presentation of a sequence of requests to which a child is likely to comply (i.e., high-probability requests) followed by a request for a behavior with a lower likelihood of compliance (i.e., low-probability request). When teacher is about to request that the student do a task for which the student has previously been noncompliant, teacher asks student (or class) to complete task(s) they prefer.	JJ was having difficulty coming to circle time, even when his teacher gave a signal and prompt several minutes ahead of time and praised him when he complied. She continued to use the signal, prompts, and praise but added HPCS by saying, "JJ, please go get my book and put it on my chair for circle time. Everyone, let's stand up and do five jumping jacks." After the preferred tasks were completed, she asked everyone to come to circle time, giving lots of praise to those who complied immediately.
Compliance (Bodrova & Leong, 2005)	Promote self-regulation by identifying and modifying classroom settings and/or routines that work against compliance.	A teacher observed that her students were most likely to be out of control as they transitioned from centers to a group read-aloud. When she simply told them to

Student Behavior (Research Support)	Intervention	Example
		clean up and come sit on the carpet, many returned to their play instead of complying, and she found herself continually "policing" cleanup and leading children one at a time to the carpet to start the read-aloud. She modified the routine to encourage self-regulation. When playtime ended, she played a tape of "Down by the Bay." She had students start putting their toys away as soon as they heard "Did you ever see a bear?" When they heard, "Llamas eating pajamas," they knew that the song would end soon and that they needed to hurry and finish. Cleanup became a great time for students to learn and practice self-regulation.
Following Procedures (Miller, 1993)	Use prompts to remind students of expectations. Although procedures teachers have set up in their classrooms may cause students to be more successful, teachers cannot expect that their students will always remember and follow them.	Before students come to circle time at the end of the day, Ms. Sanchez asks, "Who can tell me what we do before we come to circle time?" When a child answers correctly that everyone places backpacks by coats and paperwork, she says, "That's correct. We put our backpacks with our coats and paperwork so we don't forget them."

Table 2.3	Examples of Evidence-Based Instructional Interventions Applied to Preschool Behavior Problems	
Teacher Behavior (Research Support)	**Evidence-Based Principle**	**Example**
Using Praise (Brotman, Kiely Gouley, O'Neal, & Klein, 2004; Dodge & Pettit,2003; Dubow & Ippolito, 1994; Eisenberg, Cumberland, & Spinrad, 1998; Eisenberg, Fabes, & Murphy, 1996; Fagot, 1998; Gottman, Katz, & Hooven, 1997;	Coercion, negativity, and criticism are linked to increased inappropriate behavior and conduct problems. Limited reinforcement of positive child behavior and the lack of stimulation for learning in	Ms. Marquez, a beginning teacher, was having difficulty managing her classroom. Her mentor suggested that she increase her general (e.g., "Good job," "Excellent work.") and specific behavior praise (e.g., "I like the way George is

(Continued)

Table 2.3 (Continued)

Teacher Behavior (Research Support)	Evidence-Based Principle	Example
Haapasalo & Tremblay, 1994; Kamins & Dweck, 1999; Kalis, Vannest, & Parker, 2007; O'Leary, Smith Slep, & Reid, 1999; Sidman, 1989; Snyder & Stoolmiller, 2002; Wasserman, Miller, Pinner, & Jaramillo, 1996)	early childhood also contribute to conduct problems. On the other hand, frequent praise of children focusing on effort and behavior is linked to increased positive, independent behavior and increased motivation to succeed.	waiting quietly for the next assignment," or "You did a great job in music today."). During three brief self-observations, Ms. Marquez found that her rates of praise were very low. When she increased her rates of specific behavior praise, she noticed corresponding decreases in general behavior problems, such as noncompliance.
Making a Request (Barry, 2006)	Because children have shorter memories than adults, giving short, simple requests is effective. For instance, although short and simple, the request to "clean the play area" may be overwhelming and not effective because multiple tasks are involved.	Mr. Bain makes requests of children in his class one at a time using language that is very specific to the task he wants completed. Rather than a broad request to "clean the play area," he first says, "Please put the blocks away," or, "Straighten the books, or "Collect the art materials." When the request is completed, he moves to another one.
Making a Request (Cowan, 1997; Kail & Salthouse, 1994)	Given the same information, it takes children longer than adults to perceive, categorize, understand, and respond to it. Both adults and children take longer processing sentences containing negatives than those without. These two factors underline the importance of avoiding commands containing negatives and instead giving students clear directives of what to do.	Rules, procedures, and requests should be short and simple and describe what the teacher wants to see the student doing. The teacher says, "Keep your hands to yourself," instead of, "Don't hit"; "Use a quiet voice," instead of, "Don't yell"; "Show kindness toward others," instead of, "Don't use bad words."
Making a Request (Barry, 2006)	It takes longer for three- and four-year-olds to process social tasks than it does older students. Familiarity, predictability, and practice all help children become more efficient at processing information.	Practice and repetition in building any skill in children is very important. It is crucial to have students practice following rules and procedures continually. The more consistently teachers stick to a routine and teach students the rules and procedures of each routine, the more quickly students will comply with requests.

EFFECTIVE PRACTICES FOR TEACHING SOCIAL SKILLS TO YOUNG CHILDREN

In a position statement and concept paper, the Division for Early Childhood (2007) of the Council for Exceptional Children indicated that families and early educators must work together to address challenging behavior by implementing a variety of evidence-based strategies and services designed to prevent challenging behavior: "The range of interventions and supports that are effective in addressing challenging behavior can be conceptualized using the three-tier public health model of prevention and intervention approaches" (p. 2). The HighScope Perry Preschool Project, which was initiated in the early 1960s, is widely regarded as a landmark effort establishing and documenting the value of high-quality, evidence-based preschool education (Schweinhart, 2002; Schweinhart et al., 2005). The project's curriculum supports the belief that while children's first and primary social experiences take place at home, high-quality child care and preschool programs support and supplement family relationships. It also supports the belief that positive early social experiences influence children's later ability to form successful relationships with family, friends, and workmates. This approach gives adults the tools they need to help children develop social skills that contribute to their readiness for school and that enable them to solve problems without resorting to aggression or withdrawing and avoiding others. Five areas are of special importance in HighScope preschool programs:

1. Taking care of one's own needs
2. Expressing feelings in words
3. Building relationships with children and adults
4. Creating and experiencing collaborative play
5. Dealing with social conflict

HighScope teachers use a six-step process to help children settle disputes and conflicts:

1. *Approach calmly, stopping any hurtful actions.* Place yourself between the children, on their level; use a calm voice and gentle touch; remain neutral rather than take sides.

2. *Acknowledge children's feelings.* Say something simple such as "You look really upset"; let children know you need to hold any object in question.

3. *Gather information.* Ask "What's the problem?" Do not ask "why" questions as young children focus on what the problem is rather than understanding the reasons behind it.

4. *Restate the problem.* "So the problem is . . ." Use and extend the children's vocabulary, substituting neutral words for hurtful or judgmental ones (such as "stupid") if needed.

5. *Ask for solutions and choose one together.* Ask "What can we do to solve this problem?" Encourage children to think of a solution but offer options if the children are unable to at first.

6. *Be prepared to give follow-up support.* Acknowledge children's accomplishments, e.g., "You solved the problem!" Stay nearby in case anyone is not happy with the solution and the process needs repeating (HighScope, 2009).

Adults should respect children's ideas for solving problems, even if the options they offer do not seem fair to adults. What is important is that children agree on the solution and see themselves as competent problem solvers.

HighScope also emphasizes the need to create a warm and nurturing environment in preschool, not only because this helps children form trusting relationships with others but also because of its impact on learning in all areas. When the social climate of preschool classrooms is positive and supportive, children are likely to become engaged and motivated learners. Alternatively, when the climate is harsh or punitive, children are likely to turn away from school. HighScope's teaching practices illustrate a sound foundation that gives teachers the confidence and skills to relate well to children and support learning in every curriculum area. The HighScope approach also illustrates the importance of teaching social as well as academic skills when attending to the "whole child" in early education programs. Cultures of social and academic competence and effectiveness emerge from implementing systems of Positive Behavior Support in preschool programs (Stormont, Lewis, & Beckner, 2005).

The *Implementers' Blueprint and Self-Assessment* (OSEP Center on Positive Behavioral Interventions and Supports, 2005) describes Schoolwide Positive Behavior Support (SWPBS) as "a broad range of systemic and individualized strategies for achieving important social and academic outcomes while preventing problem behavior with all students" (p. 10). SWPBS is not a specific "model" but rather an approach that includes the following processes (Colvin, 1991; Colvin, Kame enui, & Sugai, 1993; Lewis & Sugai, 1999; OSEP Center on Positive Behavioral Interventions and Supports):

- Establishing a school-based collaborative team, including teachers, administrators and/or special services personnel, parents, and other stakeholders
- Defining schoolwide behavioral expectations and teaching them directly to students
- Developing procedures for acknowledging appropriate behaviors and discouraging inappropriate behaviors
- Using data to analyze, describe, and prioritize issues particular to groups of students, specific school settings, or the entire school
- Specifying measurable outcomes indicating improvement directly related to issues and context
- Selecting evidence-based practices to achieve specified outcomes and providing supports to sustain the adoption and implementation of those practices
- Monitoring the implementation of practices and progress toward outcomes
- Modifying practices based on analysis of the data

Stormont et al. (2005) provided information on establishing a team, identifying and teaching behavior expectations, using data to drive decisions, and developing support for children at risk for chronic behavior problems in preschool settings. In the following section, we provide additional information on these key features of preschool programs using systems of Positive Behavior Support

Importance of Team- and Data-Based Decision Making

The leadership team is the crucial decision-making body that matches evidence-based practices to schoolwide, group, or individual student problems:

One of the critical activities of the . . . leadership team is to develop an action plan that guides the systematic implementation of . . . systems and practices based on regular review of behavioral and academic student data and structured staff self-assessment information. (Sugai & Horner, 2006, p. 251)

Those implementing effective preschool programs have gained insight from problem-solving research that has focused on helping school-based teams update and restructure. Such changes have helped teams make more effective, efficient, and thorough data-based decisions and improve their role as conduits from research to practice. They bring evidence-based practices to teachers and make sure they implement them in the classroom to promote the achievement of all students.

This problem-solving approach is the result of federal legislation holding schools accountable for implementation and evaluation of research-based intervention prior to referring students for special education (IDEA, 1997/1999; NCLB, 2001). It is the foundation for reform practices currently referred to as Response to Intervention (RTI). In an effective preschool program, faculty and staff are active problem solvers. They have the information they need to make decisions about the academic and social behavior of children. They have efficient and effective organizational structures in place to support their decision making. They are concerned about children's progress as much as they care about outcome performance indicators. They also know the importance of implementing interventions with high fidelity, and they actively monitor the extent to which this is happening. As a fundamental part of the effective teaching of social skills, an effective team should

- meet regularly, at least once a month.
- include members responsible for organizing and facilitating an agenda, recording the activities of the meeting, and keeping track of the time limits assigned to each part of the agenda.
- share information with teachers and other professionals with regard to its decisions, actions, and supports.
- determine goals that are important to focus on each year, as well as how and when to monitor progress toward them.
- actively promote academic and social behavior expectations, assist teachers in developing the social skills of their students, and provide guidance in using data to make decisions about the progress and outcomes of efforts to teach social skills (Stormont et al., 2005).

Importance of Teaching Behavioral Expectations

Many children demonstrate inappropriate, unproductive behaviors that need to be replaced because they have not been taught appropriate, productive behaviors. A critical step in teaching social skills to young children is creating a system of expectations for schoolwide behavior. In schools implementing effective preschool programs, administrators, teachers, assistants, and staff create three to five positively stated expectations that are unified across all settings (see Figure 2.1). Throughout the year, administrators, teachers, assistants, and staff teach these expectations by demonstrating what they look and sound like; monitoring students closely as they practice them; providing positive, encouraging supportive and corrective feedback that lets students know how they are doing; and collecting data to indicate teaching success and student mastery. They acknowledge and celebrate student, classroom, and schoolwide mastery of the expectations. Children learn these social behavior expectations in the same way children who do not know how to read learn to read (i.e., through instruction, practice, feedback, and encouragement).

Figure 2.1		Illustration of Schoolwide Social Behavior Expectations for Young Children										
		Work Quietly										
		Listen										
		Keep Hands and Feet to Yourself										
		Walk										
		Stay in Your Seat										
		Raise Your Hand										

During the first week of school, teachers, assistants, and support staff not only teach the expectations but also teach procedures that create an organized, well-managed classroom where students are on-task and learning time is maximized. They use a "demonstrate, demonstrate, practice, and prove" model to teach their expectations and procedures. Throughout the day, they *demonstrate* skills that they want their children to do. They then have the children *demonstrate* these skills to indicate to the teacher that they have understood how to and can do them. As the teacher presents *practice* activities, students are able to *prove* that they have mastered the skills. This is a tried-and-true method of teaching both academic and social behavior.

Support for Teaching Appropriate and Discouraging Inappropriate Social Skills

In positive preschool classrooms, appropriate social behavior is encouraged and intentionally taught; inappropriate behavior is discouraged and not inadvertently taught. Teachers in these classrooms use specific behavior praise and rewards to encourage and teach appropriate behavior. They also make classrooms positive places for children to learn and practice appropriate social behavior.

Specific Behavior Praise

Specific behavior praise tells children that their behavior is correct, and it may also mention why. When we talk about specific behavior praise, we do not mean praise that is directed to a specific person or a specific group. *All* praise should reflect *who* (the name of the person or group) is being recognized. However, specific behavior praise also tells *what* is being recognized, while general praise does not. So "Juan, great job," or "Lilly, thumbs up!" is general praise. It is not telling the child what was done to earn your praise. General praise is fine and creates a positive classroom, but research indicates that it is not as powerful a teaching tool as specific praise. When you think about specific behavior praise, remember that it will be given to children for following classroom expectations or procedures (see Figure 2.2).

Figure 2.2   Examples of Specific Behavior Praise (Happy Talk)

Happy Talk, Keep Talking Happy Talk!

- [*Student name*], thank you for raising your hand.
- You're doing such a great job of listening to [*student name*]. You're making eye contact and smiling.
- Look at you helping [student name] clean up—what a friend!
- [*Student name*], that was a great job of saying, "Thank you."
- Wow, [*student name*], what a caring attitude you showed by helping [student or adult name] with [assisted activity or task].
- [*Student name*], everyone appreciates the way you are keeping your hands and feet to yourself!
- Nice work holding that door open for [*student or adult name*].
- [*Student name*] is doing an outstanding job of working quietly.
- [*Student name*], you are doing such a great job of staying in your seat while we are eating—thank you!
- [*Student name*], thank you for remembering to walk.
- Bravo for walking in a straight line. You are a wonderful class.

Often when educators talk about individualizing to meet children's needs, teachers think that means long, complicated plans and lessons. Using simple methods like specific behavior praise provides individualization for students by recognizing that students are mastering the behavior curriculum—the expectations and procedures of the school and classroom.

Rewards

Rewards are positive consequences provided to children after they have exhibited a desired behavior (see Table 2.4). Teachers sometimes worry about using rewards because they believe they are bribing children or because they believe children should be "intrinsically" motivated to behave appropriately. However, bribery is providing the consequence *before* the behavior happens. With bribery, we pay in advance for the "promise" of appropriate behavior, but with the reward already in hand, many children then fail to exhibit the desired behavior. Rather than buying or bribing behavior, rewards are given *after* the behavior occurs. This practice is also known as Grandma's Rule: "Finish your vegetables, and then you get dessert." The most effective approach is not to back down even in the face of arguments, noncompliance, or inappropriate behavior from the child.

Table 2.4 Social Behaviors That Are Appropriate for Rewards	
• Identifying feelings and responding appropriately	• Putting materials away correctly and carefully
• Walking quietly in line	• Staying on-task
• Raising a hand instead of speaking out	• Sharing with another child
• Using kind words while in centers or at recess	• Using friendly words like "please" and "thank you"
• Using quiet voices in the classroom	• Helping a friend or classmate who is hurt
• Participating in classroom activities	• Exhibiting appropriate bathroom behavior
• Maintaining a positive attitude	• Sitting quietly while waiting for a snack
• Helping a peer or adult without being asked or reminded	• Not responding to aggressive behavior from another child

Rewards are reasonable consequences for appropriate social behavior, but the "payment" does not have to be extravagant or expensive to be effective. In fact, most children will work for simple "tokens" of recognition and appreciation or attention as much as for other "tangibles."

Information from children is useful when deciding what rewards to use. Most teachers ask the child what types of things he or she likes (e.g., being line leader, eating lunch next to teacher), observe and record any preferred activities, or have children complete a reward menu (see Figure 2.3). It is important to be consistent in the pattern of providing rewards, but it is also good to vary them to keep children motivated.

Making Classrooms Positive Places

Making classrooms positive places means creating environments and interactions that demonstrate acceptance and care for children. Children are more motivated to learn when teachers and assistants accept them; interact positively with them; and create a supportive, cooperative learning environment for them. We recently observed in a classroom where a student was not coming to "Circle Time" right away. The teacher praised the other children as they came to the group activity. Hearing the teacher "reward" the other children, the reluctant child "made the right choice" to come join the group on time. The teacher saw the child making the correct choice and began to sing, "Here comes the sun, here comes the sun, and I say, great job, Bobby." When another child ran to the circle without cleaning up, she took a few seconds to tell him that her expectation for tomorrow was that he would stop playing when he heard the signal, clean up, and then come to circle. And if that didn't happen, the child might find that he is not allowed

Figure 2.3 Example of Preschool Reward Menu

Student ______________________________

Circle the things you like to eat.

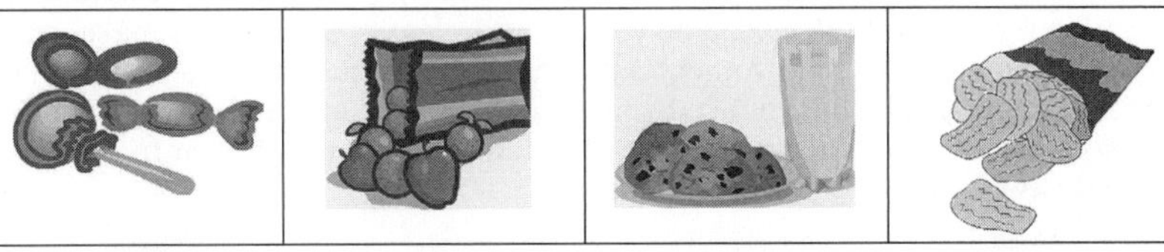

Circle the things you like to do.

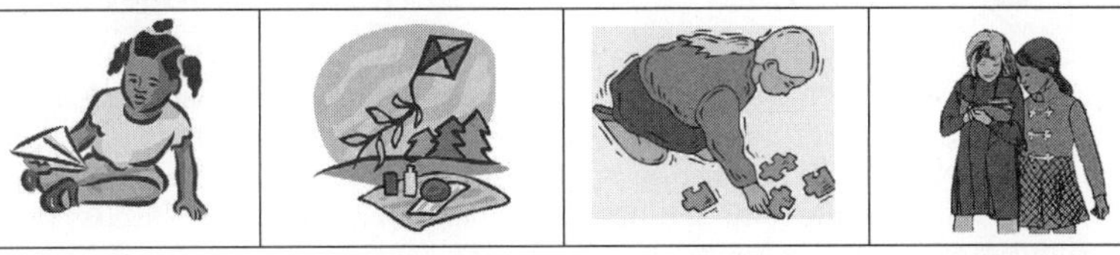

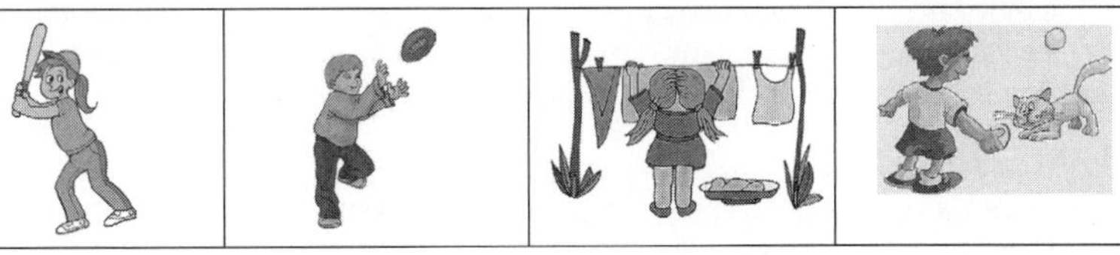

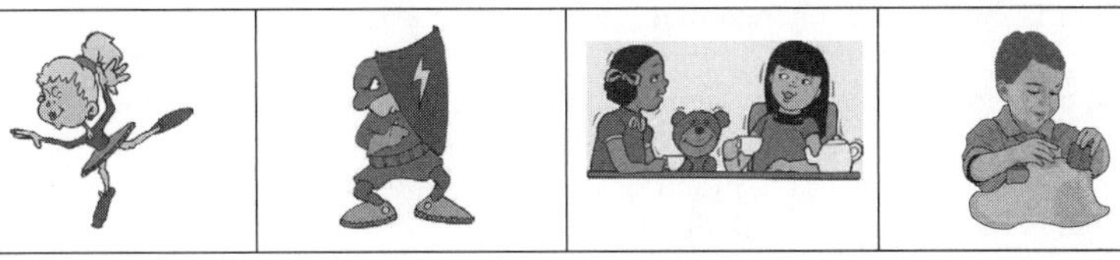

Circle what makes you feel good.

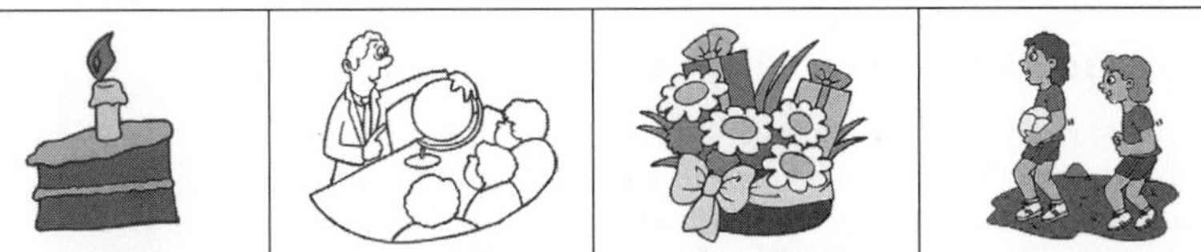

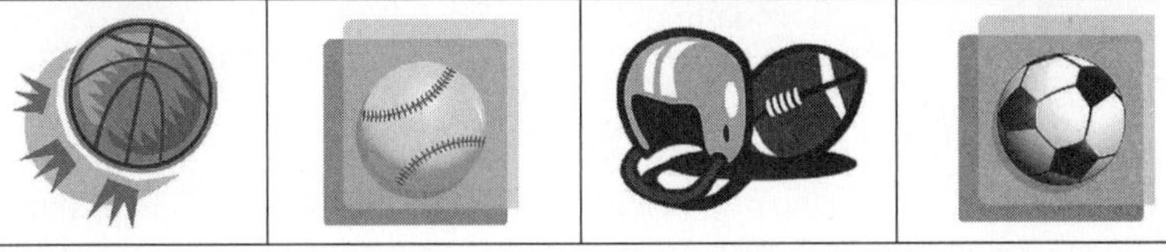

to go to his favorite center for a while because he left a mess. If it has been difficult for him to come to circle and he makes the first step, for now, she "sings his praises."

Another example . . . Imagine that you are at recess and you notice one of your children hanging back, looking sad. You can go up to her and put your arm around her shoulder and sing: "Let the sun shine in, face it with a grin, smilers never lose and frowners never win, so let the sun shine in, face it with a grin, open up your heart and let the sun shine in." If the child does decide to play and plays appropriately, make sure you praise her if she comes close to you outside and when you go inside. Use specific behavior praise: "You know, Jaylin, I noticed you were feeling sad out on the playground. I am proud of you for choosing to have a positive attitude and play with your friends. I know they loved having you play with them today."

Using Data to Plan Interventions and Monitor Progress

Once a team has been formed and schoolwide expectations have been defined and taught, a system for gathering and summarizing useful information concerning behavior and a process for using that information for decision making are established. Data are not collected for the purpose of referral for special services but to determine the best ways children can be taught in the same setting as their neighbors and peers. Discussions about this information focus on observations, assessments, surveys, and other data collection about behavior in school. Discussions reflecting the "History of the World: Parts I, II, III, and IV" or "admiring the problem" are avoided. Initial questions addressed when using data to plan interventions include the following:

- Are we satisfied with current student behavior?
- Are we implementing evidence-based practices?
- What do we already do well?
- What is the smallest change that would make the biggest difference?

Initial questions addressed when using data to monitor progress include these:

- Are we implementing the practices and systems we have agreed to implement?
- What is the impact on student social behavior?
- What is the impact on student academic behavior?

Evaluating Outcomes and Modifying Practices

A crucial responsibility for child support teams is to use data to make needed changes if the answer to the question "Are we satisfied with current student behavior?" is "No!" Expecting and/or accepting inappropriate behavior because of students' backgrounds and home life is a practice all schools must avoid. Teams, administrators, coaches, and teachers must continuously use data to identify schoolwide, group, or individual problems and write action plans identifying what will be done to solve those problems, who will complete problem-solving tasks, and how and when they will be completed. They must continuously use data to evaluate their efforts and modify their efforts. Practices that have been successful in the past in a school may become stale and ineffective. A successful intervention one year may fail the next because of a different population of children or less funding. It is not enough just to implement evidence-based practices and systems: the impact of interventions must be continuously monitored and evaluated.

Part of modifying practices, whether they be directed toward academics or behavior, is the use of data to determine the relationship between students and what it is they are expected to know. In other words, are they in the acquisition, fluency, maintenance, or generalization stage of learning? Here's an example. At the beginning of the year, a preschool teacher introduces just two centers to her students. When they have mastered the procedures for those two centers, she introduces two others. The behavior of her students suddenly changes, and there are more incidences of misbehavior. Now the team uses data (observations, conversations with students, input from the assistant) to determine what has caused the change. One change is that students have moved from the fluency/maintenance stage of learning to the acquisition stage of learning. Some children may be able to generalize skills from other centers to new centers, while others may not. The team may use the Stages of Learning Chart (see Table 2.5) to determine modifications the teacher can try in the classroom.

Table 2.5 Example of Stages of Learning Chart	
Stages of Learning	**Teacher Behavior**
Acquisition: Show and Tell	New skill or concept is introduced. *Teacher may* • Explain concretely. • Demonstrate. • Link skills or content to other ideas or concepts. • Use examples and nonexamples. • Use lots of specific praise and encourage the child when learning. • Use even more praise and encouragement.
Fluency: Practice Makes Perfect	Students use the new skill or content without a prompt. *Teacher may* • Offer multiple opportunities to practice. • Help child link skill or concept to others. • Prompt the child to use the skill or concept in new situations. • Elaborate on the skill or concept.
Maintenance: You Got It!	Students continue to use the skill or concept over time. *Teacher may* • Provide opportunities for students to use the skill or concept in new situations or with new people. • Provide opportunities within a variety of activities and in new applications. • Comment on the student's ability to maintain the skill and generalize its use.
Generalization: You REALLY Got It!	Students apply the skill or concept to new situations, people, activities, ideas, and settings. *Teacher may* • Provide opportunities for students to use the skill or concept in new situations or with new people. • Provide opportunities within a variety of activities and in new applications. • Comment on the student's ability to maintain the skill and generalize its use.

NOTE: Teaching strategies for each stage of learning may include but are not limited to adult modeling, modeling with puppets, preparing peer partners, songs, fingerplays, flannel board activities, prompts, priming, reinforcements, incidental teaching, use of games, use of children's literature, and social stories (Hemmeter & Fox, 2007).

TEACHING YOUNG CHILDREN
HOW TO BEHAVE IN SOCIAL SETTINGS

Research in the field of early childhood development indicates that social development and ability to be engaged is essential for school readiness. Children with problem behavior are at risk for both social exclusion and academic failure. Just as we teach children to read, swim, and count, we must teach them how to acquire and maintain friendships; follow rules, routines, and directions; identify feelings within themselves and others; control anger and impulses; listen and attend; and problem-solve. Preschool programs like the HighScope Perry Preschool Project, which takes responsibility for teaching social skills in an effective manner, demonstrate positive effects on the lives of their students in the areas of social responsibility, earnings and economic status, educational performance, and commitment to marriage.

Not only do programs such as the HighScope Perry Preschool Project provide guidance in teaching social as well as academic skills to preschoolers, schools and programs implementing systems of Positive Behavior Support provide insight as well. They indicate the beneficial effect on students of investing in evidence-based practices, creating a systems-based preventive continuum of behavior support, teaching and acknowledging behavioral expectations, and using data-based decisions to evaluate process and product.

An Illustration From Practice

Mountain Valley Child Development Center is a state-funded preschool program. Despite intense, high-quality programming, many children, especially those with English-language learner (ELL) needs and/or disabilities, who "graduated" from Mountain Valley entered kindergarten with wide variability in skills. They were also typically performing lower than their more privileged peers. As a result, the staff placed special emphasis on prevention of later learning problems by supporting the development of early literacy and social skills with increased instructional time, continuity of teaching, and a curriculum with a logical progression of skills precorrected and scaffolded to match the systematic instruction students received in kindergarten. Further, rich language and cognitive experiences were provided to the children to decrease the "setback" or performance gap that diverse groups of students often experience over summer vacation and to increase their potential for higher academic readiness entering kindergarten and success in later school years.

As part of the effort, the district provided opportunities for teachers to observe and participate in ongoing professional development and guided practice, thereby minimizing potential instructional fatigue resulting from the challenges of teaching young children. The bridge of scaffolded activities was also supported with increased resources, opportunities, and experiences for communities, families, and children in low-income areas to experience successful school transitions.

All children at Mountain Valley participated in an evidence-based curriculum for early literacy and language that met district expectations and standards, including 180 days of instruction targeting four areas (i.e., oral language and vocabulary; phonological and phonemic awareness; print awareness and alphabet knowledge; comprehension). Teachers and assistants regularly monitored children's progress using local norms for levels and rates of performance as a basis for adjusting what and how they were teaching. When adequate progress was not being achieved despite evidence of participation in high-quality instruction, increased opportunities to respond were provided in center-based supplemental (targeted) activities, which were supported by assistants and classroom volunteers. When appropriate, these targeted activities were provided to small groups of students with similar needs, and they were monitored regularly to identify students in need of more intensive (e.g., one-on-one) support using scripted of lessons developed by preschool teachers in the district.

REFERENCES

Agostin, T. M., & Bain, S. K. (1997). Predicting early school success with developmental and social skills screeners. *Psychology in the Schools, 34*, 219–228.

Ardoin, S., Martens, B. K., & Wolfe, L. A. (1999). Using high-probability instruction sequences with fading to increase student compliance during transitions. *Journal of Applied Behavior Analysis, 3*, 339–351.

Austin, J. L., & Agar, G. (2005). Helping young children follow their teachers' directions: The utility of high probability command sequences in pre-K and kindergarten classrooms. *Education and Treatment of Children, 28*(3), 222–236.

Barry, E. S. (2006). Children's memory: A primer for understanding children's behavior. *Early Childhood Education Journal, 33*(6), 405–411.

Bierman, K. L., & Greenberg, M. T. (1996). Social skills training in the Fast Track Program. In R. D. Peters & R. J. McMahon (Eds.), *Preventing childhood disorders, substance abuse, and delinquency* (pp. 65–89). Thousand Oaks, CA: Sage.

Bodrova, E., & Leong, D. J. (2005). Uniquely preschool. *Educational Leadership, 63*(1), 44–47.

Brigman, G. A., Lane, D., Switzer, D., Lane, D., & Lawrence, R. (1999). Teaching children school success skills. *Journal of Educational Research, 92*, 323–329.

Brigman, G. A., & Webb, L. D. (2003). Ready to learn: Teaching kindergarten students school success skills. *Journal of Educational Research, 6*, 286–292.

Brotman, L. M., Kiely Gouley, K., O'Neal, C., & Klein, R. G. (2004). Preschool-aged siblings of adjudicated youths: Multiple risk factors for conduct problems. *Early Education and Development, 15*, 387–406.

Buhs, E. S., & Ladd, G. W. (2001). Peer rejection as an antecedent of young children's school adjustment: An examination of mediating processes. *Developmental Psychology, 37*, 550–560.

Buscemi, L., Bennett, T., Thomas, D., & Deluca, D. A. (1995). Head Start: Challenges and training needs. *Journal of Early Intervention, 20*, 1–33.

Carlton, M. P. (1999). Motivation and school readiness in kindergarten children. *Dissertation Abstracts International A. The Humanities and Social Sciences, 6*(11-A), 3899A.

Colvin, G. (1991). *Procedures for establishing a proactive school-wide discipline plan.* Eugene: College of Education, University of Oregon—Eugene.

Colvin, G., & Fernandez, E. (2000). Sustaining effective behavior support systems in an elementary school. *Journal of Positive Behavior Interventions, 2*, 251–253.

Colvin, G., Kame enui, E. J., & Sugai, G. (1993). School-wide and classroom management: Reconceptualizing the integration and management of students with behavior problems in general education. *Education and Treatment of Children, 16*, 361–381.

Cowan, N. (1997). The development of working memory. In N. Cowan (Ed.), *The development of memory in childhood* (pp. 163–199). Hove, England: Psychology Press.

Davis, C. A., & Reichle, J. (1996). Variant and invariant high-probability requests: Increasing appropriate behaviors in children with emotional-behavioral disorders. *Journal of Applied Behavior Analysis, 29*, 471–482.

Division for Early Childhood (DEC). (2007). *Position statement: Identification of and intervention with challenging behavior.* Missoula, MT: Author. Retrieved October 28, 2009, from www.dec-sped.org/uploads/docs/about_dec/position_concept_papers/PositionStatement_Chal_Behav_updated_jan2009.pdf

Dodge, K. A., & Pettit, G. S. (2003). A biopsychosocial model of the development of chronic conduct problems in adolescence. *Developmental Psychology, 39*, 349–371.

Dubow, E. F., & Ippolito, M. F. (1994). Effects of poverty and quality of the home environment on changes in the academic and behavioral adjustment of elementary school-age children. *Journal of Clinical Child Psychology, 23*, 401–412.

Eisenberg, N., Cumberland, A., & Spinrad, T. L. (1998) Parental socialization of emotion. *Psychological Inquiry, 9*, 241–273.

Eisenberg, N., Fabes, R., & Murphy, B. (1996). Parents' reactions to children's negative emotions: Relations to children's social competence and comforting behavior. *Child Development, 67*, 2227–2247.

Fagot, B. I. (1998). Social problem solving: Effect of context and parent sex. *International Journal of Behavioral Development, 22,* 389–401.

Fuchs, D., & Deshler, D. D. (2007). What we need to know about responsiveness to intervention (and shouldn't be afraid to ask). *Learning Disabilities Research & Practice, 22,* 129–136.

Gottman, J. M., Katz, L. F., & Hooven, C. (1997). Meta-emotion: How families communicate emotionally. Mahwah, NJ: Lawrence Erlbaum Associates.

Haapasalo, J., & Tremblay, R. E. (1994). Physically aggressive boys from ages 6 to 12: Family background, parenting behavior, and prediction of delinquency. *Journal of Consulting and Clinical Psychology, 62,* 1044–1052.

Hart, B., & Risley, T. (1995). *Meaningful differences in the everyday lives of American children.* Baltimore: Brookes.

Hemmeter, M. L., & Fox, L. (2007). Promoting social emotional development and preventing challenging behavior: Inservice and preservice training strategies. In P. Winton, J. McCollum, & C. Catlett (Eds.), *Preparing effective professionals: Evidence and applications in early childhood and early intervention* (pp. 119–142). Washington, DC: Zero to Three Press.

Hernandez, M. J. (2003). Caracteristicas emocionales y comportamentales de los grupos sociometricos desde una perspeciiva multiple [A multiperspective of emotional and behavioral correlates of sociometric groups]. *Psicotogia Conductual, 11,* 41–60.

HighScope. (2009). *Social skills in the HighScope preschool curriculum.* Retrieved October 28, 2009, from http://www.highscope.org/Content.asp?ContentId=294

Howes, C., & Smith, E. W. (1995). Relations among child care quality, teacher behavior, children's play activities, emotional security, and cognitive activity in child care. *Early Childhood Research Quarterly, 10,* 381–404.

Huffman, L. C., Mehlinger, S. L., & Kerivan, A. S. (2000). Risk factors for academic and behavioral problems at the beginning of school. In L. C. Huffman, S. L. Mehlinger, A. S. Kerivan, D. A. Cavanaugh, J. Lippitt, & O. Moyo (Eds.), *Off to a good start: Research on the risk factors for early school problems and selected federal policies affecting children's social and emotional development and their readiness for school* (Paper 1, pp. 1–93). Chapel Hill: University of North Carolina, FPG Child Development Center. (ERIC Document Reproduction Service No. ED476378)

Individuals with Disabilities Education Act (IDEA) of 1997, 20 U.S.C. § 1400 *et seq.* (1999).

Izard, C. E., Fine, S., Schultz, D., Mostow, A., Ackerman, B., & Youngstrom, E. (2001). Emotion knowledge as a predictor of social behavior and academic competence in children at risk. *Psychological Science, 12,* 18–23.

Jacobsen, T., & Hofmann, V. (1997). Children's attachment representations: Longitudinal relations to school behavior and academic competency in middle childhood and adolescence. *Developmental Psychology, 33,* 703–710.

Jolivette, K., Gallagher, P. A., Morrier, M., & Lambert, R. (2008). Preventing problem behaviors in young children with disabilities. *Exceptionality, 16,* 78–92.

Kail, R. V., & Salthouse, T. A. (1994). Processing speed as a mental capacity. *Acta Psychologica, 86,* 199–225.

Kalis, T., Vannest, K., & Parker, R. (2007). Praise counts: Using self-monitoring to increase effective teaching practices. *Preventing School Failure, 51*(3), 20–27.

Kamins, M. L., & Dweck, C. S. (1999). Person versus process praise and criticism: Implications for contingent self-work and coping. *Developmental Psychology, 35,* 835–847.

Keane, S. P., & Calkins, S. D. (2004). Predicting kindergarten peer social status from toddler and preschool problem behavior. *Journal of Abnormal Child Psychology, 32,* 409–423.

Killu, K., Sainato, D. M., Davis, C. A., Ospelt, H., & Paul, J. N. (1998). Effects of high-probability request sequences on preschoolers' compliance and disruptive behavior. *Journal of Behavioral Education, 8,* 347–368.

Knitzer, J. E. (2002). *Building services and systems to support the healthy emotional development of young children: An action guide for policymakers* (Policy Paper No. 1). New York: Columbia University Mailman School of Public Health, National Center for Children in Poverty. Available October 28, 2009, from http://www.nccp.org/publications/pdf/text_369.pdf

Kratochwill, T. R., & Shernoff, E. S. (2004). Evidence-based practice: Promoting evidence-based interventions in school psychology. *School Psychology Review, 33*(1), 34–48.

Kupersmidt, J. B., Coie, J. D., & Dodge, K. (1990). The role of poor peer relations in the development of disorder. In S. R. Asher & J. D. Cole (Eds.), *Peer rejection in childhood* (pp. 274–305). Cambridge, England: Cambridge University Press.

Lewis, T. J., & Sugai, G. (1999). Effective behavior support: A systems approach to proactive school management. *Focus on Exceptional Children, 31*(6), 24–47.

Masten, A., & Coatsworth, J. (1998). The development of competence in favorable and unfavorable environments: Lessons from research on successful children. *American Psychologist, 53*, 205–220.

Merrell, K. W., & Buchanan, R. (2006). Intervention selection in school-based practice: Using public health models to enhance systems capacity of schools. *School Psychology Review, 35*, 167–180.

Miller, P. H. (1993). *Theories of developmental psychology* (3rd ed.). New York: W. H. Freeman.

National Research Council. (2005). *Advancing scientific research in education.* Washington, DC: The National Academies Press.

Newcomb, A., Bukowski, W., & Pattee, L. (1993). Children's peer relations: A meta-analytic review of popular, rejected, neglected, controversial, and average sociometric status. *Psychological Bulletin, 113*, 99–128.

No Child Left Behind Act of 2001, 20 U.S.C. § 6301 *et seq.* (2002). Retrieved October 28, 2009, from http://www.ed.gov/policy/elsec/leg/esea02/index.html

Normandeau, S., & Guay, F. (1998). Preschool behavior and first-grade school achievement: The mediational role of cognitive self-control. *Journal of Educational Psychology, 90*, 111–121.

O'Leary, S. G., Smith Slep, A. M., & Reid, M. (1999). A longitudinal study of mothers' overreactive discipline and toddlers' externalizing behavior. *Journal of Abnormal Child Psychology, 27*, 331–341.

O'Neil, R., Welsh, M., Parke, R. D., Wang, S., & Strand. C. (1997). A longitudinal assessment of the academic correlates of early peer acceptance and rejection. *Journal of Clinical Child Psychology, 26*, 290–303.

OSEP Center on Positive Behavioral Interventions and Supports. (2005). *School-wide Positive Behavior Support: Implementers' blueprint and self-assessment.* Eugene, OR: Author. Available October 28, 2009, at http://www.osepideasthatwork.org/toolkit/pdf/SchoolwideBehaviorSupport.pdf

Peth-Pierce, R. (2000). *A good beginning: Sending America's children to school with the social and emotional competence they need to succeed.* Chapel Hill, NC: The Child Mental Health Foundations and Agencies Network.

Pianta, R. C. (1997). Adult-child relationship processes and early schooling. *Early Education and Development, 8*, 11–26.

Pianta, R. C., Steinberg. M., & Rollins, K. (1995). The first two years of school: Teacher-child relationships and deflections in children's classroom adjustment. *Development & Psychopathology, 7*, 295–312.

Raver, C. C., & Knitzer, J. (2002). *Ready to enter: What research tells policymakers about strategies to promote social and emotional school readiness among three- and four-year-olds.* New York: National Center for Children in Poverty.

Rimm-Kaufman, S. E., Pianta, R. C., & Cox. M. J. (2000). Teachers' judgements of problems in the transition to kindergarten. *Early Childhood Research Quarterly, 15*, 147–166.

Rodgers, R., & Hammerstein, O., II. (1949). You've got to be carefully taught. In *Rodgers and Hammerstein vocal selections* (Rev. ed.). *South Pacific.* Milwaukee, WI: Hal Leonard Corporation. (Copyright 2004 by Williamson Music)

Schweinhart, L. J. (2002). *How the High/Scope Perry Preschool Project grew: A researcher's tale.* (Research Bulletin No. 32). Bloomington, IN: Center for Evaluation, Development, and Research. Retrieved October 28, 2009, from http://www.highscope.org/Content.asp?ContentId=232

Schweinhart, L. J., Montie, J., Xiang, Z., Barnett, W. S., Belfield, C. R., & Nores, M. (2005). *Lifetime effects: The High/Scope Perry Preschool study through age 40* (Monographs of the HighScope Educational Research Foundation, 14). Ypsilanti, MI: HighScope Press.

Shields, A., Dickstein, S., Seifer, R., Giusti, L., Magee, K. D., & Sprit, B. (2001). Emotional competence and early school adjustment: A study of preschoolers at risk. *Early Education & Development, 12,* 73–96,

Shonkoff, J. P., & Phillips. D. A. (2000). *From neurons to neighborhoods: The science of early childhood development.* Washington, DC: National Academy Press.

Sidman, M. (1989). *Coercion and its fallout.* Boston: Authors Cooperative.

Snyder, J., & Stoolmiller, M. (2002). Reinforcement and coercion mechanisms in the development of antisocial behavior: The family. In J. B. Reid, G. R. Patterson, & J. Snyder (Eds.), *Antisocial behavior in children and adolescents: A developmental analysis and model for intervention* (pp. 65–100).Washington, DC: American Psychological Association.

Stormont, M., Lewis, T. J., & Beckner, R. (2005). Positive Behavior Support systems: Applying key features to preschool settings. *Teaching Exceptional Children, 37*(6), 42–49.

Sugai, G., & Horner, R. H. (2006). A promising approach for expanding and sustaining School-wide Positive Behavior Support. *School Psychology Review, 35,* 245–259.

Vitaro, F., Gagnon, C., & Tremblay, R. E. (1990). Predicting stable peer rejection from kindergarten to grade one. *Journal of Clinical Child Psychology, 19,* 257–264.

Warden, D., & Mackinnon, S. (2003). Prosocial children, bullies and victims: An investigation of their sociometric status, empathy and social problem-solving strategies. *British Journal of Developmental Psychology, 21,* 367–385.

Wasserman, G. A., Miller, L. S., Pinner, E., & Jaramillo, B. (1996). Parenting predictors of early conduct problems in urban, high-risk boys. *Journal of the American Academy of Child & Adolescent Psychiatry, 35,* 1227–1236.

Wesley, P. W., & Buysse, V. (2003). Making meaning of school readiness in schools and communities. *Early Childhood Research Quarterly, 18,* 351–375.

Wong, H. K., & Wong, R. T. (1998). *How to be an effective teacher: The first days of school.* Mountain View, CA: Harry K. Wong Productions.

Wooster, A. D., & Carson, A. (1982). Improved reading and self-concept through communication and social skills training. *British Journal of Guidance and Counseling, 10,* 83–87.

3

Schoolwide Positive Behavior Support

In this chapter, we

- review why schoolwide, multitiered prevention is a preferred practice in America's schools,
- identify and describe key features of Schoolwide Positive Behavior Support,
- identify and describe characteristics of Schoolwide Positive Behavior Support systems,
- review evidence supporting the effectiveness of Schoolwide Positive Behavior Support programs, and
- provide a perspective on and an illustration from practice of Schoolwide Positive Behavior Support.

School discipline has been a recurring concern and a major problem in educational systems for several decades (Gallup & Elam, 1988; Rose & Gallup, 1999, 2007). Although there is some indication that overall school safety has slightly improved over the past few years, school violence, theft, drugs, and weapons and other less serious yet pervasive infractions such as defiance, physical conflicts, threats, profanity, and disruption continue to influence overall school climate (Algozzine, Christian, Marr, McClanahan, & White, 2008; Dinkes, Cataldi, & Lin-Kelly, 2007; Lo & Cartledge, 2007). For example, it has been reported that general education teachers faced an average of 1 in 5 students who engage in disruptive/off-task behavior and 1 in 20 students who are perceived to engage in aggressive behaviors (Myers & Holland, 2000). Problem behaviors in schools often limit teachers' ability to teach and students' ability to learn (Sprague, Sugai,

Horner, & Walker, 1999). Most recently, the 2007 report *Indicators of School Crime and Safety* presented the following striking findings (Dinkes et al.):

- Over 86 percent of approximately 83,000 public schools reported one or more serious crimes or violent incidents (e.g., physical attack, robbery, sexual battery, vandalism, possession or distribution of drugs or alcohol) in 2005–2006, totaling an estimated 2.2 million incidents, or 45.8 incidents per 1,000 students. Of these incidents, 763,000 (or 16 per 1,000 students) had police involvement.
- Approximately 19 percent of students in Grades 9 to 12 in 2005 reported that they had carried a weapon, and 6 percent reported carrying a weapon on school property in the previous month.
- In 2005, 6 percent of students ages 12 to 18 reported fear of attack or harm at school. The same percentage of students reported that they had purposely avoided a school activity or place during the previous six months due to their fear of attack and harm.
- Of surveyed teachers in 2003–2004, 35 percent agreed or strongly agreed that student misbehavior interfered with their teaching. The percentage was higher (41 percent) in urban settings.
- In 2003–2004, nearly 7 percent of public and private school teachers reported being threatened with injury by a student during the previous 12 months, with a greater percentage of the threats reported by public and city school teachers.
- In 2005–2006, 48 percent of public schools reported that they had enforced at least one serious disciplinary action, such as out-of-school suspension lasting five days or more, expulsion, or transferring a student to a specialized school, for offenses such as physical attacks, insubordination, possession, distribution or use of alcohol or illegal drugs, and use or possession of firearm or weapon.

Such challenges lead policy makers, researchers, professionals, and practitioners to continuously explore the context of school discipline to provide a learning environment where all students are able to receive the most appropriate education possible. A common response to discipline problems is detention, suspension, loss of privileges, or expulsion for the misbehaved students and the establishment of "safety watch" systems, such as metal detector or surveillance to "teach students a lesson" (Anderson & Kincaid, 2005). Unfortunately, with the use of reactive, punitive disciplinary practices, many schools have failed to reduce the very problems that are targeted for reduction; most importantly, they have failed to create an environment where students are provided with rich learning opportunities for academic and social development (Hyman & Perone, 1998; Lewis & Sugai, 1999; Skiba & Peterson, 1999, 2000; Skiba, Peterson, & Williams, 1997).

A recent emphasis in school discipline is on creating a social context that prepares all students for improvements in both academic achievement and social competence by developing a positive and effective teaching environment, establishing clear expectations and routines, teaching and encouraging socially appropriate behaviors, reducing and discouraging existing problem behaviors, and preventing future rule violations (Kilian, Fish, & Maniago, 2006; Safran & Oswald, 2003; Sugai & Horner, 2008). Schoolwide Positive Behavior Support (SWPBS) is one such approach; evidence is accumulating that it can address the current and future challenges related to social behavior commonly faced by schools (Liaupsin, Jolivette, & Scott, 2004). In this chapter, we define SWPBS and discuss its importance in relation to preventing problem behaviors, outline characteristics of SWPBS, identify and describe effective practices for implementing SWPBS, and discuss evidence of the effectiveness of SWPBS from a variety of perspectives. Our ultimate goal is to communicate a need for and the benefit of adopting the core elements of SWPBS in all U.S. schools by providing an overview of the approach and its benefits in preventing problem behaviors.

DEFINITION AND IMPORTANCE OF SWPBS

Positive Behavior Support (PBS) was initially developed as an alternative to aversive interventions used with individuals with severe disabilities who engage in extremely dangerous behavior by focusing on person-centered planning and lifestyle improvements (Carr et al., 1999, 2002; Durand, 1999; Horner et al., 1990; Meyer & Evans, 1993). It is now generally referred to the application of positive behavioral interventions resulting in socially important behavior changes (Sugai & Horner, 2002b; Sugai et al., 2000). Its application has been traditionally limited to the level of the individual. About 10 years ago, by considering the school as the "unit of analysis," PBS rapidly extended and "scaled up" to Schoolwide Positive Behavior Support (SWPBS) by shifting its focus from individuals to whole school environments (Colvin, Kame'enui, & Sugai, 1993; Horner, 2007; OSEP Technical Assistance Center on Positive Behavioral Interventions and Supports, 2004; Sugai & Horner, 2005).

SWPBS, rooted in applied behavior analysis, is a systems approach that enables schools to adopt and sustain structures and procedures using research-validated practices to address the social and academic needs of all students (Lewis & Sugai, 1999). SWPBS focuses on prevention of problem behaviors by rearranging relevant environmental variables (e.g., antecedents and consequences), directly teaching important social skills, and supporting the entire body of students with multiple levels of interventions on a continuum within the social culture of the whole school (Freeman et al., 2006). Research has suggested that no single strategy or procedure will meet all challenges of individual students and that any combination of strategies must be adopted and tailored to meet the unique cultures and needs of individual schools (Sprague et al., 1999). SWPBS is one such approach with multiple components that respond to multiple behavioral challenges faced by schools. It can effectively address a range of behavioral needs, from those of students who just need minor supports to those of students who require more intensive, in-depth behavioral services.

Elements Underlying Importance

Three foundational elements establish the importance of SWPBS.

1. The development of a problem behavior is the result of a problem context (e.g., any problem events that trigger and/or encourage the behavior occurrence). The context can teach the behavior and inadvertently shape it to increase its intensity over time (O'Neill et al., 1997). As a result, a minor problem behavior, when not addressed early, can develop into a more severe pattern, which will require increased time, resources, and effort to remedy (Walker, Colvin, & Ramsey, 1995). SWPBS provides a prevention approach for schools to teach students prosocial behaviors, prevent antisocial behaviors from occurring, and address problem behaviors during their early development stage when minimal effort will be effective. Due to its reach to all students in all settings within the whole school, effective implementation of SWPBS can lead to substantial reduction in

minor problem behaviors, allowing the school to focus on those students who need intensified interventions (Hieneman, Dunlap, & Kincaid, 2005; Miller, George, & Fogt, 2005).

2. The increased diversity in students' academic and social needs and the recent mandates (e.g., No Child Left Behind of 2001, Individuals with Disabilities Education Improvement Act of 2004) have demanded schools' increased accountability to reach out to all students, with and without disabilities. To address the unique needs of all students, schools need a mechanism to establish different levels of support simultaneously within a whole-school environment using a systematic and unified approach. Even with students who have moderate/significant disabilities or chronic behavior problems, SWPBS may provide an essential foundation such that specially tailored interventions for these individuals will be most successful (Freeman et al., 2006; Hawken & O'Neill, 2006; Lewis-Palmer, Bounds, & Sugai, 2004; Medley, Little, & Akin-Little, 2008).

3. Because each student's problem behavior is the result of the student's interactions with the environment, effective behavior change plans should address what adults and peers will do (e.g., "Teacher praises Susan when she raises her hand before talking," or "Peers ignore Jacob when he tells a joke during instruction.") and what environmental factors can be modified or rearranged (e.g., reduces alone time, breaks down long tasks, or changes seating) to change the student's behavior (Horner, Sugai, Todd, & Lewis-Palmer, 1999–2000). Carr (2007) reminded us to center our focus on "redesign[ing] the counter-productive and unfair environmental contexts" rather than on problem behaviors or problem individuals when promoting a life of quality for the individuals of concern. SWPBS centers on system arrangement and organizational structure to promote positive school climate, not on how to "change the students." As one can imagine, attributing the source of a problem to individuals can lead us nowhere but blaming the individuals and families (e.g., "KM just can't behave well due to his disabilities, and he will never learn how to be respectful.").

Defining Features of SWPBS

As described previously, the goal of SWPBS is to increase the schools' capacity to address effectively and efficiently the academic and social behavior needs of *all* students and staff. It is the application of a behaviorally based system approach to creating and sustaining positive school environments by making problem behavior irrelevant, ineffective, and inefficient and desired behavior more functional and reinforcing. For maximum outcomes, the literature suggests the following essential features of SWPBS (Cartledge & Lo, 2006; Metzler, Biglan, Rusby, & Sprague, 2001; Sugai & Horner, 2005).

Establishment of Clear Policies and Agenda

A successful SWPBS requires schools to develop a clear agenda for adopting, implementing, monitoring, and sustaining the full continuum of support. Roles of the SWPBS leadership teams must be clearly specified to guide the problem solving, action planning, and program evaluation.

Emphasis on Prevention and Teaching for All Students

SWPBS focuses on prevention and early intervention by defining and teaching three to five positively stated behavioral expectations; defining systems to acknowledge appropriate behavior; defining consistently implemented responses to problem behavior that limit its rewards; and defining and implementing classroom management systems that are consistent with those expectations, correction procedures, and systems. Horner, Crone, and Stiller (2001) advised that to educate all children effectively, schools must restructure their roles to emphasize teaching and maintaining appropriate social behaviors at the schoolwide level. Teaching is perhaps the most powerful strategy in the prevention effort, and interventions should go beyond simply reducing the problem behaviors (Carr, 2007).

Adoption of Evidence-Based Practices

The use of research-validated, evidence-based practices for promoting both academic and behavioral competence is a high priority in SWPBS. Practices that are based on a science of behavior and that "work" have long existed. SWPBS offers a system that allows schools to adopt, implement, monitor, and sustain evidence-based practices such as systematic social skill training, effective academic instruction, behavioral reinforcement technique, proactive and function-based behavioral plans, and parent training and involvement (Lewis & Sugai, 1999; Metzler et al., 2001; Sugai & Horner, 2005). Adopting strategies that have research support and that can make socially appropriate behaviors more relevant, efficient, and effective is essential (O'Neill et al., 1997; OSEP Technical Assistance Center on Positive Behavioral Interventions and Supports, 2004).

Team-Based Staff Development and Participation

Behaviorally competent personnel should be readily available to provide consistent behavioral supports for all students and staff. Throughout the planning and implementation of SWPBS, all staff members are active participants with the school administrator as the active leader. Schools with a strong and committed SWPBS leadership team are more likely to experience success in its adoption and implementation.

Data-Based Decision Making

SWPBS focuses on using data to assess fidelity and well as impact of interventions. Data-based decision making has great value because it not only strongly correlates to improved student outcomes but also increases schools' capacity to develop interventions that have a greater contextual fit to the school environments and defining concerns (Sugai, 2007). Program integrity measures, as well as quantitative and qualitative data focusing on measurable and relevant outcomes such as office disciplinary referrals, student academic performance reports, student and staff surveys, should be reviewed at least monthly to provide ongoing monitoring of student and staff behavior, to guide decision making and planning, and to determine whether the interventions are in effect (Metzler et al., 2001; Sugai & Horner, 2005).

Use of a Multisystems Approach

SWPBS involves not only students and staff but also families and communities as active participants and supporters. It addresses positive system changes in both physical environments (e.g., school structure) and adult/pupil behaviors (e.g., students, staff, family, and community members). The multisystems perspective of SWPBS considers four inter-chaining systems:

1. *Schoolwide:* Mission statement, behavioral expectations, teaching and reinforcement procedures, behavioral consequences for rule violations, and data-based decision-making procedures

2. *Classroom:* Classroom instruction and behavior management practices

3. *Nonclassroom:* Procedures for supervising and encouraging behavior in specific school settings such as bus, hallways, cafeteria, and recess

4. *Individual students:* Individualized and function-based interventions to address intensive behaviors (Sugai & Horner, 2002a)

This system-driven orientation characterizes the prevention, inclusion, and comprehensiveness of SWPBS.

Emphasis on Function-Based Approach

Taking on a functional approach, SWPBS allows the team to identify (a) the nature, frequency, intensity, and severity of problem behaviors; (b) routines, procedures, settings, or other antecedent events that are associated with problem behaviors; and (c) consequences that often follow and maintain the occurrences of problem behaviors. This function-based approach has been recognized as more meaningful and effective when compared to a non-function-based approach due to its emphasis on teaching appropriate skills to achieve the same outcomes, removing "competing" problems or irrelevant events, and supporting the performance of appropriate skills (Ingram, Lewis-Palmer, & Sugai, 2005; Vollmer & Northup, 1996). The functional approach has been widely applied across various student populations and settings (e.g., Boyajian, DuPaul, Handler, Eckert, & McGoey, 2001; Chandler, Dahlquist, Repp, & Feltz, 1999; Reid & Nelson, 2002). It applies to the interchaining systems addressing whole schools and classroom, and nonclassroom environments, as well as individual students, in an interactive approach that includes opportunities to correct and improve four key elements (see Figure 3.1) used in SWPBS (Sugai & Horner, 2002a, 2005):

1. Clearly defined and measurable *outcomes,* including academic achievement and social competence, which have socially important value for students, teachers, families, and society

2. Evidence-based *practices,* which maximize positive outcomes of students and teachers (e.g., practices for teaching and behavior management, leadership practices)

3. Effective *systems,* such as administrative leadership, team structures, guiding principles, resources, and operating processes, which can support research-validated practices to achieve outcomes

4. The use of *data* at all levels with all students and across all contexts to make informed decisions about outcomes, practices, and systems

These key features project a leveled model of support.

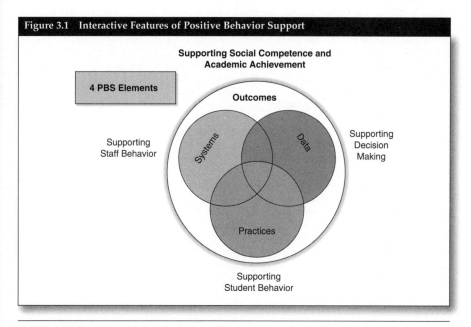

Figure 3.1 Interactive Features of Positive Behavior Support

SOURCE: 4 PBS Elements graphics from the TA Center Web site: http://www.pbis.org/school/what_is_swpbs.aspx.

The Triangle of SWPBS

Acknowledging that students' problem behaviors take a variety of forms, severity, and intensity, SWPBS addresses two continua, *scope of problems* and *intensity of support,* to reach all students with their different needs (Turnbull et al., 2002). Built on these dimensions, SWPBS is characterized by three essential components, including universal support (Tier 1; primary prevention), targeted group support (Tier 2; secondary prevention), and individual student support (Tier 3; tertiary prevention), often referred to as the "triangle" (Lewis & Sugai, 1999; Sprague et al., 1999; Turnbull et al., 2002). There are two key messages in the triangle:

1. Invest in prevention first (for all students).

2. Do not expect a single intervention to solve all problems. Multiple tiers of support that are gradually more intense will be needed (as with any system that addresses large populations).

Originated from the three-level prevention model for chronic illness, medicine, and mental health that originated in the late 1950s, the SWPBS triangle logic has evolved to serve educational contexts. It has been widely accepted in the professional literature to describe a continuum of services that require varying levels of individualization and specialization for students within a school system (Kutash, Duchnowski, & Lynn, 2006; Sugai, 2007). Similar to the recently evolving problem-solving and proactive approach of Response to Intervention (RTI), to reduce the number of special education referrals, SWPBS assesses students' needs and provides differentiated levels of support, ranging from primary prevention across all school settings with all students to specialized interventions with a limited number of those students who exhibit intensive problem behaviors. In this way, "no child is left behind" (Sandomierski, Kincaid, & Algozzine, 2008).

Universal Support

At the universal level (i.e., primary intervention), it is assumed that about 80 to 90 percent of students will arrive at school "ready" to learn basic academic and social skills. The universal level of interventions is to ensure that these students will continue to develop and sustain the use of learned skills in a variety of school settings with minimum support. It attempts to prevent problem behaviors before they start by delivering strategies universally to all students. The goal of this level is to support a maximum number of students by reducing as many problem behaviors and increasing as many socially appropriate behaviors and academic competencies as possible (Turnbull et al., 2002). Behavioral interventions, such as schoolwide social skill training, positive and proactive discipline, behavioral reinforcement systems, active supervision and monitoring, teaching behavior expectations, unified error correction procedures, and effective academic instruction, are recommended at this level (Kilian et al., 2006; Lewis & Sugai, 1999; Sprague et al., 1999; Sugai & Horner, 2002b; White, Algozzine, Audette, Marr, & Ellis, 2001). Universal academic interventions may include core early literacy programs whose effectiveness is supported by evidence and that emphasize the five essential skills of phonemic awareness, phonics, fluency, vocabulary, and comprehension (McIntosh, Chard, Boland, & Horner, 2006; National Reading Panel, 2000; Sugai & Horner, 2008).

Targeted Group Support

At the specialized group level (i.e., secondary intervention), it is assumed that some students (5 to 10 percent of the student body) at high risk for school failure (e.g., demonstrating low academic achievement, poor social skills) may continue to engage in problem behavior or academic failure even with universal support. These students will benefit from additional, more intensive academic and behavioral supports and specialized interventions (Sugai & Horner, 2002b) such as additional social skill training, self-management programs, problem solving and anger management instruction, adult mentors (checking in and checking out system), as well as intensive academic supports (McIntosh et al., 2006; Sprague et al., 1999; Sugai & Horner, 2008). The goal of targeted group support is to intensify the interventions of universal support for at-risk students without placing them for special education services.

Individual Student Support

At the individual student level (i.e., tertiary intervention), students with chronic, long-standing challenging behavior or academic underachievement (about 1 to 5 percent), for whom the universal and targeted group interventions are necessary but insufficient, need highly specialized and individualized intervention support to be successful in schools. The interventions should be based on a comprehensive functional behavioral assessment (FBA), which will inform intervention specialists about the nature of behavior problems (e.g., triggers, functions) and enable them to prescribe appropriate, hypothesis-based interventions (Sugai, Horner, & Sprague, 1999). Strategies such as intensive social skill training, individual behavior management plans, parent involvement, wraparound services, or person-centered planning are demonstrated to be effective in modifying students' chronic misbehavior and increasing their social success (Eber, Nelson, & Miles, 1997; Eber, Sugai, Smith, & Scott, 2002; Lewis & Sugai, 1999; Sprague et al., 1999). Outreach to families and communities is often a focus of tertiary intervention, as it seeks to improve the overall quality of life for students needing this level of support (Scott & Eber, 2003).

CHARACTERISTICS AND EFFECTIVE PRACTICES OF SWPBS

Even the best SWPBS plan may, unfortunately, have inadequate implementation, leading to limited success. Successful and sustainable changes in systems, practices, and behaviors require integrity, persistency, and commitment. More importantly, a supportive organizational structure should be a necessity for sustaining effective, research-based practices. Otherwise, it will be like "having scattered pieces [i.e., the effective practices] of a jigsaw puzzle spread out on a table . . . in order for the puzzle to be compete the pieces must be properly aligned and synchronized" (Miller et al., 2005, p. 559). A review of the literature on successful implementation of SWPBS suggests several characteristics.

Strong Leadership

One of the most important features that contributes to the success of SWPBS implementation is strong leadership from school administrators, typically principals who are instructional leaders (George, White, & Schlaffer, 2007). As the SWPBS team leader, a skillful administrator works with all members at school and takes on several roles:

- A *researcher* who identifies concerns affecting the success of students and staff, studies up-to-date research-based practices, problem-solves conflicts, and oversees schoolwide data collection and evaluation processes
- An *innovator* who accepts changes, articulates clear visions, initiates feasible actions, and is open for revisions
- A *motivational leader* who listens to concerns, models changes for staff, supports efforts made by staff and students, and celebrates success.

Effective SWPBS leaders know what it takes to sustain the implementation of change efforts and are fully committed to making that happen.

Agreements and Commitments

Schools' long-term capacity to adopt and sustain research-based practices to achieve positive outcomes requires a high level of agreement (at least 80 percent) on long-term commitment and investment among stakeholders such as administrators, teachers, paraprofessionals, and other school staff members (Sugai & Horner, 2002a). Muscott, Mann, and LeBrun (2008) listed 10 commitments that are consistent with the SWPBS features to which stakeholders should dedicate themselves before implementing SWPBS action plans:

1. Set SWPBS among the top three school initiatives.

2. Develop a systems approach to student behavior change with an emphasis on preventive and proactive strategies.

3. Teach socially appropriate behavior as the best prevention strategy for problem behavior.

4. Organize the three tiers of support on a continuum.

5. Develop regular and active involvement of staff members in planning and implementation.

6. Establish a comprehensive system for data collection, review, and analysis for decision making.

7. Involve families and communities.

8. Individualize support for students with intensive needs.

9. Dedicate time to professional training and regular meetings.

10. Securing at least 80 percent buy-in from school staff to embrace SWPBS.

SWPBS is not a set of quick-fix tricks or simple solutions. Rather it is a systematic effort that will take at least three to five years before desired outcomes are fully observed and sustained. Therefore, a long-term commitment from an overwhelming majority of school staff is essential. In fact, staff buy-in has been rated by school teams as the leading barrier to successfully implementing SWPBS (Kincaid, Childs, Blase, & Wallace, 2007). Buy-in can be improved by (a) presenting and sharing outcome data, (b) adopting a team planning process, (c) getting staff inputs through surveys or interviews, and (d) emphasizing existing success as well as immediate and long-term benefits to students and staff (Miller et al., 2005; Public Schools of North Carolina, 2008).

Contextual-Fit Action Plans With Integrity Checks

SWPBS action plans serve as the blueprint for its implementation. The action plans should be workable and comprehensible and should be developed based on contextual assessments indicating individual school needs, challenges, and procedures for improvement. Good action plans clarify (a) measurable outcomes; (b) members and roles of the leadership team; (c) specific activities (including interventions and data collection) across all school settings and all student levels for reaching the outcomes; (d) professional development activities; and (e) resources, including time, fiscal supports, materials for implementation, and staffing arrangement or reorganization (Sugai & Horner, 2002a). Additionally, good action plans must address contextual fit by considering (a) the natural routines of the settings; (b) the values of people in the settings; (c) available and expandable time, money, and resources, and (d) skill levels of people who will carry out the plans (O'Neill et al., 1997). For example, Bohanon et al. (2006) advised SWPBS leadership teams to consider the unique culture of each school, such as its size (e.g., small versus large numbers of students and staff), student characteristics (e.g., high school students versus elementary students), and staff characteristics (e.g., teachers trained in content areas versus teachers trained in education), when developing the action plan for implementation. For example, well-defined SWPBS action plan developed for a rural elementary school would most likely be inadequate for an urban high school. Furthermore, successful implementation of SWPBS requires not only good action plans but also high implementation integrity. Treatment integrity has been a focus of concentration in "claiming" the effects of a certain intervention in professional journals since the turn of the 21st century. Gresham, MacMillan, Beebe-Frankenberger, and Bocian (2000) reminded us that "gauging whether a given treatment 'works' is virtually impossible if nothing is known about the integrity with which it was delivered" (p. 204). SWPBS implementation requires the same level of precision as any treatment to ensure that the planned evidence-based practices lead to their maximum effectiveness. Treatment integrity of SWPBS can be improved by securing faculty buy-in and commitment, establishing ongoing support and leadership from the administration, and ensuring the quality of staff training (Anderson & Kincaid, 2005; Hieneman et al., 2005). Schools adopting SWPBS may consider two research-validated tools to examine the degree to which SWPBS is implemented adequately: (a) the *School-Wide Evaluation Tool* (SET; Horner et al., 2004), and (b) the *School-wide Benchmarks of Quality* (BoQ; Kincaid, Childs, & George as cited by Cohen, Kincaid, & Childs, 2007).

EFFECTIVENESS OF SWPBS

As of September 2008, over 8,200 schools across 43 states/territories were actively participating in SWPBS (Sugai & Horner, 2008). Some efforts had been extended from single schools to the district and state level (e.g., Freeman et al., 2006; George & Kincaid, 2008; Muscott et al., 2008; Public Schools of North Carolina, 2008). Overall, research studies have shown that a high-quality implementation of SWPBS brought about positive changes in various areas, including reduction of office disciplinary referrals (e.g., Bohanon et al., 2006; Ervin, Schaughency, Matthews, Goodman, & McGlinchey, 2007; Muscott et al., 2008; Taylor-Greene et al., 1997); reduced percentage of students repeating rule violations (e.g., Bohanon et al.; Ervin et al.); reduced number of students needing additional or intensive support (e.g., McIntosh et al., 2006); reduction of the need to use physical restraint or exclusionary time-out (e.g., Miller et al., 2005); improved classroom instructional ecology, such as on-task behavior (e.g., Algozzine & Algozzine, 2007; Marr, Audette, White, Ellis, & Algozzine, 2002); increased instructional time (e.g., Muscott et al.); increased academic performance (e.g., Nelson, Martella, & Marchand-Martella, 2002); and overall satisfaction of school personnel regarding the cost-benefit ratio of SWPBS (e.g., Ervin et al.; Nelson et al.).

To demonstrate, Taylor-Greene and others (1997) implemented SWPBS in a rural middle school to reduce high levels of problem behaviors and improve school disciplinary program during the first wave of the SWPBS initiative. The schoolwide disciplinary system consisted of an "opening day" curriculum training program in which behavioral expectations for six main school locations (i.e., classrooms, hallways, gym, cafeteria, open common areas, and bus) were clearly defined, directly taught, and systematically rewarded. The schoolwide expectation training was coupled with ongoing behavioral supports through strategies such as reminders, reinforcement of appropriate behaviors, corrective consequences, booster training procedures, and targeted support for students with chronic behavior problems. One-year implementation of the SWPBS resulted in reduction of office referrals by 42 percent. School staff also perceived SWPBS as important and effective in bringing positive changes in students.

Metzler and colleagues (2001) expanded SWPBS implementation across three middle schools by defining clear rules and expectations, teaching behavioral expectations to students, providing increased levels of praise and rewards for appropriate social behaviors, monitoring students' behavior, and utilizing frequent summary data about student behavior for decision making. The outcomes showed increases in the level of praise and reward for students' appropriate social behavior from teachers, dramatic reductions in the rates of office referrals and total number of students who received a referral, decreases in the proportion of students reporting being the target of physical or verbal aggression, and increases in the proportion of students who reported that they felt safe in schools.

To illustrate further the effects of SWPBS programs, Nelson and colleagues (2002) evaluated a comprehensive schoolwide program based on SWPBS approach to prevent and reduce disruptive behaviors in seven elementary schools serving a high percentage of students at risk for school failure. Five components constituted the program:

1. A unified schoolwide discipline program consisting of ecological arrangements of the common areas of the school, establishment of clear and consistent behavioral expectations, active adult supervision, and effective disciplinary policies and procedures (e.g., Think Time Instructional Strategy)

2. One-to-one supplemental tutoring in early literacy skills

3. A schoolwide social skills teaching program on conflict resolution

4. A video-based family management program for targeted students

5. An individualized, function-based behavior intervention plan for those students with the most challenging behaviors

Results of the comprehensive schoolwide program showed statistical declines in suspensions, emergency removals, and office referrals when compared to outcomes in the control schools. In addition, academic achievement (i.e., reading, spelling, science, and social studies) on standardized tests and overall social competence improved substantially for the target students with the most problem behaviors. These findings again pointed to the effectiveness of SWPBS at building supports at the primary, secondary, and tertiary levels to reduce students' problem behaviors and promote social adjustment of all students.

Within the implementation of SWPBS, improvements of student outcomes in specific settings such as playground, bus, cafeteria, hallways, and transition periods are of great interest to school personnel, because unstructured settings have contextual features that tend to increase students' problem behaviors. Several studies have demonstrated the positive effects of SWPBS in supporting students' behavior in these nonclassroom settings. Specific teaching and proactive procedures, such as schoolwide social skills training (e.g., on rules, routines, procedures, and desired behaviors) specific to individual settings, group contingencies, token economy system, precorrection, and active adult supervision, have resulted in noticeable reductions of student problem behaviors across various nonclassroom settings, including playgrounds, recess, hallways, and cafeterias (Kartub, Taylor-Greene, March, & Horner, 2000; Lewis, Powers, Kelk, & Newcomer, 2002; Lewis, Sugai, & Colvin, 1998; Todd, Haugen, Anderson, & Spriggs, 2002). They also have resulted in moderate improvements of adult behaviors, such as use of precorrection, acknowledgment of appropriate behavior, and positive interactions with students (Franzen & Kamps, 2008). The success of these specific-setting interventions can be partly attributed to the common set of behavioral expectations, direct and systematic teaching procedures, consistent consequences for appropriate and inappropriate student behaviors, and established overarching systems that were made available schoolwide (Lewis et al.).

The rapid expansion of SWPBS efforts can be clearly observed in the context of statewide initiatives. An example is the Positive Behavioral Interventions and Supports—New Hampshire (PBIS-NH). In an effort to address students' problem behavior and to reduce the overreliance on punitive disciplinary practices in schools, the state of New Hampshire initiated a statewide SWPBS effort to begin in 2002 (Muscott et al., 2008). The initiative underwent a five-stage system change:

1. Increasing the awareness of schools and districts

2. Obtaining schools' interest in participation

3. Ensuring school readiness in commitment

4. Executing implementation

5. Promoting sustainability

Twenty-eight schools (including 1 Head Start program, 13 elementary schools, 6 middle schools, 4 high schools, and 4 multilevel schools) participated in the initiative. Positive results were observed by the end of the second year of implementation in the high level of program fidelity, reductions of office referrals and suspension rates, increased instructional time, and increased academic achievement. Specifically, Muscott et al. (2008) reported that 88 percent of the participating schools were able to maintain an 80 percent fidelity standard by the fall of the second year. The PBIS-NH initiative resulted in a reduction of office disciplinary referrals by 6,010, or 28%; of in-school suspensions by 637, or 31 percent; and of out-of-school suspensions by 395, or 19 percent. The reductions in school violations and students' being removed from the classrooms across all participating schools translated to a recovery of 536 to 7,508 hours (89 to 1,251 days) for learning, 78 to 890 hours (13 to 148 days) for teaching, and 112 to 2,010 hours (19 to 335 days) for administrators to engage in educational leadership activities. Moreover, moderate improvements on students' statewide math and reading assessments were observed for schools with high-fidelity implementation. This evaluation evidence and that from other large-scale efforts indicate that "statewide implementation of Schoolwide Positive Behavior Support is possible and beneficial for children" (Barrett, Bradshaw, & Lewis-Palmer, 2008, p. 113). Research findings support similar conclusions.

For example, in a randomized control trial, Horner et al. (2009) assessed the effects of Schoolwide Positive Behavior Support in elementary schools in Hawaii and Illinois, where assistance was provided by regular state personnel over a three-year period. The training and professional development were functionally related to improved implementation of universal-level Schoolwide Positive Behavior Support practices, and this improved use was functionally related to improvements in the perceived safety of the school setting and the proportion of third graders meeting or exceeding state reading assessment standards. The results also illustrated that levels of office discipline referrals were comparatively low. In another randomized control trial, Bradshaw and her colleagues (Bradshaw, Koth, Bevans, Ialongo, & Leaf, in press; Bradshaw, Reinke, Brown, Bevans, & Leaf, 2008) found statistically significant effects of SWPBS on staff reports of organizational health, influence of resources, affiliations of staff, and critical features of effective intervention implementation.

Almost 800 schools in North Carolina (about one-third of those in the state) are participating in the Department of Public Instruction's Positive Behavior Support Initiative (Reynolds, Irwin, & Algozzine, 2009). For three years, rates of suspension decreased across all grade levels. Also, office discipline referrals per 100 students per school day were consistently below national averages, and schools with lower rates of office discipline referrals have higher percentages of students scoring proficient on End-of-Grade (EOG) assessments.

Collectively, SWPBS has been demonstrated to be feasible, it is being done widely, and it is associated with improved social and academic outcomes at various levels. Continuous efforts in SWPBS are being made not only in its width (i.e., across districts, regions, and states) but in its depth (e.g., refinement of techniques and sustained adoption), and they are visible in various professional publications (e.g., *Journal of Positive Behavior Interventions*) as evidence of its effectiveness.

PERSPECTIVE ON SCHOOLWIDE POSITIVE BEHAVIOR SUPPORT

The goal of education is to prepare students to be knowledgeable, independent, and responsible citizens. Increased accountability for student achievement and prevalent safety concerns related to discipline have placed additional pressure on schools as they strive to reach this goal. With the ever-increasing diversity in people and infrastructures in American schools, effective solutions are no longer found among the "quick fix," the "tough responses," the "one fits all," the "someone's problems" trick bags (Horner, Sugai, & Horner, 2000). Instead, demands are on schools, more than ever, to provide a positive schoolwide system that (a) emphasizes prevention based on scientific principles, (b) incorporates empirically validated behavior-change techniques, (c) focuses on a systemic, multilayer approach, (d) uses data for decision making, and (d) addresses ongoing professional development. SWPBS affords these features!

An Illustration From Practice

We asked a principal to share her observations about the behavior program in her school. Her words nicely illustrate the characteristics and benefits of efforts to implement SWPBS.

When you go into individual classrooms, the rules are posted, and they represent the shared set of expectations in our school. There's a behavior chart that is pretty consistent throughout the school, and we use the color system. The children know the expectations. It's very evident that they know and they comply. You can see it in their behavior. You can see it in their smiles. They are happy children because they know what the expectations are. There is nothing that they cannot accomplish. So they feel a sense of self-esteem and self-satisfaction when they meet those goals and expectations.

With a schoolwide behavior plan, of course there is an incentive attached to it because there needs to be a celebration or reward for children who are complying with the rules. We reward them with tangible items here at [our school]. Our mascot is a mustang, so when children are seen in the hall following the rules and in uniform, staff members are carrying little paper Mustangs so the children receive Mustangs. Certain days that we know tend to be difficult days, such as before a holiday, we even have Double Mustang Day. The children's faces just light up when they see an adult coming down the hall who might be a possible Mustang giver. And they are little soldiers because they can't wait for recognition of their good behavior. And they have been told they can't ask for a Mustang; they have to earn it by following the rules.

When they accumulate 25 Mustangs on a ranch that's in their room, they get a small horseshoe. When they get four of those small horseshoes, they get a golden horseshoe. And we make a big celebration in the classroom. We told them that 100 times people have said how wonderful they are—they have 100 compliments—and then they also get a fancy pencil from the principal that makes their work more fun.

SWPBS in high school requires paying attention to similar general guidelines (e.g., clearly stating and posting schoolwide expectations and creating schoolwide structures to reinforce demonstrations of expected behaviors), as well as to different considerations and consequences related to them. For example, Bohanon and colleagues (2006) established schoolwide expectations (Be Caring, Be Academically Engaged, Be Respectful, and Be Responsible) in a Chicago high school enrolling 1,800 students. They provided verbal praise and tickets that could be redeemed at a school store for students observed "doing the right thing." They also organized two "major schoolwide celebrations" (e.g., a dance held midyear and distribution of theater tickets in June), which were contingent on reductions in ODRs. As a result of implementing SWPBS, they observed consistent decreases in monthly discipline referrals and in the number of students requiring secondary and tertiary interventions and supports.

REFERENCES

Algozzine, K., & Algozzine, B. (2007). Classroom instructional ecology and School-wide Positive Behavior Support. *Journal of Applied School Psychology, 24,* 29–47.

Algozzine, K., Christian, C., Marr, M. B., McClanahan, T., & White, R. (2008). Demography of problem behavior is elementary schools. *Exceptionality, 16,* 93–104.

Anderson, C. M., & Kincaid, D. (2005). Applying behavior analysis to school violence and discipline problems: Schoolwide Positive Behavior Support. *The Behavior Analyst, 28,* 49–63.

Barrett, S., Bradshaw, C., & Lewis-Palmer, T. (2008). Maryland state-wide PBIS initiative: Systems, evaluation, and next steps. *Journal of Positive Behavior Interventions, 10,* 105–114.

Bohanon, H., Fenning, P., Carney, K. L., Minnis-Kim, M. J., Anderson-Harriss, S., Moroz, K. B., et al. (2006). Schoolwide application of Positive Behavior Support in an urban high school: A case study. *Journal of Positive Behavior Interventions, 8,* 131–145.

Boyajian, A. E., DuPaul, G. J., Handler, M. W., Eckert, T. L., & McGoey, K. E. (2001). The use of classroom-based brief functional analyses with preschoolers at-risk for attention deficit hyperactivity disorder. *The School Psychology Review, 30,* 278–293.

Bradshaw, C. P., Koth, C. W., Bevans, K. B., Ialongo, N., & Leaf, P. J. (in press). The impact of School-wide Positive Behavioral Interventions and Supports (PBIS) on the organizational health of elementary schools. *School Psychology Quarterly.*

Bradshaw, C. P., Reinke, W. M., Brown, L. D., Bevans, K. B., & Leaf, P. J. (2008). Implementation of School-wide Positive Behavioral Interventions and Supports (PBIS) in elementary schools: Observations from a randomized trial. *Education and Treatment of Children, 31,* 1–26.

Carr, E. G. (2007). The expanding vision of positive behavior: Research perspectives on happiness, helpfulness, hopefulness. *Journal of Positive Behavior Interventions, 9,* 3–14.

Carr, E. G., Dunlap, G., Horner, R. H., Koegel, R. L., Turnbull, A. P., Sailor, W., et al. (2002). Positive Behavior Support: Evolution of an applied science. *Journal of Positive Behavior Interventions, 4,* 4–16, 20.

Carr, E. G., Horner, R. H., Turnbull, A. P., Marquis, J. G., McLaughlin, D.M., McAtee, M. L., et al. (1999). *Positive Behavior Support for people with developmental disabilities: A research synthesis.* Washington, DC: American Association on Mental Retardation.

Cartledge, G., & Lo, Y. (2006). *Teaching urban learners: Culturally responsive strategies for developing academic and behavioral competence.* Champaign, IL: Research Press.

Chandler, L. K., Dahlquist, C. M., Repp, A. C., & Feltz, C. (1999). The effects of team-based functional assessment on the behavior of students in classroom settings. *Exceptional Children, 66,* 101–121.

Cohen, R., Kincaid, D., & Childs, K. E. (2007). Measuring School-wide Positive Behavior Support implementation: Development and validation of the Benchmarks of Quality. *Journal of Positive Behavior Interventions, 9,* 203–213.

Colvin, G., Kame'enui, E., & Sugai, G. (1993). Reconceptualizing behavior management and school-wide discipline in general education. *Education and Treatment of Children, 16,* 361–381.

Dinkes, R., Cataldi, E. F., & Lin-Kelly, W. (2007). *Indicators of school crime and safety: 2007* (NCES 2008–021/NCJ 219553). Washington, DC: National Center for Education Statistics, Institute of Education Sciences, U.S. Department of Education; Bureau of Justice Statistics, Office of Justice Programs, U.S. Department of Justice. Retrieved October 28, 2009, from http://nces.ed.gov/pubs2008/2008021.pdf

Durand,V. M. (1999). Functional communication training using assistive devices: Recruiting natural communities of reinforcement. *Journal of Applied Behavior Analysis, 32,* 247–267.

Eber, L., Nelson, C. M., & Miles, P. (1997). School-based wraparound for students with emotional and behavioral challenges. *Exceptional Children, 63,* 539–555.

Eber, L., Sugai, G., Smith, C. R., & Scott, T. M. (2002). Wraparound and positive behavioral interventions and supports in the schools. *Journal of Emotional and Behavioral Disorders, 10,* 171–180.

Ervin, R. A., Schaughency, E., Matthews, A., Goodman, S. D., & McGlinchey, M. T. (2007). Primary and secondary prevention of behavior difficulties: Developing data-informed problem-solving model to guide decision making at a school-wide level. *Psychology in the Schools, 44,* 7–18.

Franzen, K., & Kamps, D. (2008). The utilization and effects of Positive Behavior Support strategies on an urban school playground. *Journal of Positive Behavior Interventions, 10,* 150–161.

Freeman, R., Eber, L., Anderson, C., Irvin, L., Horner, R., Bounds, M., et al. (2006). Building inclusive school cultures using School-wide Positive Behavior Support: Designing effective individual support systems for students with significant disabilities. *Research & Practice for Persons with Severe Disabilities, 31,* 4–17.

Gallup, A. M., & Elam, S. M. (1988). The 20th annual Gallup poll of the public's attitudes toward the public schools. *Phi Delta Kappan, 70,* 33–46.

George, H. P., & Kincaid, D. K. (2008). Building district-level capacity for positive behavior. *Journal of Positive Behavior Interventions, 10,* 20–32.

George, M. P., White, G. P., & Schlaffer, J. J. (2007). Implementing school-wide behavior change: Lessons from the field. *Psychology in the Schools, 44,* 41–51.

Gresham, F. M., MacMillan, D. L., Beebe-Frankenberger, M. E., & Bocian, K. M. (2000). Treatment integrity in learning disabilities intervention research: Do we really know how treatments are implemented? *Learning Disabilities Research & Practice, 15,* 198–205.

Hawken, L. S., & O'Neill, R. E. (2006). Including students with severe disabilities in all levels of School-wide Positive Behavior Support. *Research & Practice for Persons with Severe Disabilities, 31,* 46–53.

Hieneman, M., Dunlap, G., & Kincaid, D. (2005). Positive support strategies for students with behavioral disorders in general education settings. *Psychology in the Schools, 42,* 779–794.

Horner, R. H. (2007, February). *Implementing applied behavior analysis at meaningful scales: The example of School-wide Positive Behavior Support.* Keynote presentation at the 2007 conference of the North Carolina Association for Behavior Analysis (NCABA), Wrightsville Beach, NC.

Horner, R. H., Crone, D. A., & Stiller, B. (2001). The role of school psychologists in establishing Positive Behavior Support: Collaborating in systems change at the school-wide level. *Communiqué, 29*(6), 10.

Horner, R. H., Dunlap, G., Koegel, R. L., Carr, E. G., Sailor, W., Anderson, J., et al. (1990). Toward a technology of "non-aversive" behavior support. *Journal of the Association for Persons with Severe Handicaps, 15,* 125–132.

Horner, R. H., Sugai, G., & Horner, H. F. (2000). A schoolwide approach to student discipline. *School Administrator, 57*(2), 20–23.

Horner, R. H., Sugai, G., Smolkowski, K., Eber, L., Nakasato, J., Todd, A. W., et al. (2009). A randomized, wait-list controlled effectiveness trial assessing School-wide Positive Behavior Support in elementary schools. *Journal of Positive Behavior Interventions, 11*(3), 133–144.

Horner, R. H., Sugai, G., Todd, A. W., & Lewis-Palmer, T. (1999–2000). Elements of behavior support plans: A technical brief. *Exceptionality, 8,* 205–215.

Horner, R. H., Todd, A. W., Lweis-Palmer, T., Irvin, L. K., Sugai, G., & Boland, J. B. (2004). The school-wide evaluation tool (SET): A research instrument for assessing School-wide Positive Behavior Support. *Journal of Positive Behavior Interventions, 6,* 3–12.

Hyman, J. A., & Perone, D. C. (1998). The other side of school violence: Educator policies and practices that may contribute to student misbehavior. *Journal of School Psychology, 36,* 7–27.

Ingram, K., Lewis-Palmer, T., & Sugai, G. (2005). Functional-based intervention planning: Comparing the effectiveness of FBA function-based and non-function-based intervention plans. *Journal of Positive Behavior Interventions, 7,* 224–236.

Kartub, D. T., Taylor-Greene, S., March, R. E., & Horner, R. H. (2000). Reducing hallway noise: A systems approach. *Journal of Positive Behavior Interventions, 2,* 179–182.

Kilian, J. M., Fish, M. C., & Maniago, E. B. (2006). Making schools safe: A system-wide school intervention to increase student prosocial behaviors and enhance school climate. *Journal of Applied School Psychology, 23,* 1–30.

Kincaid, D., Childs, K., Blase, K. A., & Wallace, F. (2007). Identifying barriers and facilitators in implementing Schoolwide Positive Behavior Support. *Journal of Positive Behavior Interventions, 9,* 174–184.

Kutash, K., Duchnowski, A. J., & Lynn, N. (2006). *School-based mental health: An empirical guide for decision-makers.* Tampa: University of South Florida, Louis de la Parte Florida Mental Health Institute, Department of Child and Family Studies, Research and Training Center for Children's Mental Health.

Lewis, T. J., Powers, L. J., Kelk, M. J., & Newcomer, L. L. (2002). Reducing problem behaviors on the playground: An investigation of the application of Schoolwide Positive Behavior Supports. *Psychology in the Schools, 39,* 181–190.

Lewis, T. J., & Sugai, G. (1999). Effective behavior support: A systems approach to proactive schoolwide management. *Focus on Exceptional Children, 31,* 1–24.

Lewis, T. J., Sugai, G., & Colvin, G. (1998). Reducing problem behavior through a school-wide system of effective behavioral support: Investigation of a school-wide social skills training program and contextual interventions. *School Psychology Review, 27,* 446–459.

Lewis-Palmer, T., Bounds, M., & Sugai, G. (2004). Districtwide system for providing individual student support. *Assessment for Effective Intervention, 30*(1), 53–65.

Liaupsin, C. J., Jolivette, K., & Scott, T. M. (2004). Schoolwide systems of behavior support. In R. B. Rutherford Jr., M. Magee Quinn, & S. Mathur (Eds.), *Handbook of research in emotional and behavioral disorders* (pp. 487–501). New York: Guilford Press.

Lo, Y., & Cartledge, G. (2007). Office disciplinary referrals in an urban elementary school. *Multicultural Learning and Teaching, 2*(1), 20–38.

Marr, M. B., Audette, B., White, R., Ellis, E., & Algozzine, B. (2002). School-wide discipline and classroom ecology. *Special Services in the Schools, 18*(1–2), 55–73.

McIntosh, K., Chard, D. J., Boland, J. B., & Horner, R. H. (2006). Demonstration of combined efforts in school-wide academic and behavioral systems and incidence of reading and behavior challenges in early elementary grades. *Journal of Positive Behavior Interventions, 8,* 146–154.

Medley, N. S., Little, S. G., & Akin-Little, A. (2008). Comparing individual behavior plans from schools with and without Schoolwide Positive Behavior Support: A preliminary study. *Journal of Behavioral Education, 17,* 93–110.

Metzler, C. W., Biglan, A., Rusby, J. C., & Sprague, J. R. (2001). Evaluation of a comprehensive behavior management program to improve School-wide Positive Behavior Support. *Education and Treatment of Children, 24,* 448–479.

Meyer, L. H., & Evans, I. M. (1993). Science and practice in behavioral intervention: Meaningful outcomes, research validity, and usable knowledge. *Journal of the Association for Persons with Severe Handicaps, 18,* 224–234.

Miller, D. N., George, M. P., & Fogt, J. B. (2005). Establishing and sustaining research-based practices at Centennial School: A descriptive case study of systemic change. *Psychology in the Schools, 42,* 553–567.

Muscott, H. S., Mann, E. L., & LeBrun, M. R. (2008). Positive behavioral interventions and supports in New Hampshire: Effects of large-scale implementation of Schoolwide Positive Behavior Support on student discipline and academic achievement. *Journal of Positive Behavior Interventions, 10,* 190–205.

Myers, C. L., & Holland, K. L. (2000). Classroom behavioral interventions: Do teachers consider the function of the behavior? *Psychology in the Schools, 37*(3), 271–280.

National Reading Panel. (2000). *Report of the National Reading Panel: Teaching children to read; An evidence-based assessment of the scientific research literature on reading and its implications for reading instruction; Reports of the subgroups* (NIH Publication No. 00–4754). Washington, DC: National Institute of Child Health and Human Development.

Nelson, J. R., Martella, R. M., & Marchand-Martella, N. (2002). Maximizing student learning: The effects of a comprehensive school-based program for preventing problem behaviors. *Journal of Emotional and Behavioral Disorders, 10,* 136–148.

O'Neill, R. E., Horner, R. H., Albin, R. W., Sprague, J. R., Storey, K., & Newton, J. S. (1997). *Functional assessment and program development for problem behavior: A practical handbook* (2nd ed.). Pacific Grove, CA: Brooks/Cole.

OSEP Technical Assistance Center on Positive Behavioral Interventions and Supports. (2004). *Schoolwide Positive Behavior Support implementers' blueprint and self-assessment.* Eugene, OR: Author.

Public Schools of North Carolina. (2008). *Positive Behavior Support training modules.* Retrieved October 28, 2009, from http://www.ncpublicschools.org/positivebehavior/implementation/modules/

Reid, R., & Nelson, J. R. (2002). The utility, acceptability, and practicality of functional behavioral assessment for students with high-incidence problem behaviors. *Remedial and Special Education, 23,* 15–23.

Reynolds, H., Irwin, D., & Algozzine, B. (2009). *North Carolina Positive Behavior Support Initiative evaluation report 2007–2008.* Raleigh, NC: Department of Public Instruction, Exceptional Children Division, Behavioral Support Services.

Rose, L. C., & Gallup, A. M. (1999). The 31st annual Phi Delta Kappa/Gallup poll of the public's attitudes toward the public schools. *Phi Delta Kappan, 81,* 41–56.

Rose, L. C., & Gallup, A. M. (2007). The 39th annual Phi Delta Kappa/Gallup poll of the public's attitudes toward the public schools. *Phi Delta Kappan, 89,* 33–48.

Safran, S. P., & Oswald, K. (2003). Positive Behavior Supports: Can schools reshape disciplinary practices? *Exceptional Children, 69,* 361–373.

Sandomierski, T., Kincaid, D., & Algozzine, B. (2008). Response to Intervention and Positive Behavior Support: Brothers from different mothers or sisters with different misters? *Positive Behavioral Interventions and Supports Newsletter, 4*(2). Retrieved October 28, 2009, from http://www.pbis.org/pbis_newsletter/volume_4/issue2.aspx

Scott, T. M., & Eber, L. (2003). Functional assessment and wraparound as systemic school process: Primary, secondary, and tertiary systems examples. *Journal of Positive Behavior Interventions, 5,* 131–143.

Skiba, R. J., & Peterson, R. L. (1999). The dark side of zero tolerance: Can punishment lead to safe schools? *Phi Delta Kappan, 80,* 372–382.

Skiba, R. J., & Peterson, R. L. (2000). School discipline at a crossroads: From zero tolerance to early response. *Exceptional Children, 66,* 335–347.

Skiba, R. J., Peterson, R. L., & Williams, T. (1997). Office referrals and suspensions: Disciplinary intervention in middle schools. *Education and Treatment of Children, 20,* 295–315.

Sprague, J. R., Sugai, G., Horner, R., & Walker, H. M. (1999). Using office discipline referral data to evaluate school-wide discipline and violence prevention interventions. *OSSC Bulletin, 42*(2). (ERIC Document Reproduction Service No. ED427438)

Sugai, G. (2007). Promoting behavioral competence in schools: A commentary on exemplary practices. *Psychology in the Schools, 44,* 113–118.

Sugai, G., & Horner, R. H. (2002a). The evolution of discipline practices: School-wide Positive Behavior Supports. *Child & Family Behavior Therapy, 24*(1/2), 23–50.

Sugai, G., & Horner, R. H. (2002b). Introduction to the special series on Positive Behavior Support in schools. *Journal of Emotional and Behavioral Disorders, 10,* 130–135.

Sugai, G., & Horner, R. H. (2005). Schoolwide Positive Behavior Supports: Achieving and sustaining effective learning environments for all students. In W. L. Heward, T. E. Heron, N. A. Neef, S. M. Peterson, D. M. Sainato, G. Cartledge, et al. (Eds.), *Focus on behavior analysis in education: Achievements, challenges, and opportunities* (pp. 90–102). Upper Saddle River, NJ: Pearson Education.

Sugai, G., & Horner, R. H. (2008). What we know and need to know about preventing problem behavior in schools. *Exceptionality, 16,* 67–77.

Sugai, G., Horner, R. H., & Sprague, J. R. (1999). Functional-assessment-based behavior support planning: Research to practice to research. *Behavioral Disorders, 24,* 253–257.

Sugai, G., Horner, R. H., Dunlap, G., Hieneman, M., Lewis, T. J., Nelson, C. M., et al. (2000). Applying positive behavioral support and functional behavioral assessment in schools. *Journal of Positive Behavior Interventions, 2,* 131–143.

Taylor-Greene, S., Brown, D., Nelson, L., Longton, J., Gassman, T., Cohen, J., et al. (1997). School-wide behavioral support: Starting the year off right. *Journal of Behavioral Education, 7,* 99–112.

Todd, A., Haugen, L., Anderson, K., & Spriggs, M. (2002). Teaching recess: Low-cost efforts producing effective results. *Journal of Positive Behavior Interventions, 4,* 46–52.

Turnbull, A., Edmonson, H., Griggs, P., Wickham, D., Sailor, W., Freeman, R., et al. (2002). A blueprint for Schoolwide Positive Behavior Support: Implementation of three components. *Exceptional Children, 68,* 377–402.

Vollmer, T., & Northup, J. (1996). Some implications of functional analysis for school psychology. *School Psychology Quarterly, 11,* 76–92.

Walker, H. M., Colvin, G., & Ramsey, E. (1995). *Antisocial behavior in school: Strategies and bet practices.* Pacific Grove, CA: Brooks/Cole.

White, R., Algozzine, B., Audette, B., Marr, M. B., & Ellis, E. E. (2001). Unified discipline: A school-wide approach for managing problem behavior. *Intervention in School and Clinic, 37*(1), 3–8.

4

Cognitive-Behavioral Interventions in School Settings

In this chapter, we

- provide a definition of cognitive-behavioral interventions (CBIs),
- explore the theoretical underpinnings of CBIs,
- review the current research on CBIs in school settings,
- describe one CBI appropriate for use in schools

On a daily basis, teachers and other school professionals confront student conduct issues that can range from irritating, bothersome, and simply troubling to more significant, such as noncompliance, disrespect for authority, lack of self-control, deviant levels of aggression, and illegal behavior. Behavioral excesses and deficits can increase the likelihood of students failing in school, prevent them from forming positive peer relationships, and detract from the overall learning experience in the school setting. Since the more severe forms of student behavior problems elicit negative reactions from others, they can severely limit a student's opportunity for gaining social acceptance, positive social status, and future success (Dodge & Frame, 1982).

Without interventions and effective behavior management strategies, students who engage in the more severe types of behaviors often adjust poorly to school and evidence high rates of juvenile delinquency, psychological problems, dropping out, and adult criminal activity. School professionals can find managing student behavior difficult and complex, and their attempts to find successful management strategies can tax their personal and professional resources. Persistent severe behavior problems can profoundly perplex even the most experienced teachers. According to Public Agenda (2004), nearly 8 in 10 teachers (78 percent) say that there are persistent troublemakers in their school who should be removed from regular classrooms, and more than 1 in 3 teachers say they have seriously considered quitting the profession, or know a colleague who has left, because student discipline and behavior have become so intolerable. In its polling, Public Agenda also found that 85 percent of teachers believe newcomers to the profession are particularly unprepared for dealing with problem behaviors.

It is often the case that school professionals react to student behavior problems through punitive actions such as exclusion or seclusion time out, lunch or afterschool detention, restricting access to privileges, sentence writing, and in-school and out-of-school suspension. Yet reacting to behavior problems in the absence of a more systematic and holistic approach to behavior management is incomplete, mostly ineffective, and in most cases unnecessary. Teachers should be knowledgeable about providing proactive support for students to create positive learning environments. Being proactive in managing student behavior leads to a decrease in inappropriate student behavior, allowing educators to spend more quality time planning and teaching curriculum, as well as deal effectively with the most critical behavioral issues. Succinctly, many of the behavioral problems encountered by teachers can be systematically managed by teaching replacement behaviors, thus allowing time to focus on other issues.

In a general sense, teaching students skills to regulate their own behavior is the ultimate goal of behavior management, and teaching students positive replacement behaviors is a vehicle to achieve that goal. More important, for students who exhibit behavioral problems, learning to manage their own behavior successfully would reduce their dependence on external sources of control, thereby increasing their freedom of choice, self-determination, and self-esteem (Wehmeyer, Agran, & Hughes, 2000; Worell & Nelson, 1974). Fortunately, cognitive-behavioral interventions provide a current technology for teaching these necessary replacement behaviors.

COGNITIVE-BEHAVIORAL INTERVENTIONS

The use of cognitive-behavioral interventions (CBI) to teach positive replacement behaviors to students with significant behavior problems has increased in recent years and is becoming recognized as a viable, research-based approach appropriate for use in school settings (see Mayer, Van Acker, Lochman, & Gresham, 2009; Mennuti, Freeman, & Christner, 2006; Robinson, Smith, Miller, & Brownell, 1999). Over time, CBI has gained favor in school settings because of its effective clinical use with children and adolescents in the fields of psychiatry and mental health. Cognitive-behavioral therapy in clinical settings (e.g., hospitals, residential treatment facilities, outpatient clinics) is a recommended treatment option for such conditions as obsessive-compulsive disorder (OCD), weight management, anxiety and panic disorder, social phobia, eating disorders, alcohol and drug dependency, attention deficit/hyperactivity disorder (ADHD), and problems with anger and aggression (see Butler, Chapman, Forman, & Beck, 2006; Craighead, Craighead, Kazdin, & Mahoney, 1994). Considering the effectiveness of CBI with children and youth and the role that schools play in the social and emotional development of students, it seems appropriate that school professionals consider its use in school settings.

When teachers use a CBI, they can help students learn to control their own behavior, rather than relying on external reinforcement alone (e.g., tokens for staying on-task, praise for raising hand). CBIs teach students to use their inner speech or covert self-instruction to affect or modify their underlying thinking, which in turn affects the way they behave (Mahoney, 1974; Meichenbaum, 1977). Simply put, covert self-instruction consists of talking to oneself to guide problem solving or some other behavior (Mahoney; Mahoney & Kazdin, 1979; Meichenbaum).

THEORETICAL UNDERPINNINGS OF CBI

Deficient or maladaptive self-statements or covert self-talk is believed to contribute to a variety of behavioral problems, such as poor self-esteem, impulsivity, depression, and/or disruptive and aggressive behavior (Kendall, 2000). Cognitive psychologists theorize that a person's ability to control his or her own behavior is the result of the effective use of internalized self-statements. Thus, teaching students to understand their internal self-talk and to modify their maladaptive thinking can help them prevent or change inappropriate behavior patterns.

Cognitive approaches as a way to alter maladaptive behavior patterns appeared in the late 1960s and early 1970s, as researchers began to understand the role of cognitive processes in behavior change. It was Dember's (1974) belief that a cognitive revolution occurred in psychology, as researchers gradually accepted the possible influence of cognition in the study of behavior. For example, Mahoney (1974) and Meichenbaum (1977) believed that operant and classical conditioning, the foundation of behavior therapy at the time, was not adequate to explain complex human behavior, such as violence and aggression.They posited that including underlying cognitions could enhance the effectiveness of behavior therapy. The fundamental underlying assumption was that social cognition involving expectations and appraisals plays an important role in determining behavior (Hughes, Dunn, & White, 1998; Lemerise & Arsenio, 2000; Luria, 1961; Vygotsky, 1962) and these cognitions can be examined and modified through verbal self-regulation (self-talk) to guide problem solving or other behaviors (Kendall, Ronan, & Epps, 1991; Meichenbaum, 1977). Stemming from these early theorists, CBI now comprises a promising research-based approach that focuses on social-emotional learning and the prevention or amelioration of maladaptive behavior (e.g., Mayer, Lochman, & Van Acker, 2005; Smith, Lochman, & Daunic, 2005).

Cognitive strategies can help students learn "how-to-think" rather than "what-to-think." CBIs are student operated and based on self-control; they differ from more traditional teacher-operated systems, which rely on external reward and punishment procedures (Harris & Pressley, 1991). According to Smith and Daunic (2006), most CBIs promote the understanding and use of self-talk to achieve self-control by including instructional techniques such as explicit teaching and use of modeling, role-playing, feedback, reinforcement, and cognitive components such as teacher think-alouds (i.e., cognitive modeling) to build what Kendall & Braswell (1993) called new "coping templates." Cognitive-behavioral techniques to teach effective replacement behaviors thus use a combination of cognitive, behavioral, emotive, and developmental strategies including rewards and self-evaluation (Kendall, 1993).

Since CBIs equip students with powerful self-talk strategies, students can generalize their newly learned behavior to new and novel situations outside of the training setting. When students learn effective ways to think in anger-provoking situations and engage positive "inner speech," they may be more inclined to respond appropriately in a variety of situations, not just the one in which they are rewarded (or punished) by a teacher. Covert self-instruction, therefore, can diminish overt behaviors such as hitting, pushing, or teasing, and an individual can learn to develop and regulate appropriate self-instructions to provide more constructive behavioral choices. Numerous studies demonstrate that teaching children cognitive strategies can strengthen prosocial behavior and decrease maladaptive behaviors such as hyperactivity/impulsivity, disruption, and aggression (see Abikoff, 1991; Conduct Problems Prevention Research Group [CPPRG], 1999, 2002; Lochman & Wells, 2004; Robinson, Smith, & Miller, 2002; Robinson et al., 1999).

CURRENT RESEARCH ON CBI

In a meta-analysis conducted in 1998, Beck and Fernandez analyzed 50 anger treatment studies using CBI with a total of 1,640 participants, including prison inmates, abusive parents and spouses, and college students with anger problems along with juvenile delinquents, adolescents in residential settings, and children with aggressive behavior in schools, and found an overall effect size of 0.70. Similarly, Robinson et al. (1999) found a mean effect size of 0.89 across 23 school-based studies using CBI with nonpsychotic children in K–12 settings, and 89 percent of the studies had participants who experienced greater gains on posttest and maintenance measures when exposed to treatment with a cognitive component.

Bennett and Gibbons (2000) analyzed 30 studies that used CBIs to treat antisocial behavior of children and youth 18 years and younger, finding a mean effect size of 0.48 at posttreatment (weighted 0.23) and a mean effect size of 0.66 at follow-up for the studies that included follow-up data (weighted 0.51). It was their conclusion that CBIs directed at school-aged children and youth seem to have a small to moderate effect in decreasing antisocial behavior. Interestingly, Bennett and Gibbons found that CBT has a larger effect with older than with younger school-aged students. Similar to Bennett and Gibbons, McCart, Priester, Davies, and Azen (2006) analyzed CBIs and behavioral parent training for participants 18 years old and younger who exhibited antisocial behavior such as physical or verbal aggression or delinquency. They found that, for preschool and school-aged youth, behavioral parent training had a stronger effect, whereas CBI had a stronger effect for adolescents. With a focus on school-aged populations across 21 published and 19 unpublished studies, Sukhodolsky, Kassinove, and Gorman (2004) found an overall mean effect size of 0.67 for CBI on children's anger-related problems.

Considering these meta-analyses, there is current and consistent evidence that CBIs are effective for the treatment of chronic problematic behaviors such as anger, aggression, antisocial behavior, and hyperactivity/impulsivity in school-aged populations. CBIs are easily adaptable for whole-class regular education instruction (universal prevention); small pullout group instruction (selected or secondary intervention) by school counselors, school psychologists, or behavioral resource teachers; or more restrictive venues, such as self-contained special education programs for students with emotional or behavioral disorders.

SCHOOL-BASED CBIs

There are a number of well-known CBIs for use in school settings. Many are part of multicomponent (e.g., including family intervention, academic tutoring, classroom supports, and/or systematic parent/teacher communication) and multitraining (e.g., social competence, emotional literacy, problem solving, stress reduction, coping skills, anger management, goal setting) programs. Examples are Fast Track, a comprehensive multicomponent and multisite prevention intervention; The Incredible Years, a multicomponent behavior program; and Linking the Interests of Families and Teachers (LIFT), a school-based prevention program with a parent and teacher component. These programs all contain multiple types of training (see CPPRG, 1999, 2002; Reid, Eddy, Fetrow, & Stoolmiller, 1999; Webster-Stratton, 2006), and each includes some components based on a cognitive approach. It is our view, however, that interventions that use a cognitive approach as the salient component of instruction are more applicable for a description of CBIs' effects on student behavior in schools. Promoting Alternative THinking Skills (PATHS), Second Step, Coping Power, and Tools for Getting Along are four curricula/programs that Smith, Graber, and Daunic (2009) have described as representative of interventions that have a significant cognitive training component focused on instructing children and youth to regulate their own behavior through the use of inner speech and that are applicable across grade levels, especially elementary settings.

As the universal curricular component of the Fast Track program, PATHS is intended for Grades K–6 and is a multiyear, systematic, and developmentally based program. PATHS includes a total of 131 lessons, materials, and instructions for teaching, among other areas, the use of self talk for self-control and interpersonal problem-solving skills. It was designed to be implemented along with the existing school curriculum in the regular education classroom. Lessons are to be taught three to five times per week for 20–30 minutes.

Second Step was designed to develop aspects of healthy social and emotional development such as empathy, impulse control, problem solving, and anger management. The curriculum has one application for preschool through fifth grade and another for sixth through ninth grade. Within each group, there are five teaching kits and lessons that build sequentially at each grade level. Each lesson is based on a story that demonstrates an important peer-relations skill. The stories are used to teach affective, cognitive, and behavioral social skills in a developmental sequence. In the middle school curriculum, there are three levels where teachers use discussion, role-play, homework, and a video.

The child component of the Coping Power Program includes sessions involving role-playing, interactive video vignettes, and skill-building activities in areas such as goal setting, awareness of physiological arousal, relaxation training, use of self-statements, social problem-solving skills, and dealing with peer pressure. In school-based settings, groups of four to six children typically meet for 45–60 minutes; a trained staff member and a school guidance counselor usually lead these sessions. Students also meet with staff periodically to discuss progress and focus on individual goals.

Finally, we designed Tools for Getting Along: Teaching Students to Problem Solve for middle/upper elementary school students. Our goal in the remainder of this chapter is to present in-depth information about this curriculum as one example of how the elements of a cognitive-behavioral approach to managing behavior can be translated into practice.

A CBI EXAMPLE

In this section, we provide a detailed and concrete example of what one CBI looks like in the form of a curriculum, including descriptions of lessons, activities, and implementation guidelines. The information we provide is a result of our experiences in developing the curriculum while studying its implementation over several years in collaboration with multiple school districts, schools, teachers, counselors, and students (see Daunic, Smith, Brank, & Penfield, 2006; Smith & Daunic, 2004).

Tools for Getting Along originated in materials we developed as part of a study on the effects of a conflict resolution/peer mediation program in middle schools (see Smith, Daunic, Miller, & Robinson, 2002). Based on the suggestion of Lochman, Dunn, and Klimes-Dougan (1993) to focus cognitive skills within a targeted domain, we organized the lessons around a social problem-solving framework. We also designed the curriculum to focus on understanding and managing frustration and anger, because anger is a frequent correlate of disruptive and aggressive behavior and can be preceded by frustration.

Problem Solving

In just about every daily event, people use a form of problem solving to navigate the complexities they confront. People use problem solving to find their lost keys, put together summer vacation plans, finish a crossword puzzle, and in their social lives, determine the best way to cope with a hostile coworker or resolve a dispute with a neighbor. Solving problems successfully, especially problems related to complex social situations, is one of the most useful lifetime skills that teachers can teach. When students become proficient at applying problem solving in social or personal situations, they become more proficient at developing self-control and can rely less on adult intervention when confronted with a variety of social challenges.

With some variations, solving a problem involves the following series of steps:

1. Recognizing that a problem exists
2. Defining the problem and the goal(s) of solving the problem
3. Generating multiple solutions
4. Evaluating the solutions
5. Designing a plan and carrying it out
6. Evaluating how well the plan worked

Teachers can help their students learn to apply these steps when faced with anger-provoking situations or personal dilemmas, resulting in a reduction of disruptive or aggressive behavior, increased coping skills for everyday challenges, a more positive classroom climate, and a more efficiently managed environment.

Tools for Getting Along consists of 21 lessons taught sequentially that cover six problem-solving steps, with six booster lessons for practicing learned skills. Lessons range from 30 to 40 minutes and are taught two to three times per week as a universal application, where all students in a classroom receive instruction in social problem solving. The overall goals of include the following:

- Understanding anger and how it may lead to or exacerbate social problems
- Learning how to recognize and manage anger
- Learning to use problem-solving steps effectively when in an anger-provoking situation

The goal of instruction in Tools for Getting Along is for students to learn the six problem-solving steps and then use them as covert self-talk to guide decision making. As students begin to master the problem-solving steps, they can eventually use them automatically when confronted with anger-provoking or other challenging social situations. Each lesson has specific instructions and suggested discussion material, including a cumulative review of preceding lessons, presentation of new material, and opportunities for guided and independent practice. Seven Tool Kits are situated throughout the curriculum to supplement student worksheets and activities. Each Tool Kit begins with questions about material learned previously and then provides students an opportunity to apply the learned problem-solving steps. Throughout the curriculum, numerous teaching guidelines facilitate learning of the problem-solving sequence, and specific strategies promote the generalization of problem-solving skills, including the following.

Paired or small-group learning. Teachers can structure small-group instruction (two or three per group) so students can share responsibility for learning the problem-solving strategies. Groups should include students with differing levels of social skill development and reading ability.

Self-monitoring. Each of the Tool Kits is designed to help students practice the strategies they learn and to serve as a self-monitoring device. Each Tool Kit begins by requiring students to respond to review items about steps learned previously and build skills through practice based on prior learning. The Tool Kit also provides opportunities to apply the problem-solving steps to problems they may encounter on a daily basis.

Point system. At the end of each Tool Kit is a point system that students can use to assess their own level of motivation to complete the Tool Kit. This self-assessment process aids in positive self-attribution as students become more successful, and it can act as a reinforcer, especially if teachers can incorporate the point system into their regular classroom procedures.

Cognitive modeling. Expert modeling, which teachers can provide, is considered a basic teaching strategy when using a cognitive-behavioral approach. Teachers can model for their students the behavioral and, especially, the cognitive skills they are teaching. Students can learn the essential problem-solving thinking skills by listening to teachers verbalize their thoughts when engaged in a problem-solving situation. Teachers' explanations of the cognitive strategies they use and their metacognitive awareness of those strategies (i.e., thinking about their thinking) serve as a powerful model for students to emulate (see Bandura, 1986). As part of the curriculum, therefore, it is suggested that teachers relate real-life instances in which they solved a problem of their own by "thinking out loud" to demonstrate how they used the steps, thus modeling how the problem-solving process generalizes to a variety of realistic situations. For example, when teachers think out loud as they talk about how they controlled their own anger in a real-life situation, they might say something like, "Wow, that was a mean thing for her to say to me, and I don't like it at all. I'm really angry. I need to take a deep breath and think for a moment. I shouldn't say anything back to her because that may make things worse. I will talk to her later after Ive calmed down and thought this through a little bit."

Examples of the Problem-Solving Steps

Tools for Getting Along includes six problem-solving steps focused on anger and anger-provoking social situations. The focus on anger is included because many students with problem behaviors have difficulty controlling their anger and, thus, are unable to engage rational thinking and start an effective problem-solving process.

Step 1: I know I'm angry. In the case of anger management, the recognition of anger is the necessary first step in the problem-solving skill sequence. Step 1 has three lessons designed to teach students about body signals that can help them recognize when a relatively small irritation might turn into anger and even rage. Lessons include discussions about anger-provoking situations that students may encounter and the accompanying feelings they may experience. As shown in Figure 4.1, these lessons include scripted role-plays for students to enact and discussion questions for the teacher to use to query students about whether anger escalated in the role-play situations, the levels of anger displayed, and whether the problem could have been avoided.

Figure 4.1   Student Role-Play: "Collision"

Student Role-Play: "Collision"

[Two boys are walking towards each other in the hall. Neither of them is watching where he is going, and they slam into each other.]

(COLLISION!)

Student 1: Hey, watch where you're going!

Student 2: Me!? You're the one who ran into me, you idiot!!

Student 1: [Shoves Student 2] Who are you calling an idiot!?

Student 2: Quit it! . . .

Discussion Questions

1. At what level of anger was Student 1?
2. Did Student 1 go straight to that level, or did he hit other levels on the way?
3. At what level of anger was Student 2?
4. Did Student 2 go straight to that level or hit other levels on the way?
5. Was there a turning point during the incident, or a point where the problem could have been avoided?
6. What do you think the students in each situation could have done to calm their anger?

Step 2: I calm down. For Step 2, there are three lessons designed to assist students to prevent the escalation of frustration and anger and to engage their cognition (i.e., calm down and think). In one lesson, students are taught some calming-down strategies as they build on their recognition of body signals that can aler them to the beginning of frustration or anger. After practicing these strategies together, class members are asked to describe other strategies they may have used in frustrating situations to keep themselves calm.

In another lesson, students fill in the statement *If I get angry, then I might . . .* , as part of the instruction about losing control and responding to a problem with anger. Students also respond to instruction about why reacting with aggression when angry might initially seem like a good idea and what the negative consequences of an aggressive response might be. Exercises such as these highlight for students how they might feel and the thinking process they might use when tempted to act aggressively.

Step 3: I think about the cause. The lesson for this step is designed to help students learn to define a problem in terms of goals and barriers. After recognizing that there is a problem (i.e., *I am angry and I need to calm down*; Steps 1 and 2), students need to define the cause of the problem before they decide on a course of action. The lesson instructs teachers to ask their students what they think causes most problems with other people. Following instruction, students are asked to complete a student worksheet, as shown in Figure 4.2, which queries them about the possible goals and barriers involved in a particular problem situation.

Figure 4.2   Student Worksheet: Identifying Goals and Barriers

Student Worksheet

Identifying Goals and Barriers

Name _____   Date _____

Directions: Read the story and answer the questions that follow.

Mr. Jones's class is going on a field trip to an art museum. David is the only student in the class who did not return a permission slip. He is angry and upset because he wants to go to the art museum.

What is David's goal?

What barrier is preventing him from reaching his goal?

What is David feeling?

Do you think David is getting along?

The general notion of Step 3 is that a barrier is something that a student can have some control over, as opposed to placing "blame" on another person. Students are given practice in identifying the goal(s) and the barrier(s) for several problem scenarios. A Tool Kit (see Figure 4.3) is provided at the end of the lesson so that students can think through a recent problem they have had by defining the goal(s) and barrier(s), describing the feelings they encountered (e.g., body signals, frustration, anger, rage), describing whether they remembered to calm down, and identifying what method they might have used to do so.

Figure 4.3   Tool Kit 7: Putting It All Together

Tool Kit 7

Putting It All Together

Name: _____   Date:_____

Write the steps of problem solving.

Step 1: _____

Step 2: _____

Step 3: _____

Step 4: _____

Step 5: _____

Step 6: _____

Explain why we must learn to recognize anger and frustration.

Calming down and thinking about your anger allows you to do what?

A barrier is something that keeps you from reaching your _____.

Explain why it is important to think of as many solutions as possible.

Fill in the blanks below:

When choosing a solution, you should be sure that it removes the _____, allows you to reach your_____, and does not cause negative_____.

It is important to evaluate our solutions to problems so that we can make the _____ _____ in the future.

When you choose a solution to a problem and it doesn't go so well, what should you do? (Check *all* of the items that you think are correct.)

_____ Remember that every problem is another opportunity for success.

_____ Give up.

_____ Tell yourself that even though you messed up, you know why.

_____ Don't make the same mistake again.

_____ Think more carefully about your choices.

_____ Remember that sometimes we do things right and they still don't work out.

_____ Tell yourself that nobody's perfect and that you will do better next time.

Take another look at *Tool Kit 6*. Read the description of your problem and think about the solutions you considered.

Did you choose the best solution to the problem?

Describe what happened.

How do you think it turned out?

If it didn't work out well, what do you think you could do differently next time?

How Did I Do?

Think about what you did during the *Tools for Getting Along* lesson today. Then record the number of points you think you deserve for each item below. If you get most of the points, give yourself a pat on the back!

___ I listened. (0–3 points)   ___ I participated. (0–3 points)

___ I cooperated. (0–3 points)   ___ I completed my *Tool Kit*. (0–2 points)

TOTAL _____

Step 4: I think about what I could do. The main idea of this step is to understand that there is more than one possible solution to most problems. It is one of the most important steps for students to learn. In most anger-provoking situations, the first solution generated is often unproductive because of the emotion involved. This step and the one that follows are the skill-based steps of problem solving and, thus, require the most practice. In three lessons devoted to Step 4, students learn how to figure out possible solutions to problem situations, such as by thinking about effective strategies they used in similar situations, talking with a trusted friend or adult, and/or thinking about what a parent or good friend might do. The idea is to get them to find a way to generate more than one possible solution.

After instruction on generating an array of possible solutions, teachers have students play the "What Can I Do?" game, the object of which is to come up with as many solutions as they can for prescribed problem situations. Students are asked to generate only solutions that are possible (i.e., not magical, silly, or otherwise impossible) based on the reality of the situation. At this stage, the solutions do not have to be good solutions, because the goal of the game is for students to understand that most problems have multiple solutions, including those that may not have good outcomes. Students continue to play the game using a variety of problem scenarios offered in the curriculum or ones they come up with on their own.

Step 5: I try a solution. This step is designed to help students evaluate the solutions generated in the previous step. In our curriculum, we instruct students to ask themselves what would be the best, worst, and mostly likely consequences of each choice they generate. Often in a problem-solving sequence, students do not allow for adequate time to think carefully through the multiplicity of possible consequences of implementing a particular solution. Thus, the four lessons provided to teach this step offer strategies to help students evaluate potential outcomes. To illustrate, a teacher poses an interesting social problem, shown in Figure 4.4, between Markief and his friend Tyler over an incident with a newly purchased hat. In this example, students have to consider a variety of solutions through an evaluative process.

Figure 4.4   Step 5: I Try a Solution

Step 5: I Try a Solution

Tyler was wearing his newly purchased hat when he was riding bikes with Markief in the neighborhood. Markief is always fooling around and being silly, and when he was riding off in a hurry, Markief took Tyler's hat and accidentally dropped it into a drainage ditch, getting it wet and dirty and practically ruined. Tyler shares his problem with the class, and the teacher asks the group to brainstorm some possible solutions.

The students come up with the following suggestions for Tyler:

a) Tell his mom or Markief's mom about how he lost his hat and get him in trouble.

b) Yell at Markief and tell him that he has to buy a new hat.

c) Ignore Markief's behavior and try to clean up the hat or get a new one.

d) Tell Markief that when he acts stupid, bad things happen and he needs to stop it, and then he can help Tyler with buying a new hat.

The teacher engages the class in a discussion about the best, worst, and most likely thing to happen if Tyler chooses each of the suggestions (a) through (d). After the discussion, the students summarize their evaluations of each of the suggestions.

Action	Most Likely Outcome
Tell his mom or Markief's mom about how he lost his hat and get him in trouble.	Markief gets in big trouble at home and gets grounded, and he can't play again for weeks. Also, the friendship may not be reparable.
Yell at Markief and tell him that he has to buy a new hat.	Markief just yells back and resists any effort to buy a new hat. He explains it was just an accident and Tyler should chill out.
Ignore Markief's behavior and try to clean up the hat or get a new one.	Markief doesn't stop his foolish behavior, and Tyler ends up with a ruined new hat.
Tell Markief that when he acts stupid, bad things happen and he needs to stop it, and then he can help Tyler with buying a new hat.	Markief agrees that what he did was stupid and he will talk to his mom about using his allowance money to help Tyler buy a new hat.

Using a process of generating solutions and then evaluating them, Tyler is more able to find an acceptable solution according to his goals; in this case, keeping his best friend, not getting him in trouble, and getting a new hat.

Step 6: I think about how it turned out. The final problem-solving step involves evaluating whether a selected solution, when put into action, worked in a way to accomplish established goals. If so, the curriculum instructs students to congratulate themselves on good problem solving. If the implementation of a selected solution did not turn out as planned, strategies are taught to determine whether the students had problems carrying out their plan of action or whether their selected solution was not a good one after all. Considering how even the best solution put into action may not achieve the desired goals for a variety of reasons, teachers instruct students to reward themselves for using a thoughtful process that would be more likely to provide a positive outcome most of the time. Students learn that in situations where they become frustrated or angry, using self-talk and deliberate, sequential action is a more reliable process then acting impulsively based on the emotions of the moment. The lessons for this step thus provide opportunities for students to use problem situations as opportunities for continuing skill practice. They also learn about their feelings and ability to use self-talk, and they discover how thoughtful behavior may result in consequences that will positively affect their future relationships with others and ultimately help them get what they want.

Booster Lessons

Six booster lessons in Tools for Getting Along are designed to "boost" students' knowledge and allow for further skill practice in implementing the six-step process. Following the 21 core lessons in which students learn and practice the problem-solving steps, the 6 booster lessons are taught less frequently (e.g., one every other week) and provide review and varied opportunities for students to generalize their learned skills.

Booster Lesson 1. This lesson consists of a general review of the rationale for using problem solving in social conflict situations and a substantive review of the six problem-solving steps. At the end of Booster Lesson 1, students complete a Tool Kit Revisited exercise as guided practice to review the knowledge base from previous instruction.

Booster Lesson 2. In this lesson, students can act out any or all of the six supplied scripted role-plays for the class (see Figure 4.5 for example). Opportunities to act out scripted role-plays provide students with skill practice, and teachers are encouraged to repeat the role-plays if desired. There are suggested questions for the teacher to use following each role-play to engage students in analyzing the problem situations within the context of the six problem-solving steps.

Booster Lessons 3 and 4. Here students design their own role-plays based on their ideas and/or experiences and then act them out for the class.

Booster Lessons 5 and 6. These lessons provide students an opportunity for group problem solving. Student volunteers can share real-life problems with the class, and the teacher can facilitate a whole-class discussion of the problem in light of the six problem-solving steps. Students who volunteer to share real-life social problems can report back to the class about how the chosen solutions worked out.

Figure 4.5   Problem-Solving Practice

Script 6

"The Water Fountain Incident"

[Regan and Carmen are waiting in line for the water fountain after recess when Rico and Ashton push in front of them.]

Regan: Hey watch it! Get to the back of the line! We were here first.

Rico: It's no big deal. Everyone's pushing!

Carmen: [speaking calmly] Yeah, but we were here first, and it's not fair to cut in line. We're just as thirsty as you are.

Ashton: Oh stop whining. You'll get a drink sooner or later!

Carmen: [clenching fists and thinking aloud] Whining? Oooh I'm getting mad. I need a drink, and they're making me wait longer to get one. What can I do? Maybe I should just push them back. But wait—that will probably make it worse. This isn't worth getting in trouble about. But still, I shouldn't have to go behind them. If I say something, maybe they'll get even more ugly. But maybe they won't, and maybe they won't do it again. Most likely, they'll just ignore me, but at least I'll stand up for me and Regan.

[speaking calmly] Well, it's pretty hot outside. No wonder everyone's fighting for the water fountain.

Ashton: I know—it's like 100 degrees!

Carmen: Well maybe next time you could wait your turn in line. Everyone's just as hot as you are.

Ashton: Yeah, maybe. But I couldn't help it, and I don't care if everyone else is hot or not!

Carmen: [thinking aloud] Well, I don't know if that worked or not. It was better than pushing back, I guess, because that might have started a real problem, and I kept my cool. I don't have to react just because they're acting stupid. Maybe they'll think about it next time before they push in line—at least I can hope for the best.

Regan: How about tomorrow we bring a water bottle?

Rico: Yeah—I have one I can bring.

Suggested Questions to Follow Each Script

1. What was the level of anger of [name of each character] at the beginning of the role-play? Did it go any higher?

2. Was there a turning point during the incident—a point where the problem was, or could have been, avoided?

3. How did [name of each character] keep from getting very angry?

4. What might have happened if [name] had not done . . . ?

5. What steps did [name of each character] take to solve his or her problem?

6. How do you think the incident turned out?

For incidents that did not turn out well, such as in Role-Plays #3 and #6:

7. What could [name] have done differently (or what might [name] do differently next time this problem occurs)?

Preliminary Outcome Research

Using multilevel modeling in a randomized control study to determine whether Tools for Getting Along affected measures of knowledge and behavior for 165 fourth- and fifth-grade target students, Daunic, Smith, Brank, and Penfield (2006) found significant positive effects of treatment on student knowledge of problem-solving concepts, teacher ratings of student aggression, and student reports of anger suppression. Daunic et al. also found that outcomes differed across teachers/classrooms and that teacher ratings of social validity were generally positive. A comparison of treatment with core lessons only versus treatment with core plus booster lessons indicated that the addition of booster lessons did not significantly affect treatment efficacy.

Currently, Tools for Getting Along is undergoing a four-year investigation using a randomized control field trial, with randomization at the school level. For each of the first three years, six to eight schools (approximately 43 total classrooms) were matched on size and percent of students receiving free or reduced-price lunch and randomly assigned to treatment or control conditions. We provided eight hours of training in using the Tools for Getting Along curriculum for treatment group teachers and ongoing supervision/consultation throughout the school year. We instructed teachers to implement Tools for Getting Along within a range of normal routines in the school setting. Because we know that control group teachers may deliberately or inadvertently provide some aspects of curricular constructs and information to their students, we are measuring aspects of the context/setting in which both treatment and control group students are taught in addition to using measures of treatment fidelity (treatment as delivered), problem-solving knowledge (treatment as received), externalizing behaviors, executive function, anger control, and social status. Preliminary analyses indicate that Tools for Getting Along has positive effects on executive function and externalizing behaviors as rated by both teachers and peers (Barber, Smith, & Daunic, 2009; Daunic et al., 2008).

SUMMARY

Considering the social, emotional, and academic challenges that today's youth confront on a daily basis, the effective use of a cognitive-behavioral approach to problem situations may be among the most vital skills to learn. Many students do not have the requisite skills for dealing with a myriad of social dilemmas, many of which are emotionally charged. Thus, we cannot expect students to be successful using cognitive strategies when faced with complex social problems unless we teach them explicitly and systematically. CBIs can help students with significant behavior problems learn positive replacement behaviors, and in recent years, its use in school settings has been recognized as a viable, research-based approach.

Despite the progress in establishing the research base for CBIs in schools, much more research is needed to understand better the efficacy and effectiveness of improving social and emotional outcomes for students and the factors that contribute to the successful implementation of classroom-based practice. There are many curricula available for teachers to consider, with Tools for Getting Along being one example of a CBI designed to help students approach a problem using self-awareness and inner speech. By using CBIs to supplement other evidence-based classroom management techniques, school-based professionals are in a position to have a strong influence on students' ability to become successful in managing their social and emotional needs on a daily basis.

An Illustration From Practice

It was not hard to convince Mr. Ridgeway that Tools for Getting Along provided a needed addition to his curriculum. At the beginning of the school year, students in his fifth-grade class had demonstrated time and again their inability to communicate effectively when they were in conflict. He was becoming increasingly frustrated with his students' use of verbal harassment, pushing, and general destructive behavior when they became angry with each other, as well as with the occasional fight that would break out at recess. He was also frustrated about not having an organized way to help his students arrive at constructive solutions when they were having social problems with each other and the adults around them.

Mr. Ridgeway started teaching Tools for Getting Along early in the fall twice a week for about 30–40 minutes for each lesson. Interspersed throughout his instruction, he used self-talks from his own home-based experiences that paralleled the problem-solving steps in the curriculum. One example he related to his students was about his two dogs, who were often out of control and had ripped up the screens on his porch, requiring continuous repairs. His wife was getting angry about it, and he talked to the students about how he had to calm down and think through the problem on a frequent basis. In addition, whenever he found some extra time during the week, he pointed out instances where his students could apply the skills they were learning to their own social problems.

Mr. Ridgeway also used the curriculum role-plays to great advantage. He emphasized that the role-plays were important business and would try to make them a bit like theater. The students practiced and used props, and many of them accepted their parts with real enthusiasm. Mr. Ridgeway had the students who observed each role-play watch for specific elements of what was taught in the curriculum and, following the role-play, evaluate how much they had learned.

Mr. Ridgeway facilitated the generalization of students' problem-solving skills to situations outside the classroom (e.g., between classes, in the cafeteria, at assemblies) by using transitions to remind them to use what theyd learned from the curriculum. He also talked about using their skills at home and in their neighborhoods when they had arguments with younger siblings or caregivers or when they had issues with their friends down the street. Further, Mr. Ridgeway used students' authentic outside-of-school experiences as teaching situations during and outside the Tools for Getting Along lessons. He followed up with questions about how their newly learned skills were working and what solutions they were using. At the end of the school year, Mr. Ridgeway was happy to report that he felt Tools for Getting Along had been a successful program. He had seen his students grow emotionally and observed that their use of social problem solving resulted in less verbal harassment and fewer physical altercations. In a testament to his evaluation of the program, he was planning on teaching Tools for Getting Along the following year, with administrative approval.

REFERENCES

Abikoff, H. (1991). Cognitive training in ADHD children: Less to it than meets the eye. *Journal of Learning Disabilities, 24,* 205–209.

Bandura, A. (1986). *Social foundations of thought and action: A social cognitive theory.* Englewood Cliffs, NJ: Prentice-Hall.

Barber, B. R., Smith, S. W., & Daunic, A. P. (2008, November). *Executive function skill interventions for improving behavior of students with emotional and behavioral disorders.* Paper presented at the 32nd Annual National Conference on Severe Behavior Disorders of Children and Youth, Tempe, AZ.

Beck, R., & Fernandez, E. (1998). Cognitive-behavioral therapy in the treatment of anger: A meta-analysis. *Cognitive Therapy and Research, 22,* 63–74.

Bennett, D. S., & Gibbons, T. A. (2000). Efficacy of child cognitive-behavioral interventions for antisocial behavior: A meta-analysis. *Child & Family Behavior Therapy, 22,* 1–15.

Butler, A. C., Chapman, J. E., Forman, E. M., & Beck, A. T. (2006). The empirical status of cognitive-behavioral therapy: A review of meta-analyses. *Clinical Psychology Review, 26,* 17–31.

Conduct Problems Prevention Research Group (CPPRG). (1999). Initial impact of the Fast Track prevention trial for conduct problems: I. The high-risk sample. *Journal of Consulting and Clinical Psychology, 67,* 631–647.

Conduct Problems Prevention Research Group (CPPRG). (2002). Predictor variables associated with positive Fast Track outcomes at the end of third grade. *Journal of Abnormal Child Psychology, 30,* 37–52.

Craighead, L. W., Craighead, W. E., Kazdin, A. E., & Mahoney, M. J. (Eds.). (1994). *Cognitive and behavioral interventions: An empirical approach to mental health problems.* Boston: Allyn & Bacon.

Daunic, A. P., Smith. S. W., Brank, E. M., & Penfield, R. D. (2006). Classroom based cognitive-behavioral intervention to prevent aggression: Efficacy and social validity. *Journal of School Psychology, 44,* 123–139.

Daunic, A. P., Smith, S. W., Garvan, C., Li, W., Barber, B. R., Becker, M., et al. (2009, April). *Class-wide social problem-solving intervention to address disruption/aggression: Examining efficacy using treatment as received.* Paper presented at the annual meeting of the American Educational Research Association, San Diego, CA.

Dember, W. N. (1974). Motivation and the cognitive revolution. *American Psychologist, 29,* 161–168.

Dodge, K. A., & Frame, C. (1982). Social cognitive biases and deficits in aggressive boys. *Child Development, 53,* 620–635.

Harris, K. R., & Pressley, M. (1991). The nature of cognitive strategy instruction: Interactive strategy construction. *Exceptional Children, 57,* 392–404.

Hughes, C., Dunn, J., & White, A. (1998). Trick or treat? Uneven understanding of mind and emotion and executive dysfunction in hard-to-manage preschoolers. *Journal of Child Psychology & Psychiatry, 39,* 981–994

Kendall, P. C. (1993). Cognitive-behavioral therapies with youth: Guiding theory, current status, and emerging developments. *Journal of Consulting and Clinical Psychology, 61,* 235–247.

Kendall, P. C. (2000). *Child and adolescent therapy: Cognitive-behavioral procedures.* New York: Guilford Press.

Kendall, P. C., & Braswell, L. (1993). *Cognitive-behavioral therapy for impulsive children* (2nd ed.). New York: Guilford Press.

Kendall, P. C., Ronan, K. R., & Epps, J. (1991). Aggression on children/adolescents: Cognitive-behavioral treatment perspectives. In D. J. Pepler & K. H. Rubin (Eds.), *The development and treatment of childhood aggression* (pp. 341–360). Hillsdale, NJ: Lawrence Erlbaum.

Lemerise, E. A., & Arsenio, W. F. (2000). An integrated model of emotion processes and cognition in social information processing. *Child Development, 71,* 107–118.

Lochman, J. E., Dunn, S. E., & Klimes-Dougan, B. (1993). An intervention and consultation model from a social cognitive perspective: A description of the Anger Coping Program. *School Psychology Review, 22*(3), 458–471.

Lochman, J. E., & Wells, K. C. (2004). The Coping Power Program for preadolescent aggressive boys and their parents: Outcome effects at the one-year follow-up. *Journal of Consulting and Clinical Psychology, 72,* 571–578.

Luria, A. R. (1961). *The role of speech in the regulation of normal and abnormal behaviors.* New York: Liveright.

Mahoney, M. J. (1974). *Cognition and behavior modification.* Cambridge, MA: Ballinger.

Mahoney, M. J., & Kazdin, A. E. (1979). Cognitive behavior modification: Misconceptions and premature evacuation. *Psychological Bulletin, 86,* 1044–1049.

Mayer, M. J., Lochman, J., & Van Acker, R. (2005). Introduction to the special issue: Cognitive-behavioral interventions with students with EBD. *Behavioral Disorders, 30,* 197–212.

Mayer, M. J., Van Acker, R., Lochman, J. E., & Gresham, F. M. (Eds.). (2009). *Cognitive-behavioral interventions for emotional and behavioral disorders: School-based practice.* New York: Guilford Press.

McCart, M. R., Priester, P. E., Davies, W. H., & Azen, R. (2006). Differential effectiveness of behavioral parent-training and cognitive-behavioral therapy for antisocial youth: A meta analysis. *Journal of Abnormal Child Psychology, 34,* 527–543.

Meichenbaum, D. H. (1977). *Cognitive-behavior modification: An integrative approach.* New York: Plenum Press.

Mennuti, R. B., Freeman, A., & Christner, R. W. (Eds.). (2006). *Cognitive-behavioral interventions in educational settings: A handbook for practice.* New York: Routledge.

Public Agenda. (2004). *Teaching interrupted: Do discipline policies in today's public schools foster the common good?* New York: Author.

Reid, J. B., Eddy, J. M., Fetrow, R. A., & Stoolmiller, M. (1999). Description and immediate impacts of a preventive intervention for conduct problems. *American Journal of Community Psychology, 27,* 483–517.

Robinson, T. R., Smith, S. W., & Miller, M. D. (2002). Effect of a cognitive-behavioral intervention on responses to anger by middle school students with chronic behavior problems. *Behavioral Disorders, 27,* 256–271.

Robinson, T. R., Smith, S.W., Miller, M. D., & Brownell, M. T. (1999). Cognitive behavior modification of hyperactivity-impulsivity and aggression: A meta-analysis of school-based studies. *Journal of Educational Psychology, 91,* 195–203.

Smith, S. W., & Daunic, A. P. (2004). Research on preventing behavior problems using a cognitive-behavioral intervention: Preliminary findings, challenges and future directions. *Behavioral Disorders, 30,* 72–76.

Smith, S. W., & Daunic, A. P. (2006). *Managing difficult behavior through problem solving instruction: Strategies for the elementary classroom.* Boston: Allyn & Bacon.

Smith, S. W., Daunic, A. P., Miller, M. D., & Robinson, T. R. (2002). Conflict resolution and peer mediation in middle schools: Extending the process and outcome knowledge base. *Journal of Social Psychology. 142,* 567–586.

Smith, S. W., Graber, J., & Daunic, A. P. (2009) Cognitive-behavioral interventions for anger/aggression: Review of research and research-to-practice issues. In M. Mayer, R. Van Acker, J. Lochman, & F. Gresham (Eds.), *Cognitive-behavioral interventions for emotional and behavioral disorders: School-based practice* (pp. 111–142). New York: Guilford Press.

Smith, S. W., Lochman, J. E., & Daunic, A. P. (2005). Managing aggression using cognitive-behavioral interventions: State of the practice and future directions. *Behavioral Disorders, 30,* 227–240.

Sukhodolsky, D. G., Kassinove, H., & Gorman, B. S. (2004). Cognitive-behavioral therapy for anger in children and adolescents: A meta-analysis. *Aggression and Violent Behavior, 9,* 247–269.

Vygotsky, L. (1962). *Thought and language.* New York: Wiley

Webster-Stratton, C. (2006). *The Incredible Years: A trouble-shooting guide for parents of children ages 3–8 years.* Seattle: Incredible Years Press.

Wehmeyer, M. L., Agran, M., & Hughes, C. (2000). A national survey of teachers' promotion of self-determination and student-directed learning. *The Journal of Special Education, 34,* 58–68.

Worell, J., & Nelson, C. M. (1974). *Managing instructional problems.* New York: McGraw-Hill.

5

Social Skills Instruction and Generalization Strategies

In this chapter, we

- define social skills and social competence;
- give examples of research-based curricula;
- outline effective instructional procedures and enhancements; and
- describe strategies to reinforce, maintain, and generalize prosocial behaviors beyond social skills groups.

Changes in society at the beginning of the 21st century have made social skills instruction an essential part of the course of study in public schools. Employers require skills in teamwork, communication, and problem solving. Unfortunately, economic and social pressures leave families less time to teach their children how to get along with others, and increasing numbers of children come to school with significant deficits in those abilities. At the same time, developmental theorists like Vygotsky and Bronfenbrenner have expanded educators' awareness of the impact of relationships on intellectual growth. Social learning theorists agree that learning takes place best in a healthy social environment where students and teachers encourage one another to learn and grow. Children who exhibit emotional and antisocial behaviors in the classroom hamper the learning community for themselves and others within that class. After all, "education is not preparation for life; education is life itself" (attributed to John Dewey).

Socially appropriate students are well liked, play often with friends, treat friends kindly, share, defend friends, show empathy, and help friends when they are hurt. They are more likely to settle problems with a compromise and take time to give explanations. Conversely, students who have internalizing behaviors, are extremely shy, cry frequently, or refuse to participate in group activities are gradually neglected or rejected by others. Others have externalizing antisocial behaviors. Their aggressive style of social interaction results in behavioral excesses such as arguing, shouting, teasing, blaming, and fighting. They have behavioral deficits in areas such as self-control, cooperating, problem solving, following rules, helping, sharing, making good decisions, and accepting consequences. Students with antisocial behaviors may think about interactions differently than typical students. They may blame others for their problems, believe that others want bad things to happen to them, and generally have difficulty reading social situations. They seem unable to decide cause and effect from their behaviors.

Without intervention, effects from these behavioral differences have long-lasting consequences for students. Antisocial behaviors have repercussions across environments (school, home, community) and social groups (peers, teachers, and family members). For example, peer rejection due to aggressive behavior can result in delinquency and the creation of antisocial peer groups (Patterson, Reid, & Dishion, 1992; Walker, Ramsey, & Gresham, 2004). Research has indicated that aggressive and disruptive behaviors actually result in high status and high social positions in some school settings, especially urban schools (Farmer, Van Acker, Pearl, & Rodkin, 1999; Maag, 2006; Warren et al., 2003). High status within antisocial groups is likely to have negative outcomes in the long term, such as difficulty maintaining employment and relationships with others, depression, mental illness, and contact with the legal system (Parker & Asher, 1987, reported in Maag).

A focus on prevention and school-based intervention is one of several solutions to address antisocial behaviors. Effective teaching of social skills in the natural setting of school can result in increasing social competence across peer groups, fewer inappropriate interactions, and positive long-term outcomes (Dunlap et al., 2006; Walker, Stiller, Golly, Kavanagh, & Fiel, 1998). For example, studies of resilient people who grew up in unfavorable environments often cite the following as key variables in their resiliency: adaptive social behaviors, problem-solving skills, positive social orientation including close peer friendships, warm relationships with family members, and supportive positive social networks (Doll & Lyon, 1998; Masten & Coatsworth, 1998). Thus, social skills instruction in general education classrooms is an important prevention strategy.

SOCIAL SKILLS, SOCIAL COMPETENCE, AND CURRICULA

Social competency is a very complex area of child development. A broad array of behaviors is relevant to any given social situation, appropriate responses vary according to context and persons therein, and behaviors considered appropriate in one circumstance may be punished or viewed as "uncool" in another. In this chapter, social skills are defined as behaviors that *significant* others consider appropriate for the setting and situation. In school, teachers, administrators, ancillary staff, and peers all have expectations for students' behavior; all are significant to the student. Agreement, consistency, and modeling among the adults should establish the norms for that setting. In home and community settings, parents, siblings, and the public may have differing expectations. Students need to learn how to adapt their skills from one setting to another in order to be considered socially competent.

McGinnis and Goldstein (1997) carried out a behavioral task analysis and identified 60 social skills viewed as important for building social competence, shown in Table 5.1. These vary from basic classroom skills, such as "listening," to skills for dealing with stress, such as "reacting to failure." Although this list may seem lengthy, its specificity allows the teacher to target the exact set of skills that a student or class may need.

Table 5.1   Sixty Social Skills for Elementary Students

Group I: Classroom Survival Skills	Group IV: Skill Alternatives to Aggression
1. Listening	36. Using Self-Control
2. Asking for Help	37. Asking Permission
3. Saying Thank You	38. Responding to Teasing
4. Bringing Materials to Class	39. Avoiding Trouble
5. Following Instructions	40. Staying Out of Fights
6. Completing Assignments	41. Problem Solving
7. Contributing to Discussions	42. Accepting Consequences
8. Offering Help to an Adult	43. Dealing With an Accusation
9. Asking a Question	44. Negotiating
10. Ignoring Distractions	
11. Making Corrections	**Group V: Skills for Dealing With Stress**
12. Deciding on Something to Do	45. Dealing With Boredom
13. Setting a Goal	46. Deciding What Caused a Problem
	47. Making a Complaint
Group II: Friendship-Making Skills	48. Answering a Complaint
14. Introducing Yourself	49. Dealing With Losing
15. Beginning a Conversation	50. Being a Good Sport
16. Ending a Conversation	51. Dealing With Being Left Out
17. Joining In	52. Dealing With Embarrassment
18. Playing a Game	53. Reacting to Failure
19. Asking a Favor	54. Accepting No
20. Offering Help to a Classmate	55. Saying No
21. Giving a Compliment	56. Relaxing
22. Accepting a Compliment	57. Dealing With Group Pressure
23. Suggesting an Activity	58. Dealing With Something That Isn't Yours
24. Sharing	59. Making Decisions
25. Apologizing	60. Being Honest
Group III: Skills Dealing With Feelings	
26. Knowing Your Feelings	
27. Expressing Your Feelings	
28. Recognizing Another's Feelings	
29. Showing Understanding of Another's Feelings	
30. Expressing Concern for Another	
31. Dealing With Your Anger	
32. Dealing With Another's Anger	
33. Expressing Affection	
34. Dealing With Fear	
35. Rewarding Yourself	

To acquire competency in a complex skill, students may first need to learn several basic steps. For example, in the survival skill of *following directions,* students must (1) demonstrate listening to or reading the directions, (2) mentally rehearse the required steps (self-instruction), (3) respond to the directions, and (4) monitor their own progress. Students must learn discrete behaviors for specific targeted skills, and they must also transfer or generalize the training to apply the skills in different settings. This is described as generalization of skill performance. A student's problem behaviors may impede either acquisition or performance of skills (DuPaul & Eckert, 1994; Gresham, 1995; Maag, 2006). The dual purpose of teaching social skills, therefore, should be to increase skills and their competent performance in natural settings and to decrease problem behaviors that interfere with their performance.

Choosing a Curriculum

Social skills are taught both formally and informally in the classroom. Teachers in the elementary grades frequently remind students about appropriate behaviors and use teachable moments to help the class develop greater interpersonal skills. This informal approach was sufficient when most students learned these skills from their families and the community. However, practitioners and researchers alike agree that schools now must be in the business of directly teaching appropriate social skills.

Curriculum or skills selected for use on a schoolwide basis will promote widespread use of agreed-upon skills. The use of more targeted or individualized social skills instruction is then initiated for students who need more than the primary application of the schoolwide curriculum. In these cases, selected skills are matched to the deficits of the student based on assessment. Tools such as functional assessment interviews and direct observations can assist in determining the antecedents and consequences surrounding antisocial and inappropriate behaviors (O'Neill et al., 1997). Attention to environmental variables that function to trigger and maintain antisocial (and prosocial) behaviors can then assist in selecting lessons within curricula that are a good fit to the specific child and setting. This strategic selection of skills based on individual needs (i.e., targeting skills to teach a replacement skill for the inappropriate behavior) is one critical variable in the effectiveness of social skills interventions and generalization of the skill use to natural settings (see Maag, 2006, and Scott & Nelson, 1998, for a discussion of generalization failure in social skills research). Targeting replacement skills that will appropriately serve the same function as the undesirable behavior (e.g., recruit peer attention, gain access to preferred activity or items) will also increase the likelihood that those new behaviors will occur and be reinforced in the natural environment, a phenomenon described as "behavioral entrapment" (McConnell, 1987).

Alberg, Petry, and Eller (1994) outlined an eight-step decision-making process for choosing a curriculum. Steps 1 and 2, identifying and prioritizing needs, require honest input from teachers and administrators about the needs of both students and teachers. Ideally, parents and other members of the community are involved as well. This assessment of needs can be based on formal or informal observations, a review of the reasons for office referrals, or a simple checklist, among other methods. Teachers may need encouragement to identify the specific social problems they are encountering in the classroom. Cultural differences in the student population must be taken into account when selecting curriculum programs and targeted social skills, and this needs assessment should avoid stereotyping or otherwise labeling any groups or students (Bardon, Dona, & Symons, 2008; Cartledge & Milburn, 1996). Steps 3, 4, and 5 are similar to the process for adopting any course of study: survey the literature, identify pros and cons for the most likely choices, and decide. Preparation, Step 6, consists of numerous activities: setting goals; informing families; providing training for teachers and other school personnel; planning time for practice, generalization, and maintenance of skills; and creating a plan for evaluation. Steps 7 and 8 are Implementation and Evaluation.

Battalio and Stephens (2005) similarly suggested five key steps in creating programs to support social skills development that is most likely to diminish maladaptive behaviors:

1. Assess students' behavioral characteristics and match the behavioral concern to specialized instruction to teach replacement behavior.

2. Determine if the issue is a skill deficit that needs to be taught or a performance deficit that needs to be practiced with feedback and reinforcement in natural environments (or both).

3. Choose a curriculum that uses appropriate instruction (i.e., modeling, role-playing, feedback, and generalization) and select functional lessons.

4. Collect data to show progress and match to Individual Education Program goals for students with disabilities.

5. Plan for generalization, including coaching all teachers of the specific skill/strategy in prompting and reinforcing the skill use, and for giving feedback to the program manager or consultant and team.

This same stepwise approach applies to the selection of individualized skills for teaching specific replacement behaviors for students with emotional behavioral disabilities (EBD; Maag, 2006; Quinn, Kavale, Mathur, Rutherford, & Forness, 1999).

Current concerns about safety in the schools have brought the need for training in social skills to the forefront. In response, some programs have been marketed without sufficient research to test their success. The curriculum examples used in this chapter have been selected because they are grounded in social learning principles and have a supportive research base. This short list is intended only to illustrate the variety of curricula available. The curricula mentioned focus on teaching and maintaining specific social skills and building healthy social relationships as part of the classroom and school climate. Most also include training in anger management. (See the resources list at the end of this chapter for more detail.)

Skillstreaming (McGinnis & Goldstein, 1997, 2003; McGinnis, Goldstein, Sprafkin, & Gershaw, 1984). Three versions of this popular and easy-to-use curriculum are available to address needs from preschool through high school. There are 60 separate skills outlined in the Elementary edition, making this curriculum appropriate for schools with a high proportion of students lacking basic social skills (see Table 5.1). The structured learning approach breaks each skill down into simple steps, reducing the amount of training time required for teachers before beginning the curriculum. The program provides materials for self-management, group self-report, and parent communication around homework.

ASSIST: Affective/Social Skills: Instructional Strategies and Techniques (Huggins, 1995; www.sopriswest.com). The ASSIST program was developed and validated in elementary schools in the state of Washington. Some manuals focus a specific set of lessons on social skills such as handling anger, learning friendship and cooperation skills, and avoiding sexual abuse. Others, such as *Creating a Caring Classroom* and *Building Self-Esteem*, offer a broader form of affective education with lessons that can be used in the classroom as needed.

The Tough Kid Social Skills Book (Sheridan, 1995). This program focuses on 10 social skills that are often difficult for students in groups that have a high level of aggressive behaviors. The 10 skills are recognizing and expressing feelings, using self-control, having a conversation, solving arguments, playing cooperatively, dealing with teasing, solving problems, dealing with being left out, joining in, and accepting "no." The manual guides teachers through assessing students' skills, planning for implementation, teaching the lessons, and connecting with families.

Play Time/Social Time: Organizing Your Classroom to Build Interaction Skills (Odom & McConnell, 1997; www.ici.umn.edu/products/curricula.html). In this program, primary skills are taught using scripted lessons (sharing, agreeing, play-organizing behaviors, and helping) with a focus on age-appropriate activities (e.g., playing with cars and trucks, farm animals, pretend birthday party). Following the structured teaching, students practice for approximately 10 minutes in a small group with appropriate peer models. This curriculum provides a model for delivering reinforcement during social skills practice; the teacher marks happy faces on a chart by each student's name for appropriate skills and interactions (six to eight times). At the end of sessions, the teacher provides verbal feedback, praise, and stickers or other rewards for appropriate social skills.

Bully-Proofing Your School (Garrity, Jens, Porter, Sager, & Short-Camilli, 1994). Teaching social skills is not enough in a school where bullying behavior is prevalent (Colvin, Tobin, Beard, Hagan, & Sprague, 1998). Often students are well aware of incidents of bullying long before the adults in the school tune in to it, yet they lack the skills to stop it without adult support. The *Bully-Proofing* series allows the entire student body to participate in the development of a caring climate within the school. Sample lessons include strategies for victims and changing bullying behavior (e.g., through correct social thinking, problem solving, anger management). In addition, the program provides ideas for schoolwide implementation and parent involvement.

Second Step (www.cfchildren.org). This violence-prevention program, developed by the Committee for Children in Seattle, Washington, has proven itself in numerous studies. It expands anger management by using modeling, role-playing, and generalization strategies to reduce aggressive and antisocial behaviors. It builds a core of social competencies, including problem solving, anger management, impulse control, and empathy. Socially responsible decision making becomes the basis for students adopting appropriate social behaviors. Lessons are designed to be taught by teachers, and materials are provided. Recent studies including over 500 students observed in classrooms, lunchrooms, and playgrounds have shown decreases in aggression and verbal hostility with implementation of Second Step (Frey, Hirschstein, & Guzzo, 2000).

Responsive Classroom (www.responsiveclassroom.org). The Northeast Foundation for Children considers this program to be a "social curriculum," or a way for teachers to conduct the daily routines of their classrooms and administrators to manage their schools. Components of the Responsive Classroom program are morning meeting, cooperative learning, role-playing, rules with logical consequences, and guided discovery. The purpose of the program is to create an instructional environment where (a) the way that children and teachers treat each other is as important as facts and skills; (b) feelings, values, friendships, and conflicts are fundamental elements of the curriculum; and (c) children learn the tools to confront new problems and demonstrate a responsible investment in their learning. Elliott (1999) found an increase in social skills, a decrease in problem behaviors, and improved academic competence for students in an urban elementary school using the Responsive Classroom model.

Effective Instruction of Social Skills

In a recent review of reviews of social skills studies, Maag (2006) reported a range of explicit teaching and generalization strategies reported from the literature.

> The following intervention techniques were used in studies reviewed: coaching, modeling, rehearsal, feedback, reinforcement, goal setting, instructions, discussions, peer training, problem solving training, self-instruction, self-monitoring, self-evaluation, and self-reinforcement. . . . SST [social skills training] studies incorporate both behavioral and cognitive techniques. . . . Cognitive-behavioral interventions (CBI) focus on targeting a youngster's private speech self-instruction training, problem-solving training, attribution retraining, and cognitive restructuring approaches (Maag & Swearer, 2005). In addition, virtually all effective CBI techniques with youngsters include behavioral components such as modeling, role playing, and positive reinforcement. (p. 8)

McConnell (2002), in a review of social skills interventions for children with autism, reported the following strategies and formats as effective teaching procedures: pivotal response training, adult prompting, environmental modifications, social skills groups, social stories, video modeling, and peer-mediated instruction.

Effective teaching principles must be used in teaching social skills, just as they would in teaching academic content. Table 5.2 presents a model for teaching social skills using direct instruction procedures. The teaching procedures for a social learning model involve demonstrating and modeling the skill using examples and nonexamples of the social behavior, practice and self-management by students, feedback and reinforcement from the teacher, and a performance plan for use of the skill in school and home settings with peers and adults. A complete social skills curriculum will have detailed or scripted lessons that include these effective instructional components. An example of scripted lessons is provided in the ASSIST program (Huggins, 1995).

A critical component in social skills instruction is *modeling,* which may promote skill usage beyond the lessons. An important objective in a social skills lesson is that students overlearn the steps in the skill. Thus, the models must be provided frequently enough that all students can repeat the steps to the teacher or a peer. Overlearning happens through repetition and review, observing the steps from different models (teachers and peers), and visual reminders such as posters or individual student cue cards. Lessons should be presented a minimum of two times per week for 15–20 minutes each time. Most programs recommend greater frequency, while the length of the lesson depends on the grade level of the students.

Table 5.2   Steps in Teaching Social Skills

1. Define the skill for students.

2. Model the skill.

   Use this sequence: example/nonexample/example.

   Include students in the modeling.

3. Use role-plays; have students rehearse the behavior.

   Practice a few times in front of the whole group and a few by twos, with each student in the class having a peer partner.

4. Review the skill, provide practice opportunities, and give feedback.

   Have students practice in small groups during a natural social activity (academic game, free-time activities).

   Monitor and supervise during the social activity, giving feedback to individuals on their performance.

5. Summarize the group's performance.

   Select partners to demonstrate successful examples of skill use.

6. Plan for generalization: assign homework.

   Include suggestions for using the skill in natural settings.

   Provide visual prompt card with steps in using the skill.

   Provide a process for teacher, peers, and families to report success.

7. Support use of prosocial skills in natural settings, using prompting, incidental teaching, feedback, and reinforcement of skills throughout the school day.

A second objective of a social skills lesson is that students will transfer or generalize their learning, remembering the lesson and performing the skills in natural settings. Typically, the use of adult prompting and feedback in those settings and visual reminders such as posters are recommended to promote generalization to natural settings. Figure 5.1 illustrates these features: a poster for teaching children to "ignore inappropriate behavior of peers," a point chart for acknowledging the use of this and other skills, and an abbreviated script to teach the lesson. A current research study investigating the program teaching this and other prosocial classroom skills in 24 classrooms shows that students with behavior risks who are participating in the intervention increased their on-task behavior and decreased disruptive and antisocial behaviors compared to students at risk in nonintervention classes (see Figure 5.2 on page 81).

Regarding the Skillstreaming curriculum, McGinnis and Goldstein (1997) described several key variables for effective modeling:

- Use at least two examples for each skill demonstration. If a skill is used in more than one group session, develop two new modeling displays.
- Select situations relevant to students' real-life circumstances.
- The model (i.e., the person enacting the behavioral steps of the skill) should be portrayed as a youngster reasonably similar in age, socioeconomic background, verbal ability, and other characteristics salient to the youngsters in the *Skillstreaming* group.

Figure 5.1   Poster, Point Chart, and Teaching Script for "Ignore Inappropriate Behavior"

Poster

Ignore Inappropriate Behavior

1. Keep a pleasant face.
2. Look away from the person.
3. Keep a quiet mouth.
4. Pretend you are not listening.
5. Follow directions—do your work.

Point Chart

Goal: _____   Date: _____

School: _____   Teacher: _____   Class: _____

	Groups					
Points Category	1	2	3	4	5	6
Request Assistance [Be Responsive]						
Follow Directions [Be Respectful]						
Ignore Peer Behavior [Be Responsible]						
Totals						

Script

*We are going to review the skill **Ignoring Inappropriate Behavior** [refer to poster]. We will be practicing this skill along with **How to Get the Teacher's Attention** and **Following Directions**.*

Definition

The steps for Ignoring Inappropriate Behavior are [read aloud]:

1. *Keep a pleasant face.*
2. *Look away from the person.*
3. *Keep a quiet mouth.*
4. *Follow directions—do your work.*

Now everyone read with me [students read chorally]:

Which "School Expectation" does Ignoring Inappropriate Behavior match? (Answer: Be Responsible and Be Kind.) *When you are responsible, you "take care of yourself."*

When you are Kind, you are a friend. (That means helping your classmates do the right thing, not get in trouble.)

(Continued)

Figure 5.1 (Continued)

What other ways can you Be Responsible? (Answer: Finish your work; accept outcomes of your behavior.)

Rationale

Why is it important to follow these steps for Ignoring Inappropriate Behavior? (Answers: We need to show good behavior. We don't want to give people attention for bad behaviors. We want our class to learn more things. We need to show responsibility. It is good to encourage each other to do the right thing. If we shout back or give attention to someone, they will keep doing the wrong thing.)

Role-Play

Let's practice steps for Ignoring Inappropriate Behaviors.

Use volunteers (two or three students). After each example, ask students if the volunteers ignored inappropriate behavior and to state the steps they saw (or the steps they didn't see).

Example*:* Pretend to be explaining a math problem using the board. Have one student start talking to another. Have the second student "look away" and then start working.

Nonexample*:* Pretend to be reading a story. Ask students to write three sentences about the main idea of the story. Have one student call a peer and pass a note to him or her. Have the second peer take the note, then start writing story sentences.

Nonexample: Tell students to copy five vocabulary words from the story (write on board). Tell students that when they are done, they are to go to the shelf and get a book to read. Have volunteers go to the shelf and have one start saying making faces at a peer. Have the second student say, "You're not funny!" in a loud voice, and have the first peer laugh loudly.

Example*:* Tell students to write two sentences about the brain and what it does for our body in their journals. Have a volunteer start waving a paper at another student. Have the second student look away, put a hand above the eyes to block out the distraction, then start writing quietly.

Review

You did great with the role-plays for practice.

Again, let's read together the steps to Ignore Inappropriate Behavior. [Choral read.] Let's work hard to practice this behavior today.

SOURCE: Excerpts from CW-FIT Manual; social scripts developed from Tough Kid Social Skills; Utah State BEST Practices; Skillstreaming Curricula; Mitchem, 2005. *Class-wide Function-Based Intervention Teams: A Research-to-Practice Agenda for Functional Behavior Assessment for Students with and at Risk for SBD* (Institute for Education Sciences Grant, R324A070181, Debra Kamps, Howard Wills, and Charles Greenwood).

- Modeling displays should depict positive outcomes. In addition, the model who is using the skill well should always be reinforced.
- Modeling displays should depict all the behavioral steps of the skill in the correct sequence.
- Modeling displays should depict only one skill at a time, with no extraneous content. (p. 62)

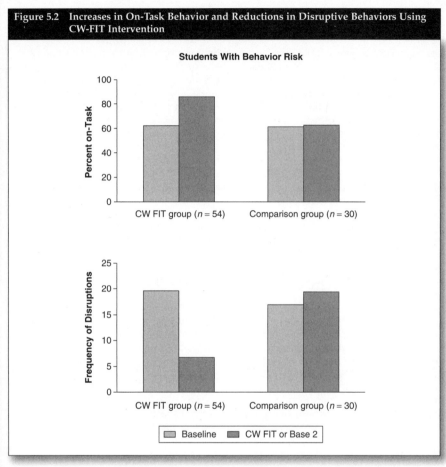

Figure 5.2   Increases in On-Task Behavior and Reductions in Disruptive Behaviors Using CW-FIT Intervention

To enhance modeling, teachers need to use models who are (a) highly skilled or expert in good social skills, (b) high-status peers, (c) friendly and helpful toward the students, and (d) in control of the rewards for appropriate social behaviors. Research clearly shows that good peer models who are valued as high-status peers can greatly influence students towards using appropriate behaviors. Examples include school athletes with appropriate social skills; students who have multiple friends and appropriate social networks; and community mentors, who might be successful high school students and adults.

Social skills programs and curricula are designed to teach a broad set of skills, including classroom survival skills (rules, work habits), interpersonal skills, and conflict resolution behaviors. Several studies have provided evidence showing the effectiveness of direct instruction in social skills for students with antisocial and aggressive behaviors. In an early exemplary study, social skills training for three students with behavior disorders (BD) in a junior high school resulted in an increase in skill use, decreases in negative behaviors, and generalization to integrated settings (Sasso, Melloy, & Kavale, 1990). Training in alternatives to aggression consisted of the following skills: accepting consequences, dealing with accusations, negotiating, responding to teasing, asking permission, and staying out of fights. Skills for dealing with stress consisted of making and answering a complaint, dealing with group pressure, showing sportsmanship, dealing with losing, and accepting "no." The third area consisted of dealing with feelings, including expressing feelings, showing understanding of another's feelings, dealing with anger of self and others, expressing gratitude, and sharing. The findings indicated that structured learning using an earlier version of the Skillstreaming curriculum (McGinnis et al., 1984), including training that utilizes modeling, role-playing, behavioral rehearsal, reinforcement, and self-recording, can be effective in teaching skills that maintain over time and generalize to untreated settings. Training occurred three times per week for 45 minutes per session, and a token system was incorporated to ensure adequate practice and generalization.

Large-scale applications of social skills interventions have also shown positive outcomes. Findings from a larger implementation of the Skillstreaming curriculum (McGinnis et al., 1984) for 70 students with emotional disturbance, for example, indicated that teachers perceived improved social competence for students (Miller, Midgett, & Wicks, 1992). Student perceptions, however, indicated higher perceived skills for the middle school students but not for the elementary-aged participants. No direct observations, however, were conducted to record students' social behaviors. In contrast, a recent report has described large-scale implementation of Second Step, a violence-prevention curriculum, with follow-up observations of students in natural settings (Frey et al., 2000). The curriculum uses modeling, role-playing, and generalization strategies to reduce aggressive and antisocial behaviors and to build a core of social competencies, including empathy, impulse control/problem solving, and anger management. Students from 12 schools and 49 second- and third-grade classrooms participated in a study with matched classrooms randomly selected to serve as experimental and control groups. A total of 588 students were observed in classroom, lunchroom, and playground settings. Decreases in aggression (down 29 percent) and verbal hostility (down 20 percent) for those who received the curriculum were noted, with increases in inappropriate behaviors observed for the control group classes (aggression up 41 percent; verbal hostility up 22 percent) (Frey et al.; Grossman et al., 1997).

Practice and Self-Management

Besides effective modeling and instruction, a key enhancement to social skills instruction is the use of multiple opportunities to respond or providing for sufficient practice of skills. Overactive students, particularly younger students, have a hard time attending to verbal instructions, the typical format for skill presentation and modeling. Thus, less time in formal instruction and more time in skill practice may be a key to effective instruction. The practice time needs to include structured yet novel and stimulating activities. Charlebois, Normandeau, Vitaro, and Berneche (1999), as an example, incorporated four critical components of effective teaching of social skills: formal lessons in problem solving, self-regulation training, hands-on activities to practice skills, and frequent individual contact with participants during small-group practice. Participants included 30 six-year-old males described as inattentive, overactive, and aggressive. The self-regulation training groups required approximately 30 percent listening to skill instruction, 70 percent practice in small peer groups, and self-regulation of skill use during small-group activities. Steps in self-regulation included the following:

1. Define what the problem is or what the objective of the task is.
2. Suggest some possible plans or operations needed to complete the task.
3. Decide what is the best plan or operation.
4. Execute the plan or operation.
5. Evaluate whether or not the plan or operation worked. (p. 141)

The authors of this study (Charlebois et al., 1999) suggested that allowing the students to self-evaluate their use of the steps in problem solving may be more effective than high rates of role-plays. The final critical component is that the teacher reduces instruction during the student practice. This time is child centered and activity based, creating a closer resemblance to children's natural social settings. The teacher's role is performance feedback for social skills, positive interaction, and effective problem solving. The researchers found much less problem behavior (e.g., disobedience, bullying, inattention, being out-of-seat, fidgeting) during this format of instruction. There are two messages here for teachers: (a) social skills lessons must include active student engagement in activities for practicing social skills, and (b) students must be able to evaluate their use of the skills along with the teacher's feedback. Current research and social skills reviews concur with these early findings, suggesting use of natural settings and activities and feedback to promote skill performance in generalized settings (e.g., Bardon et al., 2008; Franzen & Kamps, 2008; Hansen & Lignugaris-Kraft, 2005; Kamps, Tankersley, & Ellis, 2000; Robinson, Smith, & Miller, 2002).

Gresham, Sugai, and Horner and Gresham, Cook, Crews, and Kern (as cited by Bellini, Peters, Benner, & Hope, 2007), in a meta-analysis of social skills, reported that the literature shows variable effects and procedures for these interventions. Their conclusions are relevant to the structure and format for teaching social skills outlined in this chapter:

1. Social skills training should be implemented more frequently and intensely than in current practice.
2. Interventions fail to produce enough reliable maintenance and generalization.
3. Training in restricted, contrived settings restricts generalization to natural settings.
4. Use of social skill instruction that matches the skill and/or performance deficits of the focus child is most effective.
5. Interventions must be implemented with high fidelity.

GENERALIZATION OF SOCIAL SKILLS AND BUILDING PERFORMANCE COMPETENCE

Teachers can increase the impact of their classroom social skills training by encouraging their students to use their new skills in other settings. Many strategies improve transfer of training, or generalization (see Maag, 2006; Scott & Nelson, 1998; Thiemann & Kamps, 2008 for discussions of generalization). Teachers can (a) assess the target child and the natural settings to select socially valid skills (e.g., by observing peers, observing skills that the child does and doesn't perform); (b) include the assessment information in the social skills lessons by matching instructional characteristics to natural social situations, including materials, activities, and environmental supports (Kamps et al., 2002); (c) design a plan to promote generalization, including the use of visual cues and other prompts to perform the skill in natural settings when opportunities occur and the students do not use the skill autonomously; (d) reinforce students verbally when they attempt or actually use the skills in natural contexts; and (e) reward them for meeting a predetermined goal for their use of skills in natural social contexts (recess, lunchroom, free time). Sometimes opportunities must be planned and the environment arranged to create enough practice to promote maintenance and generalization. It is also helpful to observe peers and environments to determine socially valid performance goals and age-appropriate skills (e.g., typical language of classmates, joining strategies, quality and frequency of interactions).

Additional strategies for promoting generalization include the following:

- Reinforcement schedules with individual and group contracts and contingency programs
- Booster sessions to reteach skills periodically
- Peers as reinforcers and prompters during natural settings
- Training across multiple adults as intervention agents across settings
- Preferred activities, choices, and motivational procedures across settings, individuals, and new activities
- Mild consequences for antisocial behaviors coupled with reinforcement for prosocial skills
- Precorrection, or reminders of appropriate social behaviors immediately prior to social activity, followed by active supervision of social time by adults
- Environmental assessment and alteration of consequences in settings to improve social skills performance

The following sections provide examples of programs and strategies to facilitate generalization of social skills and build social competence, including (a) reinforcement systems and curricula with generalization programming, (b) peers and applications in natural settings to facilitate generalization, (c) self-monitoring, (d) group contingencies, and (e) multicomponent interventions.

Reinforcement and Generalization of Social Skills Training

The practice known as *reinforcement* applies to social skills instruction, as well as to all learning. Reinforcement is any consequence of a behavior that increases the behavior's occurrence. Behavioral "entrapment" describes recruiting a natural community of reinforcement. Peers might be reinforcing to the student and reinforce him or her in the natural setting for engaging in the behavior frequently enough that the behavior successfully generalizes. For example, when a student learns to wait in line without hitting, he repeatedly gets his turn in kickball. Kicking the ball and playing the game provides naturally occurring reinforcement, so waiting in line and requesting a turn are now learned behaviors and routinely performed (trapped) (see McConnell, 1987; Maag, 2006).

Adults must provide reinforcement throughout the instruction, generalization, and maintenance phases of social skills training if students are to transfer their skills to natural settings. Verbal praise should be specific to the behavior, delivered as immediately as possible, frequent enough to make a difference, and given with enthusiasm and eye contact. For example, on the way back to the classroom from recess, the teacher might comment to a small group of students, "That was great that your team let Tom join the soccer game!" In addition, tangible and frequent *social rewards* are necessary for reversing antisocial patterns. Examples would be extra recess, free time, time with a peer partner for study, and notes to parents. Peers can dramatically improve generalization of social behaviors if they are taught how to prompt and reinforce social behaviors of children with disabilities or behavioral problems. For younger children, adults must reinforce prosocial behaviors of *all* children and ensure that activities are fun and interactive in nature (i.e., allow for many opportunities to be social).

Research has provided evidence for several decades on the power of differential reinforcement for increasing skills and reducing antisocial or disruptive behaviors (Stage & Quiroz, 1997). Several studies have demonstrated the critical use of contingent reinforcement to enhance the effectiveness of social skills (e.g., Gonzalez-Lopez & Kamps, 1997; Lewis, Sugai, & Colvin, 1998). In an early study, Bierman, Miller, and Stabb (1987) found significant improvements in cooperative play behaviors for students when (a) tokens were rewarded for cooperation and removed for rule violations and (b) social skills instruction was provided. Thirty-two boys in Grades 1 to 3 who were rejected by their peers participated. The authors stated that the primary advantage of combining prohibitions with instructions was additive: boys who received the combined program showed immediate posttreatment decreases in negative initiations, later decreases in negative peer responses, and stable positive interactions. Kamps and colleagues similarly found that social skills instruction alone was not as effective in increasing peer interaction time as social skills plus reinforcement for skill use for Head Start and kindergarten children with antisocial and aggressive behavior (Kamps, Ellis, Mancina, & Greene, 1995; Kamps, Tankersley, et al., 2000).

DuPaul and Eckert in an early review (1994) reported (1) the successful enhancement of social skills teaching by using generalization programming and reinforcement and (2) the benefits of individualizing social skills-training curricula to incorporate features addressing "performance deficits" rather than solely using a skills-training approach. They also reported examples of using reinforcement to enhance social skills performance, including the use of peers as reinforcers and prompters during recess (e.g., Dougherty, Fowler, & Paine, 1985), social skills plus group contingencies and rewards for improved performance (e.g., Walker et al., 1983), and environmental assessment and alteration of consequences in settings to improve social skills performance (e.g., Lewis & Sugai, 1996). Current research continues to report the need for powerful reinforcement systems to promote social skill use and generalization to natural settings (e.g., Cashwell, Skinner, & Smith, 2001; Franzen & Kamps, 2008).

The Play Time/Social Time curriculum provides a model for delivering reinforcement during social skills practice. In one study, this program was used to improve prosocial skills for children at risk for behavior disorders and their peers in Head Start and kindergarten classes. Only with reinforcement were students with antisocial behaviors able to approximate the levels of appropriate interaction demonstrated by peer models. The authors also tested two ways to promote generalization. In the Head Start classes, five or six "target" students wore colored necklace tags during social activities throughout the day; the student group rotated randomly but always included students with antisocial behaviors. Teachers drew happy faces or put small stickers on the tags for appropriate use of the social skills during sessions (four to five times). In the kindergarten classes, teachers made posters that corresponded to the social skills the students had learned. A small bag was attached to the poster for the week. The teacher placed tokens in the bag when individual students were "caught" using appropriate social skills. A minimum of 20 tokens per week were used as a prompt to teachers to reinforce skills in natural settings. These strategies increased the students' use of the skills and teachers' praise for students at other times during the school day outside of the social skills lessons (Kamps, Tankersley, et al., 2000).

The Tough Kid Social Skills Book (Sheridan, 1995) suggests having students set social skills goals, with reinforcement delivered based upon meeting individual goals. The book recommends the following procedures for setting goals for students with antisocial behaviors:

- Help students choose goals that they will probably be successful in meeting (for example, skills that they sometimes exhibit, with small steps as goals for new behaviors).
- Encourage students to make specific goals, including information on what, when, where, with whom, and how the behavior is accomplished (for example, "I will play with a friend at morning recess.").
- Ensure that children choose goals over which they have control (for example, they can access the person and activity without adult assistance such as permission to go to a novel setting, transportation).
- Help students select goals that tell them what to do, rather than what not to do ("I will play soccer at recess" is better than "I will not play alone.").
- Use homework assignments from social skills lessons as a mechanism for working on goals.
- Decide with students how to keep track and evaluate attainment of goals, and deliver reinforcement. (Sheridan, 1995, p. 87–88)

These examples provide a variety of ways to incorporate reinforcement systems in social skills teaching for acquisition and performance across natural settings. *The Tough Kid Book: Practical Classroom Management Strategies* (Rhode, Jenson, & Reavis, 1992) gives examples of interesting ideas to motivate and reward children for appropriate prosocial skills (e.g., chart moves, spinners, mystery motivators, and lottery systems).

Peer-Mediated Strategies for Generalization of Prosocial Skills to Natural Settings

For several decades, researchers have reported that peers, including general education peers, can be influential in the learning and behaviors of children with disabilities, including children with behavioral problems (Delquadri, Greenwood, Whorton, Carta, & Hall, 1986; Dougherty et al., 1985; Strain, Kerr, & Ragland, 1979). A few studies have shown a collateral effect on students' positive social interactions and relationships following peer mediation in the form of academic tutoring (Fuchs, Fuchs, Mathes, & Martinez, 2002; Kamps, Barbetta, Leonard, & Delquadri, 1994). More research is needed to explore some indications that a combined social and academic intervention may be the more effective approach to addressing relationships for rejected children (Dion, Fuchs, & Fuchs, 2005). A primary rationale for including peers is that both peers and teachers are part of the social context of schools and, thus, the inclusion of peers greatly increases the likelihood of generalization. Maag (2006) suggested three conceptual issues as generalization programming tactics for social skills instruction: "selecting socially valid behaviors; focusing intervention on the peer group; and promoting entrapment" (p. 10). Functional assessment data has further indicated that both teacher and peer attention may maintain inappropriate behavior and that function-based interventions that include peers to prompt and reinforce prosocial skills and appropriate task-related behaviors can be efficient and effective (Ervin et al., 2001; Kamps, Wendland, & Culpepper, 2006; Lewis & Sugai, 1996).

Others have specifically demonstrated the value of classwide implementation of social skills training for at-risk students in the group (Bardon et al., 2008). Bardon and colleagues program used Promoting Alternative Thinking Strategies (PATHS; Kusche & Greenberg, 1994) with lessons that provided instruction for increasing skills in self-control, emotional understanding, positive self-esteem, healthy relationships, and inter-personal problem solving. Use of the lessons, incorporation of the concepts and language of the lessons throughout the school day, reinforcement, and incidental teaching resulted in improved cooperative play for three high-risk minority students referred for special education placement.

Research has also shown the benefits of peers as "trainers" for social skills (Blake, Wang, Cartledge, & Gardner, 2000; Kamps et al., 2002; Presley & Hughes, 2000). As an example, Working Together: Building Children's Social Skills Through Folk Literature is a curriculum designed for culturally diverse groups that has been used for combined teacher- and peer-mediated lessons (Cartledge & Kleefeld, 1994). Specific skills include starting a play activity, helping others to participate, following game rules, asking others to play, joining a play activity, and winning and losing. An advantage of this program is that step-by-step procedures, similar to task analysis, are defined for each skill and a script is provided for the instructor. Steps for starting a game, for example, are as follows:

> First, you need to decide on an activity. Second, you need to decide how everyone can take part. Third, you need to make sure everyone knows how to play. Then, you need to practice, if necessary. Finally you need to do the activity together. (Blake et al., 2000, p. 285)

Practice time with peers followed a direct instruction approach similar to teacher-led instruction and included role-playing situations similar to those occurring in their school settings. Teachers in this program also provided opportunities to practice skills in natural settings, and students received tickets when they were "caught being supportive" versus being "abusive" to peers. An interesting finding was that peer-mediated procedures resulted in increased positive statements and decreased negative statements for both the student trainees and for peer trainers who had behavior disorders (BD) in a subsequent intervention study. The authors and others concluded that the use of peers provides an efficient way to improve social skills and adaptive behaviors, increase positive recognition from teachers, and address generalization when peers are able to monitor in the natural school settings (Blake et al.; Prater, Serna, & Nakamura, 1999).

In some peer-training interventions, it is most efficient to recruit peers to address targeted skills. As an example, Presley and Hughes (2000) taught peer buddies to help students with BD to manage anger appropriately. This program illustrates three effective strategies: use of specific strategy steps for handling anger, use of modeling and role-playing examples derived from observations of students' interactions and student input, and combined peer and self-instruction. Senior class students taught freshman and sophomore students enrolled in a high school class for students with BD, the Triple A Strategy: ASSESS, AMEND, and ACT. This 10-step program, adapted from the Walker Social Skills Curriculum (Walker, Todis, Holmes, & Horton, 1988), taught the student to not respond to anger-provoking incidents initially but instead to assess the situation, to self-instruct on how to deal with the situation, and then to act in an acceptable manner. Students practiced using the strategy during role-plays and used a checklist to monitor their use of the 10 steps until they exhibited mastery of the steps over consecutive sessions. This strategy was encouraged for use during the school day. Examples of the role-plays were created from real-life situations in their school setting (e.g., Someone runs by your locker in a hurry and grabs something out of it while you are standing there. Someone takes your notebook out of your desk while you are out of the classroom. A student hits you and dares you to hit back. Your best friend is having a party and does not invite you.). General education peers in the study successfully taught the students with BD to master the Triple A Strategy skills. Two of the four students were observed to improve their appropriate responding during generalization probes, and the students reported that the strategy and role-plays were appropriate for high school settings. Teachers reported that more time in anger management groups/skill practice would have improved generalization. These findings confirm the recommendations for increased "dosage" of social skills instruction to maximize generalization (Bellini et al., 2007; Gresham et al., 2004; Kamps et al., 2002; Maag, 2006; Scott & Nelson, 1998).

Involving peers in social skills groups and for prompting and reinforcing prosocial behaviors in naturally occurring "social activities" at school are two very effective strategies to generalize social skills use (Kamps, Tankersley, et al., 2000; Maag, 2006). Recess and other social activities in school settings are perfect opportunities for building social relationships (Lewis, Powers, Kelk, & Newcomer, 2002). On the other hand, unsupervised recess or transition times, with limited instruction and guidance from teachers, parents, and peers, can have very negative results (Colvin, Sugai, Good, & Lee, 1997).

Colvin and colleagues (1997) investigated the effect of an elementary schoolwide intervention plan using precorrection and active supervision strategies on student behaviors in three transition settings: entering the school building, moving to the cafeteria for lunch, and exiting the school building. Procedures were developed, implemented, and facilitated by a schoolwide discipline team. All staff members identified the problem behaviors (running, pushing, yelling, hitting), identified expected or replacement behaviors (walking, keeping hands and feet to self, and using a quiet voice), and received training in precorrections and active supervision. *Active supervision* was defined as specific and overt behaviors by supervisors designed to prevent problem behavior and to promote rule following. Examples included scanning, escorting, and interacting, including general yet brief chatting, reminders of the rules, praise for rule following, and informing of rule violations with corrections. *Precorrections* were defined as antecedent instructional events designed to prevent the occurrence of predictable problem behavior and to facilitate the occurrence of more appropriate behaviors. Examples included verbal reminders just before a transition, behavioral rehearsals, or demonstrations of rule following or socially appropriate behaviors just before students entered a setting. In this study, precorrections were delivered before students entered the building, by teachers (with reminders from the principal on the intercom during initial intervention) before students went to the cafeteria, and before students left their classrooms at the end of the day.

Results showed notable decreases in problem behaviors during the three transitions and more active supervision as measured by increased teacher-student interactions. Recent intervention studies have replicated the effectiveness of precorrection, active supervision, and group contingencies to decrease recess problems (Franzen & Kamps, 2008; Lewis, Colvin, & Sugai, 2000; Lewis et al., 2002) and to improve behaviors across the cafeteria, playground, and transition settings using a social skills model and group contingencies (Lewis et al., 1998).

Walker and colleagues (Walker, Colvin, & Ramsey, 1995; Walker, Ramsey, & Gresham, 2004) recommended teaching more targeted social skills for children with antisocial, aggressive behaviors: (a) joining, maintaining, or keeping appropriate interaction going; (b) responding to teasing and bullying; (c) anger management; and (c) complying with commands and requests from teachers and peers. The researchers suggested teaching these specific behaviors to decrease antisocial behaviors, the growth of deviant peer groups, and rejection of aggressive students by students who might otherwise provide critical appropriate modeling during social times such as recess. They provided specific steps for skills. For example, appropriate behaviors to teach students to *join existing activities* include the following:

1. Select a game that you know the rules to join.

2. Stay close and wait for a natural break to initiate contact.

3. Help others and make group-oriented, positive statements while waiting.

4. Ask politely, "May I play?"

5. Respond promptly if accepted and take any offer, even if it is a small role (e.g., referee).

6. Get someone to teach you the rules quickly if necessary.

7. If refused, go look for someone who has few friends or play by yourself as an alternative.

Teachers should also confirm that students understand what *not* to do, empowering them to prevent problems. Behavior nonexamples include these: ask frequent questions or interrupt the group, talk about yourself or brag, seek attention, disagree with the group or try to instruct them in the game, be overly persistent (excessive tagging along), barge in to play or make threats to play (e.g., "Let me play, or I'll steal the ball.").

Walker and colleagues (1995, 2004) also reported that teasing is more likely to occur on the playground. Teasing is a behavior that appears to be easily ignored when done among socially appropriate friends. However, children with antisocial attitudes and beliefs often respond to teasing with intense anger, threats, and sometimes tantrums. They may need additional social skills instruction to respond appropriately to teasing on the playground. Adaptive responses to teasing include ignoring, asking the person to stop, leaving the situation, and walking toward an adult, followed by reporting to the adult if it doesn't stop. Maladaptive responses to teasing include teasing back, name-calling, getting angry, crying or acting hurt, hitting or threatening harm, having tantrums, and leaving but retaliating with a friend later.

An additional model program for improving recess behaviors for highly aggressive students is called RECESS (Walker et al., 1995; Walker, Hops, & Greenwood, 1993). The RECESS program consists of four components:

1. Scripted training in cooperative, positive social behavior for the aggressive student and all classmates

2. A response-cost point system with loss of points for inappropriate social behavior and rule infractions

3. Praise and bonus points from the consultant, teacher, and supervisor for appropriate social behavior

4. Concurrent group and individual reinforcement contingencies

The authors reported that the RECESS program is a powerful, intensive intervention for severely aggressive youth in Grades K–3. A consultant spends approximately 40 hours over a two- to three-month period assisting in implementation. Maintenance procedures ensure continued success for the students. While this appears labor intensive, one might consider the consequences of no intervention or the use of ineffective procedures: (a) continued serious aggression with potential student injury, (b) predictable delinquent behaviors by at-risk students, (c) a general trend of increasing playground aggression and an unsafe school environment (Walker et al., 2004).

The myriad research using peers as role models, prompters, and monitors and to provide reinforcement provides ample evidence for peer mediation as a teaching and generalization strategy to improve prosocial and appropriate behaviors and academic performance. In addition, specific programs (Walker et al., 2004) provide rich descriptions of "targeted skills" to match the deficits and performance needs of individual students and procedural characteristics as recommended in reviews of social skills interventions to increase their effectiveness.

Self-Management and Self-Regulation Strategies

Students with aggressive and antisocial behaviors may need to learn frequent self-management in order to facilitate generalization of social skills use to natural settings as well as in the classroom. Kern and colleagues (1995) provided a model program for using self-evaluation for students with emotional and behavioral disorders (EBD). The setting included a typical social activity, playing games with peers. Students initially exhibited high rates of inappropriate peer interaction (100+ per hour) and equal or less rates of appropriate interactions. The teacher made five-minute videotapes during the game activities, then watched them with the students. For each 30-second segment of the tape, students scored a "yes" on their score sheet ("I got along with my classmates.") or a "no." For each no rating, the student announced what the inappropriate behavior was and an acceptable replacement behavior would be. Students received points for each accurate rating and more points for yes agreements with the teacher. Negative peer interactions decreased significantly, and appropriate comments increased dramatically. The self-evaluation was faded to every other day, and eventually rewards alone maintained the appropriate behaviors. Clearly, the use of self-evaluation or self-management of behaviors by students may be a necessary component of social skills instruction for changing high rates of antisocial behaviors.

Prompts in natural settings in combination with self-management systems can be an effective way to promote generalization. As an example, the following steps were implemented as a recess program encompassing social skills instruction for students with EBD (reported in Kamps & Kay, 2002). The program taught students to join groups at recess and maintain their participation through appropriate engagement and behaviors. The components included the following:

- Teach 15-minute social skills lessons immediately prior to recess, including how to join groups, examples of appropriate/inappropriate statements, and appropriate use of hands and feet during recess.

- From a visual menu, students identify an activity they want to do during recess.
- An adult coaches individual students during recess, with prompts at two- to three-minute intervals if students are unengaged with peers and signals (e.g., thumbs-up, smiles) when students are playing appropriately.
- Students evaluate their own behavior immediately following recess by completing a "recess buddies form" with yes/no checks for specific social skills.
- The adult provides performance feedback following recess, offering and soliciting from students specific examples of appropriate and inappropriate behaviors.

The self-management form used for this program is provided in the Figure 5.3. Students increased their appropriate play with peers using the program (see Figure 5.4). In addition, students' negative behaviors and alone time decreased during recess.

Figure 5.3   Self-Management Form for Recess Buddies

Name:_____ Week of _____

		Play Games		Nice Talk		OK Hands and Feet	
		Start	Continue	Start	Continue	Start	Continue
Monday	AM	Yes No	Yes No	Yes No	Yes No	Yes No	Yes No
	PM	Yes No	Yes No	Yes No	Yes No	Yes No	Yes No
Tuesday	AM	Yes No	Yes No	Yes No	Yes No	Yes No	Yes No
	PM	Yes No	Yes No	Yes No	Yes No	Yes No	Yes No
Wednesday	AM	Yes No	Yes No	Yes No	Yes No	Yes No	Yes No
	PM	Yes No	Yes No	Yes No	Yes No	Yes No	Yes No
Thursday	AM	Yes No	Yes No	Yes No	Yes No	Yes No	Yes No
	PM	Yes No	Yes No	Yes No	Yes No	Yes No	Yes No
Friday	AM	Yes No	Yes No	Yes No	Yes No	Yes No	Yes No
	PM	Yes No	Yes No	Yes No	Yes No	Yes No	Yes No

Tag	Basketball	Football	Jump Rope	Baseball Game	Equipment

SOURCE: Images © 2009 Jupiterimages Corporation.

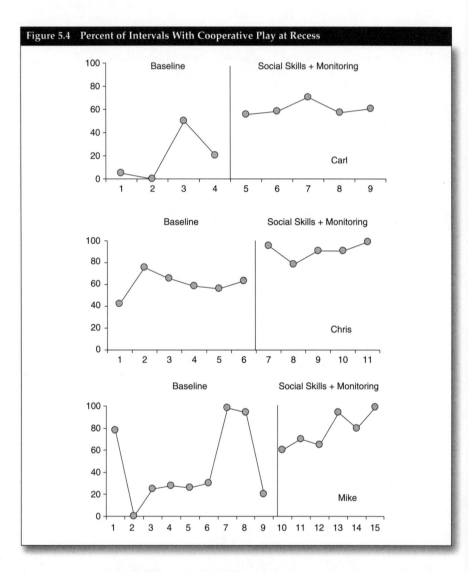

Figure 5.4   Percent of Intervals With Cooperative Play at Recess

Gumpel and David (2000), as a further example, taught three 9- to 10-year-old boys with behavior problems to self-monitor their behaviors during recess. The boys were taught to use an electronic timer to note four-minute intervals and to record on a small, pocket-size memo pad the occurrence or nonoccurrence of three behaviors: "I succeeded in playing without fighting," "I succeeded in playing without hitting," and "I succeeded in finding an activity with friends." Immediately following recess, two boys were given unconditional feedback: "It's good that you are paying attention to your behaviors!" One student who exhibited higher levels of negative behaviors was given performance feedback (i.e., "It's good that you are paying attention to your behaviors! Today you marked that you engaged in the behaviors x times, and that's more than you did yesterday! You're doing a great job!" Positive interaction behaviors increased during intervention to levels similar to those of peers, and the behaviors maintained during follow-up conditions without the self-monitoring program. Gumpel and David suggested that self-evaluation improved social skills usage by acting as a prompt to the student to perform the social skills, thus serving a self-regulatory function.

Self-management was also found to be an efficient enhancement in a study in which two sixth-grade boys tutored two kindergarten boys in social skills (Gumpel & Frank, 1999). All participants were identified by teachers as being isolated and rejected by peers. Tutors were taught, during six to eight 45-minute meetings, to engage in five social competencies: "to identify appropriate social discriminative stimuli, to enumerate possible behavioral options, to enter into that social interaction, to self-monitor, and to observe the environmental reaction" (p. 116). During cross-age peer tutoring, the sixth graders taught their young partners the steps in the model. The tutors would discuss the tutee's social behaviors since their prior meeting (four sessions per week) and review the self-monitoring sheets. Positive behaviors increased, and negative social behaviors decreased for both the tutors and the tutees during recesses, with maintenance of treatment gains following a five-week interval.

Self-instruction through use of script or prompt cards has also been used successfully for students who need help with the acquisition and performance of social skills (Petursdottir, McComas, & McMaster, 2007). Morrison, Kamps, Garcia, and Parker (2001), for example, used scripted lessons, prompt cards, and self-monitoring to improve appropriate conversational skills and decrease negative statements of middle school students with autism and their typical peers. Table 5.3 shows an example of the cue cards and the monitoring form.

These studies and reports from practitioners suggest that self-instruction, self-monitoring, and self-evaluation are important tactics to enhance social skills performance and generalization. See Mooney and colleagues for a review of self-instruction procedures (Mooney, Ryan, Uhing, Reid, & Epstein, 2005).

Group Contingencies to Promote Social Skills

Positive peer interactions and relationships are the ultimate "performance goal" of instruction in social skills. As described earlier, procedures that enable "behavioral entrapment" are most effective. It is not surprising that the use of prosocial skills is thus increased in peer groups that employ a group contingency to promote reciprocal interactions. Hansen and Lignugaris-Kraft (2005) provided a nice example of a dependent group contingency to increase positive verbal interaction and decrease negative verbalizations for middle school students with BD. In the initial intervention condition, social skills were taught to students so that they could distinguish between positive and negative peer statements. The following role play scenarios were used: greeting, encouraging while helping with schoolwork, playing together during an independent activity, sticking up for a student when a peer "puts him down," and talking to people in the lunchroom. Social skills instruction alone did not improve verbal interactions among students.

Table 5.3   Sample Prompt Cards and Self-Monitoring Form

ASKING FRIENDS FOR HELP

To ask your friends for help, you can:	Ask for help with the game.
	Ask for things from the game.
	Ask for help cleaning up.
Examples:	"Adam, how do you play this game?"
	"Mary, will you help me set up Ker-Plunk?"
	"Bill, will you read this to me?" (Looking at magazine)
	"Ned, will you help me clean up?"

COMMENTING ABOUT ACTIVITIES AND THINGS YOU LIKE

To comment, you can:	Say something about things you have done.
	Tell about things you like.
	Give compliments, say things you like about people.
Examples:	"Last night I watched *High School Musical*."
	"George, what is your favorite team?"
	"My favorite food for lunch is tacos."
	"I wonder what's for lunch today."
	"Kelly, those tennis shoes are really cool."
	"Today, let's play kickball at recess."
	"I watched the fifth graders play tag yesterday."

Self-Monitoring Chart: Name: _____   Goal: _____

Asking for Help

☐ ☐ ☐ ☐

Commenting

☐ ☐ ☐ ☐

Complimenting

☐ ☐ ☐ ☐

In the second intervention condition, a dependent group contingency was used during which two students' names were randomly selected and not revealed to the class. For the group to earn the reward, both of the two selected students had to have emitted at least four positive peer statements during a 15-minute independent work time. In addition, the teacher set a goal of four positive statements for all students during the session. Individual points were tallied on a dry erase board and praise given during sessions contingent on positive statements, so students received immediate feedback on their performance. A reinforcer preference checklist was used in advance of the intervention to select rewards that the students would want to earn.

After students earned the rewards for three consecutive days, the group contingency was faded. During fading, if the students met the group contingency goal, a die was rolled, and if numbers 3, 4, 5, or 6 came up, then the reward was received. In the final fading condition, a die roll of 5 or 6 was required (on days when the group contingency was earned) to access the reward. The authors reported increased positive statements and decreased negative statements with use of the group contingency. They also reported that the quality of the positive interactions improved (i.e., expanded and varied types of statements) and that positive statements more often served as initiations to extended conversations. They viewed these findings as evidence of "behavioral entrapment," or natural reinforcers serving to maintain the use of skills. The middle school students also reported that although it was "kind of weird at first," it made them feel good to give and to receive compliments (positive statements).

Another good example for teachers is the use of a group contingency for young children to complement direct instruction of prosocial behaviors and positive peer interactions (Cashwell et al., 2001). These authors have conducted a series of studies demonstrating successful reinforcement and group contingencies. The underlying principle of generalization is that if teachers and peers increase their awareness of prosocial behaviors throughout the classroom day, they will be more likely to attend to the behavior, which is likely to reinforce it and increase its use (Cashwell et al.; Stokes & Baer, 1977). The "tootling" intervention (Skinner, Cashwell, & Skinner, 2000) consists of (a) direct instruction in peer-monitoring of prosocial behaviors, (b) interdependent group contingencies to reinforce peer reporting of these behaviors, and (c) public progress posting to increase students' reports of their classmates incidental prosocial behaviors.

Tootling is constructed from the word *tattling*, but it means teaching peers to report prosocial rather than antisocial behaviors. Teachers also explain that tootling is like "tooting your own horn" but is tooting the horn for your peers. Students are taught to write the name of the classmate who helped, how he or she helped, and whom he or she helped on an index card that is taped to their desks. During training sessions, teachers share examples of appropriate and inappropriate tootles written by students. When adding the group contingencies, teachers set a goal for the number of tootles needed to earn a reward during a set class period (e.g., 150 in four days). A visual chart with a ladder and an icon to move up the ladder to reach the goal is posted. This strategy, "tootling plus group contingency," was successful in increasing prosocial behaviors.

Other examples of group peer monitoring and reporting include "Feed the Hungry Bee," a class contingency to increase peers' positive reporting of social behaviors for a socially rejected child (Ervin, Miller, & Friman, 1996), and use of class meetings modeled after the Teaching Family model of "family meetings" to increase peer reports of prosocial behaviors for a randomly nominated "Most Valuable Person." The intervention decreased the general occurrence of negative interactions for groups of adolescents (Bowers, Woods, Carlyon, & Friman, 2000). The authors and others suggested giving attention to procedures to maintain and expand positive reports and occurrence of prosocial behaviors, such as (a) use of indiscriminable contingencies (goals, criteria are kept secret from the students), (b) adding new target behaviors as initial social behaviors are mastered, (c) randomizing group contingency components (Kelshaw-Levering, Sterling-Turner, Henry, & Skinner, 2000), and (d) expanding reporting to include peers who help with academic assignments (Flood, Wilder, Flood, & Masuda, 2002). These reports suggest that group contingencies including peer reporting are a powerful system of reinforcement to improve prosocial behaviors for groups of students, including target students with BD.

Multicomponent Interventions

In the introduction to the chapter, we presented information regarding antisocial characteristics of children with emotional and behavioral problems and the magnitude of the effects of aggressive behaviors over time and in terms of relationships with significant others, such as peers, teachers, and family members. Many propose that a problem of this significance requires a solution that encompasses multiple dimensions to intervention. Comprehensive programs include (1) schoolwide approaches to teaching prosocial behaviors and (2) involvement of multiple persons, settings, and home-school collaboration to support intervention (Dunlap et al., 2006; Kamps et al., 2006; Sugai et al., 2000). Finally, research suggests that early identification of and intervention for serious behavior problems is directly related to students' responsiveness to intervention and offers the best prognosis for future outcomes (i.e., prevention of more serious problems is dependent on early intervention) (Dawson, 2008; Dunlap et al.; Kauffman, Mock, & Simpson, 2007; Strain & Timm, 2001; Walker & Sprague, 2007).

Schoolwide and Tiered Models

Administrators who want to begin social skills teaching as a schoolwide program in their schools can choose a curriculum from among the many available from commercial publishers (see previous discussion). The most effective approach is to use one curriculum schoolwide. Adults and children will then develop a common language for each skill. A schoolwide approach increases the opportunities for all adults, custodians, food service staff, and other support personnel as well as teachers and administrators, to reinforce appropriate behaviors. A common curriculum can also clarify home and school expectations and provide tools for home-school communications around social skills. Continued use of the curriculum can result in greater consistency between home and school and smoother transitions for students with emotional and/or behavioral issues.

Recent research has shown the benefits of Schoolwide Positive Behavior Support (SWPBS), which include

- development and teaching of school expectations and prosocial skills, as well as the use of effective academic curricula as a universal level of prevention practices;
- systematic feedback for students and consistent consequences;
- availability of resources to support teachers at the systems level; and
- data-based decision making to inform practice and indicate the need for . . .
- targeted secondary and individualized tertiary level intervention.

Figure 5.5 shows an example of schoolwide expectations across settings, including specific skills and behaviors, in an urban elementary school in the Midwest. Creating schoolwide expectations and lessons to teach the skills across settings and using a schoolwide feedback and token reinforcement system (with repetitions for demonstration of skills) dramatically reduced office referrals in the school. Schools using this schoolwide approach to teaching appropriate behaviors with high fidelity have shown improved behaviors in common settings and decreases in office referrals (see Chapter 3 for case studies in elementary schools included in a multistate national study of SWPBS) (Abbott et al., 2008; Algozzine et al., 2008; Tobin, Dickey, Horner, & Sugai, 2008).

Figure 5.5	Schoolwide PBS Expectations for an Urban Elementary School

Don Adams Elementary School

"Give Me Five" Rules

	Be Safe	Be Responsible	Be Peaceful	Be Respectful	Be Kind
Classroom	• Keep hands and feet to self. • Use material appropriately. • Sit in chairs correctly.	• Complete work. • Clean up. • Accept outcomes of your behavior. • Bring your materials to class.	• Quiet/calm voice. • Work quietly. • Make quiet transitions. • Raise your hand to talk.	• Follow directions the first time. • Be a good listener. • Take turns talking.	• Take turns. • Include others. • Use polite words. • Be a friend.
Playground	• Use equipment correctly. • Line up carefully. • Watch for others. • Keep hands and feet to self.	• Follow game rules. • Line up when called. • Take care of yourself. • Be honest. • Accept the outcomes of your behavior.	• Agree on game rules before the game starts. • Return to class quietly in a single-file line.	• Use appropriate language. • Follow all adults' directions. • Include others.	• Help others. • Include others. • Use polite words. • Accept differences of others.
Hallway	• Walk. • Keep hands and feet to self. • Watch where you are going.	• Keep the hall clean. • Take care of yourself. • Be in the correct area. • Have a hall pass.	• Voices off. • Make single-file line.	• Follow instructions. • Respect others' property. • Be timely.	• Help others in need.
Lunchroom	• Walk. • Keep all food on tray. • Chew slowly.	• Clean up. • Eat your own food. • Take care of yourself. • Be honest. • Accept the outcome of your behavior.	• Use quiet voice. • Make single-file line. • Stay at your table. • Be patient.	• Use polite language. • Follow adults' directions. • Use good manners. • Raise your hand to leave table.	• Wait your turn. • Use polite words.
Restroom	• Walk. • Keep hands and feet to self.	• Flush the toilet. • Be timely. • Wash/dry hands.	• Use quiet voice.	• Use polite words. • Respect school property.	• Take turns.

Home-School Collaboration

Individual students who show signs of emotional or behavioral problems can make large gains in their social skills when parents, peers, and teachers are involved as key players (McConaughy, Kay, & Fitzgerald, 2000; Walker et al., 2004). This is especially true when beginning early, at the preschool and kindergarten level (Dunlap et al., 2006; Kamps, Tankersley, et al., 2000; Tankersley, Kamps, Mancina, & Weidinger, 1996).

First Step to Success: Helping Young Children Overcome Antisocial Behavior is an exemplary model of school and home intervention for teaching social skills and appropriate behaviors (Walker, Kavanagh, et al., 1998). Three modules encompass the program: (a) screening of all kindergartners to determine the students most at risk; (b) a consultant-based school intervention involving the target child, peers, and teachers; and (c) parent training in caregiver skills to promote positive school adjustment and appropriate behaviors.

In the CLASS program, first the consultant and then the teacher and peers monitor the student's behavior and give him or her feedback. The HomeBase component consists of six lessons provided by the consultant during home visits. Parents learn how to teach their children the following skills: (a) communication and sharing in school, (b) cooperation, (c) limits setting, (d) problem solving, (e) friendship making, and (f) development of confidence.

Data-based studies have shown important gains in appropriate behaviors for participants. Findings following implementation of First Step to Success in kindergarten indicated increases in adaptive ratings by teachers and decreases in maladaptive ratings on the Early Screening Project scale (Walker et al., 1997), and decreases in aggression and withdrawn behaviors on teacher ratings for the Child Behavior Checklist (Achenbach, 1991). In addition, children's on-task behaviors in the classroom improved. Findings were consistently positive for two cohorts of children. Improvements continued into first and second grade for the participants for all behaviors except for withdrawn behaviors as rated by parents.

These same effects were noted in terms of pre- and posttreatment differences for a group of consultants and students in a subsequent study (Golly, Stiller, & Walker, 1998). Improved on-task behavior and decreased disruptive behaviors were noted in another study with three second and third graders with EBD risks in an urban school setting (Lien-Thorne & Kamps, 2005).These authors found that the use of an additional reinforcement system was necessary to generalize outcomes across the school day for one of the participants with more challenging behavior. Clearly, the collaboration of parents and teachers in delivering First Step to Success to address prosocial behaviors across multiple applications demonstrated increased benefits to participants. Additional replications, including use of a function-based component (Carter & Horner, 2007) and a large-scale experimental control group study, are underway using the First Step Program (Walker, Golly, McLane, & Kimmich, 2005).

The Check and Connect student engagement and dropout prevention program implemented at the University of Minneapolis is yet another example of a model that encompasses ongoing "connections" with students and families to improve social and academic outcomes (Sinclair, Christenson, Evelo, & Hurley, 1998). This program emphasizes the use of intervention within the natural setting with the following components: (a) use of a "monitor," who averaged 20 hours per week to serve 25 students by assessing absenteeism, suspensions, grades, and other indicators of school engagement via a daily monitoring form completed by school personnel (*check*); (b) providing basic intervention to all students, including regular feedback to the student, discussions of the importance of staying in school, and problem solving (*connect-basic*); and (c) providing or recruiting intensive intervention when the monitoring data indicated increased risk (*connect-intensive*). Similar to the parent liaisons in other comprehensive programs with a social skills or problem-solving component (Walker, Severson, & Feil, 1997), monitors in the Check and Connect program provide continuity across multiple natural settings and persistence in the level of support to students. The Check and Connect authors contended that these factors allowed participants (students, parents, and teachers) to establish relationships and to develop a sense of mutual trust and respect, variables contributing to better student performance. In a three-year study, 94 urban students with learning and emotional/behavioral disabilities received the Check and Connect intervention in Grades 7 and 8; half of the students (treatment group) continued to receive intervention through their first year in high school, Grade 9. These students were significantly more likely to be engaged in school than students in the control group. Specifically, students in treatment (a) were significantly more likely to be enrolled in school at the end of the year, (b) were significantly more persistent in their school attendance, (c) completed significantly more assignments, and (d) received, on average, significantly more credits during the first year of high school than control group students. Teachers also rated them as more academically competent, and general education teachers rated them as having significantly fewer behavioral problems (Sinclair et al., 1998). Recent studies continue to support the effectiveness of home-school collaboration using the Check and Connect program (Anderson, Christenson, Sinclair, & Lehr, 2004; Lehr, Sinclair, & Christenson, 2004).

These evidence-based programs provide examples of teaching social skills and problem solving as one element within *comprehensive programs* that involve relevant persons (teachers, parents, peers) as *intervention partners* in *natural settings*. Research suggests these characteristics are critical components of social skills interventions to improve student outcomes (Bellini et al., 2007; Gresham et al., 2004; Maag, 2006; Walker et al., 1997).

WHY SOCIAL SKILLS PROGRAMS SOMETIMES FAIL

Teaching social skills as an intervention can be very powerful. Program failures, however, may occur. When they do, they typically are related to poor instruction, limited reinforcement, lack of generalization planning, and negative modeling. Instructional issues include poor teaching of social skills (lecturing versus active student practice), too few sessions in social skills or limited dose of intervention, not targeting critical skills to the needs of the individual or group, and limited teaching and lack of focus on performance of the skills in natural setting (Gresham et al., 2004). Reinforcement issues include not establishing student goals and a reinforcement plan for improved social performance in natural settings or not reinforcing at a high enough level to motivate students to change. Use of visual and contextual supports and a planned schedule of feedback and reinforcement in the natural setting may be needed initially for generalization. Many researchers have recommended multiple layers of intervention with a focus on "across-the-day" intervention schedules (Goldstein, Kaczmarek, & Hepting, 1994). For example, 10 minutes of peer-mediated practice in natural settings six to eight times per week in natural settings may be more effective at promoting generalization than two 45-minute groups in a pullout session (Bellini et al., 2007; Gresham et al., 2004).

In addition, negative modeling by adults and peers may diminish the effects of social skills intervention and reinforce antisocial behaviors. Further, schools focusing on punishment procedures to address antisocial behaviors may be counterproductive to improving social competence. Grouping students with antisocial behaviors together (as sometimes occurs for social skills groups) may also be counterproductive, actually increasing problem behaviors through negative peer modeling. Dishion, McCord, & Poulin (1999) reported three experimental studies of adolescents with antisocial behavior. Guided group counseling, including social skills training, was delivered to small groups. Results actually showed an increase in problem behavior (initiation of substance use, self-reported delinquency and violent behavior) for the intervention groups when compared to control groups. The authors suggested that high-risk peers support or reinforce one another's deviant behavior; thus, group intervention with exclusively deviant peers should be avoided. The authors described this phenomenon as *deviancy training*. Antisocial peers react positively to deviant talk in the groups, a powerful reinforcement for deviancy. Nondelinquent students ignore deviant talk in favor of typical discussions. The message for conducting group social skills intervention is clear. Students with antisocial behaviors should be separated as much as possible. Small groups for practice should be at a minimum ratio of three or four good peer models for every student who has antisocial behaviors.

Administrators who institute social skills training in their schools have a special responsibility to monitor the behavior of the adults in the school toward each other and toward the students. The most powerful modeling takes place when students observe the casual social interactions that take place in their school on an everyday basis. Students will benefit from a school setting where adults model appropriate social skills and respect, where other students understand and reinforce appropriate behaviors, and where all adults use the same language in their reminders and feedback.

A final caution: It is important to note that social skills instruction is only one component of an effective behavior support plan for students identified as having EBD. Kamps and colleagues (Kamps, Kravits, Stolze, & Swaggart, 1999; Kamps, Kravits, Rauch, Kamps, & Chung, 2000), for example, found that the most effective prevention program included social skills; classroom management, including group contingencies; and academic tutoring. Outcomes of increased engagement, prosocial behaviors, and reduced disruptive behaviors demonstrated the benefits of multicomponent intervention. Thus, implementation of social skills as a single prevention strategy is limited in its effectiveness without other supportive programs (Gresham et al., 2004). Gresham stated "SST [social skills training] should not be considered as the single intervention for students with EBD, but rather as an integral part of a comprehensive intervention program for this population" (p. 44). Table 5.4 presents a summary of multiple program components for increasing effectiveness of social skills instruction to improve social competence and decrease antisocial behaviors.

Table 5.4 Components of Comprehensive Programs Designed to Improve Social Competence	
Component	**Description and Examples**
Supportive social environment	Visual schedule of session agenda, timer, marked play areas, clear expectations/rules (posted), peers available
Regular social skills teaching and practice opportunities	Social skills groups/lessons occur a minimum 3-4 times/week for 10-20 minutes each session
Naturalistic settings utilized for prompting and generalization of social skills	Modified academic work or games in small groups, centers, recess, lunch, social down time, scheduled social activities after or before school, community outings or field trips
Preferred, age-appropriate activities used for teaching prosocial skills	Recess activities, popular games, incorporate interests and familiar themes; activities should be motivating and fun for peers
Peer mediation and training incorporated into social skills lessons	Class-wide option or small group of 2-5 peers (high-status and same-age); teach 3-5 facilitative skills; teach peers to monitor skill use; use monitoring sheets, evaluation books, progress charts; adults provide prompts and feedback
Visual representations and picture cues; Written text cues and social scripts if needed	Picture books, conversation topic cards, photographs of children on cards, placemats with funny and preferred pictures; written cues or prompt cards, sample scripts
Reinforcement systems in place in social groups/natural settings; group contingencies	Use tokens, points, rewards with goal setting; use group contingencies; High levels of reinforcement and feedback initially; fade adult involvement as soon as possible
Self-monitoring and reinforcement; peer monitoring and reinforcement	Adult teaches student, peers or older children to monitor skill use with feedback sheets, markers, stickers, progress charts, graphs; peers taught to reinforce and help students self-monitor
Videotape self- or peer-modeling	Adults review and discuss taped interactions of student engaged in inappropriate behaviors or not using targeted language skills; may also review tapes of peers engaging in social interactions
Precorrection and active adult supervision	Adult reinforces positive interactions in structured and unstructured social settings; collect/evaluate self-monitoring sheets; listen to peer feedback on how groups are going
Booster sessions	Review social skills and communication targets (e.g., once every two weeks for 30-min); increase prompts
Plan for generalization	Use all strategies above to promote generalization in natural settings; adults monitor and guide; train multiple peers; provide opportunities for across-the-day interactions; coordinate home and community social events

SOURCE: Modified from Thiemann, K., & Kamps, D. (2007). Promoting Social Communication Competence of Children with Autism in Integrated Environments. R. Simpson and B. Smith Myles (eds.), p. 267-298. *Educating Children and Youth with Autism.*

GAINING COMMUNITY SUPPORT FOR SOCIAL SKILLS TRAINING

Schools play a pivotal role in society in either preventing or promoting antisocial behaviors (Mayer, 1995). Schools have opportunities to intervene around motivational variables, such as low student involvement, poor attendance at and poor participation in class, lack of homework completion, and limited involvement in afterschool activities. Schools can address variables related to individual differences with effective instructional practices, active student engagement, academic remediation, and behavioral/social support for students with problems. Schools can fail at systems support variables, including through weak or inconsistent administrative support for staff in carrying out student discipline and follow-through, staff disagreement with discipline policies, and a heavy reliance on punitive procedures. SWPBS, as previously described, includes a systems level approach: (a) practices to support positive student outcomes; (b) systems to support those practices, such as resources for implementation and teacher support; and (c) data to evaluate program fidelity and outcomes (Sugai et al., 2000).

Schools aspiring to a positive environment supporting academic and social achievement can find themselves at odds with a punishment-oriented society. Zero-tolerance policies can tie administrators' hands, limiting their ability to use mild misbehavior as a learning opportunity. Community and state systems may seem to value the results of standardized tests over breadth, depth, and self-direction in student learning. However, teaching socially valid skills in the classrooms will be supported if the community has been a part of the decision-making process in setting expectations, choosing the academic and social curricula, and arriving at agreed-upon performance goals for all students. Even when an area has great cultural diversity in its population, families can understand and appreciate the behavioral expectations of the school's culture, as long as they are explained with respect for the family's culture. The effort required to choose a good social skills program with schoolwide implementation and individualization for targeted groups should eventually pay off in student achievement. As one teacher stated, "How can you teach anything else until you teach social skills?"

Dunlap et al. (2006), in their comprehensive summary of empirical evidence related to prevention and intervention for challenging behavior, including antisocial behavior, suggested a focus on programmatic and public policy initiative to impact large numbers of children.

> Most intervention research has focused on variables affecting individual children, with little research on program procedures, systems components, and public policies that support the use of evidence-based practices with this population. . . . There is no doubt that policies and procedures at a program level can have a tremendous influence on the development and occurrence of challenging behavior (Fox et al., 2003; Knitzer, 2002; Smith & Fox, 2003; Stormont, Lewis, & Smith, 2005). (Dunlap et al., p. 39)

Descriptions of the need for social skills within the context of comprehensive programs supported by schoolwide approaches and inclusive of home, school, and community collaboration illustrate the need to focus on programmatic and public policy initiatives.

IMPORTANCE OF IMPROVING AND GENERALIZING SOCIAL SKILLS

This chapter defined *social skills* and *social competence*; provided examples of research-based curricula and effective instructional procedures; and described strategies to reinforce, maintain, and generalize prosocial behaviors beyond social skills groups. Research over the past two decades was also presented to (1) provide evidence for strategies and (2) share exemplary implementation procedures for practitioners. The procedures described incorporated findings from several recent reviews that have summarized the critical features of effective social skills programs (Bellini et al., 2007; Gresham et al., 2001, 2004; Maag, 2006). Recommendations from these reviews follow.

1. *Dosage is important.* Evaluations find that many social skills interventions are far too infrequent and too brief (Gresham et al., 2001). Bellini and colleagues (2007) stated, "School personnel should look for opportunities to teach and reinforce social skills as frequently as possible throughout the school day" (p. 160). Gresham suggested a minimum of 30 hours of intervention to effect change in social competence.

2. *Outcomes are better and show increased generalization if interventions are implemented in natural settings* "Teachers and other school personnel should place a premium on selecting social skills interventions that can be reasonably implemented in multiple naturalistic settings" (Bellini et al., 2007, p. 160).

3. *Skills for instruction should match the deficits and performance needs of the focus child or group* (Gresham et al., 2001; Maag, 2006; Scott & Nelson, 1998). Charlebois and colleagues suggested that both dosage plus characteristics at the start of intervention impact outcomes, emphasizing the importance of individualized, targeted intervention to improve social competence (Charlebois, Brendgen, Vitaro, Normandeau, & Boudreau, 2004).

4. *Intervention fidelity is important.* To be effective in terms of outcomes (acquisition and generalization to natural settings), social skills interventions must be implemented using explicit teaching models, in natural settings, with generalization programming, and with sufficient reinforcement to maintain skill use. Plans that assess children and environment well, determine behavioral function, and produce natural communities of reinforcement (entrapment) are most effective and efficient (McConnell, 1987).

Strategies from the social skills research literature mirror research findings regarding efforts to decrease disruptive and aggressive behaviors in school settings, reporting strong effects for group contingencies, self-management, and differential reinforcement; they also offer suggestions for more targeted and evidence-based interventions for students with serious conduct and behavior disorders (Eyberg, Nelson, & Boggs, 2008; Forness, 2005; Pelham & Fabiano, 2008; Smith, Lochman, & Daunic, 2005; Stage & Quiroz, 1997). The manner of implementation (i.e., fidelity, dosage, rates, length), as well as the specific intervention, may be highly influential on the intervention effectiveness. Functional assessment and inclusion of related contextual variables in intervention planning; schoolwide adoption of successful strategies; technical support from building teams and/or expert consultants; parental involvement, including home interventions; and administrative and financial support (e.g., extra staff for intensive instruction or short-term behavioral implementation) were additional variables reported as necessary for more challenging students. In summary, promising student outcomes, as reported in this chapter and the literature summarized herein, indicate that prosocial behaviors can be improved within school settings. Further, early intervention for high-risk students and an emphasis on prevention efforts can dramatically reduce later, more serious problems (e.g., delinquency, school failure and dropout) and subsequent higher treatment costs.

REFERENCES

Abbott, M., Wills, H., Kamps, D., Greenwood, C., Dawson-Bannister, H., Kaufman, J., et al. (2008). The Kansas Reading and Behavior Center's K–3 prevention model. In C. Greenwood, T. Kratowill, & M. Clements (Eds.), *Schoolwide prevention models: Lessons learned in elementary schools* (pp. 215–265). New York: Guilford Press.

Achenbach, T. M. (1991). *Manual for the Child Behavior Checklist/4–18 and 1991 profile*. Burlington: Department of Psychiatry, University of Vermont.

Alberg, J., Petry, C., & Eller, S. (1994). *The social skills planning guide*. Longmont, CO: Sopris West.

Algozzine, B., Cooke, N., White, R., Helf, S., Algozzine, K., & McClanahan, T. (2008). The North Carolina reading and behavior center's K-e prevention model: Eastside Elementary School case study. In C. Greenwood, T. Kratowill, & M. Clements (Eds.), *Schoolwide prevention models: Lessons learned in elementary schools* (pp. 173–214). New York: Guilford Press.

Anderson, A., Christenson, S., Sinclair, M., & Lehr, C. (2004). Check & connect: The importance of relationships for promoting engagement with school. *Journal of School Psychology, 42,* 95–113.

Bardon, L., Dona, D. P., & Symons, F. (2008). Extending classwide social skills interventions to at-risk minority students: A preliminary application of randomization tests combined with single-subject design methodology. *Behavioral Disorders, 33,* 141–152.

Battalio, R., & Stephens, J. T. (2005). Social skills training: Teacher practices and perceptions. *Beyond Behavior, 14*(2), 15–20.

Bellini, S., Peters, J., Benner, L., & Hope, A. (2007). A meta-analysis of school-based social skills interventions for children with autism spectrum disorders. *Remedial and Special Education, 28,* 153–162.

Bierman, K. L., Miller, C. L., & Stabb, S. D. (1987). Improving the social behavior and peer acceptance of rejected boys: Effects of social skill training with instructions and prohibitions. *Journal of Consulting and Clinical Psychology, 55,* 194–200.

Blake, C., Wang, W., Cartledge, G., & Gardner, R. (2000). Middle school students with serious emotional disturbances serve as social skills trainers and reinforcers for peers with SED. *Behavioral Disorders, 25*(4), 280–298.

Bowers, F. E., Woods, D. W., Carlyon, W. D., & Friman, P. C. (2000). Using positive peer reporting to improve the social interactions and acceptance of socially isolated adolescents in residential care: A systematic replication. *Journal of Applied Behavior Analysis, 33*(2), 239–242.

Carter, D. R., & Horner, R. (2007). Adding functional behavioral assessment to first step to success: a case study. *Journal of Positive Behavior Interventions, 9*(4), 229–238.

Cartledge, G., & Kleefeld, J. (1994). *Working together: Building children's social skills through folk literature*. Circle Pines, MN: American Guidance Service.

Cartledge, G., & Milburn, J. F. (1996). *Cultural diversity and social skills* instruction. Champaign, IL: Research Press.

Cashwell, T. H., Skinner, C. H., & Smith, E. S. (2001). Increasing second-grade students' reports of peers' prosocial behaviors via direct instruction, group reinforcement, and progress feedback: A replication and extension. *Education and Treatment of Children, 24*(2), 161–175.

Charlebois, P., Brendgen, M., Vitaro, F., Normandeau, S., & Boudreau, J-F. (2004). Examining dosage effects on prevention outcomes: Results from a multi-modal longitudinal preventive intervention for young disruptive boys. *Journal of School Psychology, 42*(3), 201–220.

Charlebois, P., Normandeau, S., Vitaro, F., & Berneche, F. (1999). Skills training for inattentive, overactive, aggressive boys: Differential effects of content and delivery method. *Behavioral Disorders, 24*(2), 137–150.

Colvin, G., Sugai, G., Good, R., & Lee, Y-Y. (1997). Using precorrection and active supervision to improve transition behaviors in an elementary school. *School Psychology Quarterly, 12*(4), 344–363.

Colvin, G., Tobin, T., Beard, K., Hagan, S., & Sprague, J. (1998). The school bully: Assessing the problem, developing interventions, and future research directions. *Journal of Behavioral Education, 8*(3), 293–319.

Dawson, G. (2008). Early behavioral intervention, brain plasticity, and the prevention of autism spectrum disorder. *Development and Psychopathology, 20,* 775–803.

Delquadri, J., Greenwood, C. R., Whorton, D., Carta, J., & Hall, R. V. (1986). Classwide peer tutoring. *Exceptional Children, 52,* 535–542.

Dewey, J. (1916). *Democracy and education: An introduction to the philosophy of education.* New York: Macmillan.

Dion, E., Fuchs, D., & Fuchs, L. S., (2005). Differential effects of peer-assisted learning strategies on students' social preference and friendship making. *Behavioral Disorders, 30*(4), 421–430.

Dishion, T. J., McCord, J., & Poulin, F. (1999). When interventions harm: Peer groups and problem behavior. *American Psychologist, 54*(9), 755–764.

Doll, B., & Lyon, M. A. (1998). Risk and resilience: Implications for the delivery of educational and mental health services in schools. *School Psychology Review, 27*(3), 348–363.

Dougherty, B. S., Fowler, S. A., & Paine, S. (1985). The use of peer monitors to reduce negative interactions during recess. *Journal of Applied Behavior Analysis, 18,* 141–153.

Dunlap, G., Strain, P. S., Fox, L., Carta J. J., Conroy, M., Smith, B. J., et al. (2006). Prevention and intervention with young children's challenging behavior: Perspectives regarding current knowledge. *Behavioral Disorders, 32*(1), 29–45.

DuPaul, G., & Eckert, T. (1994). The effects of social skills curricula: Now you see them, now you don't. *School Psychology Quarterly, 9,* 113–132.

Elliott, S. N. (1999). *Caring to learn: A report on the positive impact of a social curriculum.* Greenfield, MA: Northeast Foundation for Children. (Retrieved October 28, 2009, from http://responsiveclassroom .org/pdf_files/caring_to_learn.pdf)

Ervin, R. A., Miller, P. M., & Friman, P. C. (1996). Feed the hungry bee: Using positive peer reports to improve the social interactions and acceptance of a socially rejected girl in residential care. *Journal of Applied Behavior Analysis, 29,* 251–253.

Ervin, R. A., Radford, P., Bertsch, K., Piper, A., Ehrhardt, K., & Poling A. (2001). A descriptive analysis and critique of the empirical literature on school-based functional assessment. *School Psychology Review, 30,* 193–210.

Eyberg, S. M., Nelson, M., & Boggs, S. R. (2008). Evidence-based psychosocial treatments for children and adolescents with disruptive behavior. *Journal of Clinical Child & Adolescent Psychology, 37*(1), 215–237.

Farmer, T., Van Acker, R., Pearl, R., & Rodkin, P. (1999). Social networks and peer-assessed problem behavior in elementary classrooms: Students with and without disabilities. *Remedial and Special Education, 20,* 244–256.

Flood, W. A., Wilder, D. A., Flood, A. L., & Masuda, A. (2002). Peer-mediated reinforcement plus prompting as treatment for off-task behavior in children with attention deficit hyperactivity disorder. *Journal of Applied Behavior Analysis, 35,* 199–204.

Forness, S. R. (2005). The pursuit of evidence-based practice in special education for children with emotional or behavioral disorders. *Behavioral Disorder, 30*(4), 311–330.

Fox, L., Dunlap, G., Hemmeter, M. L., Joseph, G. E., & Strain, P. S. (2003). The teaching pyramid: A model for supporting social competence and preventing challenging behavior in young children. *Young Children, 58*(4), 48–52.

Franzen, K., & Kamps, D. (2008). The utilization and effects of positive behavior support strategies on an urban school playground. *Journal of Positive Behavior Interventions, 10,* 150–161.

Frey, K., Hirshstein, M., & Guzzo, B. (2000). Second step: Preventing aggression by promoting social competence. *Journal of Emotional and Behavioral Disorders, 8,* 102–112.

Fuchs, D., Fuchs, L., Mathes, P., & Martinez, E. (2002). Preliminary evidence on the social standing of students with learning disabilities in PALS and No-PALS classrooms. *Learning Disabilities Research and Practice, 17,* 205–215.

Garrity, C., Jens, K., Porter, W., Sager, N., & Short-Camilli, C. (1994). *Bully-proofing your school: A comprehensive approach for elementary schools.* Longmont, CO: Sopris West.

Goldstein, H., Kaczmarek, L., & Hepting, N. (1994). Communication interventions: The challenges of across-the-day implementation. In R. Gardner III & D. M. Sainato (Eds.), *Behavior analysis in education: Focus on measurably superior instruction* (pp. 101–113). Pacific Grove, CA: Brooks/Cole.

Golly, A. M., Stiller, B., & Walker, H. M. (1998). First step to success: Replication and social validation of an early intervention program. *Journal of Emotional and Behavioral Disorders, 6,* 243–250.

Gonzalez-Lopez, A., & Kamps, D. (1997). Social skills training to increase social interaction between children with autism and their peers. *Focus on Autism and Other Developmental Disabilities, 12,* 2–14.

Gresham, F. M. (1995). Best practices in social skills training. In A. Thomas & J. Grimes (Eds.), *Best practices in school psychology III* (pp. 1021–1030). Washington, DC: National Association of School Psychologists.

Grossman, D., Neckerman, H., Koepsell, T., Liu, P., Asher, K., Beland, K., et al. (1997). Effectiveness of a violence prevention curriculum among children in elementary school: A randomized controlled trial. *Journal of the American Medical Association, 277,* 1605–1611.

Gumpel, T. P., & David, S. (2000). Exploring the efficacy of self-regulatory training as a possible alternative to social skills training. *Behavioral Disorders, 25*(2), 131–141.

Gumpel, T. P., & Frank, R. (1999). An expansion of the peer-tutoring paradigm: Cross-age peer tutoring of social skills among socially rejected boys. *Journal of Applied Behavior Analysis, 32*(1), 115–118.

Hansen, S. D., & Lignugaris-Kraft, B. (2005). Effects of a dependent group contingency on the verbal interactions of middle school students with emotional disturbance. *Behavioral Disorders, 30*(2), 170–184.

Huggins, P. (1995). *Helping kids handle anger: Teaching self-control.* Longmont, CO: Sopris West.

Kamps, D., Barbetta, P., Leonard, B., & Delquadri, J. (1994). Classwide peer tutoring: An integration strategy to improve reading skills and promote peer interactions among students with autism and general education peers. *Journal of Applied Behavior Analysis, 27,* 49–61.

Kamps, D., Ellis, C., Mancina, C., & Greene, L. (1995). Peer-inclusive social skills groups for young children with behavioral risks. *Preventing School Failure, 39,* 10–15.

Kamps, D., & Kay, P. (2002). Preventing problems through social skills instruction. In R. Algozzine & P. Kay (Eds.), *Preventing problem behaviors: A handbook of successful prevention strategies* (pp. 57–84). Thousand Oaks, CA: Corwin.

Kamps, D., Kravits, T., Rauch, J., Kamps, J. L., & Chung, N. (2000). A prevention program for students with or at risk of ED: Moderating effects of variation in treatment and classroom structure. *Journal of Emotional and Behavioral Disorders, 8*(3), 141–154.

Kamps, D., Kravits, T., Stolze, J., & Swaggart, B. (1999). Prevention strategies for students at risk and identified as serious emotionally disturbed in urban, elementary school settings. *Journal of Emotional and Behavioral Disorders, 7,* 178–188.

Kamps, D., Royer, J., Dugan, E., Kravits, T., Gonzalez-Lopez, A., Garcia, J., et al. (2002). Peer training to facilitate social interaction for students with autism. *Exceptional Children, 68,* 173–187.

Kamps, D., Tankersley, M., & Ellis, C. (2000). Social skills intervention for young at-risk students: A 2-year follow-up study. *Behavioral Disorders, 25,* 310–324.

Kamps, D., Wendland, M., & Culpepper, M. (2006). Functional assessment as a tool for designing interventions for students with behavioral risks in general education classrooms. *Behavioral Disorders, 31*(2), 128–143.

Kauffman, J., Mock, D., & Simpson, R. (2007). Problems related to underservice of students with emotional or behavioral disorders. *Behavioral Disorders, 33,* 43–57.

Kelshaw-Levering, K., Sterling-Turner, H. E., Henry, J. R., & Skinner, C. H. (2000). Randomized interdependent group contingencies: Group reinforcement with a twist. *Psychology in the Schools, 37,* 523–533.

Kern, L., Wacker, D. P., Mace, F. C., Falk, G. D., Dunlap, G., & Kromrey, J. D. (1995). Improving the peer interactions of students with emotional and behavioral disorders through self-evaluation procedures: A component analysis and group application. *Journal of Applied Behavior Analysis, 28*(1), 47–59.

Knitzer, J. (2002). Promoting social and emotional readiness for school: Toward a policy agenda. In *Set for success: Building a strong foundation for school readiness based on the social-emotional development of young children* (pp. 100–122). Kansas City, MO: Ewing Marion Kaufman Foundation. (ERIC Document Reproduction Service No. ED468551)

Kusche, C. A., & Greenberg, M. T. (1994). *The PATHS curriculum.* Seattle, WA: Developmental Research and Programs.

Lehr, C., Sinclair, M., & Christenson, S. (2004). Addressing student engagement and truancy prevention during the elementary school years: A replication study of the Check & Connect Model. *Journal of Education for Students Placed at Risk, 9,* 279–301.

Lewis, T. J., Colvin, G., & Sugai, G. (2000). The effects of pre-correction and active supervision on the recess behavior of elementary students. *Education and Treatment of Children, 23*(2), 109–121.

Lewis, T., Powers, L., Kelk, M., & Newcomer, L. (2002). Reducing problem behaviors on the play ground: An investigation of the applications of School-wide Positive Behavior Supports. *Psychology in the Schools, 39,* 181–190.

Lewis, T. J., & Sugai, G. (1996a). Descriptive and experimental analysis of teacher and peer attention and the use of assessment-based intervention to improve pro-social behavior. *Journal of Behavior Education, 6,* 7–24.

Lewis, T. J., & Sugai, G. (1996b). Functional assessment of problem behavior: A pilot investigation of the comparative and interactive effects of teacher and peer social attention on students in general education settings. *School Psychology Quarterly, 11,* 1–19.

Lewis, T. J., Sugai, G., & Colvin, G. (1998). Reducing problem behavior through a school-wide system of effective behavioral support: Investigation of a school-wide social skills training program and contextual interventions. *School Psychology Review, 26*(3), 446–459.

Lien-Thorne, S., & Kamps, D. (2005). Replication study of the First Step to Success early intervention program. *Behavioral Disorders, 31*(1), 19–33.

Maag, J. W. (2006). Social skills training for students with emotional and behavioral disorders: A review of reviews. *Behavioral Disorders, 32*(1), 5–17.

Masten, A. S., & Coatsworth, J. D. (1998). The development of competence in favorable and unfavorable environments: Lessons from research on successful children. *American Psychologist, 53*(2), 205–220.

Mayer, G. R. (1995). Preventing antisocial behavior in the schools. *Journal of Applied Behavior Analysis, 28*(4), 467–478.

McConaughy, S. H., Kay, P. J., & Fitzgerald, M. (2000). How long is long enough? Outcomes for a school-based prevention project, *Exceptional Children, 67,* 1–14.

McConnell, S. (1987). Entrapment effects and the generalization and maintenance of social skills training for elementary school students with behavioral disorders. *Behavioral Disorders, 12,* 252–263.

McConnell, S. (2002). Interventions to facilitate social interaction for young children with autism: Review of available research and recommendations for educational intervention and future research. *Journal of Autism and Developmental Disorders, 32,* 351–372.

McGinnis, E., & Goldstein, A. P. (1997). *Skillstreaming the elementary school child: New strategies and perspectives for teaching prosocial skills.* Champaign, IL: Research Press.

McGinnis, E., & Goldstein, A. P. (2003). *Skillstreaming in early childhood: New strategies and perspectives for teaching prosocial skills.* Champaign, IL: Research Press.

McGinnis, E., Goldstein, A. P., Sprafkin, R. P., & Gershaw, J. (1984). *Skillstreaming the elementary school child: A guide for teaching prosocial skills.* Champaign, IL: Research Press.

Miller, M. G., Midgett, J., & Wicks, M. L. (1992). Student and teacher perceptions related to behavior change after skillstreaming training. *Behavioral Disorders, 17,* 291–295.

Mitchem, K. J. (2005). BE PROACTIVE: "Including students with challenging behavior in your classroom." *Intervention in School and Clinic, 40*(3), 188–191.

Mooney, P., Ryan, J., Uhing, B., Reid, R., & Epstein, M. (2005). A review of self-management interventions targeting academic outcomes for students with emotional and behavioral disorders. *Journal of Behavioral Education, 14,* 203–221.

Morrison, L., Kamps, D., Garcia, J., & Parker, D. (2001). Peer mediation and monitoring strategies to improve initiations and social skills for students with autism. *Journal of Positive Behavior Interventions, 3,* 237–250.

Odom, S. L., & McConnell, S. R. (1997). *Play time/social time: Organizing your classroom to build interaction skills.* Minneapolis, MN: Institute on Community Integration, University of Minnesota. (ERIC Document Reproduction Service No. ED412705)

O'Neill, R., Horner, R., Albin, R., Sprague, J., Storey, K., & Newton, J. (1997). *Functional assessment and program development for problem behavior: A practical handbook.* Pacific Grove, CA: Brooks/Cole.

Parker, J., & Asher, S. (1987). Peer acceptance and later personal adjustment: Are low-accepted children "at risk?" *Psychological Bulletin, 102,* 357–389.

Patterson, G., Reid, J., & Dision, T. (1992). *Antisocial boys.* Eugene, OR: Castalia.

Pelham, W. E., Jr., & Fabiano, G. A. (2008). Evidence-based psychosocial treatments for attention-deficit/hyperactivity disorder. *Journal of Clinical Child & Adolescent Psychology, 37*(1), 184–214.

Petursdottir, A., McComas, J., & McMaster, K. (2007). The effects of scripted peer tutoring and programming common stimuli on social interactions of a student with autism spectrum disorder. *Journal Applied Behavior Analysis, 40*(2), 353–357.

Prater, M. A., Serna, L., & Nakamura, K. K. (1999). Impact of peer teaching on the acquisition of social skills by adolescents with learning disabilities. *Education and Treatment of Children, 22*(1), 19–35.

Presley, J. A., & Hughes, C. (2000). Peers as teachers of anger management to high school students with behavioral disorders. *Behavioral Disorders, 25*(2), 114–130.

Quinn, M. M., Kavale, K. A., Mathur, S. R., Rutherford, R. B., Jr., & Forness, S. R. (1999). A meta-analysis of social skill interventions for students with emotional or behavioral disorders. *Journal of Emotional and Behavioral Disorders, 7,* 54–64.

Rhode, G., Jenson, W. R., & Reavis, H. K. (1992). *The tough kid book: Practical classroom management strategies.* Longmont, CO: Sopris West.

Robinson, R. T., Smith, S. W., & Miller, D. M. (2002). Effect of a cognitive-behavioral intervention on responses to anger by middle school students with chronic behavior problems. *Behavioral Disorders, 27*(3), 256–271.

Sasso, G. M., Melloy, K. J., & Kavale, K. A. (1990). Generalization, maintenance, and behavioral covariation associated with social skills training through structured learning. *Behavioral Disorders, 16,* 9–22.

Scott, T. M., & Nelson, C. M. (1998). Confusion and failure in facilitating generalized social responding in the school setting: Sometimes 2 + 2 = 5. *Behavioral Disorders, 23,* 264–275.

Sheridan, S. M. (1995). *The tough kid social skills book.* Longmont, CO: Sopris West.

Sinclair, M., Christenson, S., Evelo, D., & Hurley, C. (1998). Dropout prevention for youth with disabilities: Efficacy of a sustained school engagement procedure. *Exceptional Children, 65,* 7–21.

Skinner, C. H., Cashwell, T. H., & Skinner, A. L. (2000). Increasing tootling: The effects of a peer-monitored group contingency program on students' reports of peers' prosocial behaviors. *Psychology in the Schools, 37,* 263–270.

Smith, B., & Fox, L. (2003). *Systems of service delivery: A synthesis of evidence relevant to young children at risk of or who have challenging behavior.* Tampa, FL: Center for Evidence-Based Practice: Young Children with Challenging Behavior. Retrieved October 28, 2009, from http://www.challengingbehavior.org/explore/publications_docs/systems_of_service.pdf

Smith, S.W., Lochman, J. E., & Daunic, A. P. (2005). Managing aggression using cognitive-behavioral interventions: State of the practice and future directions, *Behavioral Disorders, 30,* 227–240.

Stage, S., & Quiroz, D. (1997). A meta-analysis of interventions to decrease disruptive classroom behavior in public education settings. *School Psychology Review, 26,* 333–368.

Stokes, T. F., & Baer, D. M. (1977). An implicit technology of generalization. *Journal of Applied Behavioral Analysis, 10,* 349–367.

Stormont, M., Lewis, T., & Smith, S. (2005). Behavior support strategies in early childhood settings: Teachers' importance and feasibility ratings. *Journal of Positive Behavior Interventions, 7,* 131–139.

Strain, P. S., Kerr, M. M., & Ragland, E. U. (1979). Effects on peer-mediated social initiations and prompting/reinforcement procedures on the social behavior of autistic children. *Journal of Autism and Developmental Disorders, 9*(1), 41–53.

Strain, P., & Timm, M. (2001). Remediation and prevention of aggression: A 25-year follow-up of RIP graduates. *Behavioral Disorders, 26,* 297–313.

Sugai, G., Horner, R., Dunlap, G., Hieneman, M., Lewis, T., Nelson, C., et al. (2000). Applying positive behavior support and functional behavioral assessment in schools. *Journal of Positive Behavior Interventions, 2,* 131–143.

Tankersley, M., Kamps, D., Mancina, C., & Weidinger, D. (1996). Social interventions for head start children with behavioral risks: Implementation and outcomes. *Journal of Emotional and Behavioral Disorders, 4*(3), 171–181.

Thiemann, K., & Kamps, D. (2008). Promoting social communication competence of children with autism in integrated environments. In R. Simpson & B. Myles (Eds.), *Educating children and youth with autism* (2nd ed., pp. 267–298). Austin, TX: Pro-Ed.

Tobin, T., Dickey, C. R., Horner, R., & Sugai, G. (2008). Comprehensive implementation of the three-tiered prevention approach to schoolwide behavioral support: An Oregon case study. In C. Greenwood, T. Kratowill, & M. Clements (Eds.), *Schoolwide prevention models: Lessons learned in elementary schools* (pp. 87–114). New York: Guilford Press.

Walker, H. M., Colvin, G., & Ramsey, E. (1995). *Antisocial behavior in school: Strategies and best practices.* Pacific Grove, CA: Brooks/Cole.

Walker, H. M., Golly, A., McLane, J. Z., & Kimmich, M. (2005). The Oregon First Step to Success replication initiative: Statewide results of an evaluation of the program's impact. *Journal of Emotional and Behavioral Disorders, 13,* 163–172.

Walker, H. M., Hops, H., & Greenwood, C. (1993). *RECESS: A program for reducing negative-aggressive behavior.* Seattle, WA: Educational Achievement Systems.

Walker, H. M., Kavanagh, K., Stiller, B., Golly, A., Stevenson, H. H., & Feel, E. G. (1998). First Step to Success: An early intervention approach for preventing school antisocial behavior. *Journal of Emotional and Behavioral Disorders, 6*(2), 66–80.

Walker, H. M., McConnell, S., Holmes, D., Todus, B., Walker, J., & Golden, N. (1983). *The Walker Social Skills Curriculum: The ACCEPTS program.* Austin, TX: PRO-ED.

Walker, H., Ramsey, E., & Gresham, F. (2004). *Antisocial behavior in school: Evidence-based practices* (2nd ed.). Belmont, CA: Thomson Wadsworth.

Walker, H. M., & Severson, H. H., & Feil, E. G. (1997). *Early Screening Project (ESP).* Longmont, CO: Sopris West.

Walker, H., & Sprague, J. (2007). Early, evidence-based intervention with school-based behavior disorders: Key issues, continuing challenges, and promising practices. In J. Crockett, M., Gerber, & T. Landrum (Eds.), *Achieving the radical reform of special education: Essays in honor of James M. Kauffman* (pp. 37–58). Mahwah, NJ: Lawrence Erlbaum Associates.

Walker, H. M., Stiller, B., Golly, A., Kavanagh, K., & Feil, E. G. (1998). *First Step to Success: Helping young children overcome antisocial behavior.* Longmont, CO: Sopris West.

Walker, H. M., Todis, B., Holmes, D., & Horton, G. (1988). *The Walker Social Skills Curriculum.* Austin, TX: Pro-Ed.

Warren, J., Edmonson, H., Griggs, P., Lassen, S., McCart, A., Turnbull, A., et al. (2003). Urban applications of Positive School-wide Behavior Support. *Journal of Positive Behavior Interventions, 5,* 80–91.

RESOURCES: SOCIAL SKILLS, CLASSROOM MANAGEMENT, AND PEER TUTORING

Prosocial Skills

- The ASSIST Program: Affective/Social Skills; Instruction Strategies and Techniques (Huggins, P.; Sopris West, Longmont, CO).

  Helping Kids Handle Anger

  Teaching Friendship Skills
- *Bully-Proofing Your School: A Comprehensive Approach for Elementary Schools* (Garrity, C., Jens, K., Sager, N., & Short-Camilli, C., 1994; Sopris West, Longmont, CO).
- *Getting Along With Others. Teaching Social Effectiveness to Children* (Jackson, N., Jackson, D., & Monroe, C., 1983; Research Press, Champaign, IL).
- *Play Time/Social Time: Organizing Your Classroom to Build Interaction Skills* (Odom, S., & McConnell, S., 1997; http://www.ici.umn.edu/products/curricula.html, Institute on Community Integration, University of Minnesota, Minneapolis, MN).
- *The SCORE Skills: Social Skills for Cooperative Groups* (Vernon, S., Schumaker, J., & Deshler, D., 1993; Edge Enterprises, Lawrence, KS).
- *Skill-streaming the Elementary School Child: A Guide for Teaching Prosocial Skill* (McGinnis, E., Goldstein, A., Sprafkin, R., Gershaw, N. J., & Klein, P., 1997; Research Press, Champaign, IL).
- *Tools for Citizenship & Life: Using the ITI Lifelong Guidelines and LIFESKILLS in Your Classroom* (Pearson, S., 2000: Susan Kovalik & Associates, Kent, WA).
- *The Tough Kid Social Skills Curriculum* (Sheridan, S., 1995; Sopris West, Longmont, CO).
- *Violence Prevention: Second Step* (Committee for Children, Seattle, WA).
- *The Walker Social Skills Curriculum. The ACCEPTS Program—A Curriculum for Children's Effective Peer and Teacher Skills* (Walker, H., McConnell, S., Holmes, D., Todis, B., Walker, J., & Golden, N., 1988; Pro-Ed, Austin, TX).

Behavior Management

- *Antisocial Behavior in School: Strategies and Best Practices* (Walker, H., Colvin, G., & Ramsey, E., 1995; Brooks/Cole, Pacific Grove, CA).
- *Applied Behavior Analysis for Teachers* (Alberto, P., & Troutman, A.C., 2008; Merrill, Upper Saddle River, NJ).
- *Building Positive Behavior Support and Functional Behavior Assessment in Schools* (Crone, D., & Horner, R., 2003; New York, Guilford Press).
- *CHAMPs: A Proactive and Positive Approach to Classroom Management* (Sprick, R., Garrison, M., & Howard, L., 1998; Sopris West, Longmont, CA).
- *Decreasing Classroom Behavior Problems: Practical Guidelines for Teachers* (Burke, J., 1992; Singular, San Diego, CA).
- *First Step to Success: Helping Young Children Overcome Antisocial Behavior* (Walker, H., Golly, A., Kavanagh, K., Stiller, B., Severson, H. H., & Feil, E. G., 1999; Sopris West, Longmont, CO).
- How to Improve Classroom Behavior Series (Axelrod, S., & Mathews, S. (Eds.), 2002; Pro-Ed., Austin, TX).

  How to Deal Effectively With Lying, Stealing, and Cheating

  How to Help Students Remain Seated

How to Help Students Play and Work Together
How to Help Students Complete Classwork and Homework Assignments
How to Prevent and Safely Manage Physical Aggression & Property Destruction
How to Deal With Students Who Challenge and Defy Authority
How to Help Students Follow Directions, Pay Attention, and Stay On-Task

- Preventing Problem Behavior: A Handbook of Successful Prevention Strategies (Algozzine, R., & Kay, P., 2002; Thousand Oaks, CA, Corwin).
- Responding to Problem Behavior in Schools—The Behavior Education Program (Crone, D., Horner, R., & Hawken, L., 2004; New York, Guildford Press).
- The Teacher's Encyclopedia of Behavior Management: 100 Problems/500 Plans (Sprick, R., & Howard, L., 1995; Sopris West, Longmont, CO).
- Teaching Self-Management Strategies to Adolescents (Young, K. R., West, R., Smith, D., & Morgan, D., 1997; Sopris West, Longmont, CO).
- The Tough Kid Book: Practical Classroom Management Strategies (Rhode, G., Jenson, W., & Reavis, B., 1998: Sopris West, Longmont, CO).

Peer Tutoring

- *Classwide Student Tutoring Teams: Teacher's Manual* (Maheady, L., Harper, G., Sacca, K., & Mallette, B., 1991; University of New York, College at Fredonia).
- *Together We Can! ClassWide Peer Tutoring to Improve Basic Academic Skills* (Greenwood, C., Delquadri, J., & Carta, J., 1997; Sopris West, Longmont, CO).

Parents

- *The Good Kid Book: How to Solve the 16 Most Common Behavior Problems* (Sloane, H., 1979; Research Press, Champaign, IL).
- *Little People: Guidelines for Common Sense Child Rearing* (4th ed.) (Christopherson, E., 1998; Overland Park Press, Shawnee Mission, KS).
- *SOS: Help for Parents; A Practical Guide for Solving Behavior Problems* (3rd ed.) (Clark, L., 2005; SOS Programs, Bowling Green, KY).
- *The Tough Kid Parent Book: Practical Solutions to Tough Childhood Problems* (Jenson, W., Rhode, G., & Hepworth, M., 2003; Sopris West, Longmont, CO).

6

Conflict Resolution, Peer Mediation, and Bullying Prevention

In this chapter, we

- review the rationale for conflict resolution, peer mediation, and bullying prevention;
- describe effective conflict resolution, peer mediation, and bullying prevention programs and practices;
- describe critical features that support implementation and maintenance of conflict resolution, peer mediation, and bullying prevention programs; and
- review evidence of effectiveness of conflict resolution, peer mediation, and bullying prevention programs.

Professionals who work with school-aged children and adolescents have been concerned for decades about antisocial behavior problems such as harassment, discrimination, and destructively aggressive behavior (Rose & Gallup, 2000; Smokowski & Kopasz, 2005; Tulley & Chiu, 1995). These issues are not new, but the topic of school safety has become more pressing as high-profile violent events have occurred in schools across the country in recent years (U.S. Surgeon General, 2001). For example, in a recent survey for the World Health Organization, as many as 20 percent of students reported being bullied, and 20 percent identified themselves as bullies (Heydenberk, Heydenberk, & Tzenova, 2006). These statistics imply serious consequences for all students and school professionals who experience a decreased sense of safety in their school environment, such as heightened levels of emotion (e.g., fear, anxiety, anger) and a decreased ability to engage higher-order thinking processes.

Nothing is more critical to student success across all grade levels than for school professionals to ensure a safe and orderly school environment and a climate conducive to learning. Attempts to engender high academic achievement and social-emotional competence enable children and adolescents to interact with others effectively in an ever-changing and increasingly complex world. In light of No Child Left Behind Act of 2001, school administrators and teachers are often pressed to focus on academic progress and improve test scores, yet this emphasis is often at the expense of equally important social and emotional learning. Students who do not have the skills to handle increasing levels of independence and accompanying social challenges as they matriculate through school may not be successful socially *or* academically.

To address these academic and behavioral issues, school administrators, particularly at the middle and high school levels, continue to seek out programs and procedures that help prevent serious incidents of violence and work to reduce overall student harassment, discrimination, bullying, and aggression. Since adult-directed practices, such as detention or suspension, tend to be punitive and do little to teach positive conflict management (Kauffman, 2005; Polsgrove & Smith, 2004), researchers and school-based professionals over the past few decades have invested in more proactive, preventive approaches that combine student-centered, skill-building interventions with substantive changes in the ecological context of the schools and classrooms in which student behaviors occur (Andrews, 1995).

An approach to prevention that combines schoolwide efforts to improve the learning environment with student-centered strategies designed to build constructive behavioral repertoires can be grouped under the general heading of conflict resolution education (CRE). CRE can include teaching students about conflict resolution, helping them develop and use peer mediation skills, and addressing bullying at both the schoolwide and individual student levels. These strategies are evidence-based efforts to promote all aspects of successful adjustment (Fonagy, Twemlow, Vernberg, Sacco, & Little, 2005; Garrard & Lipsey, 2007; Zins, Bloodworth, Weissberg, & Walberg, 2004). These programs focus on teaching students constructive conflict management and on creating environments that empower students, foster independence, and provide opportunities to practice developing skills. Moreover, because chronic student behavior problems demand considerable time and attention from teachers and administrative staff, CRE in the broadest sense can contribute to academic achievement for practical reasons, as well as conceptual ones.

CRE has been defined as programs designed to facilitate the constructive resolution of interpersonal conflicts (Garrard & Lipsey, 2007). It can include interventions that target violence prevention, character education, social skills training, and antibullying. These efforts proliferated during the 1960s and continue to provide educators with an alternative to reactive, adult-centered approaches. Like the Positive Behavior Supports (PBS) model (Lewis & Sugai, 1999), CRE programs and other forms of violence prevention interventions can be viewed as occurring at multiple levels of school functioning. The broadest is the schoolwide level, at which social systems are defined and understood so that efforts to teach and reward correct behavior can be coordinated among all school-based personnel. CRE programs can be situated at this broadest level as a proactive approach to conflict management and bullying prevention. A common language can develop among all constituents at the school, and students are more likely to be immersed in a culture that views conflict constructively, has no tolerance for unacceptable, antisocial behavior, and promotes a warm and caring atmosphere in which to learn.

CRE programs can also operate at the classroom level, where teachers promote behavior management on a daily basis and have the opportunity to reinforce schoolwide norms and teach specific skills. Conflict resolution principles, including an introduction to peer mediation, can be taught within the classroom, and teachers can lead discussions about specific topics, such as bullying. Students who do not respond sufficiently to schoolwide and classwide efforts may need more intensive services; they may benefit from instruction delivered through small-group settings or individualized counseling sessions for bullies and bully victims.

Regardless of level of implementation, the primary goal for CRE programs is to facilitate the constructive resolution of interpersonal conflicts, which can consist of ego-threatening provocations or disputes over possessions or relationships (Garrard & Lipsey, 2007). Secondary or longer-term program goals can include increasing prosocial behaviors and the prevention of aggression and violence across the school environment through the development of specific conflict resolution and social problem-solving skills (Daunic, Smith, Brank, & Penfield, 2006; Heydenberk et al., 2006). Antibullying programs, in particular, may be imbedded in more general CRE, but their goal is to create a schoolwide zero-tolerance policy with regard to bullying and a safe, consistent, and nurturing school atmosphere (Smokowski & Kopasz, 2005).

In this chapter, we will (a) describe CRE programs (i.e., conflict resolution, peer mediation, antibullying) and their rationale within a developmental framework, (b) review effective program characteristics, (c) describe recommendations for successful implementation and program maintenance, and (d) review some of the current evidence concerning the efficacy of particular interventions.

SOME PROGRAM DEFINITIONS

Conflict resolution is typically a school-based program that includes instruction to help students view the conflict they will inevitably encounter as a constructive, rather than destructive, process. Thus, training in conflict resolution is designed to be preventive. Ideally, conflict resolution concepts should be taught to all students in a school in classwide or small-group settings, Conflict resolution concepts can be infused into other academic content, such as social studies or health education, and/or be more specialized for selected groups of students who may serve as peer mediators or who might benefit from more intensive training (see Smith, Daunic, Miller, & Robinson, 2002).

Peer mediation is typically used as an intervention, often in conjunction with a conflict resolution curriculum. Specially trained students who serve as peer mediators follow formal procedures to help peers who are having a dispute negotiate a positive, mutually acceptable resolution. While conflict resolution curricula are designed to teach students general concepts about constructive approaches to conflict in daily life, peer mediation is a more structured and focused opportunity for mediators to practice skills they have learned in formal training. Peer mediation may be taught to selected cadres of students, or it can be implemented as a universal approach in which each student has an opportunity to act as a mediator.

Bullying prevention programs can be viewed as falling under the umbrella of CRE, but they typically have features that distinguish them from programs that involve peer mediation. Since bullying by definition involves an imbalance of power (Garbarino & de Lara, 2003; Smokowski & Kopasz, 2005), conflicts that involve a bully and a victim might not be well suited to mediation by peers, and students are generally encouraged to report incidents of bullying to a trusted teacher, school counselor, or school psychologist.

Bullying prevention programs can focus on direct intervention with either the bully or the victim, and they can concurrently address bullying systemically, focusing on antisocial behaviors at multiple levels within the school, as previously described. They are compatible with the overall goal of CRE: to provide school-based prevention in the service of safe and consistently nurturing educational environments.

A DEVELOPMENTAL FRAMEWORK

The primary developmental tasks of early and middle adolescence have been described as (a) achieving emotional independence from parents and other adults, (b) desiring and achieving socially responsible behavior, and (c) acquiring a set of values and an ethical system to guide behavior in the future (Havighurst, 1972). Students who develop positive coping strategies for the environmental demands they encounter during this critical transition have an improved chance of growing into emotionally healthy adults. Such development requires that they learn new ways of conceptualizing and dealing with situations when their prior responses are no longer effective. Developmental psychologists call this process of creating new cognitive structures *accommodation* (Berger, 1994). Accommodation occurs most readily under conditions that provide optimal levels of both *challenge* and *support* (Ivey, 1991). Sufficient challenge is required to create a need to develop new ways of solving problems; sufficient support is needed to create a climate in which the individual feels safe enough to risk trying new coping strategies. Successful development thus occurs when a challenge is balanced with available support.

A significant source of challenge, particularly for adolescents, is conflict with peers. These conflicts are troublesome and can significantly affect a school, the families involved, and even an entire community (Heydenberk et al., 2006). Teaching CRE principles can make important contributions to an adolescent's social adjustment and self-esteem, especially when coupled with opportunities to practice learned skills through peer mediation and antibullying strategies. Indeed, results of a meta-analysis of the effects of CRE on antisocial behavior in schools suggest that adolescence may represent a window of opportunity wherein increased need for resolving social conflict aligns with developmental readiness to benefit from conflict resolution and bullying prevention programs (Garrard & Lipsey, 2007).

It is helpful to view the role of CRE in the prevention of chronic and destructive behavior problems through this developmental frame of reference. Although younger children can learn conflict resolution and antibullying strategies, we think CRE becomes particularly relevant during the middle school years, when children are naturally becoming increasingly independent of adults and more heavily influenced by peers. For appropriate types of conflict, peer mediation can offer a support system for the social challenges students experience, and along with other forms of CRE, it can contribute to a nurturing school environment. Although antibullying programs are typically implemented at the elementary as well as middle school level, they, too, may be especially critical for preadolescents, who are increasingly vulnerable to their peers' opinions.

CHARACTERISTICS OF EFFECTIVE CRE PROGRAMS

Conflict Resolution: Providing a Schoolwide Context

Conflict resolution programs typically include a curriculum designed to provide basic knowledge to students about individual differences, changing win-lose situations to win-win solutions, and using negotiation to resolve conflicts effectively (Carlsson-Paige & Levin, 1992; Daunic, Smith, Robinson, Miller, & Landry, 2000). A conflict resolution curriculum can focus on social skills, such as empathy training, effective communication, and stress and anger management; attitudes about conflict; bias awareness; and/or negotiation and large-group problem solving. Teachers or other school professionals help students learn a process for handling interpersonal conflict by focusing on skill development within a general conceptual framework rather than on how to solve an immediate, specific problem.

Students typically tend to view conflict situations as occasions in which there are winners and losers (Carlsson-Paige & Levin, 1992). Introducing them to scenarios where all parties can win offers a framework within which to view conflict as a learning opportunity to solve mutual problems and strengthen social relations. Johnson and Johnson (1996) argued that conflict, if managed constructively without violence, may actually be desirable. CRE is thus a recommended strategy for addressing positively and proactively the conflict that is inevitable in schools. Conflict resolution curricula can introduce students to the productive aspects of conflict instead of focusing on eliminating or preventing it. Programs may be especially effective when teachers use cooperative learning strategies to foster integrative, rather than competitive, approaches to learning (Stevahn, Johnson, Johnson, & Real, 1996).

Effective conflict resolution programs are student rather than adult centered. Adults are not always available to help students negotiate solutions to their day-to-day conflicts, and programs that depend solely on adult decision making fail to teach students appropriate social skills to use in the absence of adult supervision (Smith & Daunic, 2004). The task in teaching effective conflict resolution is to help all students realize that their *approach* to conflict, rather than the existence of conflict itself, determines their successful social development. Through a variety of learning experiences, such as discussion, role-plays, and simulations, and through a focus on student empowerment, conflict resolution curricula can (a) facilitate the understanding of conflict and its determinants; (b) teach students effective communication, problem solving, and negotiation; and (c) provide a foundation for education about peace and nonviolence.

Example: Working Together to Resolve Conflict

Through a funded research project, we developed and evaluated a middle school conflict resolution program, Working Together to Resolve Conflict (WTRC, www.coe.ufl .edu/CRPM/CRPMhome.html). Lessons were designed to help students learn that dealing with conflict could be a productive exercise. WRTC thus fostered a problem-solving approach to conflict and encouraged students to seek mutually agreeable solutions. We designed twelve 40- to 50-minute lessons within four topic areas: understanding conflict, effective communication, understanding anger, and handling anger. An additional lesson provided an introduction to the process of peer mediation.

Lessons included student activities and role-plays for practicing newly learned skills. For example, students learned about the "Relax-Breathe-Think" model to practice thinking through difficult situations, rather than reacting impulsively, in a lesson on handling anger. Teachers who implemented the lesson presented students with several scenarios and instructed them in each case to answer the question, "Who's the boss, me or the problem?"

Administrative personnel in each of the schools in our study determined how the CR lessons would be integrated into their overall school programming. In one case, a newly instituted course in critical thinking for students at all three grade levels provided an appropriate vehicle. In another school, a homeroom period at the beginning of the day was long enough to allow teachers to deliver the curriculum schoolwide. Since all students in the school were taught the lessons, a consistent language around conflict and its peaceful resolution could emerge within the school culture.

Peer Mediation: A Preventive Alternative to Adult Intervention

Not only should adults teach students about conflict, they must also provide students with opportunities to practice in real-life conflict situations. Students are constantly exposed to violence and aggression in the media, often presented as a win-lose situation, and they may see similar scenarios in their homes and communities. To counter the effects of such negative models, students need opportunities to observe appropriate, positive negotiations and to practice conflict resolution skills in supportive environments. Peer mediation, an explicit intervention in which students help their peers solve conflicts, offers such an opportunity. When mediators and disputants can resolve disputes with minimal adult supervision, school professionals are relieved of paying time-consuming attention to frequently occurring conflicts, and students are empowered to take responsibility for negotiating these challenging situations successfully.

Schoolwide peer mediators are typically a group of students who receive formal, intensive training in mediation (e.g., Smith et al., 2002). There are several models of mediation, but all tend to follow the same general process: mediators (a) provide a supportive environment, (b) help disputants focus on mutually identified problems, (c) help disputants develop a list of possible solutions through brainstorming, and (d) guide disputants to mutually agreed-upon resolutions. The negotiation skills required for mediators and disputants include self-control, effective communication, problem solving, critical thinking, and appropriate planning.

For students trained as mediators and those who attend mediation as disputants, the opportunity to participate in a formal resolution process should contribute to their self-esteem and to a school climate that fosters peaceful solutions to interpersonal problems. Following the experience of settling their own disputes in a supportive and safe environment, most students are more self-motivated and better able to accept the structure and guidance offered by adults (see Smith et al., 2002). Other positive outcomes include (a) regard for conflict as a learning opportunity; (b) a nonpunitive method of discipline with long-lasting benefits; (c) reduction in violence, other antisocial behaviors, vandalism, and absenteeism; and (d) better understanding of individual differences (see Heydenberk et al., 2006; Schrumpf, Crawford, & Usadel, 1991).

Example: Peer Mediation Training

Through our research project in middle schools, we provided peer mediation training and helped school personnel select implementation strategies, but each school developed its own method for selecting mediators and establishing mediation protocols. Peer mediation training included concepts similar to those covered by the schoolwide conflict resolution curriculum but added a focus on the influence of culture, the specific procedures of the mediation process, and the need for confidentiality. Training also included role-plays and mediation simulations, and successful students were able to execute the mediation process with minimal supervision by adults.

For any student, participation in the peer mediation process was always voluntary, and a schoolwide referral process was readily accessible. At the conclusion of each mediation, mediators and disputants signed an agreement form that included the date, type of conflict, and agreed-upon resolution. According to teachers, students' feelings of independence in handling their own disputes positively influenced their attitude toward the program and their willingness to take their responsibilities seriously (Smith et al., 2002).

Some challenging aspects of implementing mediation programs include the following:

- Assuring that mediations occur as soon as possible after a referral is made
- Providing ample opportunities for all trained mediators to mediate disputes
- Matching mediators appropriately with disputants (e.g., age, gender)

As part of our research, we helped school personnel pair mediators for mutual support during mediations, provide mediation opportunities on a rotating basis, and facilitate discussion during debriefings. We found the availability of a class period during which program facilitators could schedule mediations and meet regularly with mediators to debrief (e.g., a homeroom period) to be a help, if not a necessity. Academic considerations also need be given appropriate priority to prevent mediators from missing a test or another important class activity.

To summarize, setting up a peer mediation program requires significant planning and school resources. Those in charge of its implementation should address the following questions as they consider the logistics of making referrals and implementing the mediation process:

- How and by whom will students be referred?
- What kinds of conflicts are suitable for mediation?
- Where will mediation take place?
- Who will supervise the mediations?
- How will the mediators be made available?
- How often will mediators miss class?
- Can teachers refuse to release a mediator (or disputant) from class to attend a mediation?

Selection of Peer Mediators

The selection of peer mediators usually occurs through student applications, student nominations, or teacher nominations. In our experience, the "successful" or "leader-type" students are most often chosen. In our study, the attitudes of peer mediators toward conflict, school, communication, and openness were significantly more positive than those of a control group matched on individual variables (i.e., school, grade level, gender, race, socioeconomic status (SES), and placement in special program) *prior* to training in mediation. Understandably, school staff must consider how serious, conscientious, and competent students would be in the role of peer mediator, but a dilemma arises when only the "best" students, or the leaders, are chosen for the job. Other students, particularly those who are or are becoming disenfranchised from school, may view mediators as a select group who are less apt to understand their problems, or they may see the whole program as "belonging to the establishment" and, therefore, less appealing (Robinson, Smith, & Daunic, 2000). The social acceptability of mediation as an alternative response to school conflict depends in part on its appeal to a broad range of students, particularly those most likely to engage in disruptive, aggressive, or antisocial behavior.

Moreover, peer mediation training includes problem-solving steps that are part of several well-researched interventions aimed at reducing aggressive student behavior (e.g., CPPRG, 2004; Lochman, Dunn, & Klimes-Dougan, 1993). Program coordinators miss an opportunity to engage students who may otherwise become socially isolated if they restrict training to school leaders (Daunic et al., 2000). Although not specific to peer mediation, there is recent evidence that students with pronounced behavioral problems can become positive influences when training their peers in social interaction skills via a formal social skills curriculum (Blake, Wang, Cartledge, & Gardner, 2000). In Blake and colleagues study, both peer trainers and student trainees showed an increase in positive peer interactions. Thus, students with high levels of interpersonal conflict at school might have the potential to become effective peer mediators and, in so doing, enhance a program's overall acceptability.

In sum, CRE that includes peer mediation (Benson & Benson, 1993; Deutsch, 1994; Schrumpf et al., 1991) is a significant move away from reactive, punitive, and seclusionary methods of discipline. Its proponents suggest that mediation training can achieve the following:

- Provide students with a framework for resolving conflicts.
- Give students an opportunity to assume responsibility for their own behavior.
- Lower teacher stress by reducing the number of student conflicts they have to handle.
- Increase instructional time.
- Help students understand how diverse cultural backgrounds can affect interpersonal communication and human interactions.

Bullying Prevention: Addressing a Specific Form of Conflict

Bullying is typically defined as some form of aggressive behavior against someone perceived as having lesser power or an inability to defend himself or herself (Bauer, Lozano, & Rivara, 2007; Garbarino & deLara, 2003; Olweus, 2003; Smokowski & Kopasz, 2005). Bullying can involve physical violence, terrorizing, or social isolation. It is one of the most prevalent forms of school violence and a significant problem, with some estimates running as high as one in every three children involved as either a bully or a victim. Although the U.S. Department of Education reports that 77 percent of middle and high school students surveyed reported being bullied at some point in their school career, many students are also involved as bystanders, and few of these students intervene on behalf of the victim (Garbarino & deLara; Olweus). In a study using surveys, semistructured interviews, and focus groups, Garbarino and deLara reported that students often feel powerless and ashamed, contributing to a dysfunctional social system that diminishes the ability to concentrate on learning.

One of the first steps in an effective schoolwide antibullying program is for school professionals to assume responsibility and take an active role in determining the facts about bullying situations (Cooper & Snell, 2003). Playground supervisors, for example, may wrongly assume that a student's aggression is some form of play and consequently fail to intervene. School professionals may also falsely assume that bullying is limited to physical aggression occurring mostly among boys, when malicious gossip and social exclusion by girls are just as harmful. Once an accurate picture of bullying behavior in a schoolhouse is drawn, a more effective bullying prevention program can be implemented.

Bullying frequently occurs in nonclassroom locations, such as the playground, hallway, or school bus. Most bullying prevention programs, therefore, involve attempts to improve supervision and establish procedures and guidelines for student behaviors in these less structured environments. Although students at the middle and high school level may want to manage most social situations themselves, a majority believe that adults should intervene in bullying situations long before they actually do (Frey et al., 2005; Garbarino & deLara, 2003). Monitoring and supervision thus become cornerstones of an effective schoolwide antibullying program.

Effective bullying prevention programs involve everyone in a school building and fit under the general umbrella of a schoolwide discipline and antiviolence plan and, thus, a CRE framework. A strong antibullying policy is front and center, and adult responsibility, in addition to student involvement, is key. Cooper and Snell (2003) recommended the following components for a successful policy:

- Commitment to creating a safe, caring, and respectful learning environment for all students
- Provision of a clear definition of bullying with concrete examples
- Clear consequences for bullying within the framework of the school discipline code
- Provision of a common framework through which students, parents, and school personnel can recognize and respond to bullying

Example: Olweus Bullying Prevention Program

Perhaps the best-known program is the Olweus Bullying Prevention Program, developed and evaluated over 20 years (Bauer, Lozano, & Rivara, 2007; Olweus, 2003). The program builds on four key principles derived from studies of problem behaviors, specifically aggression. The four principles are designed to create a school environment characterized by (1) warmth and positive interest/involvement from adults, (2) firm limits on anti-social behavior, (3) consistent application of nonpunitive sanctions for rule violations, and (4) adults who act as authorities and positive role models. The school's social environment is the vehicle through which these principles are carried out, so teachers, administrators, students, and parents all play key roles. A major focus is to provide fewer opportunities and rewards for bullying.

The Olweus Bullying Prevention Program has implemented measures of program effectiveness at the school, classroom, and individual student levels, using questionnaires, discussion groups, regular classroom meetings, parent meetings, and individual meetings with bullies, victims, and their parents (Bauer et al., 2007; Olweus, 2003). The general program prerequisite is the awareness and involvement of adults in the school, including formation of a Bullying Prevention Coordinating Committee, training of staff, formation of classroom and school rules about bullying, and individual intervention plans. Part of Norway's National Initiative Against Bullying, the Olweus program is offered on a large scale through a train-the-trainer strategy of dissemination in which trainers at a national research center train and supervise key persons from a number of different schools, who are then responsible for leading each participating school's staff discussion groups. Modified to accommodate cultural differences and practical constraints, the program has been implemented through this model in the United States, providing an example of a long-term, research-based approach to the prevention of bullying and the provision of a nurturing school environment.

HOW TO SUSTAIN CRE AND BULLYING PREVENTION PROGRAMS

The success of any new program in a school is a function of the school's community and culture. Moreover, school schedules, competing curricular demands, available space and resources, and the priority assigned to any schoolwide program can facilitate or impede its effective implementation. Given these parameters, and with insight gained from our experience and that of other researchers, we suggest that program developers consider the following factors as key to implementing and sustaining schoolwide programs in CRE and bullying prevention: committed leadership; consistency of promoting and monitoring the program; and, in the case of peer mediation programs, mediator selection.

Committed Leadership

The following characteristics are typically addressed in discussions of effective schools and the programs within them:

- A clear and focused mission on learning for all
- Instructional leadership
- High expectations of all stakeholders
- Opportunity to learn and student time on-task
- Frequent monitoring of student progress
- Safe and orderly environment for learning
- Positive home/school/community relations

The importance of administrators, teachers, and other school personnel cannot be overemphasized. They will lead the efforts to realize these goals as they implement CRE and bullying prevention programs to enhance the social and academic development of their students.

Administrators

Schools are under increasing pressure from parents and community members to provide safe environments for the children they serve. Many administrators, particularly those immediately responsible for schoolwide discipline, are compelled to develop responsive antiviolence and safe-school programs. Coupled with escalating demands for academic improvement in schools with increasingly diverse student populations, the urgency to demonstrate antiviolence measures often makes it tempting to initiate new programs without fully exploring the resources and effort necessary to make them effective. To ensure a program's long-term success—in this case, programs that include CRE and bullying prevention—one or more school administrators must commit to providing essential resources and responsible follow-through. For example, a committed administrator would (a) assign to an individual (or team) the primary responsibility for program implementation, (b) make sure that person (or team) has time to perform the required duties effectively, and (c) solicit feedback periodically about program status and needs. This administrative commitment is probably the single most important factor in sustaining a viable program.

Faculty and Other School Personnel

Along with engaging the commitment of top-level administrators, we suggest that establishing a school mediation or antibullying "team," including teachers from each grade level and administrators or guidance counselors who would be directly involved in program supervision, enhances program success. In a study about the implementation of a CR/PM program in one middle school, Matloff & Smith (1999) argued that the buy-in of this core group is critical. The researchers found that if team members view CRE as potentially beneficial to both staff and students, they naturally encourage the involvement of the remaining faculty. Conversely, if a school administrator assigns responsibility for a program to a teacher or group of teachers without their input, any incentives, or a commitment to follow through, those teachers interest in the program's success is seriously diminished. It was Matloff and Smith's contention that teachers with the most information and direct experience with program components are most likely to feel comfortable using it.

Even willing faculty who enthusiastically support CRE can be cautious about taking advantage of peer mediation or bullying prevention services if they lack relevant experience. Only after teachers or other school professionals have become knowledgeable and directly involved are they likely to be fully committed. Further, the school implementation team must make a variety of decisions about curriculum delivery, program logistics, counseling services, and, where relevant, peer mediator selection. They must make these decisions according to the needs of each school and cannot rely on "packaged" prescriptions. Team members need incentives for these efforts, along with sufficient planning time and resources. When time and resources are lacking, the team cannot be expected to invest the effort required to initiate and sustain a comprehensive schoolwide effort.

Finally, if educators truly wish to affect school culture as a whole and help students develop lasting constructive and cooperative conflict resolution strategies, they need to examine how conflict is addressed among faculty as well as students. Through exposure to conflict resolution concepts, either taught specifically or infused throughout curricula, students can learn to respond appropriately to simulated and real conflict situations. Students will also be heavily influenced by the larger school culture. Adults are not likely to be effective role models if students see that they are not constructive conflict managers themselves. Conversely, modeling respect for students is critical to the success of CRE programming (see Cassinerio & Lane-Garon, 2006). School personnel need to foster an environment conducive to the peaceful and constructive resolution of conflicts and a zero tolerance for bullying and other forms of antisocial behavior, whether it occurs among students or adults.

Consistency of Promotion and Follow-Up

In the case of CRE programs that involve peer mediation, students may need frequent reminders about program availability. Those who have experienced traditional, adult-dependent school discipline may not consider mediation as a way to help settle interpersonal disputes and may continue to call on readily available adults unless they are actively and consistently encouraged to use mediation. Thus, school professionals should address on an ongoing basis how they publicize the availability of peer mediation as a disciplinary option. Some suggestions for publicizing peer mediation to students and faculty are these:

- Frequent announcements to remind students and teachers of mediation as an alternative to discipline referrals
- Posters advertising the program
- Flyers distributed to homeroom teachers
- T-shirts worn by peer mediators
- School- and districtwide recognition of the contributions of peer mediators

Also important to the integrity and sustainability of a peer mediation program is an ongoing check on how the disputants view the process, such as having disputants complete a brief survey a few days following mediation. A member of the school mediation team can administer a questionnaire, such as the one in Figure 6.1, to disputants to solicit their perspectives about (a) the value of the mediation process, (b) whether required steps were followed by the mediators, (c) how helpful the mediation was in settling their dispute, and (d) how well they adhered to the signed agreement. This kind of follow-up is important in assessing the fidelity of the mediation process and its social validity.

Figure 6.1 CR/PM: Client Questionnaire

NAME _____ GRADE _____

SEX (circle one) M F

Directions: Please answer these questions about your recent peer mediation. Circle the number that *best* matches how much you agree with each item. A "1" means the HIGHEST level of agreement, and a "5" means the LOWEST level of agreement.

Example:

	Strongly Agree		**Strongly Disagree**	

1. I like to study science. 1 2 3 4 5

		Strongly Agree				Strongly Disagree
1.	The final agreement signed during peer mediation was fair.	1	2	3	4	5
2.	The peer mediators did a good job.	1	2	3	4	5
3.	The peer mediation was helpful to me.	1	2	3	4	5
4.	The final agreement signed during the mediation will work.	1	2	3	4	5
5.	Peer mediation is useful.	1	2	3	4	5
6.	I was satisfied with the peer mediation.	1	2	3	4	5
7.	I was satisfied with the final agreement signed during the peer mediation.	1	2	3	4	5
8.	The peer mediators did not take sides.	1	2	3	4	5
9.	I thought the agreement we signed was a good one.	1	2	3	4	5
10.	The other student thought the agreement we signed was a good one.	1	2	3	4	5
11.	I think I can stick to the agreement we signed.	1	2	3	4	5
12.	I don't think the peer mediators will talk about the mediation to others.	1	2	3	4	5
13.	I think the peer mediators will keep our mediation confidential.	1	2	3	4	5
14.	The agreement we signed will help to solve our conflict.	1	2	3	4	5

		Strongly Agree				Strongly Disagree
15.	The other student and I were equally satisfied with the agreement we signed.	1	2	3	4	5
16.	Peer mediation helped me resolve the conflict.	1	2	3	4	5
17.	Peer mediation helped me understand my feelings.	1	2	3	4	5
18.	Peer mediation will help me to assist others in resolving their conflicts.	1	2	3	4	5
19.	I think mediation could help others understand conflict.	1	2	3	4	5
20.	I think mediation could help others resolve conflicts.	1	2	3	4	5

Directions: For each of the following, circle **Yes** if it definitely happened or **No** if it did *not* happen.

1.	At the beginning of the mediation, the peer mediators explained the rules.	**Yes**	**No**
2.	Most of the time, I stated my feelings and concerns without being interrupted.	**Yes**	**No**
3.	Most of the time, I listened to the feelings and concerns of the other student.	**Yes**	**No**
4.	The peer mediators helped me make my feelings and needs clear.	**Yes**	**No**
5.	The peer mediators helped make the other student's feelings and needs clear.	**Yes**	**No**
6.	I got to suggest solutions to the conflict.	**Yes**	**No**
7.	The other student got to suggest solutions to the conflict.	**Yes**	**No**
8.	The peer mediators suggested solutions to the conflict.	**Yes**	**No**
9.	The peer mediators helped us come up with several ways to solve the conflict.	**Yes**	**No**
10.	The agreement we reached combined both the other student's and my ideas.	**Yes**	**No**
11.	I have kept my part of the signed agreement since the mediation.	**Yes**	**No**

Circle the answer:

12.	The agreement we signed was	a) my idea. b) the other student's idea. c) the peer mediator's idea. d) a solution that combined our ideas.

Equally important are frequent opportunities for mediators and teachers to discuss their experiences. The mediation process requires sophisticated and sometimes subtle skills that are difficult even for adults to master. We cannot expect students to become overnight experts or to maintain the skills they learned during training without regular meetings to review concepts and debrief about their experiences. Effective program implementation thus requires a built-in time for mediators to debrief with school mediation team members, who can monitor how well the students are following specified procedures, provide an opportunity to learn from experience, and discuss how to enhance the desirability of mediation for fellow students.

In the case of bullying prevention programs, consistent vigilance is critical if such programs are to be effective in changing the culture of a school. Smokowski and Kopasz (2005) suggested that bullying prevention is often best linked to comprehensive violence prevention programming, with a focus not only on eliminating undesirable behaviors but also on constructing a school environment that is inconsistent with bullying and coercion. Maintaining a zero-tolerance policy that includes swift and serious consequences for bullying behaviors is key to program effectiveness. Success becomes more likely when everyone in the school cooperates to eliminate positive social payoffs for bullies and those who support or tolerate them.

We suggest that a way to offer those who have previously been rewarded by bullying an alternate form of personal recognition is to involve them in CRE—potentially even as peer mediators. As we discussed previously, students who engage in proactive forms of aggression, which can include bullying, are sometimes those who have leadership qualities and are influential with peers. If at least some of these students can be enlisted to support peer mediation actively, the context of the school will benefit. In addition, Smokowski and Kopasz (2005) suggested the following evidence-based strategies for helping to shape a school culture that promotes mutual respect:

- Reach out to victims.
- Set and enforce clear rules and consequences for bullying behavior.
- Supervise students during breaks, especially in nonclassroom settings.
- Engage students in class discussions and activities about bullying to encourage everyone to take a more active role in its prevention.
- Encourage active participation by parents and other adults in the community.

Efficacy Evidence From CRE and Bullying Prevention Research

Examining more than 25 years of evidence from a comprehensive set of experimentally controlled studies, Garrard and Lipsey (2007) synthesized findings to assess the overall effectiveness of CRE programs for reducing antisocial behaviors in K–12 schools. Programs included met five criteria: (1) a primary goal of constructive resolution of conflict; (2) primary target behaviors of opposition, provocations, or disputes; (3) intervention that involved institutional or individual capacity building; (4) program content focused explicitly on the nature of conflict and constructive options for responding; and (5) direct instruction, modeling, and guided practice to build competence. Effect sizes from 36 studies meeting these criteria indicated improvements in antisocial behaviors in CRE participants compared to control groups, with the largest effects occurring for early to mid-adolescence as compared to middle childhood. Effect sizes were similar across programs using direct instruction or peer mediation, and the fidelity with which programs were implemented was more critical than how much instruction participants received. In a less rigorous analysis focused on peer mediation outcomes in school-based settings (Burrell, Zirbel, & Allen, 2003), results likewise indicated a high degree of conflict resolution and participant satisfaction.

The Conflict Resolution/Peer Mediation Project

Our work in three middle schools provides a specific example of typical disputants, conflict issues, mediation resolutions, and office referral patterns. Though specific to these participants, our findings generally correspond to those of other researchers (e.g., Cantrell, Parks-Savage, & Rehfuss, 2007; Cassinerio & Lane-Garon, 2006; Nix & Hale, 2007) and provide insight into how students use peer mediation and whether they consider it a viable alternative to less constructive conflict resolution strategies.

Disputants, Issues, and Resolutions

In our study (Smith et al., 2002), younger middle school students appeared to be more open than their older peers to using mediation, in that sixth-grade students were involved in the majority of referrals. It is possible that the types of disputes handled appropriately through mediation, such as conflicts over relationship issues or feelings, may occur more often among sixth graders than among seventh or eighth graders. From a developmental standpoint, moreover, an increasing need for independence in settling conflicts, including independence from the help of peers, may account for fewer referrals among older students. For example, one mediator told us that students sometimes felt embarrassed about going to mediation and didn't want to risk their reputation with friends. We also found that more girls than boys participated in mediation, possibly because boys may have perceived its use as a sign of weakness (Smith et al.). These results are consistent with those of Garrard and Lipsey (2007), who reported effect sizes for mediation programs to be almost twice as large among females as males.

We found verbal harassment (e.g., name-calling, threatening, or insulting a family member) to be the most frequent reason for mediations in our middle school research, along with spreading rumors or talking behind someone's back (i.e., gossiping). Boys were more likely than girls to be involved in mild forms of physical aggression (e.g., pushing, hitting), and girls were more likely to be concerned with relationship issues, such as broken friendships or gossip. It is important to note that many forms of verbal aggression are often used as a means to establish dominance, intimidate, or maintain social status and, therefore, fall under the definition of bullying. The prevention of these behaviors has implications for stemming the occurrence of more violent forms of behavior. Aggression theorists (e.g., Bandura) assert that verbal taunting, name-calling, or threats can escalate into physical aggression. This may especially be the case for students who are deficient in the verbal skills necessary for diffusing potentially violent situations. For these students, peer mediation is an opportunity to resolve hostile conflicts by practicing effective verbal strategies in a structured environment and potentially avoiding a spiral of destructive events. If mediation can diffuse the consequences of verbal threats or harassment before they escalate, it will serve an important preventive function. Some researchers (Lochman et al., 1993) have suggested that an inverse relationship exists between level of verbal skill and use of physical aggression among preadolescents. The more verbally skilled a child is, the *less* likely he or she may be to use physical force in resolving conflicts. If so, it is important to teach students to negotiate and to give them opportunities to practice. Thus, properly implemented peer mediation programs provide a vehicle for enhancing verbal skills during a critical developmental period.

During several years of our observing schools implement WTRC, more than 95 percent of mediations in the middle school study resulted in a resolution acceptable to both disputing parties. This finding is consistent with those of other researchers (see Burrell et al., 2003) and supports the notion that middle school students can, at the very least, successfully follow a structured procedure and help disputants reach a mutually agreeable conflict solution. Students most frequently resolved to avoid each other, stop the offending behavior, or "agree to get along," supporting findings from other studies of peer mediation at the elementary or middle school level (see Johnson & Johnson, 1996, for a thorough review). Although agreements reached through peer mediation may appear somewhat superficial, we suggest that the willingness and ability of 11- and 12-year-old mediators and disputants to follow a process of negotiation through to any acceptable conclusion is a significant achievement. It provides a foundation for lifelong negotiation skills and acts as a significant force in the prevention of school violence.

Overall Program Effects

To determine program efficacy, we examined school discipline records and administered teacher and student attitude surveys about school conflict and school climate. Although we found no significant changes in survey responses following program implementation, there was a promising downward trend in disciplinary incidents, particularly at the school where staff were most involved. Despite little evidence of schoolwide attitude change, both the mediators and disputants expressed high levels of satisfaction with the mediation process and its capacity for solving conflicts.

Olweus Bullying Prevention Program

Large-scale evaluation of multilevel bullying prevention programs has generally yielded promising but somewhat mixed results (see Frey et al., 2005). Probably the most widely recognized bullying prevention program designed to be implemented by teachers and school staff, the Olweus program was initially studied in Norway. Findings indicated that it was responsible for substantial reductions (50 percent or more) in the frequency with which students reported being victimized and acting as bullies themselves, and it was associated with reductions in reports of antisocial behavior and improvements in the social climate of the school (Frey et al.; Smokowski & Kopasz, 2005). Study replications in similar settings indicated consistent, though somewhat more modest, results. In a nonrandomized controlled trial with 10 public middle schools to examine the effectiveness of the Olweus Bullying Prevention Program in the United States, Bauer and colleagues (2007) used pre- and posttreatment school survey data about relational and physical victimization to determine program effects. They also examined whether the program improved student attitudes toward bullying. No overall effect on student victimization was found, but the study did show effects for white students in treatment schools, regardless of gender or grade level. Students in intervention schools were more likely posttreatment to see other students as intervening actively in incidents of bullying. Given these findings, the researchers cautioned school administrators to monitor program outcomes carefully and pay particular attention to the potential influences of culture and family.

Steps to Respect

Another program that has been studied in the United States is Steps to Respect: A Bullying Prevention Program. This program focuses on addressing adult and systemic factors through schoolwide policies and training, coupled with promoting prosocial beliefs and social-emotional learning through a classroom-based curriculum (Frey et al., 2005). In a randomized control study using direct observations to evaluate intervention effects on bullying and bystander behavior on playgrounds, researchers found significant decreases in bullying and argumentative behavior and bystander encouragement, increases in "agreeable interactions," and more active adult responsiveness in schools using the Steps to Respect program. The trend toward reductions in bystander approval was particularly heartening, since the potential reinforcement of bullying through peer approval may lead to long-term benefits in behavioral norms. Finally, in a study of a bully prevention program that incorporated training in affective vocabulary, social-emotional literacy, and conflict resolution skills, student and staff questionnaire responses indicated gains in constructive conflict resolution, including self-regulation and problem solving, a decrease in bullying, and an increased sense of safety (Heydenberk et al., 2006).

CONCLUDING THOUGHTS

Although there is much to be learned about the effectiveness of CRE programs, it is safe to say that students benefit from learning about conflict and its prosocial resolution. They learn how to make conflict a constructive opportunity for effective communication, critical thinking, and problem solving. They also develop skills for dealing with intimidating situations, such as bullying and social isolation. Students can learn formal mediation procedures, help their peers negotiate positive solutions to conflicts, and contribute to a school environment that does not tolerate bullying. Even though many of the issues involved may seem relatively harmless and typical, particularly for middle school students, low-level conflicts can escalate to more serious levels and/or contribute to feelings of alienation and low self-esteem.

Teaching students how to resolve disputes and be more in control of the outcome helps them develop lifelong social skills. These skills and a proactive approach to countering violence and alienation increase time for academic learning and, indeed, may be critical to social and academic success. Although some published conflict resolution and bullying prevention programs can be costly to implement, others are available for minimal cost and training. The bottom line is that the general guidelines outlined in this chapter go a long way toward ensuring a safe and effective school: committed personnel, including top administrators; open communication among teachers, students, and parents; a schoolwide framework for talking about and handling conflict; encouragement of student responsibility; and consistent monitoring and evaluation.

Our experience as researchers of WTRC taught us that we can learn from attending to how students engage in the process of resolving conflict, as well as to how well their efforts translate into measurable outcomes. Offering students a socially acceptable process as an alternative to violence is an important preventive measure in itself. Students who have requisite skills for mediation (i.e., students with leadership qualities, high social status, effective communication skills) can constitute an effective mediator cohort, with the primary intervention target being the attitudes and behavior of students referred to mediation. Conversely, training in CRE can be focused on developing or remediating *all* students' social behaviors. Students who lack skills in leadership and communication and those across the social status spectrum could work with student leaders to learn and practice the skills required in formal mediations. Students with learning, behavioral, or social problems that place them at risk for school failure could learn to deal more effectively with conflict by serving as peer mediators themselves. Although this approach might not be as efficient initially, its value could be far-reaching and contribute to the culture of the school as a whole.

The work conducted in the field of CRE and bullying prevention shows promise. A further understanding through longitudinal studies of well-implemented programs that track student learning is needed. In particular, studies can be designed to focus on the attitudes of bullies, victims, and disputants; the nature of student resolutions and responses to bullying over time; and program effects on aggressive and violent behavior. To effect schoolwide change, school professionals need to make constructive conflict resolution and antibullying sentiment an integral part of school culture. As CRE is studied over the long term, much can be learned about how school communities can benefit from a unified, consistent, and proactive approach.

An Illustration From Practice

Located in a small urban environment in North Central Florida, Jonesville Middle School has just under 1,000 students, 70 percent from ethnically diverse backgrounds and over 37 percent eligible for free or reduced-price lunch. After our research team talked with the principal and assistant principal (AP) about instituting a conflict resolution and peer mediation program at the school, it was agreed that the AP would take responsibility for overseeing the program if the faculty agreed to participate. The AP enlisted faculty input at a meeting with the research project director to give teachers a sense of what would be expected and to get their input on when and where the schoolwide conflict resolution lessons would be taught. A critical thinking class had just been added to the schoolwide curriculum, so it was decided that this would be the ideal place to teach conflict resolution and peer mediation. Lessons in topics such as understanding conflict, effective communication, understanding and handling anger, and peer mediation would provide a background context for all students in the school so that they would have some understanding about constructive conflict resolution and the mediation process.

Following the initial faculty meeting, the sixth-, seventh-, and eighth-grade team leaders met with the research project director to brainstorm ways to implement the peer mediation component of the program. Together they decided that each grade-level leader would be responsible for selecting and training student mediators (following a train-the-trainer inservice conducted by our research staff), scheduling and conducting mediations, and debriefing regularly with student mediators. The teachers chose a combination of student applications and teacher recommendations to select peer mediators, and they agreed to seek a diverse group of students for these positions. Team leaders then selected approximately 25 student mediators from a combination of grade levels.

Since all students began the day with a 30-minute homeroom, this provided an ideal time to conduct mediations. Schoolwide referral procedures were established once mediators had been selected and trained and had practiced several simulated mediations. Referral procedures involved making sure that (a) referral forms were available in classrooms and offices so that students or teachers (with student consent) could make referrals to mediation, (b) forms were turned in to team leaders in a timely way, (c) mediations were scheduled as soon after the referral as possible, and (d) referral procedures were publicized regularly through school announcements. Publicity included information about the types of conflict appropriate for mediation (i.e., fighting or other egregious violations of the code of conduct would not be appropriate, but mediation could help prevent the escalation of typical disputes such as social misunderstandings, verbal harassment, and accusations and the subsequent need for adult intervention).

Team leaders also established a mediator rotation process so that no individual was called upon excessively. Although fewer mediations than expected took place over the year, the number of referrals provided an opportunity for all trained mediators to conduct at least one mediation, and students had ample opportunities to debrief as a group with team leaders and learn from their collective experience. Following the code of confidentiality learned during training, they discussed only general information about mediation issues so that the group could brainstorm solutions that might benefit everyone. When asked to fill out a questionnaire about their experience, the mediators reported using their training in informal situations as well as in formal mediations and noted the conflict resolution/peer mediation program benefits to both mediators and disputants. The total number of discipline referrals at Jonesville was significantly lower following implementation of the program, and both administrators and teachers reported that it was a positive influence on overall school climate.

REFERENCES

Andrews, D.W. (1995). The adolescent transitions program for high-risk teens and their parents: Toward a school-based intervention. *Education and Treatment of Children, 18*(4), 478–498.

Bauer, N. S., Lozano, P., & Rivara, F. P. (2007). The effectiveness of the Olweus Bullying Prevention Program in public middle schools: A controlled trial. *Journal of Adolescent Health, 40,* 266–274.

Benson, A. J., & Benson, J. M. (1993). Peer mediation: Conflict resolution in schools. *Journal of School Psychology, 31,* 427–430.

Berger, K. S. (1994). *The developing person through the life span* (3rd ed.). New York: Worth.

Blake, C., Wang, W., Cartledge, G., & Gardner, R. (2000). Middle school students with serious emotional disturbances serve as social skills trainers and reinforcers for peers with SED. *Behavioral Disorders, 25*(4), 280–298.

Burrell, N. A., Zirbel, C. S., & Allen, M. (2003). Evaluating peer mediation outcomes in education settings: A meta-analytic review. *Conflict Resolution Quarterly, 21*(1), 7–26.

Cantrell, R., Parks-Savage, A., & Rehfuss, M. (2007). Reducing levels of elementary school violence with peer mediation. *Professional School Counseling, 10*(5), 475–481.

Carlsson-Paige, N., & Levin, D. E. (1992). Making peace in violent times: A constructivist approach to conflict resolution. *Young Children, 48*(1), 4–13.

Cassinerio, C., & Lane-Garon, P. S. (2006). Changing school climate one mediator at a time: Year-one analysis of a school-based mediation program. *Conflict Resolution Quarterly, 23*(4), 447–460.

Cooper, D., & Snell, J. L. (2003). Bullying—Not just a kid thing. *Educational Leadership, 60*(6), 22–25.

Conduct Problems Prevention Research Group (CPPRG). (2004). The effects of the Fast Track program on serious problem outcomes at the end of elementary school. *Journal of Clinical Child and Adolescent Psychology, 33*(4), 650–661.

Daunic, A. P., Smith. S. W., Brank, E. M., & Penfield, R. D. (2006). Classroom based cognitive-behavioral intervention to prevent aggression: Efficacy and social validity. *Journal of School Psychology, 44,* 123–139.

Daunic, A. P., Smith, S. W., Robinson, T. R., Miller, M. D., & Landry, K. L. (2000). Implementing schoolwide conflict resolution and peer mediation programs: Experiences in three middle schools. *Intervention in School & Clinic, 36*(2), 94–100.

Deutsch, M. (1994). Constructive conflict resolution: Principles, training, and research. *Journal of Social Issues 50*(1), 13–32.

Fonagy, P., Twemlow, S. W., Vernberg, E., Sacco, F. C., & Little, T. D. (2005). Creating a peaceful school learning environment: The impact of an antibullying program on educational attainment in elementary schools. *Medical Science Monitor, 11*(7), 317–325.

Frey, K. S., Hirschstein, M. K., Snell, J. L., Van Schoiack Edstrom, L., MacKenzie, E. P., & Broderick, C. J. (2005). Reducing playground bullying and supporting beliefs: An experimental trial of the Steps to Respect program. *Developmental Psychology, 41*(3), 479–491.

Garbarino, J., & deLara, E. (2003). *And words can hurt forever: How to protect adolescents from bullying, harassment, and emotional violence.* New York: Free Press.

Garrard, W. M., & Lipsey, M. W. (2007). Conflict resolution education and antisocial behavior in U.S. schools: A meta-analysis. *Conflict Resolution Quarterly, 25*(1), 9–38.

Havighurst, R. J. (1972). *Developmental tasks and education* (3rd ed.). New York: McKay.

Heydenberk, R. A., Heydenberk, W. R., & Tzenova, V. (2006). Conflict resolution and bully prevention: Skills for school success. *Conflict Resolution Quarterly, 24*(1), 55–69.

Ivey, A. E. (1991). *Development strategies for helpers.* Pacific Grove, CA: Brooks/Cole.

Johnson, D. W., & Johnson, R. T. (1996). Conflict resolution and peer mediation programs in elementary and secondary schools: A review of the research. *Review of Educational Research, 66*(4), 459–506.

Kauffman, J. M. (2005). *Characteristics of emotional and behavioral disorders of children and youth* (8th ed.). Upper Saddle River, NJ: Pearson.

Lewis, T. J., & Sugai, G. (1999). Effective behavior support: A systems approach to proactive schoolwide management. *Focus on Exceptional Children, 31,* 1–24.

Lochman, J. E., Dunn, S. E., & Klimes-Dougan, B. (1993). An intervention and consultation model from a social cognitive perspective: A description of the Anger Coping Program. *School Psychology Review, 22*(3), 458–471.

Matloff, G., & Smith, S. W. (1999). Responding to a schoolwide conflict resolution-peer mediation program: Case study of middle school faculty. *Mediation Quarterly, 17,* 125–141.

Nix, C. L., & Hale, C. (2007). Conflict within the structure of peer mediation: An examination of controlled confrontations in an at-risk school. *Conflict Resolution Quarterly, 24*(3), 327–348.

No Child Left Behind Act (NCLB) of 2001, Pub. L. 107-110, 115 Stat. 1425 (2002).

Olweus, D. (2003). A profile of bullying at school. *Educational Leadership, 60*(6), 12–17.

Polsgrove, L., & Smith, S. W. (2004). Informed practice in teaching self-control to children with emotional and behavioral disorders. In R. B. Rutherford, M. M. Quinn, & S. R. Mathur (Eds.), *Handbook of research in emotional and behavioral disorders* (399–425). New York: Guilford Press.

Robinson, T. R., Smith, S. W., & Daunic, A. P. (2000). Middle school students' views on the social validity of peer mediation. *Middle School Journal, 31*(5), 23–29.

Rose, L. C., & Gallup, A. M. (2000). The 32nd annual Phi Delta Kappa/Gallup poll of the public's attitudes toward the public schools. *Phi Delta Kappan, 82,* 41–48.

Schrumpf, F., Crawford, D., & Usadel, H. C. (1991). *Peer mediation: Conflict resolution in the schools.* Champaign, IL: Research Press.

Smith, S. W., & Daunic, A. P. (2004). Research on preventing behavior problems using a cognitive-behavioral intervention: Preliminary findings, challenges and future directions. *Behavioral Disorders, 30*(1), 72–76.

Smith, S. W., Daunic, A. P., Miller, M. D., & Robinson, T. R. (2002). Conflict resolution and peer mediation in middle schools: Extending the process and outcome knowledge base. *Journal of Social Psychology, 142*(5), 567–586.

Smokowski, P. R., & Kopasz, K. H. (2005). Bullying in school: An overview of typees, effects, family characteristics, and intervention strategies. *Children & Schools, 17*(2), 101–110.

Stevahn, L., Johnson, D. W., Johnson, R. T., & Real, D. (1996). The impact of a cooperative or individualistic context on the effect of conflict resolution training. *American Educational Research Journal, 33,* 801–823.

Tulley, M., & Chiu, L. H. (1995). Student teachers and classroom discipline. *The Journal of Educational Research, 83*(3), 164–171.

U.S. Surgeon General. (2001). *Youth violence: A report of the Surgeon General.* Retrieved October 28, 2009, from www.surgeongeneral.gov/library/youthviolence/toc.html

Zins, J. E., Bloodworth, M. R., Weissberg, M. C., & Walberg, H. J. (2004). The scientific base linking social and emotional learning to school success. In J. E. Zins, R. P. Weissberg, M. C. Wang, & H. J. Walberg (Eds.), *Building academic success on social and emotional learning* (pp. 3–22). New York: Teachers College Press.

7

Classroom Interventions and Individual Behavior Plans

In this chapter, we

- review relationships between Schoolwide Positive Behavior Support and Response-to-Intervention approaches to prevention,
- define and discuss targeted classroom interventions, and
- define and discuss intensive individual interventions.

S ince 1996, there has been an increasing emphasis on the use of Schoolwide Positive Behavior Supports (SPBS) to improve students' social behavior. Chapter 3 of this text provides a thorough overview of the background, essential features, and research findings from the past 10 years of implementing SPBS. A critical feature of this three-tiered model is that school staff must work cohesively in a proactive, strategic manner across the school to enhance social behavior and reduce problem behavior of students.

The purpose of this chapter is to discuss how the techniques of SPBS and the current approach known as Response to Intervention (RTI) can be applied in elementary school classrooms to enhance the social behavior of students. Since schools are now attempting to use RTI as both an academic and behavioral approach, this chapter will discuss the relationship between these RTI and SPBS and show how they can be aligned to meet the needs of students and teachers in classroom situations. Our intention is to provide administrators, educators, and family members with a conceptual model and practical educational techniques. Since Chapter 3 reviewed universal approaches across the first tier of the SPBS model, we focus our discussion on important classroom approaches for teachers to support students with behavior problems.

WHAT EDUCATORS SHOULD KNOW ABOUT THE RTI MODEL

The RTI language in the Individuals with Disabilities Improvement Act of 2004 (IDEIA) requires schools to assess, provide necessary instruction, and evaluate progress of students with learning difficulties prior to identifying the students as having a learning disability. These students would be considered to be receiving Tier II interventions, since their performance at Tier I was found to be lagging behind that of other students in the classroom. When students receive and are responsive to Tier II instructional approaches, according to the RTI model, they are more likely to be receptive to the ongoing academic instruction in their classroom. Tier II interventions are, therefore, able to thwart the development of further, more chronic academic problems that might require special education services.

The behavioral side of the RTI model is analogous to this instructional approach. In short, when a student in a general education classroom is displaying behavior that doesn't meet social expectations and schoolwide behavior program (Tier I), teachers can refer a student for Tier II supports and interventions in an attempt to ameliorate the behavior problem and teach the student more effective behavior for school success. The Tier II intervention should be efficient and accessible and have a standard assessment approach and criteria for entering the intervention. While assessment and intervention approaches vary at present, it is generally agreed that this system should be systematic and accessible within one to two weeks to students in general education (see Hawken, Vincent, & Schumann, 2008).

RTI AS A SCHOOLWIDE AND CLASSROOM MANAGEMENT APPROACH

There is mounting evidence that schools that universally employ an SPBS approach are also high-achieving schools (Horner, 2007). Concurrently, when students demonstrate classroom behavior problems in high-achieving schools, competent teachers are better situated to address the student's behavior problem within their classrooms. These teachers know how to work with school and district colleagues to use behavior plans that link directly to their SPBS system. (We again refer the reader to Chapter 3 for a review of schoolwide procedures that serve as foundational and critical features in improving school environments.) We move beyond Tier I schoolwide approaches to discuss how teachers can improve their classroom management strategies and use Tier II and III approaches with students who have behavior problems.

EFFECTIVE CLASSROOM MANAGEMENT APPROACHES

By *effective classroom management procedures*, we are referring to practices that have been used over the past 30 years that have led to diminished behavior problems in classrooms. The strategies we support are backed by evidence from a number of sources but are nicely summarized and presented in Evertson and Emmer (2009) and Sprick, Garrison, and Howard (1998). Evertson and Emmer have been researching and applying effective classroom management procedures for the past three decades, while Sprick and colleagues integrated these classroom procedures into a classroom system known as CHAMPS. Both approaches have been very useful for improving students' classroom behavior. Table 7.1 shows the essential features that accomplish this outcome.

	Observed		
Feature	**Yes**	**No**	**Plan for Improvement**

1. Effective Classroom Arrangement/Layout
  a. High traffic/low congestion
  b. Teacher is eye to eye with all students.
  c. Teaching materials are at hand
  d. Students see whole class presentations ad displays			

2. Walls and Ceilings Available for the Following:
  a. Classroom expectations/rules
  b. Daily schedule/assignments
  c. Calendar
  d. Student of the week, other honors
  e. Emergency procedures			

3. Social Expectations Posted
  a. Rules/behaviors for the expectations are posted.
  b. Expectations/rules are frequently discussed.			

4. Transitions Taught and Monitored
  a. Leaving/entering room
  b. Beginning/ending day			

5. Classroom Procedures Taught and Monitored
  a. Small- and large-group instruction
  b. Independent work
  c. Materials
  d. Drinks
  e. Restroom			

6. Schoolwide Expectations Posted and Taught
  a. Hallways
  b. Cafeteria
  c. PE/specialists
  d. Playground
  e. Library			

Table 7.1   Essential Features of Classroom Organization and Management

(Continued)

| | Observed | | |
Feature	Yes	No	Plan for Improvement
7. Daily Routines Taught/Practiced a. Attention signal b. Homework in/out c. Classroom assignments d. Assignment standards e. Attendance/tardy procedures			
8. Whole-Group Instruction Emphasizes the Following: a. Prevention of misbehavior b. Managing pace of and on-task behavior through momentum and smoothness c. Maintaining focus through alerting, accountability, and participation			
9. Appropriate Student Behavior Maintained by the Following: a. Monitoring and supervising all student behavior b. Being consistent across behavior c. Identifying and acknowledging students using positive social skills d. Using proximity and eye contact when students are off-task or misbehaving e. Providing reminders and redirection to those off-task f. Verbal statements to stop misbehavior g. Using individual and group reinforcement programs			
10. Clear Communication Skills a. Behaviorally specific b. Calm and direct c. Assertive body posture d. Empathy and concern e. Questioning and problem solving			

Table 7.1 (Continued)

In collaborative schools that value peer and administrative guidance and feedback, Table 7.1 can be used as a tool to observe and make a plan of action for a classroom teacher. Some teachers use many of these recommended practices in their classrooms, but when most teachers are observed, they will be found to have some areas in need of improvement. The following example describes how one teacher benefitted from a peer observation.

Example: Classroom Management Observation and Plan

Ms. Tomaz is a third-grade classroom teacher with seven years of teaching experience at Sunset Elementary. She has received positive yearly evaluations from her principal, which typically have included a few comments about improving her classroom management approaches. Until this year, however, Ms. Tomaz has never had specific goals or activities for improving her management skills.

She and another teacher agreed to use some collegial support and supervision around management procedures. With the principal's agreement, they planned observations of each other's classroom for two hours. The principal substituted for the teachers so that they could visit and observe in each other's classroom. The teachers used Table 7.1 during their observations so that they could specify a few items for improvement and develop a plan of action to help each other.

The observing teacher concluded that Ms. Tomaz had discussed and taught social expectations and had a daily schedule, but communicated these only verbally in class. There were no posters or other visual reminders in the room about their Schoolwide Positive Behavior Support program. The observer recommended that the program poster with its social expectations be posted and that a daily schedule be written on the classroom whiteboard. This would give the students and the adults in the room a place to look at and review these items throughout the day when necessary. It would also give Ms. Tomaz referents for students who were misbehaving. She could ask the students to refer to the expectations or schedule to identify what they should be doing at the specific time. The students could respond, make commitments to show expected behavior within the scheduled activity, and then get back to the activity.

This type of reminding about social expectations through posted visual material is helpful in improving classroom management. While this is a brief and straightforward example, one can see that many possible recommendations can come from classroom management observation. Teachers and administrators should use the information to develop goals that are achievable within the classroom, without overwhelming a teacher with too many goals at any one time.

TIER II BEHAVIOR PLANS FOR STUDENTS

Even when teachers have developed a strong, systematic approach to classroom management, some students will need additional behavior supports and interventions. Following an SPBS model, these students are considered to be a targeted group who are at risk of school failure due to their behavior. These students show consistent and somewhat enduring behavior problems. Sometimes this is evident through teacher discussion and nomination. That is, teachers often know in a comparative manner when a student is not meeting classroom and school expectations. They will then refer the student to a school student support team meeting to review progress and brainstorm ideas in the classroom.

Systematic Identification of Tier II Students

Systematic approaches for identifying students for Tier II interventions have been developed over the past 20 years. The two most common approaches are *systematic screening* and *frequency of office discipline referrals*. Walker and Severson (1992) developed the

Systematic Screening for Behavior Disorders (SSBD) to identify students at risk for severe behavior problems. The SSBD requires teachers to nominate students and rate their behaviors to determine if they are at risk for behavioral failure. This screening tool has three assessment steps, or gates, that narrow the pool of students who may need Tier II or III interventions.

1. Teachers rank all of their students for externalizing (e.g., aggression, defiance) or internalizing (e.g., shy, anxious, withdrawn) behavioral characteristics, as defined and explained in the SSBD.

2. Teachers complete rating scales on critical events and maladaptive and adaptive behaviors on the three highest-ranked internalizing and externalizing students.

3. Students who meet criteria based on a normative sample are considered at risk for school failure and, with parent consent, enter the Tier II interventions.

We have used this approach in several intervention studies to identify students. Further elaboration of the SSBD can be found in Walker and Severson (2007); Walker, Cheney, Blum, and Stage (2005); and Cheney, Flower, and Templeton (2008). The SSBD is used early in the school year, in the first 30–45 days, and is an efficient and valid method, taking only about 90 minutes of a teacher's time, for forming a pool of students in need of Tier II intervention.

Irvin and his colleagues (Irvin, Tobin, Sprague, Sugai, & Vincent, 2004; Irvin et al., 2006) have reviewed the use of office discipline referrals (ODR) as a practical and valid approach for identifying students in need of Tier II interventions. This approach can be useful after a school has met all requisites of implementing universal Tier I interventions. Using ODRs requires that teachers and administrators review and align the types of behavior problems that can lead to an office referral and those that can be managed in classrooms. Once this alignment has been made and, for example, only significant behavior problems (e.g., aggression, defiance, peer provocation, repeated noncompliance within a one-day period) are referred to the office, a behavior support team can set criteria for admitting a student into a Tier II intervention. The criterion is typically set at three to five ODR. Use of this procedure has been described and evaluated in several recent studies (e.g., Fairbanks, Sugai, Guardino, & Lathrop, 2007; Filter et al., 2007; Hawken, MacLeod, & Rawlings, 2007).

BEHAVIOR PLANNING FOR TIER II STUDENTS

Once a teacher needs assistance with a student, SPBS requires an approach that is efficient, effective, and accessible. The Tier II strategy and its techniques should also be directly linked to the schoolwide system of social instruction. This integration has led to the development and evaluation of strategies that incorporate several evidence-based practices in the classroom. These include increased supervision and monitoring through the use of daily behavior report cards, regular positive instructional feedback regarding social behavior, increased reinforcement for positive social behavior, improved relationships with adults at school, regular parental involvement, and systematic progress monitoring. This type of behavior planning is based on 15 years of research on established programs (e.g., Check & Connect, Behavior Education Program), which has been described in several articles.

Check & Connect (Sinclair, Christenson, Evelo, & Hurley, 1998) has been identified as an evidence-based intervention by the U.S. Department of Education's What Works Clearinghouse (http://ies.ed.gov/ncee/wwc/). This intervention has been demonstrated to maintain school engagement and reduce problem behavior in general education settings for middle and high school students with learning disabilities and emotional disturbances (ED). C&C relies on an adult mentor to supervise, monitor, provide feedback to, and problem-solve with students regarding their behavior in school.

The *check* component of the program consists of an adult mentor employing daily monitoring procedures for school risk factors: tardiness, absenteeism, behavior referrals, detention, suspension, course grades, and credits. The *connect* refers to the mentors forming positive relationships with students so that they can implement two levels of intervention for monitoring student progress in terms of risk factors. Progress monitoring is shared with students daily and weekly through a report card system. Additional supports are provided to students in the intensive program, including social skills groups, individualized behavior contracts, academic tutoring, problem-solving sessions with parents, and help developing alternatives to out-of-school suspensions with school personnel.

Randomized studies of both elementary- and secondary-level students have found positive improvement for students in C&C in the areas of attendance, school completion, school engagement in academic and social activities, and overall improved social functioning (Lehr, Sinclair, & Christenson, 2004; Sinclair, Christenson, & Thurlow, 2005).

The Behavior Education Program is similar to C&C in that it uses relational, supervisory, and feedback systems, although it was explicitly developed as a Tier II intervention to support students who are at risk of developing more serious behavior problems in meeting schoolwide social expectations while reducing their problematic behavior (Crone, Horner, & Hawken, 2004; Hawken & Horner, 2003). As a Tier II behavioral intervention, BEP has shown promise with elementary and middle school students, reducing ODR and improving teachers' perceptions of student social and academic performance. Hawken (2006), for example, reported that in a small sample of 10 middle school students, 70 percent had a reduction in office discipline referrals after at least eight weeks of BEP intervention. This finding was replicated when Hawken and colleagues (2007) used the BEP to decrease office referrals with a sample of elementary-aged students.

Supervision and Monitoring of Tier II Students

Behavior planning for Tier II students relies on the availability of two adults, a coach/mentor and the classroom teacher, to provide increased supervision and monitoring of students. Students follow prescribed steps like those outlined in the BEP and C&C models. They first get a daily behavior progress report (DPR) card developed by the school's behavior support team. The DPR lists the schoolwide expectations (e.g., respect, responsibility, safety) for at least three grading periods to rate student progress against clearly stated expectations. This card provides a rubric for the teacher to rate the student's behavior during the school day. It is designed to prompt the teachers to provide students with positively stated feedback about their behavior and specific behavior they need to improve to be successful in the classroom. Figure 7.1 provides an example of a DPR.

Figure 7.1   Daily Progress Report for Buzzy Bee Club

Buzzy Bee Club

Checked in	Yes	No
Checked out	Yes	No
Parent Signature	Yes	No

Bee Respectful   Bee Responsible
Bee Safe   Bee a Hard Worker

Student:_____ **Date:**_____ **Goal:**_____

	Reading				Math				Afternoon				
Expectations	**Tough Time**	**OK**	**Good**	**Way to Go!**	**Tough Time**	**OK**	**Good**	**Way to Go!**	**Tough Time**	**OK**	**Good**	**Way to Go!**	**Totals**
Bee Respectful	1	2	3	4	1	2	3	4	1	2	3	4	
Bee Responsible	1	2	3	4	1	2	3	4	1	2	3	4	
Bee Safe	1	2	3	4	1	2	3	4	1	2	3	4	
Bee a Hard Worker	1	2	3	4	1	2	3	4	1	2	3	4	

DAILY TOTAL _____

Way to Go! (4): Met expectations with positive behavior; worked independently without any reminders or corrections.
Good (3): Met expectations with only 1 reminder or correction.

OK (2): Needed 2–3 reminders or corrections.
Tough Time (1): Needed 4 or more reminders or corrections.

Parent Signature:_____	**TOTAL:** _____
Comments:	**Comments:**

In our development and evaluation of the Social Response to Intervention System (SRIS; Cheney & Lynass, 2009), students checked in with their coach daily for an eight-week period, the minimum time allowed for students to benefit from SRIS's instruction, supervision, and reinforcement on social expectations. Check-in, which lasted two to three minutes, occurred before school and accomplished the following:

- Assured that students were ready and had their school materials.
- Reviewed their daily goals.

- Gave students verbal encouragement to meet their goals.
- Checked for parent signatures on the previous day's DPR.

At check-in, students received their daily progress report (DPR) card. The DPR listed the schoolwide expectations (e.g., Bee Respectful, Bee Responsible) for at least three grading periods so that student progress could be rated against the expectations. This card established clear student expectations and provided a rubric for the teacher to rate the student's behavior during the school day. The card was designed to prompt the teachers to provide students with positively stated feedback about their behavior and specific behaviors to improve so they would be successful in the classroom.

Regular Feedback During Instructional Periods

Throughout the school day, teachers are expected to give students regularly scheduled feedback on their social behavior. Teachers rate the student's behavior at set intervals (e.g., morning reading, recess, morning math, lunch, afternoon science/social studies, etc.) on the DPR. Students are rated based on their ability to meet schoolwide expectations without teacher reminders. The teacher meets briefly (two minutes) with students at the end of each period and discusses student behavior, provides positive feedback about what the student did well, and gives corrective feedback if needed. Teacher feedback and a DPR score are given throughout the day at the set times. In our work, we ask teachers to score students based on the number of teacher reminders given to a student on the social expectations. For example, a score of 4 indicates that the student met the expectation without any reminders from the teacher. A 3 represents one teacher reminder, a 2 indicates two to three teacher reminders, and a 1 indicates four or more teacher reminders. (Figure 7.1 presents an example of a DPR developed in the evaluation study of SRIS.)

To learn how to give these reminders and scores, teachers participate in a four-hour training on use of the DPR and giving positive feedback to students. Teachers are first given information on the use of the DPR by watching a DVD produced by the BEP (Hawken, Peterson, Mootz, & Anderson, 2006) and then practice giving feedback in role-plays. After the training session, teachers are observed in classrooms and provided feedback on the use of this system. Our research indicates that most teachers can implement the program with fidelity and report that the system works effectively with students in their classrooms (Cheney, Lynass, Flower, Waugh, & Iwaszuk, in press).

Increased Reinforcement for Positive Social Behavior

Three decades of research has consistently concluded that increasing the rate of positive interactions and tangibles with students results in greater improvements in students' social and academic performance. For Tier II classroom interventions, therefore, it is recommended that teachers increase their rates of acknowledgment and reinforcement to improve students' social behavior in school. This suggests that the teacher and coach need to identify systematic ways to increase the types of verbal and tangible reinforcement. Within the Tier II intervention, the DPR serves as a means to make sure this reinforcement occurs.

The DPR requires teachers to give students points after identified time periods. The points are used to set daily goals for the student. Daily goals are typically set between 75 and 85 percent of the total points. In Figure 7.1, for example, there are 48 total points on the DPR, so a student would have to earn 36 points if the daily criteria/goal was 75 percent. The number of points expected is written on the point card for students to see. After each period, students can calculate the points they have earned. When a student meets his or her daily goal, the student receives a daily reinforcer, which is either verbal praise, a sticker, or a visible acknowledgment on a string of beads or a bar graph. As students meet their goals over a week or month, the coach and student celebrate these larger stretches of success in more socially valid and valuable ways. For example, a one-week celebration may be additional free time with peers, while a one-month reinforcer might be a special lunch with the teacher or coach.

Progress Monitoring

The hallmark of determining a student's progress in Tier II interventions is the collection and close monitoring of performance data. In reading programs, we often use fluency data of words read per minute. Results are then charted, and teachers can review the progress of students by how students increase their words per minute in relation to a target or goal. The same is true for social behavior in a Tier II intervention. When students have a DPR, the data from it can be charted, performance criteria set, and goals for program success set at a four- to eight-week intervals.

This process starts when the coach enters students' DPR data into a database, such as an Excel file or an online database system that can chart student progress. The number of points earned daily on the DPR is converted to a percentage of total points and then charted. Weekly goals can be set that are equal to or slightly higher than the points earned in a student's baseline period. Figure 7.2 shows a chart for one student in the Social Response to Intervention System (Cheney & Lynass, 2009). The example shows that the student initially had difficulty earning daily points and after the first seven days had earned 64 percent of points. Days when the student did not meet criteria were below the vertical goal line, which was set at 75 percent. The team determined the daily criteria should be lowered for the student, and it was set at 70 percent. After that, the student started having success with the daily point card and gradually improved his performance to averaging over 80 percent of points earned by the 10th week of the program. While the chart does not show all of the student's data, this student's criteria were shifted from 75 to 80 and finally to 85 percent of daily points. The student was successful with the program and finally graduated after 15 weeks of the intervention.

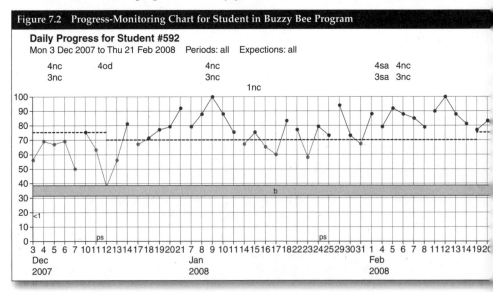

Figure 7.2   Progress-Monitoring Chart for Student in Buzzy Bee Program

This use of charted data for progress monitoring demonstrates how Tier II interventions can be based on wise use of daily performance data. Data are used for the decision-making process, and students, teachers, and parents are kept informed about how the student progressing in the program and toward ultimate goals. The data can be collected efficiently, and once a mentor checks the student out daily, student data can be entered in 15-minutes using a Web-based application.

Improved Relationships With Adults at School

Researchers have concluded that the *quality* of students' relationships with staff and faculty is connected to their school outcomes (Finn, 1989; McPartland, 1994). Sinclair and her colleagues (1998) emphasized this in their discussion of why building connections with students is important in school (see Chapter 5). The type of interpersonal relationships that teachers and students develop and the types of school activities a student becomes involved in are major factors in a child's positive social development (Connell & Welborn, 1991; McPartland, 1994). Additionally, when children do not develop positive relationships with their parents or guardians, they are likely to develop behavior problems at home and in school. Finally, behavior problems are related to poor academic performance and school failure (Anderson, Christenson, & Sinclair, 2004; Sinclair et al., 1998).

Developing relationships with children in a Tier II intervention may be perplexing sometimes, rewarding at other times, and very challenging with a few students. This is due to the backgrounds and experiences of children, some of which may make the child hesitant in or resistant to forming relationships with adults. Trust with these children has to be developed over time and comes from repeated interactions that are consistent and positive.

Interviews with at-risk children indicate that they value coaches or mentors who are trustworthy, attentive, empathetic, available, positive, respectful, and virtuous. Behaviors that illustrate these characteristics include doing what you say you will, putting the child at the center of concern, looking at how the child feels, willingly making time for the child, genuinely saying positive things about the child, involving children in decisions that affect them, and being a role model. When you couple the notion of being strength based with the values and actions above, you will be developing what psychologists refer to as "unconditional positive regard."

This is not always an easy stance to take with a child who is displaying a behavior problem. When a student has shoved another student, knocked over a desk in classroom, or argued with the teacher, a typical adult reaction might be to blame the child for misbehavior and then punish him or her for the behavior. We are encouraging coaches to take another approach, considered "authoritative," which is neither overly "authoritarian" nor overly "permissive." When students misbehave, we expect the coach to be available and attentive to the children's needs. We expect that the coach would spend time listening to the children explain their perceptions of any problems they encountered and attempt to have the children discuss how they behaved and what they "got" from the misbehavior. This is often called identifying the "function" or "purpose" of a child's behavior. The following suggestions are provided for coaches to improve their relationships with students:

- Use appropriate volume, tone of voice, and language.
- Do not take the student's frustration personally.
- Tell the student, "I am listening to you so we can solve the problem together."
- Let the student explain his or her feelings, without interrupting, while maintaining safety.

- Calmly explain why some things cannot happen or are not allowed in school.
- Offer alternatives to students when necessary.
- Use empathetic words like "I can see that you're frustrated."

Regular Parental Involvement

Whenever students are exhibiting classroom behavior problems that merit behavioral interventions, it is important to involve parents, family members, or guardians in the intervention work. In Tier II BEP and SRIS, it is recommended that a daily home note goes to parents/guardians so that they can review student progress and participate in reinforcing and encouraging school success. Communication among the coach, teachers, and parents is not always easy to accomplish, but it should be maintained as an important goal in behavior plans and planning process.

Many parents of students with behavior problems have received countless telephone calls relating problems that occurred at school. Communication with parents attempts to build greater trust, collaboration, and cooperation. Therefore, it makes sense that phone calls and home notes should emphasize the positive aspects of students' social progress. Even if the child has had difficult day, the teacher or coach involved with the parent should stay positive and suggest ways to help the student learn and use positive social skills. When there are significant behavioral issues at school, we suggest that the teacher or coach make a personal call to the parent and review the issues and make any further program adjustments with the parents involvement. Overall, it is good practice to coordinate communication efforts to families with other staff members, such as office staff, the teacher, and/or the counselor, to ensure that families are not overwhelmed or confused by multiple contacts.

SUMMARY OF TIER II BEHAVIOR PLANNING

This section has presented the steps and examples for implementing a Tier II Behavior Plan. To summarize, Tier II interventions are embedded in and consistent with a SPBS system. In this case, we described the Buzzy Bee program from the SPBS and then showed how it can be applied systematically with one to three students in a classroom. The students are identified through teacher nomination, systematic screening, or from review of ODR data. Once a student is identified, he or she is assigned to a coach, who explains the DPR, the system of checking in and out, and how points can be exchanged for reinforcement. The coach supervises and monitors student progress by charting data daily or weekly and by having frequent discussions with the teacher. The coach and teacher work hard to improve the student's social relationships with them as adults and with other peers in the classroom. Finally, the coach, teacher, and parents/guardians work collaboratively to have a unified system for improving student social skills. This approach has been shown to be highly effective with about 75 percent of students who use the intervention within a school practicing SPBS (see Cheney et al., in press; Hawken et al., 2008; Todd, Campbell, Meyer, & Horner, 2008).

INDIVIDUALIZED BEHAVIOR INTERVENTION PLAN (BIP)

The Tier II intervention approach described above, with a coach, daily report card, daily goals, reinforcement, and progress monitoring, was developed for students with emerging behavior problems that put them at risk of school failure. SRIS and BEP approaches are for groups of students and, thus, are typically not individualized to any great extent so they can be quickly and efficiently implemented with any student. When a student is not responsive to a Tier II intervention, however, teachers should work with their school behavior support teams to modify and develop an individualized behavior plan for the student.

Individualized behavior plans have been emphasized in both the Individuals with Disabilities Education Act (IDEA) of 1997 and IDEIA of 2004 within the language of Positive Behavioral Supports (PBS) "in the case of a child whose behavior impedes the child's learning or that of others" (20 U.S.C. § 1414[d][3][B][I]). Behavior intervention plans (BIP) should be strength based (Horner, Sugai, Todd, & Lewis-Palmer, 2000) and based on results from a functional assessment (FA). The goal of the BIP is to develop interventions that will significantly decrease problem behaviors while concurrently teaching and sustaining positive social skills. Development of the BIP requires the involvement of behavior support team members, who will assist the teacher so that the student be more successful over the course of his or her academic career (Bambara & Kern, 2005).

Roles and Input for Behavior Plans

Classroom teachers should rely on the expertise of other professionals and family members of the student. A typical behavior support team consists of parents/guardians, the student when appropriate, general education teacher(s), special education teacher, an administrator, school psychologist, and school counselor (Horner, Sugai, Todd, & Lewis-Palmer, 2000). Other members from the community and school may be involved when they can provide additional insight into the student's behaviors and ideas for effective strategies. Each team member is important, offering valuable information for the development and implementation of an effective behavior intervention plan.

Formal and Informal Assessment by Team Members

At the initial team meeting, each member should be assigned the task of collecting some baseline information on the student's functioning. This information will be used to help develop an effective BIP. Information collected falls into two categories: formal assessments and informal assessments. Formal assessments are any materials that document the student's behaviors, abilities, or personal history. Examples are a list of medications, legal proceedings with family and/or child, expulsions/suspensions, disciplinary actions, absences, staff/parent/student interviews, office discipline referrals, and any direct observations of the student. Just as important is informal information, which is any undocumented life changes, naturalistic observations of the child, interactions with community members, student self-reports, and discussions between teachers and school staff (Sugai, Lewis-Palmer, & Hagan-Burke, 2000). To be effective and efficient for the classroom and, possibly, home settings, assessments should occur within a two-week period and reported back to the team so that initial intervention work can begin.

The assessments enable the team to answer multiple questions in relation to each problem behavior. Team members should be able to describe the behaviors of concern; identify when, where, and to what extent each behavior occurs or does not occur in multiple environments; classify different consequences that maintain or deter the behaviors; and write a summary statement for each behavior. Such assessments will allow the team to develop clear descriptions for each problem behavior.

Example: Addressing Student Behavior Problems

Returning to the work done by Ms. Tomaz at Sunset, recall that she had followed the schoolwide Buzzy Bee program, had made some environmental improvements after a peer observation, and had used the Tier II Bee program with three of her students. After reviewing the progress-monitoring notes for the students, she concluded that two of her three students were successful and meeting classroom social expectations on a daily basis. However, one student, Laurence, was not successful, and after eight weeks of using the DPR and charting daily performance data, he was still only meeting his daily goals about 50 percent of the time. Laurence was, therefore, a candidate for a Tier III behavior plan. The teacher met with the behavior support team, and all agreed to start the Tier III planning and intervention process for Laurence.

The first step was to agree on clear descriptions of each problem behavior that would be addressed in the Behavior Intervention Plan. Clear, objective definitions enabled team members to understand what the behavior clearly looked like. The team used clear behavioral definitions for discussing when, where, and to what extent they had or had not seen the specific behaviors. It is important to acknowledge when and where behaviors occur because this information dictates the types of interventions that will ultimately developed by the team. Next, the team discussed current consequences that maintain the identified behaviors. With this information, the team helped the teacher write a summary statement (also known as a hypothesis statement), which concisely identified the antecedent events that triggered the behavior, described the problem behavior, and identified the consequence (Bambara & Kern, 2005; O'Neill et al., 1997). Summary statements provide a clear picture of the behavior to facilitate the team's development of interventions focused on decreasing problem behaviors while providing school-appropriate replacement/alternative behaviors.

Developing and Evaluating Interventions

Once all summary statements are completed, the team can begin developing interventions for each problem behavior. It is important that all members of the team are encouraged to contribute ideas or recommendations. Allowing parents, community members, and school staff to participate will support the incorporation of culturally appropriate strategies (Kea, Cartledge, & Bowman, 2002). Using culturally appropriate strategies will support the plan, along with maintaining the student's and family's beliefs and values.

Prior to the meeting, support parents in becoming involved by brainstorming techniques they have used in the past to reduce their child's problem behaviors. These solutions will be discussed during the brainstorming part of the meeting. During brainstorming, which should be around 15 minutes, write down everyone's ideas on a board, computer screen, or someplace else where the entire group can see everyone's ideas. Once brainstorming is complete, the group starts analyzing each idea for appropriateness and effectiveness. Both appropriateness and effectiveness can be analyzed by making sure strategies are supported in peer-reviewed literature (i.e., journal articles or books). The ideas must also be culturally significant and beneficial to the individual student, family, and community (Kea et al., 2002). Multicultural research offers many interventions, which are peer reviewed, to support a child. Thus, school team members should review culturally appropriate, peer-reviewed literature prior to the meeting.

Using Evidence-Based Practices

The Individuals with Disabilities Education Improvement Act of 2004 (IDEIA) requires interventions "based on peer-reviewed research to the extent practicable" (20 U.S.C. § 1414[d][1][A][i][IV]). *Peer-reviewed research*, as defined in IDEIA, is research that has been published in a scholarly journal article that is reviewed and edited by experts in the field (peers). The interventions or strategy suggested by an article will not be published if peers do not find the research valid and reliable. Many Positive Behavior Supports for students needing a behavioral intervention plan are published in peer-reviewed literature.

Some ideas for the BIP may come from the student or family or community members with little or no basis in peer-reviewed research. These interventions should not be dismissed, as it is important to incorporate culturally appropriate interventions that work in terms of the student's diverse and individual needs. The team can compromise by making small modifications of the peer-reviewed intervention to incorporate the student's culture.

While collaborating on culturally appropriate and peer-reviewed interventions, the group should also remember there is more than one solution to a problem behavior. Multiple solutions may be needed due to different environments, times of day, and other student factors. If multiple interventions exist for a problem behavior, there is nothing wrong with picking one to start off with, then changing to a different intervention if data show the first intervention is unsuccessful (Walker, Ramsey, & Gresham, 2004).

To help keep everyone focused providing appropriate interventions for the student's problem behaviors, the case manager or special education teacher should create a summary of the plan. This plan should define specific behaviors, strategies to use for each problem behavior, replacement/alternative skills the student will learn, person/people responsible for implementing/using particular intervention, and a re-evaluation schedule.

Table 7.2 is the BIP that was developed by Ms. Tomaz and her team for Laurence. The team worked with Ms. Tomaz to narrow areas of concern down to two primary behaviors. The first was a class or group of behaviors that was defined as "refusing to do work"; these included arguing, talking back, being out of his seat, and disrupting peers with talking during math time. The second was fighting on the playground during recess. The team proposed two beginning interventions for Laurence: one in class, which included self-monitoring and reinforcement of cooperative classroom skills, and the other on the playground, which included instruction and reinforcement of game skills. The team planned to meet and evaluate Laurence's progress during a scheduled weekly evaluation time.

Table 7.2 Behavior Intervention Plan	
BEHAVIOR INTERVENTION PLAN	Date Created: 07/06/2009
Student's Name: Laurence Shiro	Grade: 3
Section A	
Description of Problem Behaviors	1. Refuses to work (argues with teacher, talks back, is out of seat, and disrupts peers by talking) on individual math assignments, such as worksheets. 2. Fights (yells, physically pushes, or places his body in close proximity to others' faces) with peers on the playground during recess.

(Continued)

Table 7.2 (Continued)	
Section A	
Antecedents	1. Laurence struggles with math. It is his hardest subject. He also struggles with staying focused during individual time. 2. Laurence does not understand how to share, ask to enter into a game, or play by someone else's rules.
Consequences of Behaviors	1. When Laurence does not complete his individual math assignments, he is removed from the classroom and put in the hallway. He gains the teacher's attention, and she works through assignment with him. 2. Laurence loses recess privilege and stands on "wall." Students give Laurence the item and walk away. Students fight back with Laurence.
Behavioral Objectives	1. Laurence will work on grade-level individual math assignments during designated time and finish assignments. 2. Laurence will interact positively with his peers by sharing school equipment, asking to play with others, and participating in a game with someone else's rules during recess.

Data to Be Collected: Discipline referrals from recess fights, amount of individual math work completed, frequency of disruptions during individual math time

Section B		
Antecedent/Environment: **(Individual Math Time)** 1. Self-Management: Monitor his behavior (Smith & Sugai, 2000).	**Replacement/** **Alternative Skill:** 1. Laurence will self-monitor behaviors during math class and check in with teacher at the end of math period. He will receive positive reinforcements for using cooperative class skills when he meets his predetermined criteria.	**Contact:** 1. Ms. Block, School Counselor 2. Ms. Tomaz, General Education Teacher 3. Mr. & Mrs. Shiro, Parents

Evaluation Schedule: General education teacher and school counselor will review progress weekly and report to parents via e-mail or phone call.

| **Antecedent/Environment**
(Recess):
1. Teach cooperative play skills.
2. Assign peer buddy.
3. Use point card and reinforcement for cooperative play. | **Replacement/**
Alternative Skill:
1. Laurence will use cooperative play skills to join and play games at recess.
2. Laurence will listen to and talk with his peer buddy about game rules.
3. Laurence will follow game rules and participate appropriately in game for 10–20 minutes. | **Contact:**
1. Ms. Block, School Counselor
2. Ms. Tomaz, General Education Teacher
3. Mr. & Mrs. Shiro, Parents
4. Laurence, Student Carter, Peer Buddy |

Evaluation Schedule: The school team (school counselor, behavior support team, recess staff, and general education teacher) will review Laurence's progress weekly, and the school counselor will check in with both Laurence and his peer buddy. Laurence's parents will be notified through e-mail or a phone call on Laurence's progress each week.

Addressing the Function of Behavior

Interventions to address the problem behaviors should focus on answering the question "Why?" Why was Laurence, for example, refusing to work on individual math homework and fighting with peers during recess? Students may use these behaviors because they do not have positive social skills to obtain a teacher's or peers attention or to escape situations, such as a difficult or uncomfortable task. Students can have many reasons for obtaining and escaping; interventions must gradually work toward desirable social skills while considering the preferred function for the behavior.

Table 7.3 displays how the two interventions chosen for Laurence can meet the perceived function of his behavior. If Laurence is seeking attention, then both the self-monitoring and the peer assistance approaches should increase the amount of attention by the teacher and peers. The teacher can attend to this issue by positioning the student closer to her and checking in with him more often. Peers can be used in the process by serving as buddies and tutors. If Laurence is finding math too difficult or frustrating, he may be refusing to work because he thinks he will ultimately fail anyway and feel embarrassed. His arguing, defiance, and peer interruptions may be a result of his motivation to escape the math work. Ms. Tomaz can use this knowledge to design the intervention by decreasing his frustration and giving him work that is closer to his level.

Table 7.3 Evidence-Based Strategies Matching Interventions by Function (Obtain Attention/Objects or Escape From Difficult/Unwanted Tasks)

Function	Intervention Strategy	Example	Research
Attention	Student support	• Answer questions as a team with a peer or peers. • Engage in peer tutoring/learning.	Armendariz & Umbreit, 1999; Bacon & Bloom, 2000; Morrison, Kamps, Garcia, & Parker, 2001; Shukla, Kennedy, & Cushing, 1999
	Increased proximity to student	• Move seating arrangement. • Use explicit routines and expectations within the classroom.	Scott & Nelson, 1999; Shukla et al., 1999
	Self-management of activities	• Student tallies behaviors and receives reward when levels achieved. • Completes work and demonstrates appropriate behaviors.	Barry & Messer, 2003; Brooks, Todd, Tofflemoyer, & Horner, 2003; Callahan & Rademacher, 1999; Lee, Simpson, & Shogren, 2007; Smith & Sugai, 2000; Todd, Horner, & Sugai, 1999
Function	**Intervention**	**Example**	**Research**
Escape	Modifing difficulty of the task	• Shorten sentences required for paragraph. • Provide breaks during lesson. • Reduce number of pages required. • Provide more challenging work.	Moore, Anderson, & Kumar, 2005; Umbreit, Lane, & Dejud, 2004

(Continued)

Function	Intervention	Example	Research
Table 7.3 (Continued)			
	Providing choices	• Allow student to choose ○ sequence of completing tasks. ○ where to work on task. ○ whom to work with on task (peer).	Dunlap et al., 1994; Vaughn & Horner, 1997
	Self-monitoring of activities/behaviors	• Student monitors work and checks off when completed. • Reinforced after completion of predetermined number.	Smith & Sugai, 2000; Stahr, Cushing, Lane, & Fox, 2006; Todd et al., 1999

Addressing Skill Deficits

The interventions listed above along with others developed by the team can only be successful if the student has learned the appropriate behaviors necessary to replace the problem behaviors. Many students do not have the necessary skills to demonstrate appropriate school behaviors. Alternative skills provide students with replacement behaviors to use during situations they they may want to obtain attention or escape situations. Replacement skills (behaviors) teach students effective, socially acceptable behaviors that allow the student to obtain the desired outcomes without using an inappropriate problem behavior. These skills may provide students with coping, tolerance, or general adaptive skills (Bambara & Knoster, 1998). Students with problem behaviors can acquire these skills by receiving social skills lessons. Social skills training is an effective intervention to help students learn alternative and/or replacement skills, resulting in a decrease in problem behaviors (Cook, Gresham, Kern, Barreras, & Crews, 2008). Providing a student with a set of school-appropriate social skills can increase his or her chances of success in future academic work.

Developing and implementing behavior intervention plans with Positive Behavior Supports sets up the team to support the student in being successful in school. The multidisciplinary team works together to provide the student with culturally relevant, peer-reviewed interventions that decrease problem behaviors. Decreasing the problem behaviors will increase the student's prosocial behaviors, which has been correlated to increase in academic engagement in the classroom (Kilian, Fish, & Miniago, 2007). The student increases his or her chances of decreasing problem behaviors when the team works together to provide an effective behavior intervention plan.

CONCLUSION

This chapter has provided a process for developing behavior plans for teaching positive, prosocial skills while reducing problem behaviors. We recommended and provided examples of using the SPBS model and have attempted to show how it is similar to an RTI model. Figure 7.3 summarizes the building blocks of the process we have discussed. The foundation is a block of schoolwide features that are formulated, monitored, and evaluated by a leadership team and implemented by all staff. Within classrooms, teachers need to focus on the next block, effective classroom management. When schoolwide features and classroom management approaches don't reach a few students, Tier II and III interventions need to be implemented. These four blocks form the primary structures and strategies for impacting positive school social behavior. Teachers who follow these recommendations should see an improved classroom environment and enhanced student social and academic performance.

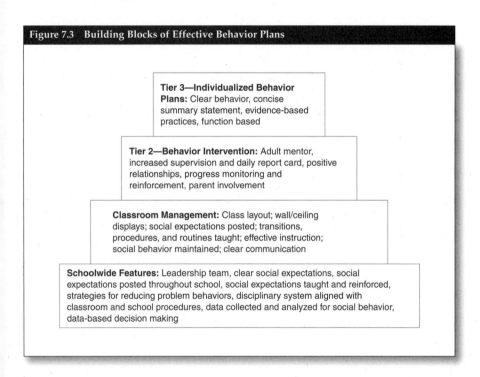

Figure 7.3 Building Blocks of Effective Behavior Plans

Tier 3—Individualized Behavior Plans: Clear behavior, concise summary statement, evidence-based practices, function based

Tier 2—Behavior Intervention: Adult mentor, increased supervision and daily report card, positive relationships, progress monitoring and reinforcement, parent involvement

Classroom Management: Class layout; wall/ceiling displays; social expectations posted; transitions, procedures, and routines taught; effective instruction; social behavior maintained; clear communication

Schoolwide Features: Leadership team, clear social expectations, social expectations posted throughout school, social expectations taught and reinforced, strategies for reducing problem behaviors, disciplinary system aligned with classroom and school procedures, data collected and analyzed for social behavior, data-based decision making

REFERENCES

Anderson, A. R., Christenson, S. L, & Sinclair, M. F. (2004). Check & connect: The importance of relationships for promoting engagement with school. *Journal of School Psychology, 42*(2), 95–113.
Armendariz, F., & Umbreit, J. (1999). Using active responding to reduce disruptive behavior in a general education classroom. *Journal of Positive Behavior Interventions, 1*, 152–158.

Bacon, E., & Bloom, L. (2000). Listening to student voices. *Teaching Exceptional Children, 32*, 38–43.

Bambara, L. M., & Kern, L. (2005). *Individualized supports for students with problem behaviors: Designing positive behavior plans.* New York: Guilford Press.

Bambara, L. M., & Knoster, T. (1998). Designing Positive Behavior Support plans. In *Innovations* (No. 13). Washington, DC: American Association on Mental Retardation.

Barry, L. M., & Messer, J. J. (2003). A practical application of self-management for students diagnosed with attention-deficit/hyperactivity disorder. *Journal of Positive Behavior Interventions, 5*, 238–248.

Brooks, A., Todd, A. W., Tofflemoyer, S., & Horner, R. H. (2003). Use of functional assessment and a self-management system to increase academic engagement and work completion. *Journal of Positive Behavior Interventions, 5*, 144–152.

Callahan, K., & Rademacher, J. A. (1999). Using self-management strategies to increase the on-task behavior of a student with autism. *Journal of Positive Behavior Interventions, 1*, 117–122.

Cheney, D., Flower, A., & Templeton, T. (2008). Applying response to intervention metrics in the social domain for students at risk of developing emotional or behavioral disorders. *Journal of Special Education, 42*, 108–126.

Cheney, D., & Lynass, L. (2009). *Social Response to Intervention System.* Seattle: University of Washington.

Cheney, D., Lynass, L., Flower, A., Waugh, M., & Iwaszuk, W. (in press). The Check, Connect, and Expect program: A targeted, tier two intervention in the School-wide Positive Behavior Support model. *Preventing School Failure.*

Cook, C. R., Gresham, F. M., Kern, L., Barreras, R. B., & Crews, S. D. (2008). Social skills training for secondary students with emotional and/or behavioral disorders. *Journal of Emotional and Behavioral Disorders, 16*, 131–144.

Crone, D. A., Horner, R. H., & Hawken, L. S. (2004). *Responding to problem behavior in schools: The behavior education program.* New York: Guilford Press.

Evertson, C., & Emmer, E. (2009). *Classroom management for elementary teachers* (8th ed.). Upper Saddle River, NJ: Pearson.

Finn, J. D. (1989). Withdrawing from school. *Review of Educational Research, 59*, 117–142.

Dunlap, G., DePerczel, M., Clarke, S., Wilson, D., Wright, S., White, R., et al. (1994). Choice making to promote adaptive behavior for students with emotional and behavioral challenges. *Journal of applied behavior analysis, 27*, 505–518.

Fairbanks, S., Sugai, G., Guardino, D., & Lathrop, M. (2007) Response to Intervention: Examining classroom behavior support in second grade. *Exceptional Children, 73*, 288–310.

Filter, K. J., McKenna, M. K., Benedict, E. A., Horner, R. H., Todd, A. W., & Watson, J. (2007). Check in/check out: A post-hoc evaluation of an efficient, secondary-level targeted intervention for reducing problem behaviors in schools. *Education and Treatment of Children, 30*(1), 69–84.

Hawken, L. S. (2006). School psychologists as leaders in the implementation of a targeted intervention: The behavior education program. *School Psychology Quarterly, 21*, 91–111.

Hawken, L. S., & Horner, R. (2003). Implementing a targeted intervention within a school-wide system of behavior support. *Journal of Behavioral Education, 12*, 225–240.

Hawken, L. S., MacLeod, K. S., & Rawlings, L. (2007). Effects of the Behavior Education Program (BEP) on office discipline referrals of elementary school students. *Journal of Positive Behavior Interventions, 9*, 94–101.

Hawken, L. S., Peterson, H., Mootz, J., & Anderson, C. (2006). *The Behavior Education Program video: A check-in, check-out intervention for students at risk.* New York: Guilford Press.

Hawken, L., Vincent, C., & Schumann, J. (2008). Response to Intervention for social behavior. *Journal of Emotional and Behavioral Disorders, 16*, 213–225.

Horner, R. (2007). *Is School-wide Positive Behavior Support an evidence-based practice: A research summary.* Eugene: Technical Assistance Center on PBIS, University of Oregon.

Horner, R., Sugai, G., Todd, A., & Lewis-Palmer, T. (2000). Elements of behavior support plans: A technical brief. *Exceptionality, 8*, 205–215.

Individuals with Disabilities Education Act (IDEA) of 1997, 20 U.S.C. § 1400 *et seq.*

Individuals with Disabilities Education Improvement Act (IDEIA) of 2004, 20 U.S.C. § 1400 *et seq.*

Irvin, L. K., Horner, R. H., Ingram, K., Todd, A. W., Sugai, G., Sampson, N., et al. (2006). Using office discipline referral data for decision-making about student behavior in elementary and middle schools: An empirical investigation of validity. *Journal of Positive Behavior Interventions, 8,* 10–23.

Irvin, L. K., Tobin, T., Sprague, J., Sugai, G., & Vincent, C. (2004). Validity of office discipline referral measures as indices of school-wide behavioral status and effects of school-wide behavioral interventions. *Journal of Positive Behavioral Interventions 6,* 131–147.

Kea, C. D., Cartledge, G., & Bowman, L. J. (2002). Interventions for African American learners with behavioral problems. In B. A. Ford & F. Obiakor (Eds.), *Creating successful learning environments for African American learners with exceptionalities* (pp. 79–94). Austin, TX: Pro-ED.

Kilian, J. M., Fish, M. C., & Maniago, E. B. (2007). Making schools safe: A system-wide school intervention to increase student prosocial behaviors and enhance school climate. *Journal of Applied School Psychology, 23,* 1–30.

Lee, S., Simpson, R. L., & Shogren, K. A. (2007). Effects and implications of self-management for students with autism: A meta-analysis. *Focus on Autism and Other Developmental Disabilities, 22,* 2–13.

Lehr, C. A., Sinclair, M. F., & Christenson, S. L. (2004). Addressing student engagement and truancy prevention during the elementary years: A replication study of the Check & Connect model. *Journal of Education for Students Placed at Risk, 9*(3), 279–301.

McPartland, J. M. (1994). Dropout prevention in theory and practice. In R. J. Rossi (Ed.), *Schools and students at risk: Context and framework for positive change* (pp. 255–276). New York: Teachers College. (ERIC Document Reproduction Service No. ED366695)

O'Neill, R. E., Horner, R. H., Albin, R. W., Sprague, J. R., Storey, K., & Newton, J. S. (1997). *Functional assessment and program development for problem behavior: A practical handbook.* Pacific Grove, CA: Brooks/Cole.

Scott, T. M., & Nelson, C. M. (1999). Using functional behavioral assessment to develop effective intervention plans: Practical classroom applications. *Journal of Positive Behavior Interventions, 1,* 242–251.

Sinclair, M. F., Christenson, S. L., Evelo, D. L., & Hurley, C. M. (1998). Dropout prevention for high-risk youth with disabilities: Efficacy of a sustained school engagement procedure. *Exceptional Children, 65*(1), 7–21.

Sinclair, M. F., Christenson, S. L., & Thurlow, M .L. (2005). Promoting school completion of urban secondary youth with emotional or behavioral disabilities. *Exceptional Children, 71*(4), 465–482.

Smith, B. W., & Sugai, G. (2000). A self-management functional assessment-based behavior support plan for a middle school student with EBD. *Journal of Positive Behavior Interventions, 2,* 208–217.

Sprick, R., Garrison, M., & Howard, L. (1998). *CHAMPs: A proactive and positive approach to classroom management,* Longmont, CO: Sopris West.

Stahr, B., Cushing, D., Lane, K., & Fox, J. (2006). Efficacy of a function-based intervention in decreasing off-task behavior exhibited by a student with ADHD. *Journal of Positive Behavior Interventions, 8,* 201–211.

Sugai, G., Lewis-Palmer, T., & Hagan-Burke, S. (2000). Overview of the functional behavioral assessment process. *Exceptionality, 8,* 149–160.

Todd, A. W., Campbell, A. L., Meyer, G. G., & Horner, R. H. (2008). The effects of a targeted intervention to reduce problem behaviors. *Journal of Positive Behavior Interventions, 10,* 46–55.

Todd, A. W., Horner, R. H., & Sugai, G. (1999). Self-monitoring and self-recruited praise: Effects on problem behavior, academic engagement, and work completion in a typical classroom. *Journal of Positive Behavior Interventions, 1*(2), 66–122.

Umbreit, J., Lane, K. L., & Dejud, C. (2004). Improving classroom behavior by modifying task difficulty: Effects of increasing the difficulty of too-easy tasks. *Journal of Positive Behavior Interventions, 6*(1), 13–20.

Vaughn, B. J., & Horner, R. H. (1997). Identifying instructional tasks that occasion problem behaviors and assessing the effects of student versus teacher choice among these tasks. *Journal of Applied Behavior Analysis, 30,* 299–312.

Walker, B., Cheney, D., Stage, S., & Blum, C. (2005). Schoolwide screening and Positive Behavior Support: Identifying and supporting students at risk of school failure. *Journal of Positive Behavior Interventions, 7,* 194–204.

Walker, H. M., Ramsey, E., & Gresham, F. M. (2004). *Antisocial behavior in school: Evidence-based practices.* Belmont, CA: Thomson/Wadsworth.

Walker, H. M., & Severson, H. H. (1992). *Systematic screening for behavior disorders* (2nd ed.). Austin, TX: Pro-Ed.

Walker, H. M., & Severson, H. H. (2007). Proactive, early screening to detect behaviorally at-risk students: Issues, approaches, emerging innovations, and professional practices. *Journal of School Psychology, 45,* 193–223.

8

Effective Home-School Partnerships

In this chapter, we

- review why home-school partnerships are important,
- describe characteristics of home-school partnerships,
- identify and describe effective home-school partnership programs and practices,
- describe critical features that support the implementation and effective use of home-school partnership programs, and
- review evidence of effectiveness of home-school partnership programs.

Parent involvement has been a core value in special education since the passage of the Education for All Handicapped Children Act of 1975. The law required schools to include parents of children with disabilities in educational program planning, decision making, and evaluation. Since this initial mandate, the role of families has changed significantly with each reauthorization of the law. The parents of children with disabilities are involved with their child's education on multiple levels. Part C of the Individuals with Disabilities Education Act of 1997 (IDEA) calls for family-centered services that address the need of the whole family of infants and toddlers with disabilities. Early interventions design and implement programs that use family strengths to facilitate the child's development and learning, while assisting the family in finding resources for meeting their needs. Such family-centered approaches are the recommended practices: they tend to encourage a sense of self-efficacy and greater parent satisfaction with services (Trivette, Dunst, Boyd, & Hamby, 1995).

Moreover, for children with disabilities ages 3 to 21 years, the law requires that parents are to be included in decisions regarding assessment, placement in special education, educational program planning, and confidential treatment of records, as well as whether to participate in mediation to solve disputes or not to participate at all. These are considered basic rights concerning the family's participation, but educators are encouraged to go beyond the minimum legal requirements to develop truly collaborative home-school partnerships (Smith, Gartin, Murdick, & Hilton, 2006), including offering meaningful opportunities to participate in their child's education at school and at home.

In addition to IDEA, the passage of the No Child Left Behind Act of 2001 (NCLB) expanded parental involvement and parents options with regard to their children's education. NCLB requires local school districts, working in collaboration with parents, to develop written polices for parent involvement. In addition, school districts are to strengthen teachers' and staff members capacity to work effectively with families, provide parents with material and training that will help them improve student achievement, and design and conduct parent involvement activities that help guide their children's learning. The goal of parental involvement as specified by by both laws is to maximize the learning potential of children.

The provisions in these laws and the research on the effects of parental involvement on school achievement clearly indicate the importance of schools and families working together, suggesting that the relationship is mutually supportive; that is, the relationship between families and schools is one in which both contribute and benefit. The current focus is on forming partnerships. Ideally, a home-school partnership is a collaborative relationship in which all partners are valued for their knowledge, judgment, and experiences to improve outcomes for students (Turnbull, Turnbull, Erwin, & Sodak, 2006).

THE IMPORTANCE OF HOME-SCHOOL PARTNERSHIPS

Epstein (2001) described three overlapping spheres of influence that are the major contexts for children's development and learning: the family, the school, and the community. Time, experiences in families, and experiences in schools control the degree of overlap among the three. Students engage in activities that influence their school success in all three areas and are influenced by their peers, teachers, and families. Ultimately, the theory hypothesizes that students will learn more when home, school, and community work together.

Research conducted over the last three decades provides a persuasive argument for the critical role that families play in facilitating their children's educational success. Several comprehensive reviews of the research on parent involvement (Fan & Chen, 2001; Henderson & Berla, 1994; Henderson & Mapp, 2002; Jeynes as cited in Jeynes, 2005) document the benefits to students in schools, including improved motivation, homework completion, and academic performance; fewer absences; increased self confidence; and higher graduation rates and rates of postsecondary education.

The benefits to schools have also been documented. One benefit is that schools with strong home-school connections are likely to exhibit higher levels of trust than those without, resulting in better student morale and a more positive climate (Hoy, 2002), better teacher morale, and higher ratings of teachers by parents (Decker & Decker, 2003). Building trusting relationships within schools makes them more inviting places for parents. Parents who feel that they can trust the professionals who work with their child are more inclined to participate in their child's education. When they feel welcomed in their child's classroom and school, parents participate in more informal and open communication with professionals (Soodak & Erwin, 2000).

Families and professionals can benefit significantly from each other. Hallahan, Kauffman, and Pullen (2008) posited that parents and teachers have a "symbiotic relationship" in which both groups can benefit from each other. As we know, parents have a wealth of information about their child in terms of background information and medical history that may help understand child learning and behavior. Working together, parents and teachers can determine child interests, strengths, and needs that are helpful to planning and implementing effective academic and social instruction. Parents can follow up on teacher instruction by helping at home with assigned tasks and behavior plans. Teachers, on the other hand, can enable parents to become more actively involved in their child's education by providing information on school progress, including them in the teaching and reinforcing of social skills, and helping them to stay abreast of opportunities for their children.

A belief in sharing the responsibility for educating children is a characteristic of home-school partnerships, which emphasize collaborative problem solving and shared decision-making strategies to provide students with consistent, congruent messages about learning and behavior. Building relationships and finding ways to work together to promote the educational experiences and school successes of all students is essential. In home-school partnerships, both parents and teachers are valued for their contributions to child growth and development.

PRINCIPLES AND KEY FEATURES OF HOME-SCHOOL PARTNERSHIPS

Because families, schools, and communities are so different, no single model for establishing home-school partnerships exists. In fact, if anything is true, it is that one size does not fit all when it comes to planning and implementing home-school connections. Partnerships are more effective if they are site-specific in development (Kagan, 1984). That is, school personnel, in collaboration with family members, determine the elements of their home-school program. Smith and colleagues (2006) offered the following set of interrelated principles to guide educators work with families of children with disabilities to develop partnerships:

- *Develop a sense of community.* When families and professionals feel they are a part of a community, they are more committed to its success. A school that promotes community building is dedicated to an open, welcoming, and accepting environment.
- *Promote equality between family members and professionals.* Considering the wealth of information parents have about their child, they must be recognized for their important role in their child's education. To establish equality, it is important to recognize parents as knowledgeable resources and value them as key to their child's success.
- *Share responsibility and decision making.* Shared decision making assumes that academic and social outcomes result from the interaction of qualities that the child brings from home with the qualities of the school. As such, family members should participate in decision making with regard to all aspects of schooling (i.e., they are recruited to be members of school advisory groups and school governance, as well as to plan for their own child's education). The notion of shared responsibility for educational outcomes is at the heart of home-school partnerships.
- *Consider family culture.* It is critical to recognize, value, and affirm the strengths of families, especially when families are from culturally diverse backgrounds. Boethel (2003), in reviewing the literature on diversity and school-family connections,

found that regardless of ethnicity, culture, or income, most families have high expectations for their children, and many are involved in their child's school programs. However, the form of that involvement on the part of families of lower socioeconomic status and/or of ethnic minorities generally differs from that of white, middle-class families. In addition, economic stressors will impact the extent and type of involvement among low-income families.

- *Focus on collaboration.* Collaboration is fostered when each partner shares a common goal of student success. Epstein's (2001) perspective of overlapping spheres of influences showed that families, schools, and communities have a common mission around children's learning. This common mission compels them to work together to produce the best outcomes for children.
- *Protect the integrity of the family.* The family is seen as a whole unit that collectively demonstrates strength and cohesion at multiple levels. Recognition of the family as a unit is crucial. Note that each family differs, and the primary caregiver for each child may not be a parent.
- *Improve family members advocacy skills.* Involving parents as partners recognizes that they are advocates of education and key resources to improve their child's growth and development. Families empowered as advocates for quality education, for their child and for all children, can also be supportive of needed systems change in today's schools (Shaheen & Spencer, 2001).

Christenson (2002) suggested that there are four important features of home-school collaboration:

1. Recognize that both home and school are microsystems that are used to operating autonomously. Collaborating with schools or families will require a change of beliefs about responsibility for teaching and learning, as well as growth and development.

2. Home-school collaboration is not restricted to a specific area. It may concern a child-centered issue (e.g., behavior, academic learning) or systems-level issue (e.g., school policy).

3. Home-school collaboration is a preventive rather than a remedial activity. The purpose of home-school collaboration is to improve student success and prevent conflict and alienation.

4. While parent-teacher relationships are crucial to student successful outcomes, home-school collaboration is a broader concept. It includes the primary home contact person, who may be a parent, grandparent, or even a neighbor. Likewise, school partners may be teachers, administrators, or other support personnel that contribute to the student's success.

In their analysis of 80 studies of parental involvement, Henderson and Mapp (2002) found that many forms of family involvement positively affect outcomes both socially and academically for children. They concluded that four aspects of home-school partnerships were evident across all studies:

Programs that successfully connect with families and community invite involvement, are welcoming, and address specific parental and community needs.

Parent involvement programs that are effective in engaging diverse families recognize cultural and class differences, address needs, and build on strengths.

Effective connections embrace a philosophy of partnership where power is shared—the responsibility for children's educational development is a collaborative enterprise among parents, school staff, and community members.

Organized initiatives to build parent and community leadership aimed at improving low-performing schools are growing and leading to promising results in low-income urban areas and the rural South. (p. 1)

CHARACTERISTICS OF EFFECTIVE HOME-SCHOOL PARTNERSHIPS

Research on effective home-school partnerships suggests that they have six central characteristics: communication, commitment, equity, respect, trust, and competency (Blue-Banning, Summers, Frankland, Nelson, & Beegle, 2004; Smith et al., 2006; Turnbull et al., 2010). Each will be discussed.

Communication

Communication is the foundation for successful home-school partnerships. The methods of communication that teachers, administrators, and family members use take many forms. The most important aspect of communication to keep in mind is that it is a two-way process. Families and school professionals have the opportunity to give input and be heard on all matters related to child outcomes and school policy. Communication between home and school should be positive, understandable, and respectful. Effective methods for communication take into consideration the cultural and linguistic backgrounds, lifestyles, and work schedules of families and school staff. Communication content to and from families can include information about the child, information on resources available to support the child in school and home, as well as school and family events. Effective communication style includes speaking positively and listening to one's partner.

While communication between home and school can take many forms, parent-teacher conferences are a regular occurrence in most schools and can be an extremely effective way to share information. These conferences are most successful if they are well planned and positive. Even if the conference focus is on poor achievement or behavior, teachers who are diplomatic and include positive information about the child will find parents are more willing to work together to solve the problem. If teachers present the attitude that they want each child to succeed, parents will respond positively and actively participate in a plan to help the child improve.

Scheduling conferences is crucial to success. Making times available that meet the lifestyles and schedules of families will increase attendance. Offering to come to their homes may be the only way to ensure meetings with some families will take place because of limited resources and transportation. It is important that the family is open to a home visit; they should know you are coming, and you should be cautious to avoid making them feel uncomfortable. When allowed, home visits can be very helpful in building the relationship, including mutual trust and reciprocity, because families see that teachers are willing to be flexible and supportive (Allen, 2008).

There are a number of other methods of communication between home and school. Home-note programs have been utilized to communicate with parents as part of a behavior management system when help is needed to reinforce certain behaviors. These are most successful if parents and teachers have agreed philosophically about the behavior management approach (Hallahan et al., 2008). Journals that go back and forth between school and home can help keep families and teachers apprised of important events. They are particularly useful with children with severe disabilities when they are well organized and jargon-free and include appropriate space for commenting. Also, procedures for their use should be agreed upon by teachers, therapists, and parents (Hall, Wolfe, & Bollig, 2003). E-mail is yet another form of written communication between home and school. Homework hotlines and homework Web sites are also becoming available in many schools. Although computer technology offers new streams of communication, schools will need to determine the appropriateness of their use based on their availability to the families in the school area. Communication methods are limited only by the imagination. Each school and classroom should investigate and use the methods that are most useful to the partners.

Commitment

Commitment refers to all members of the partnership sharing a sense of confidence in their mutual loyalty to the child and the family and a belief in the importance of the goals set for the child's success. This commitment goes beyond the point of service compelled by law. In their research, Blue-Banning and colleagues (2004) found that family members looked for an attitude of commitment from professionals that indicated their work was more than "just a paycheck." Other terms used to describe professionals who are committed are *flexible*, *available*, and *accessible*. For example, school professionals may arrange their own schedules so that families are able to get in touch with them or arrange times other than the workday to hold conferences. When professionals are willing to look beyond themselves, family members will see them as committed and are more likely to work with them to improve their child's educational outcomes.

Equity, Respect, and Trust

These three concepts are closely related. The concept of equality in home-school partnerships assumes that all partners have the same capacity to influence decisions made with regard to the child. When equity is apparent in the partnership, then family members, as well as professionals, are recognized for their knowledge, skills, and expertise. In promoting equality in the relationship, teachers work to understand the knowledge that family members have of their children, particularly experiences and cultural influences that may account for children's development, learning, and behavior, while providing opportunities for sharing this information.

When respectful partnerships are in place, each partner judges all others to be valuable members. In communicating with one another, respect is demonstrated when teachers, family members, and students treat each other with dignity (Turnbull, Turnbull, & Wehmeyer, 2009). Families suggest that respectful teachers are courteous to them (Blue-Banning et al., 2004). The simple gesture of calling parents by their last names or asking permission to use their first names is an example many parents appreciate. Other ways to be respectful of family members are being on time for meetings, acknowledging the time parents are taking to attend a meeting, and recognizing the contributions family members make to the discussion as important.

Respectful partnerships also honor cultural diversity. A number of barriers may limit home-school partnerships with families from culturally and linguistically diverse backgrounds. These include language differences, a lack of understanding of the American public school system, miscommunications, and past negative experiences with schools. Two possible solutions for these issues are interpreters and liaisons (Parette & Petch-Hogan, 2000). Liaisons with the community can help to inform family members, as well as build trust between school personnel and families. The liaison should be someone respected and trusted by the community. Interpreters can facilitate communication between home and school. It is essential that interpreters be adequately trained to ensure that information is exchanged accurately, and ideally they should have knowledge of the local community.

Honoring cultural diversity also includes developing a deeper understanding of and sensitivity to family priorities, needs, and resources (Parette & Petch-Hogan, 2000). To do this, school professionals need to understand cultural norms related to social behavior, family values, and communication styles (Harry, 2008) yet to do so without overgeneralizing specific characteristics to all families with whom they work. Allen (2008) described several school settings in which teachers worked with family members to address cultural differences. Activities included reading and discussing published cultural memoirs (i.e., autobiographies or short stories) and gathering photographs and other cultural artifacts to share.

As mentioned previously, a trustful environment is a necessity if home-school partnerships are to be successful. When parents feel they are welcomed to the table in a respectful manner and that their input is valued, their participation will be strengthened. Family members identify trust with regards to schools in three ways: reliability, safety, and discretion (Blue-Banning et al., 2004). Reliability refers to knowing that you can depend on someone (i.e., they will do what they say they will). For example, school professionals are reliable if they are careful not to make promises they can't keep. All parents need to know that their children are safe at school, and parents want their children to be nurtured and cared for both physically and emotionally (Baker, 1997/2001; Blue-Banning et al.). Finally, discretion refers to parents being certain that school professionals can be trusted with confidential information. We have discussed the value of information that parents and other family members share about their child that can benefit plans for the child's learning and behavior. As we encourage families to share this information, we must assure them that it will be treated with discretion.

The families that Soodak and Erwin (2000) spoke with stressed the importance of building trusting relationships between school professionals and families. To these parents, trusting relationships resulted from interactions that were open and mutually respectful. Parents felt welcomed to the school through a variety of formal opportunities to participate and through informal interactions with school personnel. Continued efforts to build respectful and trusting relationships sustain connections that support student learning (Allen, 2008).

Competency

Competency refers to being highly qualified for one's professional role (Turnbull et al., 2009). Several researchers have found that family members are very aware of the skill level of their child's teacher and other school professionals (Baker, 1997/2001; Blue-Banning et al., 2004). They want school professionals to demonstrate knowledge of "best practices," to be able to individualize instruction, and to differentiate instruction. Both NCLB and IDEA state that teachers should have high expectations for all students and that outcomes are driven by high educational standards. Parents have this expectation as well. Competent teachers are also lifelong learners who strive to improve their skills and are always open to new knowledge and experience.

While school professionals maybe extremely competent in their roles as teachers, related service providers, and school administrators, they may not have adequate skill in collaboration and team building to develop effective partnerships with families. Investigations of teacher preparation programs indicate that education on collaboration is limited (Broussard, 2000; Hoover-Dempsey, Walker, Jones, & Reed, 2002). Therefore, it may be necessary to provide this training as part of the design and development of a home-school partnership. Training provided to both teachers and other school personnel together may foster effective collaboration (Whitbread, Bruder, Fleming, & Park, 2007).

The principles for and characteristics of effective home-school partnerships indicate the complex nature of what may seem to be a simple endeavor. For schools to establish and maintain effective home-school partnerships, they must be willing to invest the necessary time and energy. Remembering that there is no "one-size-fits-all" approach to partnerships, schools will identify what teachers, administrators, staff, and family members determine to be the strengths, interests, and needs of their community and design appropriate strategies to respond. Once the partnership is established, members must regularly assess its effects based on the desired outcomes. While this approach may not be easily accomplished, the evidence clearly indicates the results for students (i.e., improved academic and social outcomes) are worth it.

HOME-SCHOOL PARTNERSHIPS AND CHALLENGING BEHAVIOR

Recent attention to home-school partnerships has been noted in the literature on Positive Behavior Intervention and Support, particularly as applied at the schoolwide level. One example of a successful application of Schoolwide Positive Behavior Supports and home-school partnerships is Positive Behavioral Interventions and Supports New Hampshire (PBIS-NH; Muscott et al., 2008). The PBIS-NH project identified family-friendly schools as incorporating the following values, which include the essential characteristics of home-school partnerships:

Families are informed of school activities in a variety of ways.

Families have access to information about how they can support their child's learning.

Families have access to information about how they can be involved in supporting learning in school through volunteering and assisting.

Families know what resources are available and how to access those resources. (p. 11)

The schools participating in the PBIS-NH program used Epstein's (2002) framework for developing home-school partnerships. The program developed the following activities that included key components of that framework.

- *Parenting and learning at home.* Parents were taught PBIS strategies so they could create a home environment conducive to studying and completing homework.

- *Two-way communication strategies.* Several schools created a monthly newsletter that featured a write-in parent advice section. Periodic surveys assessing parents' feelings of connectedness were distributed, and follow-up was done with nonresponders and non-English speakers.
- *Volunteering and shared decision making.* A variety of opportunities for volunteering were provided, and family members were encouraged to participate in leadership teams and other committees making decisions that affected schools, teachers, administrators, families, and students.

The PBIS-NH project has taken the concepts of effective home-school partnerships and applied it to an effective program for preventing behavioral problems. PBS easily lends itself to the concept of home-school partnerships. Lucyshyn, Horner, Dunlap, Albin, and Ben (2002) defined *family partnerships* in PBS as

> the establishment of a truly respectful, trusting, caring, and reciprocal relationship in which interventionists and family members believe in each other's ability to make important contributions to the support process; share their knowledge and expertise; and mutually influence the selection goals, the design of behavior support plans, and the quality of family-practitioner interactions. (p. 12)

This definition underscores the importance of the relationship to the success of PBS. Practicing adherence to this definition will encourage partnerships and increase the likelihood of full participation by families.

Families of children at risk for or exhibiting challenging behaviors are likely to present with difficulties that may inhibit establishing a home-school partnership. Friend (2008) described several issues that may pose barriers to these families. One key issue is the likelihood of multiple negative interactions between teachers and parents. The teacher's frustration with the child may lead to a negative perception of the family. The resulting interactions between parent and teacher may be negative. Continued requests for parents to participate in a behavior plan in whose development they had no input increases parental frustration. When parents are unable to comply with the plan or their efforts are unsuccessful, the frustration of both the parent and teacher escalates. Negative interactions may carry over into parent conferences. Parents who are anxious about hearing of yet another problem related to their child may seem combative. Negative opinions are again formed about the family and the student.

It is important to recognize that families of children with challenging behaviors want their child to behave appropriately and will do anything to they can to help that child (Hallahan et al., 2008). Blaming parents for their child's behavior is nonproductive. They need supportive resources, which are best provided in concert with the family. It is essential that teachers make every effort to form partnerships with these families and work collaboratively to help their children.

These problems may be avoided if schools actively promote strong home-school partnerships. School professionals who view partnerships as important will see families for their strengths and their knowledge of their children. Families who feel that they are welcomed, respected, and supported are more likely to be involved with their children's education and in their children's schools. As we've discussed, the benefits of this involvement to the child and the school are enormous and worth the efforts of school professionals to establish.

An Illustration From Practice

Ms. Sams, the behavior resource teacher at Larchmont Elementary, is preparing for a 3:00 PM meeting with Doug Johns, a fourth grader; his parents; and Ms. Graham, his classroom teacher. Doug has recently been struggling in the classroom academically and socially. He seems unable to complete his work in class or his homework, and his grades are suffering. Ms. Graham has noticed that he is spending more time alone and argues with the boys who have been his friends since kindergarten. Ms. Sams is concerned about Doug and is anxious for the meeting.

Mrs. Graham has arranged for the meeting in the conference room. She is prepared for the meeting with her observation notes and examples of Doug's work. She has also spoken with the music teacher and PE coach. When she spoke with Doug's parents, they preferred to come to school for the meeting, and due to Mr. Johns's work schedule, immediately after school was best. Mrs. Graham agreed, and the meeting was scheduled.

Mr. and Mrs. Johns are driving to a meeting with their son's classroom teacher and the school's behavior resource teacher. They had noticed a change in Doug's behavior lately and that his grades have fallen slightly. They weren't surprised to get the call from Mrs. Graham and are hopeful that the meeting will be helpful for Doug. In preparing for the meeting, Mrs. Johns has made her own notes about Doug's behavior and has prepared a list of her concerns.

The parent-teacher conference is an extremely important method for sharing information and working collaboratively with parents to solve problems and promote student success. Larchmont is a small rural elementary school with 535 preschool through fifth-grade students, 75 percent of who qualify for free or reduced lunch. For Larchmont Elementary, located in a sparsely populated rural community, these meetings may be the only chance for teachers to have meaningful conversations with parents. The faculty and administration realize this and during the past few years have worked to improve the tone and outcomes of meetings with family members. Their goal is to conduct meetings in which family members and teachers felt respected and valued as members of a team and participate meaningfully and that both be willing to follow up with plans. Meetings are scheduled to meet parent timelines and locations. Teachers are prepared for meetings with information on the child, including notes on strengths as well as concerns. The staff developed checklists for both teachers and parents to use to prepare for conferences. They also developed guidelines for conducting the conference.

The meeting with Mr. and Mrs. Johns, Ms. Sams, and Mrs. Graham resulted in a plan to address Doug's needs. Mrs. Graham conducted the meeting and began with introductions. She then asked Mr. and Mrs. Johns to address their concerns. By asking them to talk about their child, Mrs. Graham was letting them know that what they have to say is important and that they are a primary source of information. Both felt comfortable discussing their concerns and offered insights into the problem. As Mrs. Graham and then Ms. Sams discussed their observations, the Johns interjected their own comments. Ms. Sams offered several ideas for assisting Doug. Together, Ms. Sams, Mrs. Graham, and the Johns talked through a plan and agreed on actions that each could take. They will monitor his progress through a journal that will travel between school and home. They agreed to give the plan four weeks and set a follow-up meeting date.

This conference was designed to succeed. The parents were included in all decisions, beginning with setting the time and place, and they were encouraged to add important information about their child. The conference ended in agreement on a solution. When teachers recognize and value family input, parent-teacher conferences are more likely to end like this one. When parents feel they have input in designing an intervention, they are also more likely to follow through at home. These parents left with the idea that they are partners.

REFERENCES

Allen, J. (2008). Family partnerships that count. *Educational Leadership, 66*(1), 22–27.

Baker, A. J. L. (2001). Improving parent involvement programs and practice: A qualitative study of parent perceptions. In S. Redding & L. G. Thomas (Eds.), *The community of the school* (pp. 127–154). Lincoln, IL: Academic Development Institute. (Originally published in 1997, *School Community Journal, 7*(1), 9–35.) Retrieved October 28, 2009, from http://www.adi.org/journal/cots/2001SCJBook.pdf

Blue-Banning, M., Summers, J. A., Frankland, C., Nelson, L. G. & Beegle, G. (2004). Dimensions of family partnerships: Constructive guidelines for collaboration. *Exceptional Children, 70,* 167–184.

Boethel, M. (Ed.). (2003). *Diversity: School, family, & community connections (Annual synthesis 2003).* Austin, TX: National Center for Family & Community Connections with Schools. Southwest Educational Development Laboratory. Retrieved October 28, 2009, from http://www.sedl.org/connections/research-syntheses.html

Broussard, A. C. (2000). Preparing teachers to work with families: A national survey of teacher education programs. *Equity and Excellence in Education, 33,* 41–49.

Christenson, S. L. (2002). *Supporting home-school collaboration.* Retrieved October 28, 2009, from the Children, Youth, and Family Consortium Web site: http://www.cyfc.umn.edu/schoolage/resources/supporting.html

Decker, L. E., & Decker, V. A. (2003). *Home, school, and community partnerships.* Lanham, MD: Scarecrow Press.

Education for All Handicapped Children Act of 1975 (Public Law 94-142), 20 U.S.C. § 1411–1420.

Epstein, J. L. (2001). *School, family, and community partnerships: Preparing educators and improving schools.* Boulder, CO: Westview Press.

Epstein, J. L. (2002). *School, family, and community partnerships: Your handbook for action.* Thousand Oaks, CA: Corwin.

Fan, X. T., & Chen, M. (2001). Parental involvement and students' academic achievement: A meta-analysis. *Educational Psychology Review, 13,* 1–22.

Friend, M. (2008). *Special education: Contemporary perspectives for school professionals.* Boston: Pearson.

Hall, T. E., Wolfe, P. S., & Bollig, A. A. (2003). The home-to-school notebook: An effective communication strategy for students with severe disabilities. *Teaching Exceptional Children, 36*(2), 68–73.

Hallahan, D. P., Kauffman, J. M., & Pullen, P. C. (2008). *Exceptional learners: An introduction to special education* (11th ed.). Boston: Allyn & Bacon.

Harry, B. (2008). Family-professional collaboration with culturally and linguistically diverse families: Ideal vs. reality. *Exceptional Children, 72*(3), 372–388.

Henderson, A., & Berla, N. (Eds.). (1994). *A new generation of evidence: The family is critical to student achievement.* Washington, DC: Center for Law and Education.

Henderson, A. T., & Mapp, K. I. (2002). *A new wave of evidence: The impact of school, family, and community connections on student achievement* [Key Findings Abstract]. Austin, TX: Southwest Educational Development Laboratory. Retrieved October 28, 2009, from http://www.sedl.org/connections/resources/Keyfindings-reference.pdf

Hoover-Dempsey, K. V., Walker, J. M., Jones, K. P., & Reed, R. P. (2002). Teachers Involving Parents (TIP): An in-service teacher education program for enhancing parental involvement. *Teaching and Teacher Education, 18*(7), 843–867

Hoy, W. K. (2002). Faculty trust: A key to student achievement. *Journal of Public School Relations, 23,* 88–103.

Individuals with Disabilities Education Act (IDEA) of 1997, 20 U.S.C. § 1400 *et seq.*

Jeynes, W. H. (2005). *Parental involvement and student achievement: A meta-analysis* (Family Involvement Research Digest). Cambridge, MA: Harvard Family Research Project. Retrieved October 28, 2009, from http://www.hfrp.org/family-involvement/publications-resources/parental-involvement-and-student-achievement-a-meta-analysis

Kagan, S. L. (1984). *Parent involvement research: A field in search of itself.* Boston: Institute for Responsive Education.

Lucyshyn, J. M., Horner, R. H., Dunlap, G., Albin, R.W., & Ben, K. R. (2002). Positive behavior support with families. In J. M. Lucyshyn, G. Dunlap, & R. W. Albin (Eds.), *Families and positive behavior support: Addressing problem behavior in family contexts* (pp. 3–43). Baltimore, MD: Brookes.

Muscott, H. S., Szczesiui, S., Berk, B., Staub, K., Hoover, J., & Perry-Chisholm, P. (2008). Creating home-school partnerships by engaging families in schoolwide positive behavior supports. *Teaching Exceptional Children, 40*(6), 6–14.

No Child Left Behind Act of 2001 (NCLB), 20 U.S.C. § 6301 *et seq.*

Parette, H. P., & Petch-Hogan, B. (2000). Approaching families: Facilitating culturally/linguistically diverse family involvement. *Teaching Exceptional Children, 33*(2), 4–10.

Shaheen, J. A. C., & Spencer, C. C. (2001). *Take charge! Advocating for your child's education.* Albany, NY: Delmar.

Smith, T. E. G., Gartin, B. C., Murdick, N. L., & Hilton, A. (2006). *Families and children with special needs: Professional and family partnerships.* Upper Saddle River, NJ: Pearson Merrill.

Soodak, L. C., & Erwin, E. J. (2000). Valued member or tolerated participant: Parents' experiences in inclusive early childhood settings. *The Journal of the Association for Persons with Severe Handicaps, 25,* 29–44.

Trivette, C. M., Dunst, C. J., Boyd, K., & Hamby, D. W. (1995). Family-oriented program models, help giving practices and parental control appraisals. *Exceptional Children, 62,* 237–248.

Turnbull, A. P., Turnbull, R., Erwin, E., & Soodak, L. (2006). *Families, professionals, and exceptionality: Positive outcomes through partnerships and trust.* Upper Saddle River, NJ: Merrill/Prentice Hall.

Turnbull, A., Turnbull, R., & Wehmeyer, M. L. (2009). *Exceptional lives: Special education in today's schools* (6th ed.). Upper Saddle River, NJ: Merrill/Prentice Hall.

Whitbread, K. M., Bruder, M. B., Fleming, G., & Park, H. J. (2007). Collaboration in special education: Parent-professional training. *Teaching Exceptional Children, 35,* 6–14.

9

Community and Interagency Partnerships

In this chapter, we

- examine one school-linked service program that illustrates the importance of community development and interagency partnerships in preventing problem behavior,
- identify and describe effective elements of a 15-year-old community partnership program that serves low-income families and their children at multiple sites in an affluent suburban community, and
- describe an evaluation of the program at one site.

L ow-income families and immigrant families face monumental challenges in raising their children and supporting them in school. When non-native-English-speaking parents and other families lack material and social supports, their ability to nurture their children as students is compromised. Those families, particularly the ones who have recently immigrated, often face an additional difficulty: "they do not speak the language of the school" (Harry, 1992, p. xiii). The process of relocating to a new country can have both material and psychological costs. Helping families and their children can prevent the development of emotional or behavioral problems in school and promote academic achievement. Too often, fragmented service systems fail to meet the most basic needs of disadvantaged families (Anderson-Butcher et al., 2008; Schorr, 1989).

AUTHOR'S NOTE: The names of the families described in the text boxes are pseudonyms. Some information about families has been altered to protect families' anonymity.

In response to the needs of low-income and immigrant families and their school-age children, Montgomery County, Maryland, developed an interagency program, Linkages to Learning (LTL), in the early 1990s. In 1993, the program began serving youth and families in two elementary schools and one health center. By 2000, the program had expanded to seven elementary and two middle schools. Currently, LTL serves students and families at more than 30 elementary, middle schools, and health centers at 28 sites in the county. While initially designed to provide a flexible and coordinated service delivery system, it has evolved at some sites into a community development model in which public and private agencies collaborate to support families and develop neighborhoods that promote the healthy development and achievement of children. In general, families participating in the program report a high degree of satisfaction with services (Leone, Lane, Arlen, & Peter, 1996; Meisel, 1997). A quasi-experimental study at one Linkages site and a control school site showed improved social behavior and decreased emotional distress among children whose families were enrolled in the program (Fox et al., 1999).

Linkages to Learning is a collaborative effort of the Montgomery County Department of Health and Human Services, the Montgomery County Public Schools, and four primary service providers—Guide Youth Services, Kensington-Wheaton Youth Services, the City of Rockville, and the Silver Spring YMCA—which are linked with various schools. The program provides social services (including financial and food assistance), counseling, physical and mental health care, translation, and educational support. This chapter describes the development and evolution of collaborative interagency services and supports serving low-income and immigrant families and their children in one of the wealthiest counties in the United States. We begin by describing the forces that led to the development and growth of the program over the past 16 years. We then turn to a discussion of how the Linkages approach to service delivery helps prevent emotional and behavioral disorder in children through supporting families and developing communities, and we discuss implementation of the program at one site. We conclude with a discussion of the core principles that guided the development and sustainability of the program.

POVERTY, IMMIGRANT STATUS, AND RISK

With a median family income of more than $91,000 per year, Montgomery County ranked seventh in the United States in 2007 (Bishaw & Semega, 2008). Obscured by the relative opulence of the county are large numbers of children and families living in poverty and near-poor frugality. Of the 163 elementary and middle schools in the county, approximately 62 schools serve student populations in which more than 50 percent of families are eligible for the Free and Reduced Meal Programs (FARMs). In 2005–2006, more than 33,000 children out of a population of more than 140,000 students in the Montgomery County Public Schools received support through FARMs (Linkages to Learning, 2006). Within Maryland, Montgomery County has the highest percentage of children of immigrants attending the public schools. Montgomery County is part of the Washington, D.C., "emerging gateway" for immigrants. This influx of émigrés, which accelerated in the 1990s and continues to the present, is characterized by families with low levels of formal education, extreme poverty, and low levels of English proficiency (Singer, 2004). Historically, low-income and immigrant families in Montgomery County have been served by an array of social service agencies that were centrally located at several sites. In addition to the duplication of effort and inefficiency associated with multiple service providers, low-income families struggled with transportation to social services, health, and mental health offices. These families and their children were considered at risk because of their poverty, inadequate access to health care, the children's performance in school, and their lack of familiarity with the social service and mental health care systems.

In Maryland and across the United States, children living in poverty and immigrant children, who are often nonnative English speakers, are at greater risk for failure to complete high school and experience a host of other less-than-desirable adult outcomes than their peers. For example, data from the 2007 and 2008 U.S. Census Bureau surveys show that the median income for individuals without a high school diploma was $19,000 per year, while the median income for those with a high school diploma was $27,000 per year (Crissey, 2009). Similarly, the rate of unemployment was highest for those without a high school diploma and lowest for those with advanced graduate degrees. In 2007, individuals with less than a high school diploma had an unemployment rate of 7.1 percent. In contrast, high school graduates averaged a 4.4 percent unemployment rate, and those completing a bachelor's degree had a 2.2 percent unemployment rate (Bureau of Labor Statistics, 2009). Similarly, on measures of health, individuals with higher levels of education have lower rates of chronic illness, such as heart disease and diabetes, and greater life expectancy (National Poverty Center, 2007). Researchers have found these differences independent of demographic and labor market factors.

INTERAGENCY APPROACHES TO PREVENTING PROBLEM BEHAVIOR

For more than 50 years education, psychology, medicine, and related human services professions have engaged in efforts to prevent problem behavior and respond to emergent and chronic behavior problems of children in school. In the 1950s and 1960s, responses to "disturbed behavior" in school children were often associated with counseling and psychoeducational approaches (Bower, 1960; Morse, Cutler, & Fink, 1964). Emerging in the 1960s and continuing to the present day have been approaches based on applied behaviorism that use operant conditioning to shape student behaviors in socially acceptable ways (Haring & Philips, 1962; Kauffman & Lewis, 1974; Rhodes & Tracy, 1977). Concurrent with the rise of applied behaviorism were ecological, cognitive-behavioral, and pharmacological approaches to the treatment of behavioral problems (Kaufmann, 1977, 1997).

While traditional, microlevel approaches targeted at changing the child dominate how the professions respond to behavior problems in children, in recent years programs have supplemented traditional approaches with early prevention efforts designed to support families and children (Dryfoos, 1994). For example the Chicago Longitudinal Study (CLS) has shown that early intervention services for at-risk, urban children have the potential for strong returns on the investment (CLS, 1999). Reynolds, Temple, Robertson, and Mann's (2002) cost-benefit analysis of the Chicago program showed that preschool participation in one of the city's Child Parent Centers provided a return to society of $7.14 for every dollar invested. Increased tax returns and the reduction of public expenditures for remedial education, criminal justice involvement, and restitution to the victims of crime resulted in benefits to families and the community. Lower, yet still positive, returns were seen with the older participants. Children who participated in the program through age 6 showed a return of $6.11 per dollar invested, while school-age participants yielded a return of $1.66 per dollar invested.

Similarly, Linkages to Learning has adopted an early intervention approach that does not discard traditional child-change strategies but rather attempts to place those approaches in the context of community development and family support. That is, improved performance of children in school is grounded in interagency partnerships that support and develop families and neighborhoods. Figure 9.1 illustrates the iterative cycle of family support and improved child academic and social behavior that underlies Linkages to Learning. A major emphasis of the program has been on preventing and reducing the social, emotional, and health problems of children that interfere with their ability to succeed in school. Part of the process of reducing risk factors for children has involved supporting their families and giving them the skills that enable them to help their children independently of the program.

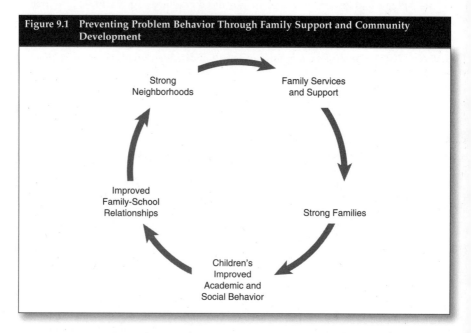

Figure 9.1   Preventing Problem Behavior Through Family Support and Community Development

CORE PRINCIPLES AND GOVERNANCE STRUCTURE

While each Linkages site has unique features that have been developed in response to parent and community needs, core defining principles connect all Linkages programs and supports. These principles include (a) collaborative services; (b) interdisciplinary teams; (c) integrated, seamless service delivery; (d) responsive programming; (e) multilingual and culturally competent staff; (f) community-based services; and (g) strengths-based programming (Linkages to Learning, 2008).

As a *collaborative* program, Linkages involves both public and private agencies working together toward a common goal: improved well-being of children and their families. In addition to the major partners—the department human services, the public school system, and local direct service providers—local businesses, churches and synagogues, and recreation programs are also part of Linkages.

As an *interdisciplinary* program, Linkages staff includes educators, social workers, psychologists, and health professionals. This feature enables the development and delivery of . . .

integrated, seamless services to children and families. Because staff from various agencies and professions work in the same offices adjacent to or in schools they serve, duplication and inefficiencies are minimized or eliminated.

Responsive programming, as the term implies, means that each site working with school improvement teams plans and delivers services in response to local community needs.

Multilingual and culturally competent staff, another defining principle of Linkages, ensures that families' needs are understood and that staff can communicate with immigrant families in their own languages. Cultural competence among staff includes an awareness and understanding of the differences between the dominant American culture and the *high-context* culture of many families served by the program. For example, in high-context cultures, communication involves connecting with others in ways that they recognize, understand, and value. This means developing respectful, welcoming relationships with families as a prerequisite to working with or helping them. From this perspective, a necessary step before parents will use program resources is building a trusting relationship.

Community-based services means that. in contrast to traditional mental health and social service delivery systems, agencies and supports come to neighborhoods where children and families live and where children spend the majority of their time in school.

Finally, *strengths-based programming*, in contrast to a deficit-based approach, begins with the assumption that the personal and social assets of children and their families provide a vehicle for communication, support, and the development of better functioning in school and the community.

These program principles have enabled the program to build effective partnerships between the Linkages staff and the local schools staffs.

Linkages is directed by a three-person Linkages Resource Team. This group provides technical assistance, administrative support, and leadership on accountability and strategic planning to the sites. The Resource Team also coordinates staff development activities and initiatives and works closely with the Advisory Group, composed of more than 30 representatives of partner agencies, local businesses, civic organizations, parents, and faith groups. The Advisory Group, which meets quarterly, has been essential in the development of strategic plans, including site selection and policy development. Although some glitches are inevitable when multiple agencies and professionals representing different disciplines work together to deliver services and provide support, during the past 15 years, Linkages has evolved and thrived.

LINKAGES TO LEARNING IN ACTION

In many respects, Linkages programs operate like the settlement houses in the United States in the late 19th and early 20th centuries that offered social services and support to the urban poor (Day, 2002). In contrast to settlement houses, which were often privately run and sometimes religiously affiliated, Linkages operates though private and public partnerships. In some neighborhoods, Linkages has connections with faith-based organizations, but it is not affiliated with or sponsored by any church, synagogue, or religiously affiliated group.

While each Linkages site operates somewhat differently, some common elements can be found at each school-linked site. A basic belief, embedded in the principles enumerated above, is that a primary purpose of the programs is to help families and their children thrive, not just survive. Accordingly, many families after receiving support become mentors and part of a support system for new families. Strong families become part of the social capital of their neighborhoods, which in turn strengthens local communities. For example, Linkages families have organized neighborhood walks, developed partnerships between families, and organized moms' groups. For some families, Linkages represent a safe haven where those who speak their language help them connect with their children's teachers and the principal and provide mental health or social services.

Families whose children attend elementary and middle schools that are Linkages sites receive mental health, social, education, and health services at the school or in a building near the school. The range of services includes mental health assessments, individual and group counseling, health services, support groups for parents, and staff development for teachers. Social services include translation and transportation assistance, housing assistance, afterschool and summer recreation programs, and assistance in connecting with other agencies. Education support has ranged from tutoring and mentoring for children to offering adult education classes and groups in English and computer literacy for parents. Students have also obtained basic health care services through Linkages, such as hearing and vision screening, emergency services, immunizations, referrals, and case management. Each site has an emergency fund that can be used for housing, food, transportation, or other essential short-term support. Linkages staff often use these funds to match support provided by faith-based or civic groups. Beyond basic mental health, social services, education, and health services, parents identify needs for specific programs and supports at each site.

Broad Acres Elementary School

The program site at Broad Acres Elementary School provides a window through which we can view the development and evolution of Linkages to Learning. The program at Broad Acres was initially designed as a health center in 1995 to serve one of the poorest communities in the County. With support from Robert Wood Johnson Foundation, a health care center adjacent to the school was developed. The school principal, with support from the school district, invited a local private nonprofit agency to send a clinician to Broad Acres after school to provide therapy for children and families on a fee-for-services basis. A research and demonstration grant from the U.S. Department of Education through the University of Maryland was used to provide additional clinical staff during school hours and to fund an evaluation of the program. Paid staff were supplemented by graduate interns in social work and psychology from several local universities. The Montgomery County Department of Health and Human Services set up a trailer outside the school for the program. During the first four years of the program at Broad Acres, strong support within the school district and from the county council made the difference between losing the program and growing the program. Political capital at the system level and the ability of the principal to access it was essential.

As the program evolved at Broad Acres, the staff found that taking the time to build relationships with families was essential. In high-context cultures, like those of the immigrant families served at Broad Acres, nonverbal communication and the setting are essential. Cultural competence at the program level meant structuring time to be flexible and responsive to build relationships and communicate with families. Connecting with parents meant less reliance on flyers, letters, and posted announcements and more phone calls, home visits, and informal contacts outside the school. The Linkages staff at Broad Acres developing families' trust by talking with individuals informally and often at unscheduled times.

Being culturally competent at Broad Acres sometimes meant that the Linkages office stayed open weeknights and weekends, when parents were free to visit. Also, spending the time with a parent when the opportunity presents itself can wreak havoc on scheduled appointments with school staff. By necessity, most public school cultures in the United States are low context and highly scheduled. The need to structure the program to be responsive to parents from a higher-context culture can precipitate a problem for any regularly scheduled meetings between school staff and Linkages staff. A common example of this phenomenon on the practice level occurs when a teacher schedules back-to-back, half-hour parent-teacher meetings and a parent arrives half an hour late. The teacher feels that she has no flexibility to meet with the late parent (it's not fair to the next parent) and politely tells him or her to reschedule the meeting. The parent probably walks away feeling dismissed, not because of the content of the message but because of the brevity of the conversation. As Linkages at Broad Acres evolved, staff became adept at understanding parents' needs and developing ways in which to communicate effectively with them.

In the program at Broad Acres, the staff has used a weekly two-hour staff meeting as an opportunity for training and consultation with the school on acculturation and cultural competence issues. For example, Linkages staff members participated in meetings involving parents, a teacher, and the principal. These situations provided an opportunity to discuss with the principal and school staff how the differences in culture (high versus low context) played out in the ongoing miscommunication with some families.

Staff commitment to a collaborative culture were essential as the program developed at Broad Acres. The Linkages staff and school staff developed a shared vision of the anticipated outcomes for children and families and a commitment to working together to reach common goals. In part because the team was culturally

The Badasu family moved from West Africa to a neighborhood served by a Linkages site several years ago. Mr. Badasu possessed a green card, but the family was not eligible for health care insurance in Maryland because they had lived in the United States less than five years. Their son Ansa experienced significant mental health problems and reported hearing voices. Through Linkages, Ansa was seen by a psychiatrist, who provided sample medication that the family would not have been able to afford. Linkages staff were instrumental in supporting a requested waiver of health insurance regulations so that the family could apply for and receive essential mental health services and support.

Ms. Hurtado, a single mother of four from Central America, reported that she was dying of cancer when she was first introduced to Linkages staff through a neighbor. Her ability to care for her children and their success in school were seriously compromised by her illness. Through Linkages, she received medical attention and a correct diagnosis of her medical condition. The knowledge that she does not have cancer and support from Linkages staff have transformed Ms. Hurtado into a volunteer in her children's school, an employee at a local community center, and a mentor to families new to the community.

diverse and came from different organizational cultures (school, child welfare, private provider business), a collaborative program culture was essential. The collaborative culture that evolved at Linkages included responsiveness to children and families from different ethnic backgrounds and to program and school staff from different professional and organizational cultures.

As the collaborative culture at Broad Acres developed, Linkages staff learned to understand the perspectives, needs, and stresses experienced by teachers in the school. By the same token, school staff developed realistic expectations about what Linkages therapists and case managers could and could not do and an understanding of the importance of confidentiality between clients and therapists. The Linkages and school staffs worked out referral procedures, integrated educational and mental health teams, and coordinated policies for crises within a collaborative culture. This could not have happened in an environment where staff failed to trust one another and felt the need to compete for resources. Over time, the Linkages therapist participated in the weekly educational support team meetings in the school, and the Linkages site coordinator became part of the school planning committee. Linkages staff members regularly participated in the meetings to coordinate parent programs in the school, and the principal became a member of the Linkages advisory board. Both staffs participated in each other's meetings to develop vision and mission statements.

At the end of each school year, the Linkages staff and the school staff met to evaluate the program and promote communication. At these meetings, staff members were asked to evaluate how well staff from the other program (school or Linkages) met their expectations. As each staff member presented critical and positive feedback at these meetings, other staff quietly listened without questions. After discussion, the common points were identified, and both staffs chose the top three priorities on which to work during the next school year. Building a collaborative culture between Broad Acres Elementary School and the Linkages staffs took a large commitment of time during the first few years. Without the investment of time to create and sustain the relationships through feedback sessions, retreats, and team meetings, it would have been difficult to create a collaborative culture.

EVALUATING THE EFFECT OF LINKAGES TO LEARNING ON CHILDREN AND FAMILIES

Several studies of Linkages to Learning have been conducted. During the initial years of the program, a formative evaluation of one of the first two Linkages schools suggested that while parent satisfaction with the program and services was very high, staff perceived the relationship between parents and the school much more positively than did the parents (Leone et al., 1996).

A second, more extensive investigation was conducted to assess the effects of the LTL program on children and families. In that study, researchers compared one of the four existing Linkages sites at that time, Broad Acres Elementary School, with a non-Linkages elementary school serving families and children with similar characteristics. This quasi-experimental study, like the earlier investigation, involved interviewing families who were representative of those served by the program. The outcomes reported in this chapter summarize findings presented elsewhere and the findings from our parent satisfaction study (see Fox et al., 1999).

The evaluation design compared children and families at Broad Acres with a comparison or control school. Over four years, a total of 119 children and 69 parents participated in the study. The sample consisted of families from whom data were collected just before Linkages started at Broad Acres and again three years later. The small size of the sample, relative to the number of children and families served by Linkages, reflected the unusually high mobility rates at both the experimental and control schools. Because this project was designed as a comparison-school study, we expected that children and families at both schools would share many common characteristics. Unfortunately, major differences existed. Differences in ethnicity, income level, education, and length of time in the United States were just some of the schoolwide demographic differences found. Overall, the experimental school, Broad Acres, served a population at greater risk for difficulties than the control school. The control school was selected by public school administrators and not by the researchers for the project. Other elementary schools whose demographic profile more closely resembled Broad Acres were not selected, in part because they were receiving other special programs and compensatory services.

Many parents who declined to participate in the evaluation of Linkages were part of the program, and they and their children received Linkages services. However, an analysis of the children and families participating in the evaluation and those not participating revealed no significant differences on any measures. Measures of child behavior problems and academic performance from the pretest did show children at Broad Acres having more difficulties than children at the control school. For example, we found that according to teachers, the children at Broad Acres demonstrated more acting-out behaviors, such as being disruptive in class, and more learning difficulties, such as poor concentration, than students at the control school. According to mothers, children at Broad Acres demonstrated more total problem behaviors, such as symptoms of aggression and depression, than children at the control school. And Broad Acres students demonstrated poorer academic performance on measures of math, reading, and writing abilities.

Procedure

During the fall of the first project year, information about the Linkages to Learning evaluation project was distributed to all parents with children in Grades K–2 at the experimental and control schools. Bilingual staff distributed informational flyers and answered questions at parent meetings, PTA functions, and other school activities. All flyers and consent forms were available in English, Spanish, and Vietnamese. In addition, teachers in Grades K–2 distributed to all children in their classrooms consent forms and endorsement letters from the principals. Parents or guardians who agreed to participate in the evaluation of Linkages to Learning and their children were interviewed and assessed each year. In addition, teachers were asked to complete two questionnaires each year and assess the behavior of each child participating in the program.

Parent Report of Emotional and Behavioral Outcomes

Parents at Broad Acres reported a significant decrease of children's negative behaviors over three years. Decreases were reported on both the externalizing and internalizing subscales of the Child Behavior Checklist. Children at Broad Acres exhibited more negative behaviors than children in the control school before the start of the project. By the end of the third year, children at Broad Acres had fewer negative behaviors than children at the control school. This suggests that Linkages may have had a positive, schoolwide impact on the prevalence of parent-reported behavior problems.

Differences in CBCL Scores by Services

We also evaluated differences among children in three groups. We examined children at the control school, children at Broad Acres who had received direct services through Linkages, and children at Broad Acres who had not received services. Over time, we found significant differences among the three groups on both the externalizing and internalizing subscales of the CBCL. Children who had the highest scores on the CBCL were those who were receiving Linkages services. This suggests that the children who needed services most were the ones who received them. The externalizing problem scores for children receiving services were, on average, more than 2 points higher than those of children not receiving services in the same school and 4 points higher than scores of children in the control school.

By the end of the study, parent-reported problems for children receiving services at Broad Acres had dropped to the level of problems for children at the control school. We found that children at Broad Acres who were not receiving services also showed a dramatic decline in parent-reported problem behaviors. In fact, the decline for this group was even greater than for those receiving services, particularly on the internalizing subscale. Since even parents of those children not directly receiving services were reporting significant improvements in the behaviors of their children, the Linkages to Learning program may have affected the emotional climate of the school. Perhaps these children, whose behavioral problems were less severe and entrenched than those of children receiving services, were more likely to make behavioral gains with even a minimal level of intervention (e.g., program presence in the school, program impact on teacher or parent attitudes). Evidence also suggests that several students at Broad Acres with emotional and behavioral disorders were able to remain at the school and not be placed in a specialized and segregated treatment program, an expected outcome without intervention.

Teacher Report of Emotional and Behavioral Outcomes

Data on children's behavior in the classroom were collected from teachers using the Teacher-Child Rating Scale (T-CRS). Teachers completed checklists each year to document the behavioral strengths and weaknesses they observed among their students. The T-CRS groups items into positive and negative behaviors. Negative behaviors include things like being disruptive in class, poor motivation, and defiant behavior. Examples of positive behaviors include coping well with failure, being sensitive to other children's feelings, and tolerating frustration well. Our evaluation found differences between groups on negative behaviors but not on positive behaviors.

Overall, children at the control school demonstrated an increase in negative behaviors as they got older, while children at the experimental school did not show a similar trend, though they had more risk factors. One possible explanation for this trend at the control school is that the classroom becomes a more structured environment as children move from primary to intermediate grades. Accordingly, negative, acting-out behaviors become more apparent, particularly among children at risk for academic and behavioral problems. It is also possible that as children get older, teachers' expectations for conforming behaviors get higher. Also, when children fall behind academically, they may be more likely to respond by acting out in an attempt to distract from their academic difficulties or to express frustration, anger, or poor self-image.

Child Report of Emotional Outcomes

Children were asked about their own emotional well-being. For this measure, children reported on the extent to which they experienced anxiety, depression, distractibility, and poor self-esteem. At the beginning of the evaluation, Broad Acres and the control school were significantly different from each other, with children at the control school reporting significantly lower levels of emotional distress. Over the three-year period, however, levels of distress among children at Broad Acres remained stable, while the scores for the children in the control school increased significantly, exceeding the distress scores for children at Broad Acres.

We can only speculate about the reasons for an increase in distress symptoms among children at the control school. As children mature and develop greater self-awareness, they are more able and more likely to report on their internal experiences of sadness, anxiety, or low self-concept. Common stresses experienced by school-aged children include those related to academic success, social acceptability, and family factors such as divorce. Many children are first referred for special education services for emotional disturbance during the first few years of school when they exhibit behavior problems. While we would expect that children at both schools would be similarly vulnerable to the effects of such stresses, only those at the control school showed increases in distress levels over time. This finding suggests that Linkages at Broad Acres may serve as a protective factor against increases in emotional distress.

Academic Outcomes

The academic performance of children within the two groups at Broad Acres were different. While the children not receiving direct services from Linkages started with higher math achievement scores, by the end of the study, the children receiving services had made such gains that they were now approaching the achievement scores of their peers in the no-service group.

This positive impact of the Linkages to Learning program on math achievement was not found for either the reading subscale or the writing subscale of the achievement measure. One important consideration is the fact that a significant number of the children at Broad Acres had limited English proficiency, which could have confounded reading and writing scores. Math scores, because they are less language dependent, may be less influenced by this factor.

Parent-Reported Outcomes

Our evaluation of parenting practices showed that parents at Broad Acres who received Linkages services made the greatest gains in consistency of parenting skills over time, while parents at the control school showed slight increases. We also examined parents' satisfaction with the program and the extent to which it met their needs. We conducted a series of interviews with parents and identified aspects of the program that they found most useful (Meisel, 1997). In general, parents were very satisfied with the program. They identified improved academic, behavioral, and social skills of children; improved communication with school staff; and improved parenting skills as the most important outcomes of the program. Parents said that individual and group counseling, academic tutoring, and afterschool and summer activities were the most important services their children received. For themselves, parents reported that English language classes, access to other social service agencies, and parenting classes were most helpful.

One parent, in response to a question about her satisfaction with the program, said, "The Linkages services helped my daughter very much. She would inflict harm on herself when she was reprimanded, and would frequently fight with her siblings and classmates. She received counseling, and I did too, and now life is much smoother for us." Another commented, "I have only had a few appointments, but I feel like I see the Linkages staff all the time because I am in the school a lot . . . so I can talk to them for a few minutes without an appointment and clear up simple things that way."

Community Partnerships

An outcome more difficult to quantify than changes in children's social behavior or academic performance involves the partnerships that developed through the Linkages to Learning program. In addition to the private mental health agency, the public schools, and the social service agency, the Linkages staff has developed and continues to develop partnerships with groups such as the Vietnamese Professional Association of America, Bikes for Tykes, a local food bank, local businesses, and several local congregations. These partnerships provide additional links and supports and opportunities for Linkages families.

PREVENTING PROBLEM BEHAVIORS WITH COMMUNITY PARTNERSHIPS

Linkages to Learning may be a promising approach to meeting the needs of low-income and immigrant families. We believe that the core elements described earlier were essential in setting the stage for the positive outcomes for children and parents. Findings from the evaluation at Broad Acres Elementary School are quite encouraging. Anecdotal information from other Linkages sites and other sources likewise suggests positive outcomes for children and families.

A challenge faced by programs serving low-income and immigrant families and their children is the sustainability of community-based initiatives, particularly in times of fiscal crisis and high unemployment. Too often, interagency and collaborative initiatives fail when evidence of program impact is not measured, is ignored, or is never publicized. When innovations are perceived as faddish or the program is championed by a single individual or small group of individuals, they are more easily discarded (Slavin, 2004). Research has shown that one of the key factors of program sustainability is the institutionalization of the practice into the school and community culture. Taylor (2006) found that the retention of key staff and continuing professional development were more critical to the continuation of practices than the stability of the original district-level policy or personnel. Through the development of support for Linkages to Learning within neighborhoods, the Montgomery County Public Schools, the Department of Health and Human Services, the Montgomery County Council, private service providers, and other local partners the program have created a broad base of support for the program. Because each program site has some unique features, is collaborative, and is tailored to family and community needs, a rigid Linkages bureaucracy has not developed.

Some evidence suggests that Linkages is an effective way of preventing problem behavior through community development, interagency partnerships, and school-linked services to low-income and immigrant families and their children. The ongoing ability of Linkages to Learning to support children and families may hinge on its ability to continue to document positive and lasting changes in children, families, and communities.

REFERENCES

Anderson-Butcher, D., Lawson, H. A., Bean, J., Flaspohler, P., Boone, B., & Kwiatkosski, A. (2008). Community collaboration to improve schools: A new model from Ohio. *Children and Schools, 30,* 161–172.

Bishaw, A., & Semega, J. (2008). *Income, earnings, and poverty: Data from the 2007 American Community Survey* (American Community Survey Reports [ACS] 09). Washington, DC: U.S. Department of Commerce, Bureau of the Census. Retrieved October 28, 2009, at http://www.census.gov/prod/2008pubs/acs-09.pdf

Bower, E. M. (1960). *Early identification of emotionally handicapped children in school.* Springfield, IL: Charles C. Thomas.

Bureau of Labor Statistics. (2009). *Education pays . . .* [Data from Current Population Survey]. Retrieved October 28, 2009, from http://www.bls.gov/emp/ emptab7.htm

Chicago Longitudinal Study (CLS). (1999). *A study of children in the Chicago public schools: User's guide* (Version 6). Madison: University of Wisconsin.

Crissey, S. R. (2009). *Educational attainment in the United States: 2007* (Current Population Reports P20-560). Washington, DC: U.S. Census Bureau, U.S. Department of Commerce. (ERIC Document Reproduction Service No. ED505040)

Day, P. J. (2002). *A new history of social welfare* (4th ed.). Boston: Allyn & Bacon.

Dryfoos, J. (1994). *Full-service schools: A revolution in health and social services for children, youth, and families.* San Francisco: Jossey-Bass.

Fox, N., Leone, P., Rubin, K., Oppenheim, J., Miller, M., & Friedman, K. (1999). *Final report on the Linkages to Learning program and evaluation at Broad Acres Elementary School.* College Park: University of Maryland. Retrieved October 28, 2009, from http://www.montgomerycountymd.gov/content/Linkages/pdfs/baesexec.pdf

Haring, N. G., & Phillips, E. L. (1962). *Educating emotionally disturbed children.* New York: McGraw-Hill.

Harry, B. (1992). *Cultural diversity, families, and the special education system.* New York: Teachers College Press.

Kauffman, J. M. (1977). *Characteristics of children's behavior disorders.* Columbus, OH: Charles E. Merrill.

Kauffman, J. M. (1997). *Characteristics of emotional and behavioral disorders of children and youth* (6th ed.). Columbus, OH: Charles E. Merrill.

Kauffman, J. M., & Lewis, C. D. (Eds.). (1974). *Teaching children with behavior disorders: Personal perspectives.* Columbus, OH: Charles E.Merrill.

Leone, P. E., Lane, S. A., Arlen, N., & Peter, H. (1996). School-linked services in context: A formative evaluation of Linkages to Learning. *Special Services in the Schools, 11*(1/2), 119–133.

Linkages to Learning. (2006). *Linkages to Learning six-year strategic plan: FY 2008–2013.* Rockville, MD: Department of Health and Human Services.

Linkages to Learning. (2008). *Program overview.* Rockville, MD: Department of Health and Human Services.

Meisel, S. M. (1997). *Evaluation of low-income families' satisfaction with school-linked social services.* Unpublished manuscript, Department of Special Education, University of Maryland.

Morse, W. C., Cutler, R. L., & Fink, A. H. (1964). *Public school classes for the emotionally handicapped: A research analysis.* Washington, DC: Council for Exceptional Children.

National Poverty Center. (2007). *Education and health* (National Poverty Center Policy Brief #9). Ann Arbor: University of Michigan, Ford School of Public Policy. Retrieved October 28, 2009, from http://www.npc.umich.edu/publications/policy_briefs/brief9/policy_brief9.pdf

Reynolds, A. J., Temple, J. A., Robertson, D. L., & Mann, E. A. (2002). Age 21 cost-benefit analysis of the Title I Chicago Child-Parent Centers. *Educational Evaluation and Policy Analysis, 24*(4), 267–303.

Rhodes, W. C., & Tracy, M. L. (Eds.). (1977). *A study of child variance: Vol. 2. Interventions.* Ann Arbor: University of Michigan Press. (ERIC Document Reproduction Service No. ED135121)

Schorr, L. (1989). *Within our reach: Breaking the cycle of disadvantage.* Garden City, NY: Doubleday.

Singer, A. (2004). *The rise of new immigrant gateways* (The Living Cities Census Series). Washington, DC: Brookings Institution, Center on Urban and Metropolitan Policy. Retrieved October 28, 2009, from http://www.brookings.edu/~/media/Files/rc/reports/2004/02demographics_singer/20040301_gateways.pdf

Slavin, R. E. (2004). Education research can and must address "what works" questions. *Educational Researcher, 33*(1), 27–28.

Taylor, E. (2006). A critical analysis of the achievement gap in the United States: Politics, reality, and hope. *Leadership and Policy in Schools, 5,* 71–87.

10

Culturally Responsive Teaching

In this chapter, we

- review the cultural context that is common in America's schools,
- identify and describe key features of culture that impact learning and behavior,
- identify and describe characteristics of culturally responsive teaching,
- review features of a culturally responsive teaching model,
- review culturally responsive teaching practices,
- describe a culturally responsive teaching model,
- describe a culturally responsive teaching program, and
- provide a perspective on culturally responsive teaching.

It is abundantly clear that great diversity exists within our schools, communities, and nation. For example, more than one-third of the children in elementary and secondary schools are culturally and linguistically diverse (CLD) students (National Center for Educational Statistics, 1993), about 1 in 5 lives in poverty (Children's Defense Fund, 2001), and about 1 in 10 has limited proficiency in English (Kindler, 2002). Today's teaching force, however, remains overwhelmingly White, middle class, and monolingual (Ladson-Billings, 2001) with about 85 percent of teachers being female and 15 percent male. Increasingly, general and special educators are faced with overwhelming challenges to prepare CLD students to live in a world where some groups have greater societal benefits than others primarily because of race, class, gender, language, religion, ability, and/or age (Gollnick & Chinn, 2002). Many scholars and educators (e.g., Bennett, 1995; Burstein & Cabello, 1989; Dilworth, 1990; Huber, 1991; Obiakor, 2001, 2003; 2007, 2008; Obiakor & Beachum, 2005; Sleeter, 1995; Smith, 1991; Utley & Obiakor, 2001) have suggested that teachers who are sensitive to the diverse cultures that students bring to the classroom have the ability to understand cultural cues of different ethnic and social groups and are able to provide learning experiences that meet their needs.

In an effort to prepare and teach students effectively, social as well as academic behavior in the classroom needs to be addressed, monitored, and promoted. Targeting all three of these elements must be done by implementing effective classroom plans. Few would argue that teaching appropriate behavior is one of the more difficult areas that beginning teachers must address. This holds particularly true for those teaching in urban schools (Obiakor & Beachum, 2005; Utley & Obiakor, 2001). Research indicates that needs in urban schools are more pervasive than in rural or suburban schools. In the urban school setting, teachers and service providers must gain students' cooperation in participating, while also ensuring that their learning involves their culture, ethnicity, social identity, language, and safety, as well as their academics (Brown, 2003).

Many of these personal growth issues are handled in the home, but a lack of resources and time in the home shifts some responsibility to teachers and other service providers. Often, these professionals lack the knowledge to deal effectively with CLD learners, especially when they exhibit gaps in and inappropriate patterns of academic and social behaviors. As a result, they engage in exclusionary and other punitive administrative practices, which worsen difficult situations and increase the incidence of problem behaviors (Lewis-Palmer, Sugai, & Larson, 1999; Mendez & Knoff, 2003). It has also been noted that these actions are often administered for minor infractions to the students with the greatest need for school support (Mendez & Knoff; Morrison, Anthony, Storino, & Dillon, 2001). Clearly, acquiring a greater understanding of culture within the school setting provides teachers and service providers with the foundation to infuse the curriculum with culturally rich experiences, fostering not only academic achievement but also social empowerment. The use of culturally responsive teaching allows for the necessary academic content to be taught while also teaching students how to act, respond, and get along with others. This is the strategic focus of this chapter.

CULTURE AND TODAY'S CLASSROOMS

Culture has an impact on learning and behavior (Obiakor, 2001). When investigating student behaviors in various cultures, African American and Native American students are the most likely to be excluded, and Hispanic American students have higher exclusion rates than do White students. Even more disturbing are the findings that indicate these harsh punishments are (a) ineffective (e.g., Krezmien, Leone, & Achilles, 2006); (b) prime predictors of poor school outcomes (Obiakor, 2001, 2007); and (c) tied to issues related to disproportionality in special education (Skiba, Michael, Nardo, & Peterson, 2002; Skiba, Poloni-Staudinger, Simmons, Feggins-Azziz, & Chung, 2005). Few would argue the need to teach appropriate behavior in the classroom in order to achieve an optimal learning environment, but how can students learn if they are not in attendance? Excluding students from the academic setting is not the answer, and teachers need to learn and practice more appropriate ways to teach behavior while also acknowledging cultural differences.

How can teachers and service providers optimize learning in today's classroom setting when they are ill prepared or unprepared to teach behavior? Wilson and Corbett (2001) and Delpit (1995) noted that today's classroom environments should be places in which expectations are clearly stated and inappropriate behaviors are dealt with immediately. Attempting to meet the needs of students requires that teachers and service providers develop an awareness of and explicitly respond to students ethnic, cultural, social, emotional, and cognitive characteristics (Brown, 2003). Delpit indicated that many children expect many more direct verbal commands than perhaps teachers may expect to give or provide. If students interpret commands as questions, teachers and administrators may perceive them as uncooperative and insubordinate without understanding their failure to comprehend what is expected and why they choose not to comply.

More than a decade ago, Delpit (1988) advocated the (a) fostering of more meaningful interpersonal relations in schools, (b) affirmation of the beliefs that all learners are capable of learning, (c) establishment of high academic standards for all learners, and (d) use of learners' communicative styles in teaching. Clearly, academic success demands the acquisition of the mainstream culture, which means, in part, acquiring the communicative codes of those in power. Those who do not belong to the power group should be taught explicitly the means of access to power, including the linguistic forms and ways of talking, writing and interacting used by the powerful. Equally important, those in power (in this case, teachers and service providers) should be taught to value ethnic distinctions and be helped to learn about cultures and languages of students of disenfranchised/disadvantaged groups. Gaining students' cooperation in today's classrooms involves establishing a classroom atmosphere in which teachers are aware of, and address, students' cultural, linguistic, social, emotional, and cognitive needs (Brown, 2004). Most significant perhaps to each child or adolescent is the willingness and ability of an educator or service provider to genuinely touch his or her social and emotional persona. As Brown (2003) pointed out, the development of a comfortable learning environment for teachers and service providers often overpowers the use of effective curricular and instructional strategies in terms of influencing students' growth.

CULTURALLY RESPONSIVE TEACHING

Culturally responsive teaching, a foundational concept of multicultural education, involves the infusion of curriculum with rich connections to students' cultural and linguistic backgrounds within family and community contexts (McCaleb, 1994; Reyhner, 1992). Students become active generators of knowledge, building new academic knowledge by making connections to cultural, community, and home-based experiences. Reyhner argued that validating students' cultural and linguistic experiences leads to their empowerment, collaborative goal setting, and meaningful learning. These forms of growth are especially crucial for students presenting problem behaviors.

Culturally responsive teaching facilitates and supports the achievement of all students. It requires teachers and service providers to create learning environments where all students are welcomed, supported, and provided with best opportunities to learn regardless of their cultural and linguistic backgrounds. To do so effectively, these professionals need to use the three dimensions of a culturally responsive teaching framework:

1. *Academic achievement*—making learning rigorous, exciting, challenging, and equitable with high standards

2. *Cultural competence*—knowing and facilitating the learning process with consideration for the needs of students' cultural and linguistic groups

3. *Sociopolitical consciousness*—recognizing and assisting students in the understanding that education and schooling do not occur in a vacuum (Gay, 2002).

The interaction of all three dimensions can significantly help teachers and service providers to meet the needs of a diverse student population. Whether teachers and service providers will act to implement culturally responsive teaching with their students is strongly influenced by their own knowledge of and comfort with ethnicity and diversity, as well as their confidence about being able to teach in a culturally responsive manner (Gay, 2002).

Culturally responsive teachers and service providers recognize the fact that students who do not believe they are valued in school settings are likely to develop inaccurate self-esteem, alienating them further from school learning. Validating cultural experiences of CLD learners in the schooling process and content is a way to affirm their identity. It creates multiple ways of seeing and perceiving a viable experience of all in a culturally diverse society. Jackson (1994) suggested that to build culturally responsive teaching, teachers and service providers must (a) build trust, (b) become culturally literate, (c) build different methodological approaches, (d) use effective questioning techniques, (e) provide effective feedback, (f) analyze instructional materials, and (g) establish positive home-school relations. These strategies are especially critical for students experiencing problems with social behavior.

Culturally responsive teaching uses the child's culture to build a bridge to success in school achievement. In addition, it places other cultures alongside the middle-class mainstream, macrocultures at the center of the classroom instruction paradigm. It leads to deeper studies of one's own culture and to the studies of other cultures. Finally, it recognizes the power of teaching while fully realizing that, without accompanying changes in all other aspects of schooling and society, the very best teaching will not be able to accomplish the systemic reforms needed for CLD students to receive genuine educational equity and achieve excellence (Pewewardy, 1998). Table 10.1 lists the specific behaviors that teachers should initiate when using a culturally responsive teaching model (Sandhu & Rigney, 1995).

Table 10.1   A Three-Step Culturally Responsive Teaching Model

Step One: Awareness

Teachers and service providers

- actively seek information regarding other cultures and ethnic groups through all means available to them, including books, films, and community resource people.
- learn to create learning conditions for students from diverse ethnic backgrounds that are equitable. They do this by, among other methods, becoming aware of culturally specific learning styles, communication patterns, behaviors, and values.
- examine their own values, behaviors, and beliefs and how they might have positive or negative effects upon culturally different/distinct learners.

Step Two: Acceptance

This is the step whereby teachers and service providers

- accept that cultural diversity is valuable and an asset to all students.
- believe that all learners can learn and have the potential to excel in their areas of interest, no matter what their background or disability.
- respect divergent thinking and different viewpoints of their learners. Everyone brings a unique and worthwhile perspective to the table—acknowledge it.

Step Three: Action

Teachers and service providers

- empower their learners through encouragement, support, and personal attention.
- practice behaviors that are free from biases, prejudice, and stereotypes; encourage their learners to do the same; and, finally, lead by example.
- are genuine, empathetic, and considerate with their students both in and outside the classroom.
- are committed to promoting cultural diversity and are open to new experiences and challenges.
- are committed to incorporating cultural diversity into the curriculum and into all learning experiences.

TEACHING APPROPRIATE BEHAVIOR

The actions of a teacher are important, and students often notice them. Teachers use verbal and nonverbal language when they teach and interact with students, and students tend to recognize nonverbal language more than verbal responses to their behaviors and comments. They notice teachers' facial expressions and other body movements, especially when they believe teachers should be listening to them (Brown, 2004). Often, teachers fail to recognize the communication signals they are channeling through nonverbal actions. Teacher behaviors often indicate that a student's nonverbal communication is used in decision-making processes. Teachers who have an understanding of the diverse meanings of gestures along with the sociocultural heritages of their students have an opportunity to enhance learning in a diverse classroom (Gaythwaite, 2005).

Similarly, teachers shoul employ a great deal of caution when reading nonverbal cues. This caution is of particular relevance when addressing students from diverse settings. For example, if a student is identified as cheating on a test or the teacher suspects that the student copied an assignment from another student, the teacher may confront the student about the event. Some people believe that if a student does not look you directly in the eye when answering a question that he or she is lying. However, in the case of children from specific regions or CLD backgrounds, looking directly at a person when confronted may be a sign of disrespect.

Creating a safe climate is a prerequisite for helping CLD students with behavior problems to develop awareness of who they are. Within this learning environment, personal and professional assumptions and biases can be challenged, and cultural content can be explored (Weinstein, Tomlinson-Clarke, & Curran, 2004). Teachers and the school environment are critical protective factors for fostering resilience. Critical school factors identified by Benard (2004) and Henderson and Milstein (1996) include the following:

- *Developing caring relationships with adults and peers*—teaching social skills, establishing unconditional positive regard, creating a culture of care and respect, and consistently providing care and support
- *Setting high and clear expectations for academic performance and classroom behavior*— teaching cooperation and conflict resolution, consistent implementation of rules and procedures, and communicating an expectation that students are capable of high-level academic performance
- *Providing opportunities for meaningful participation in learning*—structuring the curriculum so that every child succeeds, linking the curriculum to students, validating home language, providing experiential learning, and using group processes throughout the curriculum

These must all be considered for students to have the optimal learning environment possible.

A teacher or service provider who is authoritative and sensitive to the cultural norms of students holds their attention by (a) using the communicative style of their culture, (b) appealing to affiliation rather than authority to maintain order, and (c) believing it is unnecessary to use coercive means to control them. Allowing students to vent frustrations and disagree with school-imposed or perceived teacher-imposed constraints builds a community that works together to find a solution acceptable to all rather than an authoritarian atmosphere of "because I said so" (Bondy, Ross, Gallingane, & Hambacher, 2007). These tasks include (a) creating a physical setting that supports academic and social goals, (b) establishing and maintaining expectations for behavior,

(c) enhancing students' motivation, (d) organizing and managing instructional formats, (e) working with families, and (f) using appropriate interventions to assist students experiencing problems (Weinstein et al., 2004).

Clearly, supportive classroom environments encompass all the critical school factors that foster resilience in CLD students. In contrast, teachers and service providers who create nonsupportive environments are authoritarian, stress both power and control, convey low expectations, and rely on extrinsic motivation to get students to work. This can create problems for many different types of students, including students from diverse backgrounds. In creating a supportive environment, teachers and service providers can develop an understanding that cultures vary in terms of their emphasis on the group or the individual (Franklin, 2001). They can begin to appreciate the importance of conducting home visits and consulting with parents and community members. In addition, teachers and service providers can learn what questions to ask about CLD students' family backgrounds, educational experiences, and cultural norms and values (Grossman, 1995; Kottler, 1994; Sileo & Prater, 1998). Table 10.2 lists some questions that teachers and service providers can explore as they interact with CLD students.

Table 10.2 Questions to Explore When Building Culturally Responsive Teaching Practices

- *Family Background and Structure*: Where did your family come from? How long have you been in this country? What is the hierarchy of authority in your family? What responsibilities do you have at home? Is English a second language for you and your family?
- *Education*: How much previous schooling have you had? What kinds of instructional strategies are you familiar with? In your former schools, was there an emphasis on large-group instruction, memorization, and repeating of information? What were the expectations for appropriate behavior in your previous school? Were you expected to be active or passive? Peer oriented or teacher oriented?
- *Interpersonal Relationship Styles*: Do cultural norms emphasize working for the good of the group or for individual achievement? What are the norms with respect to interaction between males and females? What constitutes a comfortable personal space? Do students obey or question authority figures? Are expressions of emotion and feelings emphasized or hidden?
- *Discipline*: Do adults act in permissive, authoritative, or authoritarian ways? What kinds of praise, reward, criticism, and punishment are customary for you? Are these behaviors administered publicly or privately? To the group or the individual?
- *Time and Space*: How do you think about time? Is punctuality expected, or is time considered flexible to you and your family? How important is speed in completing a task to you and your family?
- *Religion*: What restrictions are there concerning topics that should not be discussed in school related to religion? Do you need to miss any school for any religious reasons?
- *Food*: What are you used to eating? What have you not eaten before? Is there anything that you are allergic to? Are there any foods that you are not allowed to eat?
- *Health and Hygiene*: How are illnesses treated and by whom in your family or culture? What are the norms with respect to seeking professional help for emotional and psychological problems?
- *History, Traditions, and Holidays*: Which events and people are sources of pride for your cultural group? To what extent does your cultural group in the United States identify with the history and traditions of your country of origin? What holidays and celebrations are considered appropriate for observing in school?

Clearly, teachers' knowledge about and attitudes toward cultural diversity are powerful determinants of learning opportunities and outcomes for CLD students. For some students, they facilitate achievement; for others, they obstruct learning (Gay, 2002). The physical features, emotional tone, and quality of interactions among students and between students and teachers have a tremendous impact on how or whether learning occurs.

Classroom climates that are "cold," hostile, isolative, and stressful are not conducive to the best learning for any students, and CLD students in particular perform much better in emotionally warm, caring, and supportive classroom climates (Gay, 2001; Howard, 1999). As Howard discovered, students preferred "teachers who displayed caring bonds and attitudes toward them, and teachers who establish community- and family-type classroom environments" (p. 131). The best quality education for CLD students is as much *culturally responsive as it is developmentally appropriate,* which means using their cultural orientations, background experiences, and ethnic identities as conduits to facilitate teaching and learning. This applies to students in both regular and special education (Gay, 2002).

Teachers and service providers should begin by asking themselves a few questions: Do I know the cultural background of each of my students? Do I integrate literature and resources from their cultures into my lessons? Do I consistently begin my lessons with what students already know from home, community, and school? Do I understand the differences between academic language and my students' social language, and do I find ways to bridge the two (Kopkowski, 2006)? To a large measure, children's experiences outside the classroom greatly affect their success at school, especially when children's home experiences are not those of the mainstream culture (Heath, 1983; Moll & Dias, 1987). This makes it even more important for teachers and service providers to know their students and their families and to stay in constant communication with them. Knowing this information will help teachers develop a positive learning environment and will help them to understand students and what they are going through and to communicate more effectively with them. For example, students may exhibit inappropriate (according to the teacher or service provider) social skills in the classroom. If the teacher or service provider has a mutual line of communication open with the student and family, the teaching process for those students becomes much more manageable.

When teaching social skills to CLD learners, teachers must be careful to respect the children's cultures, even if it is necessary to teach a skill that is contrary to the behaviors in which a child has been socialized. For example, many children living in violence-prone areas are taught to be tough and physically aggressive as a means of survival. This instruction, however, is contrary to the expectations of the school culture. In teaching nonaggressive alternatives to conflict, teachers need to acknowledge an understanding of parents' lessons but point out the need for students to learn alternative skills to be successful in school (Cartledge, Singh, & Gibson, 2008). Today's foremost challenge in education is to create learning environments that maintain the cultural integrity of every child while enhancing educational success (Wlodkowski & Ginsberg, 1995). Positive interventions are critical for students at risk for behavior problems.

Social skill instruction is a proactive, positive intervention that is especially important for CLD learners, who may be at odds with the culture of the school and, as a result, may tend to experience unduly punitive and ineffective consequences. A major concern for young CLD learners is that they are likely to be punished excessively for their specific behaviors rather than receive instruction to develop replacement behaviors. CLD students need to be taught behaviors that are critical for success in general education classrooms. The model for teaching social skills is essentially to tell the student what the behavior is, show him or her how to perform the behavior, give the student ample opportunities to practice the behavior with corrective or reinforcing feedback, and present programs for behavior maintenance and transfer (Cartledge & Milburn, 1995, 1996). To be culturally relevant, social skill instruction needs to reflect the lifestyle and experiences of the CLD learner. Instruction needs to reflect the learner's immediate experiences or environment, include culturally specific models, and involve skills that he or she needs to develop (Cartledge et al., 2008).

TEACHING BEHAVIOR TO CLD LEARNERS

Teaching behavior for maintaining an appropriate learning environment is as much an art as it is science, according to researchers and teachers (Brown, 2004). Effectively teaching student behaviors generally involves the ability to develop a classroom social environment in which students agree to cooperate with teachers and fellow students in pursuit of academic growth (see Brown). For the classroom to be an optimal learning environment, acceptable behaviors need to be exhibited by all. With awareness of our own taken-for-granted assumptions, knowledge of our students' cultural backgrounds, and understanding of the broader context, we can begin to reflect on the ways that classroom practices promote or obstruct equal access to learning (Weinstein, Tomlinson-Clarke, & Curran, 2004).

Culturally responsive classroom management (CRCM) is connected to a teacher's ability to use culturally responsive curricular materials and instructional processes to manage behaviors (Brown, 2004). Brown interviewed teachers and found most were primarily nonpunitive in their approach to handling disruptive behavior—they relied on their strong relationships with students built on trust, rather than fear or punishment, to maintain a cooperative learning environment. Each teacher demonstrated mutual respect for students through congruent communication patterns that honored students' ethnic and cultural needs. Teachers spoke of creating caring learning communities and demonstrating genuine interest in each student. All the teachers with at least five years of experience established clearly stated expectations for behavior and used an assertive demeanor when necessary to establish their authority as a teacher. These same teachers also described how they established a businesslike classroom learning environment with explicitly stated expectations for student behavior and academic progress (see Brown).

Teaching students in a way that creates a smoothly operating learning environment involves a series of highly fluid and dynamic actions (Brown, 2003). Discipline enters into the process when classroom disruption prohibits appropriate behavior or creates other problems (Cartledge et al., 2008). First, we need to monitor our behavior in terms of equitable treatment (Nieto, 2000). Some critical questions deserve to be answered; for instance, Are we more patient and encouraging with some? Are we more likely to chastise others? Do we base stereotypical judgments of our students' character and academic potential on their hairstyle and dress? Second, we need to question traditional assumptions of "what works" in classroom instruction and be alert to possible mismatches between existing strategies and students' cultural backgrounds. Third, we need to consider when to accommodate students' cultural backgrounds and when to expect students to accommodate (Grossman, 1995), or what Nieto (2000) called *mutual accommodation*.

In mutual accommodation, teachers accept and build on students' language and culture but also equip them and their families to function within the culture of the school in key areas needed for academic progress and order (e.g., attendance, homework, and punctuality). To implement culturally responsive classroom management, teachers and service providers must (a) recognize their ethnocentrism and understand the broader sociopolitical context to know that definitions of appropriate classroom behavior are culturally defined, (b) develop knowledge of their students' cultural backgrounds, (c) use culturally appropriate classroom-management strategies, and (d) build caring classroom communities. CRCM makes it explicit that instruction is grounded in teachers' judgments about appropriate behavior and that these judgments are informed by cultural assumptions (Bondy et al., 2007). Moreover, teacher educators and researchers interested in effective classrooms must begin to make cultural diversity an integral part of the conversation. We need to ask whether diversity requires different approaches to instruction, to examine the kinds of cultural conflicts that are likely to arise in ethnically diverse classrooms, and to consider the best ways to help preservice teachers become competent in multicultural settings (Weinstein et al., 2004).

Making good choices in a classroom setting is important for students to be successful. For example, a program such as CHA CHA might be a good choice. CHA CHA encourages students' individual accountability for responsible decision making, positive social behavior, meeting homework deadlines, and being present and punctual. The behavioral criteria associated with CHA CHA are the following:

- Students treat peers and adults with respect as measured through compliance with school and classroom rules.
- Students arrive to school on time.
- Students complete all homework each day. (Students may stay after school every day for homework help with one teacher from each grade level, or they may call the district's homework hotline.)
- Students must attend school every day and arrive on time, or if they are absent, the absence must be excused (King, Harris-Murri, & Artiles, 2006).

The following individually focused approaches are components of the CHA CHA and Rights and Responsibilities programs. These approaches are designed to meet the needs of students who have difficulty meeting the success criteria for these programs, as defined above (see King et al., 2006). If a particular student shows a pattern of behavior in need of remediation, the classroom teacher meets with the principal, and they develop an action plan for supporting the student through school and community resources, including school counseling, assignment to a GEAR UP mentor, and participation in the peer mediation program. Additionally, any further negative behaviors by the student do not impact the referral-free status of the class, since a plan is in place for him or her and the teacher and principal are in close communication regarding his or her progress (see King et al.). This is just one example of a program that can be implemented to teach students how to be successful in the classroom and prevent problem behaviors.

CONCLUSION

Today, educators are faced with overwhelming challenges to prepare students from CLD backgrounds to live in a society and world where some groups have greater societal benefits than others. To prepare students, behavior in the classroom needs to be addressed, monitored, and taught effectively. We know that many key factors can play into how a student responds to a teacher in a classroom; these include the student's culture and where he or she lives. Culturally responsive teaching facilitates and supports the achievement of all students. In addition, it requires teachers to create learning environments where all students are welcomed, supported, and provided with the best opportunities to learn, regardless of their CLD backgrounds. Having a supportive classroom environment that encompasses all students will foster resilience and acceptance. Teachers' knowledge about and attitudes toward cultural diversity are powerful determinants of learning opportunities and outcomes for ethnically different students and must be considered as a part of the learning process. Children's experiences outside the classroom greatly affect their success at school, especially when their home experiences are not those of the mainstream culture. This makes it even more important for teachers and service providers to know their students and their families. Culturally responsive classroom management is a technique that can be implemented to address behavior. This technique is connected to a teacher's ability to use culturally responsive curricular materials and instructional processes to teach students content and proper behaviors. Students need to be taught how to act, respond, and get along with others, as well as content, to be successful in the classroom and prevent problem behaviors that could persist for many years.

Illustrations From Practice

Classroom to Community and Back (Saifer, Edwards, Ellis, Ko, & Stuczynski, 2005) is a professional development resource that describes how "educators can use the knowledge and culture students bring to school" (p. v) to support their success. The book includes several examples (paraphrased below) illustrating how teachers used the experiences, understandings, views, concepts, and ways of knowing of the students sitting in the classroom to engage in culturally responsive instruction.

A first-grade student and her mother are taking turns reading to the class from a book the child has made as part of a project to use parents' knowledge at home and in school. The mother reads a few lines in Vietnamese, and then her child reads the English translation. The rest of the students are listening and actively engaged in taking notes on clipboards provided by the teacher. Some sketch quick drawings or jot down words in the six spaces available on their papers. The story concludes with a moral about the importance of the family sticking together like a "bunch of chopsticks," because separately they are not as strong. It is a familiar story that the child's mother heard when she was a little girl in Vietnam. Maps and handwritten posters listing titles of stories, main characters, plots, and other information about the children's books are displayed around the room—all in their native languages. Almost every day for two-and-a-half weeks, different families repeat the storytelling. During this time, the children hear parents' favorite stories from their childhoods in Russia, Ukraine, Mexico, and the Philippines, and home languages, cultures, family histories, and community values become central elements of the school's curriculum (Saifer et al., "Fairy Tales, Folktales, and Family Stories," pp. 91–92).

Nearly half the students at Woodmere Elementary School in Portland, Oregon, are from families who immigrated to the United States from Eastern Europe, Southeast Asia, and Mexico. Their classmates and peers are from mostly lower-income White families who have lived in the neighborhood for many years. The fifth-grade teacher's goal for the "Heritage Dolls" activity was to have students become more connected to each other and more interested in learning by dressing a cardstock cut-out figure in the native costume of the country of their ancestors. The teacher sent a letter home explaining the activity so that parents could assist. Students conducted original research to establish the authenticity of their doll's dress and to gather background information on the culture, language, food, geography, climate, housing style, transportation, games, special products, industries, and employment opportunities found in the countries represented by the dolls. What they have learned is placed on 3 × 5 inch cards, which are used to prepare for an oral report to the class. The teacher engages the children in the activity by having them answer questions about why they chose their country, how they researched it, how they made the doll, and what they learned about the culture (Saifer et al., "Heritage Dolls," pp. 124–125).

The middle school library has become a gallery of black-and-white and color portraits displayed on the tops of bookcases and tables. The pictures of students with their families and teachers invite visitors to take a closer look into their diverse worlds. As students walk through the exhibit, they have been given the assignment of jotting down "similarities or differences to their own families, or something in the photos they want to know more about." When they return to their tables in groups of five or six, the conversations begin. Many of the students have questions about the "stories" in the photographs, and they are asked to use words, pictures, or symbols to answer questions about their own family experience: What does your family look like? How does your family support you to be the best you can be in school? What happens when home and family come together? What does your teacher need to know about your family to teach you better? The afterschool teachers who brought their students to participate in this lesson are encouraged to continue the conversation about family diversity and to create activities that infuse the information from the students' discussions back in their classrooms (Saifer et al., "Heritage Dolls," p. 90).

Accepting that improvements in the quality of their communities have an impact on everyone's lives, students at Aberdeen High School (AHS) create a Collaborative Action Research Project as the "crowning achievement" of their senior year in high school. Teams of up to four students gather information as a basis for developing an action plan for solving a community-based problem, such as

- unfair athletic practices in their school;
- poor quality of food in the school cafeteria;
- rundown and hazardous conditions in city parks; or
- limited appreciation of teachers in some schools.

Teams have also worked on projects with broad community benefits:

- A Handbook for Improving the City of Aberdeen
- Creating Harmony in Teenage Relationships
- Solutions Regarding Parking at AHS
- Creating a Junior High Pregnancy Prevention Program

The Collaborative Action Research Project culminates in a 20-minute professional presentation to a panel of judges, including the school board president, district superintendent, principal of the high school, director of technology, and the curriculum/instruction/assessment director. Although the presentation can be stressful, participants all realize the value of celebrating the good work being done and of honoring the changes students have initiated in their community (Saifer et al., "Heritage Dolls," p. 131).

REFERENCES

Benard, B. (2004). *Resiliency: What we have learned*. San Francisco: West Ed.

Bennett, C. I. (1995). *Comprehensive multicultural education: Theory and practice* (3rd ed.). Boston: Allyn & Bacon.

Bondy, E., Ross, D. D., Gallingane, C., & Hambacher, E. (2007). Creating environments of success and resilience: Culturally responsive classroom management and more. *Urban Education, 42*(4), 326–348.

Brown, D. F. (2003). Urban teachers' use of culturally responsive management strategies. *Theory Into Practice, 42*(4), 277–282.

Brown, D. F. (2004). Urban teachers' professed classroom management strategies: Reflections of culturally responsive teaching. *Urban Education, 39*(3), 266–289.

Burstein, N. D., & Cabello, B. (1989). Preparing teachers to work with culturally diverse students: A teacher education model. *Journal of Teacher Education, 40*, 9–16.

Cartledge, G., & Milburn, J. F. (1995). *Teaching social skills to children and youth: Innovative approaches* (3rd ed.). Boston: Allyn & Bacon.

Cartledge, G., & Milburn, J. F. (1996). *Cultural diversity and social skills instruction: Understanding ethnic and gender differences*. Champaign, IL: Research Press.

Cartledge, G., Singh, A., & Gibson, L. (2008). Practical behavior-management techniques to close the accessibility gap for students who are culturally and linguistically diverse. *Preventing School Failure, 52*(3), 29–38.

Children's Defense Fund. (2001). *The state of America's children yearbook 2001*. Washington, DC: Author.

Delpit, L. D. (1988). The silenced dialogue: Power and pedagogy in educating other people's children. *Harvard Educational Review, 58*(3), 280–298.

Delpit, L. D. (1995). *Other people's children: Cultural conflict in the classroom*. New York: New Press.

Dilworth, M. E. (1990). *Reading between the lines: Teachers and their racial/ethnic cultures*. (Teacher Education Monograph No. 11). Washington, DC: ERIC Clearinghouse on Teacher Education and American Association of Colleges for Teacher Education. (ERIC Document Reproduction Service No. ED322148)

Franklin, J. (2001). The diverse challenges of multiculturalism. *Education Update, 43*(2), 1, 3, 8.

Gay, G. (2001). Educational equality for students of color. In J. A. Banks & C. A. M. Banks (Eds.), *Multicultural education: Issues and perspectives* (4th ed., pp. 197–224). Boston: Allyn & Bacon.

Gay, G. (2002). Culturally responsive teaching in special education for ethnically diverse students: Setting the stage. *Qualitative Studies in Education, 15*(6), 613–629.

Gaythwaite, E. (2005). Didn't you see what I meant? *Curriculum and Teaching Dialogue, 7*(1/2), 97–108.

Gollnick, D. M., & Chinn, P. C. (2002). *Multicultural education in a pluralistic society*. Upper Saddle River, NJ: Merrill Prentice-Hall.

Grossman, H. (1995). *Classroom behavior management in adverse society* (2nd ed.). Mountain View, CA: Mayfield.

Heath, S. B. (1983). *Ways with words: Language, life, and work in communities and classrooms*. New York: Cambridge University Press.

Henderson, N., & Milstein, M. M. (1996). *Resiliency in schools: Making it happen for students and educators*. Thousand Oaks, CA: Corwin.

Howard, G. R. (1999). *We can't teach what we don't know: White teachers, multiracial schools*. New York: Teachers College Press.

Huber, T. (1991, October). *Restructuring to reclaim youth at risk: Culturally responsible pedagogy*. Paper presented at the 13th annual meeting of the Mid-Western Educational Research Association, Chicago, IL. (ERIC Document Reproduction Service No. ED341655)

Jackson, F. R. (1994). Seven strategies to support a culturally responsive pedagogy. *Journal of Reading, 37*(4), 298–303.

Kindler, A. L. (2002). *Survey of the states' limited English proficient students and available educational programs and services, 2000–2001 summary report*. Washington, DC: U.S. Department of Education, National Clearinghouse for English Language Acquisition and Language Instruction Educational Programs.

King, K. A., Harris-Murri, N. J., & Artiles, A. J. (2006). *Proactive culturally responsive discipline.* Retrieved October 28, 2009, from the National Center for Culturally Responsive Educational Systems Web site: http://www.nccrest.org/Exemplars/exemplar_culturally_responsive_discipline.pdf

Kopkowski, C. (2006, November). *It's there: Talk about it. Race and poverty don't need to be the elephants in the classroom. As culturally responsive teaching takes root, these issues can actually help your students learn.* Retrieved September 23, 2008, from National Education Association Web site: http://www.nea.org

Kottler, E. (1994). *Children with limited English: Teaching strategies for the regular classroom.* Thousand Oaks, CA: Corwin.

Krezmien, M. P., Leone, P. E., & Achilles, G. M. (2006). Suspension, race, and disability: Analysis of statewide practices and reporting. *Journal of Emotional and Behavioral Disorders, 14,* 217–226.

Ladson-Billings, G. (2001). *Crossing over to Canaan: The journey of new teachers in diverse classrooms.* San Francisco: Jossey-Bass.

Lewis-Palmer, T., Sugai, G., & Larson, S. (1999). Using data to guide decisions about program implementation and effectiveness. *Effective School Practices, 17*(4), 47–53.

McCaleb, S. P. (1994). *Building communities of learners: A collaboration among teachers, students, families, and community.* New York: St. Martin's Press.

Mendez, L. M. R., & Knoff, H. M. (2003). Who gets suspended from school and why: A demographic analysis of schools and disciplinary infractions in a large school district. *Education and Treatment of Children, 26,* 30–51.

Moll, L. C., & Dias, S. (1987). Change as a goal of educational research. *Anthropology and Education Quarterly, 18,* 300–311.

Morrison, G. M., Anthony, S., Storino, M., & Dillon, C. (2001). An examination of the disciplinary histories and the individual and educational characteristics of students who participate in an in school suspension program. *Education and Treatment of Children, 24,* 276–293.

National Center for Educational Statistics, U. S. Department of Health, Education, and Welfare. (1993). *Digest of educational statistics.* Washington, DC: Government Printing Office.

Nieto, S. (2000). *Affirming diversity: The sociopolitical context of multicultural education* (3rd ed.). White Plains, NY: Longman.

Obiakor, F. E. (2001). *It even happens in "good" schools: Responding to cultural diversity in today's classroom.* Thousand Oaks, CA: Corwin.

Obiakor, F. E. (2003). *The eight-step approach to multicultural learning and teaching* (3rd ed.). Dubuque, IA: Kendall/Hunt.

Obiakor, F. E. (2007). Multicultural special education: Effective intervention for today's school. *Intervention in School and Clinic, 42*(3), 148–155.

Obiakor, F. E., & Beachum, F. D. (2005). Developing self-empowerment in African American students using the comprehensive support model. *Journal of Negro Education, 74*(1), 18–29.

Pewewardy, C. D. (1998, November). *Culturally responsive teaching for American Indian learners.* Paper presented at the 1998 Kansas Institute on Effective Teaching Practices for Indian Education, Lawrence, KS. (ERIC Document Reproduction Service No. ED459981)

Reyhner, J. (1992). Bilingual education. In J. Reyhner (Ed.), *Teaching American Indian students* (pp. 59–77). Norman: University of Oklahoma Press.

Saifer, S., Edwards, K., Ellis, D., Ko, L., & Stuczynski, A. (2005). *Classroom to community and back: Using culturally responsive, standards-based teaching to strengthen family and community partnerships and increase student achievement.* Portland, OR: Northwest Regional Educational Laboratory. Retrieved June 20, 2009, from http://www.nwrel.org/partnerships/c2cb/c2c.pdf

Sandhu, D. S., & Rigney, J. R. (1995). Culturally responsive teaching in U.S. public schools. *Kappa Delta Pi Record, 31*(4), 157–162.

Sileo, T. W., & Prater, M. A. (1998). Creating classroom environments that address the linguistic andcultural backgrounds of students with disabilities: An Asian Pacific American perspective. *Remedial and Special Education, 19*(6), 323–337.

Skiba, R. J., Michael, R. S., Nardo, A. C., & Peterson, R. (2002). The color of discipline: Sources of racial and gender disproportionality in school punishment. *Urban Review, 34,* 317–342.

Skiba, R. J., Poloni-Staudinger, L., Simmons, A. B., Feggins-Azziz, R., & Chung, C.-G. (2005).Unproven links: Can poverty explain ethnic disproportionality in special education? *Journal of Special Education, 39,* 130–144.

Sleeter, C. E. (1995). An analysis of critiques of multicultural education. In J. A. Banks & C. A. McGee Banks (Eds.), *Handbook on research on multicultural education* (pp. 81–94). New York: Simon & Schuster Macmillan.

Smith, G. P. (1991). *Parameters of the knowledge base for a culturally responsive pedagogy for teacher education.* Paper presented at the American Association for Colleges of Teacher Education, University of North Florida, Jacksonville.

Utley, C., & Obiakor, F. E. (2001). *Special education, multicultural education, and school reform: Components of quality education for learners with mild disabilities.* Springfield, IL: Charles C. Thomas.

Weinstein, C. S., Tomlinson-Clarke, S., & Curran, M. (2004). Toward a conception of culturally responsive classroom management. *Journal of Teacher Education, 55*(1), 25–38.

Wilson, B. L., & Corbett, H. D. (2001). *Listening to urban kids: School reform and the teachers they want.* Albany: State University of New York Press.

Wlodkowski, R. J., & Ginsberg, M. B. (1995). A framework for culturally responsive teaching. *Educational Leadership, 53*(1), 17–21.

11

Monitoring Student Progress and Evaluating Prevention Practices

In this chapter, we

- review the context and need for regular monitoring of progress when implementing prevention practices,
- identify and describe key features of effective progress-monitoring measures,
- review evidence supporting the use of progress monitoring to support behavioral interventions,
- review the context and need for program evaluation when implementing prevention practices,
- identify and describe key features of effective program evaluations, and
- provide a perspective on progress monitoring and evaluation of prevention efforts.

Problem solving is central to prevention practices. In all approaches to problem solving, a difference between expected and actual behavior is the basis for identifying a problem and for developing plans for the "who, what, where, when, and how" for changing it. Data and assessment are central to the process.

Ray Jones's desk is covered with data defining the status of the students in his school. The latest "pile" just arrived from "downtown" illustrating his school's position in the district's documentation of performance in the state's high-stakes testing program.

As more and more data appear regularly on his computer, Mr. Jones knows that the condition of education at his school is "attracting attention" and the challenge is how to use all of it to bring about the greatest improvement in the learning and behavior of the students in his school. He also knows that he needs practical, proven methods for providing support to prevent learning and behavior problems. The teachers and other professionals in his school need to know that what they are doing is producing desired effects. District administrators and school board members need to know how these methods are working so that they can continue or change them. Policy makers need ways of documenting success in implementing prevention strategies to ensure continued support.

The Behavior and Reading Improvement Center (BRIC) has been implementing preventive interventions in elementary schools in the Charlotte-Mecklenburg Schools (CMS) district for several years, using a continuum operationalized into three tiers of support: primary, secondary, and tertiary. Participating schools were assigned a Center Support Coordinator (CSC) to direct and monitor the implementation of project-sponsored interventions. At the onset of our restructuring of these schools, we put a behavior instruction system into place. We had unified schoolwide and classroom expectations and used a unified correction script when students broke rules and procedures. Our ongoing professional development included whole-group sessions in which we set goals together (e.g., created five positively stated schoolwide expectations, developed a matrix to link expected behaviors in specific locations to schoolwide expectations) and small-group and individual coaching to provided guided practice to teachers needing help in teaching, prompting, and reinforcing expected behaviors. We conducted regular procedural fidelity observations and noted that the success of our efforts was directly related to the level at which the interventions were implemented. This came as no surprise, since systematic monitoring of progress and outcomes is the foundation on which all successful teaching efforts are based.

MONITORING STUDENT PROGRESS IN PREVENTIVE INTERVENTIONS

A growing body of research supports the belief that in order for students to behave appropriately in school, they must be exposed to effective behavior instruction, including direct teaching focused on clear and positive schoolwide and classroom expectations, monitoring of progress toward mastery of those expectations, provision of feedback to all stakeholders concerning progress, and the collection and use of data to make instructional decisions. The current method of choice for preventing problems relies on graduated support through tiered intervention models.

The assumption is that the first-level, primary, or universal intervention consists of systematic direct instruction of behavior or academic skills that lead to students meeting schoolwide and classroom expectations. If students fail to meet these goals, they qualify for secondary or tertiary interventions. With regard to behavior instruction at the primary level, Lane and Menzies (2003) suggested that in the ideal situation, a wide range of data, including standardized reading test scores, behavior rating scales, curriculum-based measurements, and direct observation measures would be collected on every student participant. Yet, due to resource and time constraints, this range of measures often is not feasible, particularly when monitoring student responsiveness to primary interventions. Some primary interventions conducted to date have collected a limited range of outcome variables (e.g., office referrals, rewards allocated), which has made it difficult for researchers and practitioners to detect changes in the targeted domain.

The Individuals with Disabilities Education Improvement Act (IDEA) and No Child Left Behind Act (NCLB) underline the increased need for progress monitoring and outcomes-based assessment of efforts to adopt, implement, and sustain effective services for students in our public schools (Kratochwill, Volpiansky, Clements, & Ball, 2007). Of course, no single assessment can be used for all purposes, and using too many assessments can be problematic and prohibitive. The focus of preventive interventions is to develop, maintain, and improve systems for teaching appropriate behavior and replacing inappropriate behavior. Evaluating the effectiveness of these systems typically involves the use of multiple measures, including but not limited to existing data from a variety of sources and current systematic observations, global rating scales, and curriculum-based and norm-referenced tests; however, classroom-based ratings of target behaviors over a specified period of time are increasingly popular tools for addressing these formative and summative assessment needs (Chafouleas, Riley-Tillman, & Sugai, 2007; Salvia, Ysseldyke, & Bolt, 2010).

The broad term *direct behavior ratings* (DBRs) is used for brief assessments of behavior over a specified period of time (Chafouleas, Riley-Tillman, & Sugai, 2007). These measurements show promise both as progress-monitoring planning and teaching tools and as outcomes-based behavior assessments (Chafouleas, Riley-Tillman, & McDougal, 2002; Riley-Tillman, Chafouleas, & Briesch, 2007). For example, Chafouleas, Riley-Tillman, and McDougal suggested that they may be feasible, acceptable, effective in promoting positive student behavior, and successful in increasing parent/teacher communication. Perspectives on the use of DBRs among a sample of educators suggest that they are highly acceptable as an intervention tool and as a way to measure behavior (Chafouleas, Riley-Tillman, & Sassu, 2005). Riley-Tillman, Chafouleas, and Briesch indicated that such a brief assessment offers a considerable advantage in that data can be collected and feedback provided frequently in a feasible manner and the active role of the classroom teacher in this data collection process likely increases the acceptability and use of it. The teacher's role as a participant observer also provides a "fidelity check" for the intervention implementation by serving as a consistent reminder of the agreed-upon plan. We believe DBRs show great promise as tools with which to record, monitor, and assess student progress toward mastering schoolwide and classroom expectations, as well as for assessing overall effectiveness of prevention efforts.

What We Know About the Use of Daily Behavior Ratings

The DBR (also known as daily behavior report card [DBRC], home-school note, and other, similar names) is a measure in which a specified behavior is rated at least daily and the information is shared with someone other than the rater (Chafouleas et al., 2002; Chafouleas, Riley-Tillman, & Sugai, 2007; Riley-Tillman, Chafouleas, Sassu, Chanese, & Glazer, 2008; Wright, 2002).The DBR has been reviewed in the literature as an intervention tool but recently has received attention as an assessment tool as well. If used as an assessment tool to monitor behavior, comparing data collection across multiple points, it may be referred to as a "systematic" DBR (Riley-Tillman, Chafouleas, & Briesch, 2007). Systematic DBRs have the following characteristics: the targeted behavior is defined operationally, the observations are conducted under standardized procedures to ensure consistency in data collection, the data collection occurs for a specific time and place, and the data are scored and summarized in a consistent manner (Riley-Tillman et al.). To date, some studies have examined the characteristics of these measures for estimating behavior, but most of the literature has focused on them as intervention tools.

Studies of the efficacy of DBRs as assessment tools have focused on monitoring the effects of medication on children with attention deficit/hyperactivity disorder (ADHD).

For example, two studies have compared concurrent, performance-based daily behavior ratings and systematic direct observation ratings in special education (Steege, Davin, & Hathaway, 2001) and general education settings (Chafouleas, McDougal, Riley-Tillman, Panahon, & Hilt, 2005) to determine their accuracy. Both studies found moderate to high associations between behavior rating and direct observation data, thereby indicating an adequate level of accuracy and reliability. In a recent study, Chafouleas, Riley-Tillman, Sassu, LaFrance, and Patwa (2007) stated that

> the overall consistency found in this study lends support to the use of DBRCs as tools to estimate global classroom behavior, dependent on how data will be used. Considering the previously discussed need for reliable, feasible methods for monitoring student behavior, the results of this study provide an exciting base for future consideration. (p. 36)

A recent survey conducted by Chafouleas et al. (2006) supported the general acceptability and reported use of daily behavior ratings by classroom teachers. However, Riley-Tillman et al. (2007) cautioned:

> Some potentially significant limitations to the use of [DBRs] should be noted. First, similar to rating scale data, data collected via [DBRs] will be influenced by rater perception of student behavior (e.g., the teacher). This limitation should therefore discourage use of the [DBR] in isolation or in high-stakes decisions (e.g., eligibility for services). Second, the response format of the [DBR] (a Likert scale from 1–5 or 1–7) invariably makes it less sensitive to change than SDO [systematic direct observation] procedures such as frequency counts or time sampling. In addition, the limited number of [DBR] items may impact the reliability of the device. These limitations suggest that use of a [DBR] might best be used in low-stakes cases (e.g., monitoring the effect of a pre-referral intervention) and as a supplement, rather than a wholesale replacement, to more established methods such as SDO. (p. 80)

Riley-Tillman et al. (2007) recommended using the DBRC if the collection of any other type of data would be unreasonable (e.g., lack of time and number of school psychologists to conduct SDOs), when monitoring less severe (e.g., time-on-task, out-of-seat) or low-frequency (e.g., running out of classroom) behaviors, and when data will be used to manage interventions rather than inform specific diagnosis decisions. Chafouleas et al. (2005) stated:

> It may be that a key to deciding whether a DBRC is appropriate is the level of precision needed. For example, if it is critical to measure actual behavior at a specific time, then perhaps the DBRC is not a good tool. However, if a summary of overall behavior, such as from across various observation points, is desired, then maybe the DBRC can provide an appropriate level of precision. Future research needs to examine these issues, such as the number of DBRC data points needed to provide a precise estimate of behavior. (p. 674)

There is a clear and present promise in using DBRCs to improve social skills and behaviors that support academic and other important school-related outcomes. In the proposed project, we will test the efficacy of this intervention for improving classroom ecologies, skills of teachers, and behavioral and academic performances of children. The work will extend what is currently known about a widely used intervention with evidence of its effectiveness in a large-scale, randomized control trial. The trial will be completed in an urban district enrolling large numbers of children who are at risk of failure and likely to need additional or alternative forms of instruction, either to supplement or supplant conventional instruction.

Using Daily Behavior Ratings

A DBR provides systematic performance feedback to students from the classroom teacher that is also usually shared with parents, other teachers, and administrators. When using DBRs, the teacher divides the instructional day into set periods for purposes of recording and giving performance feedback. The teacher then targets specific behaviors for recording and giving performance feedback. At the end of a set period, the teacher rates the student's performance for each behavior using a rating scale. The teacher then shares the results of the recordings with the student on some schedule. Feedback can be provided at the end of each rating period, once in the morning and once in the afternoon, or at the end of the day. When the DBR is used in the context of a preventive behavior support intervention, the teacher's performance feedback challenge is to accentuate reinforcement of behavioral success and, if need be, encourage improvement on behaviors with lower ratings. Most implementations of DBRs reported in the literature have a parent feedback component. Students bring the recorded daily results, including any teacher comments, home. The parents typically are asked to sign the report and given the opportunity to make comments on it, and the child returns the signed form to the teacher the next day.

Chafouleas et al. (2002) pointed out that daily behavior ratings can vary according to the goal of the rating (academic, behavioral, increase or decrease in target behavior), the target of the rating (individual, classwide), the frequency (daily, more than daily, weekly) of the rating, the rating systems used (checklist, scale), the person (child, teacher, other individual) providing the rating, the frequency with which information is shared with another person (daily, weekly), the consequence (positive, negative) of the rating, and the setting for providing the consequence (home, school, other). Table 11.1 presents questions and focusing activities to use in developing a DBR. Steps to follow in creating a DBR include the following:

1. Identify the target behavior.

2. Identify functional pieces of the rating (e.g., who, what, where, when, and how).

3. Design the form to use to record the rating (see Figure 11.1).

4. Identify functional pieces of consequences (e.g., who, what, where, when, and how).

5. Confirm the acceptability of the DBR with individuals involved in using it.

While DBRCs are typically used with individual students, a form can be developed and displayed using an overhead projector or whiteboard for monitoring classroom behavior performance and progress (see Figure 11.2 on page 201).

When the form is ready for use, the procedure for using it is presented and discussed to ensure that the target behavior(s) and the conditions of using the DBR are understood. A procedure for documenting acceptability and implementation fidelity also should be in place. Decisions about continued or modified use are made only after reviewing effectiveness data (see Figure 11.3 on page 201).

Table 11.1 What to Address in Developing a DBR	
Question	Focusing Activity
What is your goal?	• Identify a SMART objective. Is it specific? Can it be measured? Is it aligned with school expectations? It is rigorous but achievable? Is it worthy of instructional time? • Identify desired outcome (increase, maintain, or decrease).
Who will be rated?	• Identify specific individual. • Identify specific group.
When will rating occur?	• Identify time of day. • Identify frequency and duration.
Where will rating occur?	• Identify setting or settings.
How will rating occur?	• Identify scale and format for rating. • Identify rater.
How will rating be used?	• Identify outcome of rating, including person responsible for it. • Identify frequency of outcome.

SOURCE: Adapted from S. Chafouleas, T. C. Riley-Tillman, & G. Sugai (2007), *School-based behavioral assessment*. New York: The Guilford Press.

Figure 11.1 Sample Daily Behavior Report Card for Individual Student			
What We Are Working On: Following schoolwide expectations for appropriate behavior.			
Name:			
Date:			
	Rating		
	2 = Great!	**1 = OK**	**0 = Difficulty**
	Schoolwide Expectation		
Time:	**Be Safe**	**Be Respectful**	**Be Responsible**
Morning [Classroom]			
Morning [Cafeteria]			
Afternoon [Playground]			
Today's Goal: 15–18 points	**Today's Points:**		
Consequence: Share and discuss with parents.			
Teacher Comments:	**Parents Comments:**		

Figure 11.2   Sample Daily Behavior Report Card for Entire Class

What We Are Working On: Following schoolwide expectations for appropriate behavior.

Today's Date:			

	Rating		
	2 = More Than 80% of Class	1 = 50%–80% of Class	0 = Less Than 50% of Class
	Schoolwide Expectation		
Time:	Be Safe	Be Respectful	Be Responsible
Morning [Classroom]			
Morning [Cafeteria]			
Afternoon [Music]			

Today's Goal: 15–18 points	Today's Points:

Consequence: Bank $10 for classroom party (total needed = $100).

Additional Comments:

Figure 11.3   Summary of Progress With Use of DBR

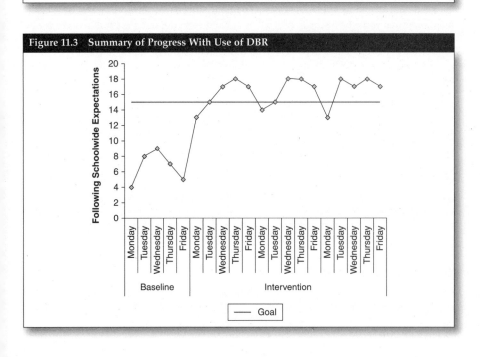

EVALUATING OUTCOMES OF PREVENTION EFFORTS

Effective evaluations "tell the story" of the program. They document the extent to which the program is meeting its goals; using appropriate activities; being implemented as intended; and succeeding in a manner that is generating evidence suitable for continuation, replication, or renewal. They detail information needed to justify initiation and continuation of a program, as well as to sustain, replicate, and scale up implementation efforts. High-quality evaluations are grounded in scientific methods in which data are used to answer important questions about the value or worth of a program or project.

The CIPP (Context, Input, Process, Product) model credited to Stufflebeam and his colleagues (Stufflebeam, 1968, 1983, 2003; Stufflebeam & Shinkfield, 2007) is commonly used to define the methodological framework for an evaluation. Context indicators document the program's goals, objectives, and activities and serve as a foundation for judging progress and performance, as well as a basis for generalization. Input indicators document what was done to meet the needs, address the problems, and manage the opportunities of a program as a basis for planning and replanning efforts and allocating resources. Process indicators document how faithfully the program was implemented relative to its original design and focus. Product indicators document intended and unintended outcomes and provide a basis for continuations, revisions, and improvements. A complete and effective evaluation is a thorough, feasible, and appropriate documentation of the goals, activities, implementation, and outcomes of a program using indicators directly related to them and grounded in quantitative and qualitative information. This information is the evidence that policy makers, administrators, teachers, and other professionals need to justify, sustain, replicate, and scale up a program.

Each component of CIPP evaluations is tied to a different set of decisions and documentation that must be addressed in planning and carrying out a comprehensive evaluation of an ongoing educational program. As Gall, Borg, and Gall (1996) indicated, typically three broad tasks drive this type of evaluation: "delineating the kinds of information needed for decision making, obtaining the information, and synthesizing the information so that it is useful in making decisions" (p. 703). The Joint Committee on Standards for Educational Evaluation (1994) held that evaluations are conducted to establish the worth or merit of a program and to help improve it. Evaluation is the process of documenting key aspects of a program. In this regard, evaluation should not be viewed as something that is separate from, or added to, a program. It should also not be seen as simply providing "thumbs-up" or "thumbs-down" decisions. Rather, evaluation is most effective when it is focused on and developed from ongoing and continuous use of evidence or indicators to support the claims of the program.

A system of context, input, process, product, and replication, sustainability, and improvement indicators is essential to answering these questions and documenting the general and specific qualities of prevention interventions and programs. Guidelines, examples, and templates for use in planning, implementing, and using evaluations grounded in context, input, process, and process indicators are presented in the following sections.

Documenting Context

Context indicators for an evaluation detail the goals, objectives, and activities of the program and serve as a foundation for judging progress and performance, as well as a basis for generalization. The information verifies the extent to which expected systems and practices grounded in prevention science theory and research evidence are part of the program. This component of the evaluation is a measure of the congruence of expectations and practices. It is a marker of whether support that should be available is available, as well as a report of who is providing it and who is receiving it.

Context indicators and assessments represent data gathered before a program is implemented or as part of planning to implement it. Typically documented features include the support that was provided, the individual(s) providing the support, and the individual(s) receiving the support. The goal is to illustrate the extent to which expected systems and practices were put in place to support the likelihood of a prevention program's achieving its goals. Typically, the "game" and the "players" are described so that others can see specific aspects of the program; information about other sources of support can also be used to provide a picture of the implementation efforts. The benefit in documenting context indicators is that claims such as "We've tried everything!" can be supported.

Documenting Input

Input indicators detail what should be or was done to meet the needs, address the problems, and manage the opportunities of a prevention program as a basis for planning and replanning efforts and allocating resources. They document critical aspects of professional development and illustrate key features of training and technical assistance provided as part of the implementation process. The focus is on describing the training events, who participates in them, and their perceived value to the participants. Input indicators and assessments represent data gathered after a program is planned but before it is implemented. Input indicators provide evidence that key aspects of prevention programs are presented to the individuals responsible for implementing them. Analysis of the content and form of professional development opportunities and of the characteristics of participants provides a basis for evaluating the appropriateness of the programs. Perceptions of the participants about the experience and markers of knowledge and skills that were gained provide fundamental evidence of the value of professional development.

Documenting Process

Process indicators detail how faithfully the prevention program was implemented relative to its original design and focus. They reflect the extent to which professional development has resulted in change in the practices used in participating schools or classrooms and in the behavior of administrators, teachers, and children, as well as others in their schools. Gilliam, Ripple, Zigler, and Leiter (2000) pointed out the importance of documenting process evaluation indicators:

> Outcome evaluations should not be attempted until well after quality and participation have been maximized and documented in a process evaluation. Although outcome data can determine the effectiveness of a program, process data determine whether a program exists in the first place. (p. 56)

Process indicators and assessments represent data gathered while a prevention program is implemented as evidence of its fidelity (O'Donnell, 2008). They illustrate the extent to which change in practices has occurred in participating schools and in the behavior of administrators, teachers, and children, as well as others in their schools. Process indicators typically include information about schoolwide, nonclassroom, and classroom support systems, as well as those for individual students. The school's discipline handbook; improvement plan goals; annual action-planning documents for providing behavior support; behavior instruction materials and implementation timelines; and summary reports of office discipline referrals, suspensions, and expulsions are other process indicators of interest.

Documenting Product

Product indicators detail intended and unintended outcomes and provide a basis for continuations, revisions, and improvements. As Fixsen, Naoom, Blase, Friedman, and Wallace (2005) pointed out,

> [A] test of evidence-based practice or program effectiveness at implementation sites should occur only after they are fully operational, that is, at the point where the interventions and the systems supporting those interventions within an agency are well integrated and have a chance to be fully implemented. (p. 18)

Information from product evaluation indicators reflects the extent to which targeted outcomes are being and/or are likely to be achieved. Office discipline referrals (ODRs), suspensions, expulsions, levels of behavior risk, attitude surveys, and end-of-grade and other achievement assessments are widely used markers for behavioral and other changes resulting from high-fidelity implementation of prevention programs. Product indicators and assessments represent data gathered after a program is implemented as evidence of its outcomes and the extent to which intended outcomes were achieved.

Office discipline referrals are widely used indicators of problem behavior and the social climate of schools (see Ervin, Schaughency, Goodman, McGlinchey, & Matthews, 2006; Ervin, Schaughency, Matthews, Goodman, & McGlinchey, 2007; Horner, Sugai, Todd, & Lewis-Palmer, 2005; Irvin, Tobin, Sprague, Sugai, & Vincent, 2004; McIntosh, Chard, Boland, & Horner, 2006). The School-Wide Information System (SWIS) includes a Web-based computer application for entering, organizing, managing, and reporting ODR data for use in decision making by teachers, administrators, and other staff (Irvin et al., 2006). Numbers of suspensions and numbers of students at risk for continued problems are also important indicators of behavior change. All three are useful markers for documenting changes in the general social climate of the school and improvements in problem behavior resulting from implementation of problem behavior prevention programs. In addition to behavior, it is important to document time allocated to instructional activities, academic achievement, and other aspects of schooling (e.g., attitudes, school safety, and teacher turnover) when evaluating prevention programs.

DESIGNING PROGRAM EVALUATIONS

Selecting participants for intervention and identifying the measures that are sensitive to the effects of prevention programs are important aspects of program evaluation (see Shadish, Cook, & Leviton, 1991, for detailed discussion of evaluation designs). Another important step in program evaluation involves selecting an evaluation design that can provide evidence of the effect (or absence of effect) of the prevention program. Measuring changes in students' behavior is not difficult. The challenge for evaluators is to use an evaluation design that clearly and unequivocally enables them to link changes in behavior to the implementation of the program. A good program design will enable administrators to rule out other factors besides the program itself as potential explanations for improved behavior or performance among program participants. Examples of such other factors are developmental maturation of participants, changes in school personnel, or changes or additions in other school programs or curricula. The first step in choosing an evaluation design is to decide whether the focus will be on single cases or groups of participants.

Single-Case Designs

Single-case or single-subject designs are most suitable for measuring program effects when the intervention has targeted a limited number of participants or sites and when a control or comparison group is either unfeasible or unavailable. Single-case designs have the advantage of showing changes over time for specific individuals. In single-case evaluation designs, individual students, teachers, classrooms, or schools can represent a single case that is compared to itself or to another comparable single case. A distinguishing feature of single-case designs is multiple or continuous measurement of key behaviors or other indicators of program effects.

In single-case designs, evaluators must carefully define what is measured, when it is measured, and how it is measured. Often this involves direct observations of clearly defined discrete behaviors. It may also involve ratings of behaviors by teachers or other persons or tallies of specific types of problems or desired positive behaviors. For example, in a single-case design targeted at individual students, an evaluator might count the number of classroom rule violations and the number of classroom or recess behavior problems reported by a student's teacher. Or an evaluator might record direct observations of on-task or off-task behavior over a discrete time period.

In a single-case design where a classroom or a school serves as the case, an evaluator might count the number of office discipline referrals or the number of students participating in afterschool recreational activities. These data could be collected on a daily or weekly basis. Many of the descriptive outcome measures listed in Table 10.3 are appropriate for single-case evaluation designs. Functional behavior assessment (see Chapter 5) is another form of single-case assessment in which an evaluator examines antecedents and consequences of particular behavior. For evaluating the effects of prevention programs, two types of single-case designs, multiple-baseline and changing-criterion designs, are most appropriate, as discussed below.

Multiple-Baseline Designs

A multiple-baseline design begins with data collection during a baseline period before implementation of a program. The strength of the program, or intervention, is measured by comparing performance after intervention with performance during baseline. In the multiple-baseline design, the baseline period is a different length of time for each case, and program effects are anticipated as each case moves from baseline to intervention. The intervention is systematically introduced to each case or subject independently at different points in time. Program effects are demonstrated when targeted behaviors or indicators change in the expected direction after the intervention is introduced. Changes in behavior for each of the cases (students, schools, or classrooms) at different points in time are generally considered convincing evidence of program effects.

Changing-Criterion Designs

The changing-criterion design also begins with a baseline condition followed by the introduction of an intervention. In contrast to the multiple-baseline design, the changing criterion design demonstrates the effectiveness of the intervention by improved behavior at increasingly higher criteria for successful performance. That is, as participants reach a predetermined criterion of performance in the program, expectations and reinforcing conditions are changed to a higher level. For example, if a peer mediation program was designed to decrease "name-calling," "bullying," and "fighting" during recess, a changing criterion design might initially aim for 30 percent, then 60 percent, then 90 percent reduction in the target behaviors over time.

Analysis of single-case evaluation data usually involves visual inspection of graphed data points over time for the various cases to reveal the extent to which the prevention program is having its anticipated effect. Statistical analysis of single-case data is also possible, but if the data provide sufficient information without additional labor, let them speak for themselves.

Group Designs

Group designs can use descriptive outcome measures and/or standardized instruments to measure participants' behavior or performance before and after the implementation of a prevention program. In contrast to single-case designs, group designs require gathering data from many participants and computing averages for the performance of participants at two or more points in time.

Experimental Group Designs

Experimental group designs compare the performance of a group participating in a program to a comparable group (a control group) that does not participate in the program. When the group receiving the program shows greater changes in behavior than a comparable control group, evaluators can conclude that the changes were due to the program and not other factors that might affect both groups equally, such as developmental maturation. For example, beneficial effects of Tier II interventions can be demonstrated by greater changes in the behavior of participating students than of matched nonparticipating peers in the same classrooms. Whenever possible, experimental group designs are preferable to group designs without control groups.

Designs Without Control Groups

When control groups are not feasible, a group evaluation design can compare the performance of a group after the implementation of a program to the same group's performance before the program began. This is sometimes referred to as pre- and post-treatment comparison. Scores on standardized instruments for program participants can also be compared to the similar scores of the normative sample that was used to develop the standardized assessment instrument. For example, if outcome data include teacher ratings on a standardized instrument, then group averages on the scales for the program participants can be compared to average scores on the same scales for the normative sample, assuming this information is available in the instrument's technical manual.

Evaluators need to be cautious when interpreting results of group designs without control groups. Control groups "control" for other possible explanations of changes in scores when they share the same characteristics of the group receiving a program or "treatment." Without comparisons between the treatment group and control group, however, there is no way to test whether changes in performance might have been due to a factor besides the program being tested.

Statistical Analyses

In contrast to single-case evaluation designs, group designs typically rely on statistical analyses of outcome data. Analyses of group performance can be based on descriptive or inferential statistics. Descriptive analyses might involve examining the percentage of students in a prevention program who exhibit specific problem behaviors before and after implementation of the program. In experimental group designs, evaluators can compare differences in the percentages of students exhibiting the problem behaviors in the group with the program versus a control group without the program. Descriptive statistics, like chi-square, test differences in the proportion of students in each group who show the problems versus the proportion in each group who do not show the problems.

Inferential statistics, such as the t-test, analysis of variance, and multivariate analyses, test differences in averages, or mean scores, relative to the variance in scores for each group or sample. Inferential statistics are more powerful than descriptive statistics for showing changes in scores as evidence of program effects. Inferential statistics enable evaluators to judge whether changes or differences between groups are random or chance effects (unexplained variance) or program effects (explained variance). Inferential statistics can also be used to determine whether characteristics of specific subgroups of participants are associated with types of outcomes.

Whether evaluators use descriptive or inferential statistics to examine program outcomes, it is essential that they have the necessary statistical expertise or that they confer with measurement and evaluation specialists to ensure that they are using statistical techniques appropriately. The choice between descriptive or inferential statistics with group evaluation designs may also be influenced in part by the stakeholders for whom the evaluation is being conducted. For example, prevention programs implemented within a single classroom or single school may be subjected to less intense levels of scrutiny than are programs that involve a number of classrooms, schools, or school districts. For evaluations of single-class or single-school interventions with relatively few participants, single-case deigns or group designs using descriptive statistics may be all that is necessary to demonstrate program effectiveness. However, even in these instances, evaluators need to think carefully about outcome measures and the type of evaluation design most appropriate for their particular program.

MEASUREMENT ISSUES

Regardless of whether evaluators choose single-case or group designs to measure program effects, it is essential that the measurement procedures have well-demonstrated reliability and validity. *Reliable* measurement procedures are stable and consistent over repeated applications. An instrument or procedure has good test-retest reliability when it provides the same or very similar results when administered at two different times without any intervening changes in a given situation. An instrument or procedure has good inter-rater reliability when it provides the same or very similar results when administered by two different individuals at about the same point in time. The best instruments show both high test-retest and high inter-rater reliability.

Valid measurement procedures measure what they purport to measure. Validity can be tested in several ways; for example, by comparing subjects' scores on a particular instrument to scores on a similar measure (construct validity) or by testing the predictive power of the measurement procedure (criterion-related validity). Evaluators should examine the technical manuals for published instruments for studies on validity.

It is also important to examine the items and scores of an instrument to determine whether they measure the specific types of behavior or outcomes that might be reasonably expected from a given prevention program. For example, if a prevention program was designed to reduce the occurrence of aggressive behavior among primary grade students, then a valid outcome measure might involve direct observations of the children's aggressive behavior or ratings of children's aggressive behavior by appropriate informants. While the academic performance of the students might also be of interest, data on academic performance would not be a valid measure of program effectiveness.

COMMON HAZARDS IN PROGRAM EVALUATION

Several potential hazards exist in evaluating prevention programs. Anticipating hazards in advance can help reduce or eliminate their negative impact on evaluation results.

Nonequivalent Treatment and Comparison Groups

One potential hazard is the use of nonequivalent treatment and comparison groups. To avoid this problem, it is essential that students in any comparison group, whether selected at the classroom or school level, share common characteristics with students participating in the prevention program. For example, if students are selected for a prevention program based on a high number of risk factors or severity of their behavior problems, a comparison group without the program should also have similarly high risk factors or similarly severe behavior problems. If the two groups differ on these selection factors, it will be extremely difficult to show that the program produced beneficial effects for the targeted group.

For example, the lack of a nonequivalent comparison group was a problem encountered by the Linkages to Learning Project (see Chapter 9), where the participating school had more high-risk students than did the comparison school. This inequality occurred because the schools were selected by school district administrators rather than by the program evaluators. As a result, outcomes for students at the two schools had to be interpreted with caution because of differences between schools that existed before the program began.

Regression to the Mean

A hazard not dissimilar to nonequivalent treatment and comparison groups is a statistical phenomenon termed "regression to the mean." In this commonly observed statistical artifact, scores at the extreme ends of a distribution of scores tend to move closer to the average, or mean, on a second assessment. Regression to the mean can occur when the participants in a prevention program are selected on the basis of extreme scores on a pretest or preprogram measure and the same measure is used later to assess outcomes of the program. Participants who obtained extreme scores on the pretest measure are more likely to score closer to the mean the next time they are assessed, regardless of whether they received the program or not. Regression to the mean thus undermines interpretations of changes as due solely to the program itself. The problem of regression to the mean can be avoided by selecting program participants based on eligibility criteria that do not include pretest scores on one of the outcome measures.

Maturation of Participants

A third hazard for evaluators is maturation of participants during the course of the program. Educators and mental health professionals are often interested in promoting the social, emotional, and academic maturation of the children with whom they work. However, unless adequately accounted for in an evaluation design, the maturation of program participants might explain changes in behavior over time better than the effects of the prevention program itself. An evaluation design that uses a comparison group that is about the same age and/or grade level as the group participating in the program is less likely to mistake maturation for program effects. Because of the frequent measurement associated with single-case designs, maturation effects are less of a potential problem in these studies than they are with group designs.

Influence of History

A fourth hazard concerns the influence of history on program effects. Evaluators and measurement specialists use the term *history* to refer to unique experiences of participants or aspects of programs that might affect outcomes. For example, if baseline or pretreatment data were collected on student behavior just prior to a major holiday, the level of inappropriate behavior might be higher than normal. Comparisons to this unusually high level of troublesome behavior after the introduction of a prevention program would artificially inflate program effects shown by reductions in problems. The effect of history can also occur when new staff members are hired after the start of the prevention program, when the schedule or location of the program changes, and when other changes to the students' routines occur after the program is introduced. Good communication between program evaluators and program staff can help to identify history that might influence outcomes.

Conclusion

Most evaluation hazards can be avoided when individuals evaluating programs are aware of the larger contexts within which the program operates, have a good understanding of how the program is implemented, and have the opportunity to observe the program in operation. Evaluators need to be involved in preliminary discussions with staff about evaluation design, program implementation, data collection, and data analyses. When evaluation is not considered during the planning of the prevention program, it can be very difficult to extract meaningful program effects from existing data. Thus the threats to the validity of an evaluation implemented after a program has been implemented or has been completed are considerable.

DISSEMINATING EVALUATION INFORMATION

A primary reason for program evaluation is to learn whether or not a particular program produced the desired effects. Demonstrated efficacy should be the first consideration in decisions about whether to continue a prevention program in the future. A well-conducted, clearly presented evaluation report that shows the success of a program can bolster arguments for sustaining the program, especially when budget constraints threaten its continuation. Conversely, programs that may appear promising will be more vulnerable to budget cuts when administrators are unable to provide convincing evidence of their positive impact on participants.

An evaluation report should disseminate findings to key stakeholders in an objective and unambiguous manner. To do this effectively, report writers need a clear sense of the intended audience. For example, professional audiences or journal editors usually expect a report to include a literature review and details about statistical analyses, as well as discussion of methods, results, and conclusions. Other audiences, such as school administrators, school boards, or legislators, are usually most interested in descriptions of what a program does, whom it serves, and how it was evaluated. Reports for these audiences should present clear and concise descriptions of the major features of the program, evaluation methods, key findings regarding efficacy, limitations, and conclusions. Additional information concerning evaluation instruments, statistical analyses, and background literature can be placed in footnotes or appendixes for further examination by interested parties.

MEASURING SUCCESS OF PREVENTION PROGRAMS

We know what we need to know . . . that's why we are asking the questions. All research and evaluation activities begin and end with questions. Good teaching is an iterative process of asking and answering questions. Effective problem solving involves answering questions. Effective prevention efforts can only be achieved with positive answers to key questions:

1. What problem needs changing?
2. What do we currently know about the problem?
3. What do we need to know about the problem?
4. What intervention will likely change the problem?
    a. Who will implement it?
    b. Where will it happen?
    c. When will it happen?
    d. How will it happen?
5. How will we know the intervention worked?
6. What will we do if the intervention does not work?

This chapter focused on procedures for measuring the success of prevention programs. Each school year, administrators and school boards face decisions on how to allocate their resources to best meet the needs of all children. Often these decisions involve sorting through competing demands for funding, staffing, and building space. Political pressures can also influence decisions regarding school resources and programs. In the face of such challenges, careful program evaluation is essential to preserve and sustain effective prevention programs. Without sound evidence of their success, prevention advocates will be hard pressed to convince decision makers to continue such efforts, regardless of their positive outcomes for children.

REFERENCES

Chafouleas, S. M., McDougal, J. L., Riley-Tillman, T. C., Panahon, C. J., Hilt, A. M. (2005). What do daily behavior report cards (DBRCs) measure? An initial comparison of DBRCs with direct observation for off-task behavior. *Psychology in the Schools, 42*(6), 669–676.

Chafouleas, S. M., Riley-Tillman, T. C., & McDougal, J. L. (2002). Good, bad, or in-between: How does the daily behavior report card rate? *Psychology in the Schools, 39*, 157–169.

Chafouleas, S. M., Riley-Tillman, T. C., & Sassu, K. A. (2006). Acceptability and reported use of daily behavior report cards among teachers. *Journal of Positive Behavior Interventions, 8*, 174–182.

Chafouleas, S. M., Riley-Tillman, T. C., Sassu, K. A., LaFrance, M. J., & Patwa, S. S. (2007). Daily behavior report cards: An investigation of the consistency of on-task data across raters and methods. *Journal of Positive Behavior Interventions, 9*(1), 30–37.

Chafouleas, S. M., Riley-Tillman, T. C., Sugai, G. (2007). *School-based behavioral assessment: informing intervention and instruction.* New York: Guilford Press.

Ervin, R. A., Schaughency, E., Goodman, S. D., McClinchey, M. T., & Matthews, A. (2006). Merging research and practice agendas to address reading and behavior schoolwide. *School Psychology Review, 35*, 198–223.

Ervin, R. A., Schaughency, E., Matthews, A., Goodman, S. D., & McGlinchey, M. T. (2007). Primary and secondary prevention of behavior difficulties: Developing a data-informed problem-solving model to guide decision making at the school-wide level. *Psychology in the Schools, 44*, 7–18.

Fixsen, D. L., Naoom, S. F., Blase, K. A., Friedman, R. M., & Wallace, F. (2005). *Implementation research: A synthesis of the literature* (FMHI Publication #231). Tampa, FL: Florida Mental Health Institute, National Implementation Research Network.

Gall, M. D., Borg, W. R., & Gall, J. P. (1996). *Educational research* (6th ed.). White Plains, NY: Longman.

Gilliam, W. S., Ripple, C. H., Zigler, E. F., & Leiter, V. (2000). Evaluating child and family demonstration initiatives: Lessons from the Comprehensive Child Development Program. *Early Childhood Research Quarterly, 15*(1), 41–59.

Horner, R. H., Sugai, G., Todd, A. W., & Lewis-Palmer, T. (2005). School-wide Positive Behavior Support: An alternative approach to discipline in the schools. In L. M. Bambara & L. Kern (Eds.), *Individualized supports for students with problem behavior: Designing positive behavior plans* (pp. 359–390). New York: Guilford.

Irvin, L. K., Horner, R. H., Ingram, K., Todd, A. W., Sugai, G., Sampson, N. K., et al. (2006). Using office discipline referral data for decision making about student behavior in elementary and middle schools: An empirical evaluation of validity. *Journal of Positive Behavior Interventions, 8*(1), 10–23.

Irvin, L. K., Tobin, T. J., Sprague, J. R., Sugai, G., & Vincent, C. G. (2004). Validity of office discipline referral measures as indices of school-wide behavioral status and effects of school-wide behavioral interventions. *Journal of Positive Behavior Interventions, 6*, 131–147.

The Joint Committee on Standards for Educational Evaluation. (1994). *The program evaluation standards.* Thousand Oaks, CA: Sage.

Kratochwill, T. R., Volpiansky, P., Clements, M., & Ball, C. (2007). Professional development in implementing and sustaining multitier prevention models: Implications for response to intervention. *School Psychology Review, 36*(4), 618–631.

Lane, K. L., & Menzies, H. M. (2003). A school-wide intervention with primary and secondary levels of support for elementary students: Outcomes and considerations. *Education and Treatment of Children, 26*(4), 431–451.

McIntosh, K., Chard, D. J., Boland, J. B., & Horner, R. H. (2006). Demonstration of combined efforts in school-wide academic and behavioral systems and incidence of reading and behavior challenges in early elementary grades. *Journal of Positive Behavior Interventions, 8,* 146–154.

O'Donnell, C. L. (2008). Defining, conceptualizing, and measuring fidelity of implementation and its relationship to outcomes in K–12 curriculum intervention research. *Review of Educational Research, 78,* 33–84.

Riley-Tillman, T. C., Chafouleas, S. M., & Briesch, A. M. (2007). A school practitioner's guide to using daily behavior report cards to monitor student behavior. *Psychology in the Schools, 44*(1), 77–89.

Riley-Tillman, C. T., Chafouleas, S. M., Sassu, K. A., Chanese, J. A. M., & Glazer, A. D. (2008). Examining the agreement of direct behavior ratings and systematic direct observation data for on-task and disruptive behavior. *Journal of Positive Behavior Interventions, 10*(2), 136–143.

Salvia, J., Ysseldyke, J. E., & Bolt, S. (2010). *Assessment in special and inclusive education* (10th ed.). Florence, KY: Cengage Learning.

Shadish, W. R., Cook, T. D., & Leviton, L. C. (1991). *Foundations of program evaluation: Theories of practice.* Newbury Park, CA: Sage.

Steege, M. W., Davin, T., & Hathaway, M. (2001). Reliability and accuracy of a performance-based behavioral recording procedure. *School Psychology Review, 30,* 252–261.

Stufflebeam, D. L. (1968, January). *Evaluation as enlightenment for decision-making.* Address to the Working Conference on Assessment Theory, Sarasota, FL. (ERIC Document Reproduction Service No. ED048333)

Stufflebeam, D. L. (1983). The CIPP Model for Program Evaluation. In G. F. Madaus, M. Scriven, & D. L. Stufflebeam (Eds.), *Evaluation models: Viewpoints on educational and human services evaluation.* (pp.117–141) Boston: Kluwer Nijhof.

Stufflebeam, D. L. (2003, October). *The CIPP Model for Evaluation: An update, a review of the model's development, a checklist to guide implementation.* Paper presented at the Annual Conference of the Oregon Program Evaluators Network, Portland, OR. Retrieved October 28, 2009, from http://www.wmich.edu/evalctr/pubs/CIPP-ModelOregon10-03.pdf

Stufflebeam, D. L., & Shinkfield, A. J. (2007). *Evaluation theory, models, and applications.* San Francisco: Jossey Bass.

Wright, J. (2002). *Teacher behavior report card generator* [Internet software]. Retrieved October 28, 2009, from http://www.jimwrightonline.com/php/tbrc/tbrc.php

12

Building and Sustaining Effective Prevention Practices

In this chapter, we

- review effective current prevention practices to stop school violence,
- provide information about how to sustain effective violence prevention programs, and
- provide a summary of the critical features of programs and practices for preventing problem behaviors.

As school administrators, teachers, and educational researchers know all too well, violence in schools threatens the establishment of learning environments that are conducive to student success. Incidents of disrespect, noncompliance, bullying, and verbal harassment and acts of extreme physical violence result in schools where learning becomes secondary to issues of personal safety, and students, their parents, and their communities are adversely affected. Although evidence suggests that between 1992 and 2005, public school safety improved (Dinkes, Cataldi, Kena, & Baum, 2006), any incident that compromises the well-being of students and staff is one too many.

Part of a joint effort by the U.S. Department of Education's National Center for Education Statistics and the U.S. Bureau of Justice Statistics, the *Indicators of School Crime and Safety: 2006* report (Dinkes et al., 2006) contributes to an understanding of our nation's schools and the conditions surrounding school-related crime, its perpetrators, and its victims. Specifically, the report covers topics such as victimization, fighting, bullying, student perceptions of school safety, weapons issues, teacher injury, and drugs and alcohol. According to the survey, 78 percent of public schools reported one or more violent incidents in 2005–2006. Among students ages 12 to 18,

- 4 percent reported being victimized at school during the previous 6 months,
- 3 percent reported theft,
- 1 percent reported violent victimization,
- 28 percent reported the occurrence of bullying, and
- 8 percent reported bullying as an almost daily occurrence.

Among students in Grades 9–12,

- 25 percent reported that drugs were made available to them on school property, and
- 8 percent had been threatened or injured with a weapon on school property in the previous 12 months.

Beyond affecting the individuals directly involved, incidents of violence may cause disruptions in the school setting, affect bystanders, and alarm the surrounding community (Henry, 2000; Vossekuil, Fein, Reddy, Borum, & Modzeleski, 2002). When considering these incidents, however, it is important to remember that students are twice as likely to be victims of serious violent crime *away* from school than they are to experience it in school settings.

BUILDING EFFECTIVE PREVENTION PRACTICES

Administrators, teachers, and other school personnel have access to multiple sources of advice on how to make schools more safe and effective. In the late 1990s, the Departments of Education and Justice developed a guide to help adults keep schoolchildren out of harm's way, and it is still as relevant today as it was then. *Early Warning, Timely Response: A Guide to Safe Schools* (Dwyer, Osher, & Warger, 1998) presents a brief summary of the research on violence prevention, intervention, and effective responses to crisis in schools. It describes the characteristics of safe schools, early warning signs that relate to violence and problem behavior, and interventions that school personnel can implement "to prevent violence and other troubling behavior, to intervene and get help for troubled children, and to respond to violence when it occurs" (U.S. Department of Education, 1998, pp. 1–2). Using information available in a public domain publication (Office of Special Education and Rehabilitative Services, 1998) and presented by Dwyer, Osher, and Hoffman (2000), we summarize the guidelines here because they support, reinforce, and promote the research-based practices that are the focus of this book.

Characteristics of Safe, Responsive Schools

Most schools in the United States can be safe environments when appropriate, expected academic and social behaviors are a prominent focus and are adequately supported. As detailed by the chapters in this book, schools that support learning effectively encourage excellent teaching and foster socially appropriate behaviors that are foundational to safe and secure environments. Safe schools foster positive relationships between staff and students (see Chapters 1, 3, 6, and 10) and promote meaningful parental and community involvement (see Chapters 8 and 9). The most effective prevention programs address multiple factors and recognize that safety and order are related to the social, emotional, and academic development of students. According to Dwyer and colleagues (1998), strategies that facilitate positive outcomes in all of these areas operate in schools that do the following:

Focus on positive expectations. People working in effective schools believe that all students can learn and behave appropriately. They communicate their expectations clearly and teach students that meeting them is their responsibility, both inside and outside of school. Their administrators provide the resources that are needed to support programs that help students to achieve and behave in socially desirable ways.

Actively involve families. When families are included in schooling, students are more likely to experience success and less likely to engage in inappropriate academic or social behavior. Effective schools welcome family involvement, reduce obstacles to family participation, actively engage families, and support them when they express concerns about their childrens' education or behaviors that cause concern.

Develop links to the community. School improvement requires resources, including commitment from and collaboration and partnerships with families, professional support services, police and law enforcement agencies, and church and other faith-based memberships, as well as communities at large. Conditions that increase the risk of school violence and decrease opportunities to provide support strengthen when linkages among community partners weaken.

Emphasize positive relationships. Effective schools create and support opportunities for students and adults to interact and develop connections that guide, foster, and direct interpersonal competencies. Research has consistently shown that a positive relationship with an adult is a critical factor in preventing student violence at school. Administrators and teachers in effective schools make sure ample opportunities are available for teachers and students to spend quality time together. They also encourage students to develop positive interpersonal relations by helping each other and assisting each other when help is needed.

Focus on safety issues directly. Because children come to school with different levels and types of experience related to violence, school personnel should actively teach them appropriate strategies for dealing with feelings, expressing anger, and resolving conflicts. They should also teach that individuals are responsible for their own actions and that the choices they make have consequences for themselves and others.

Treat students with respect. Conflicts in many schools arise from bias and unfair treatment of students by staff, peers, and others as a result of ethnicity, gender, race, social class, religion, disability, nationality, sexual orientation, physical appearance, or some other factor. When students are treated unfairly or become scapegoats and/or targets of violence, they sometimes react in aggressive ways or harm themselves. In effective schools focused on safety, all children are valued and treated with respect, and often there is a deliberate and systematic effort to establish a climate that demonstrates this by displaying children's artwork, posting academic work prominently throughout the building, and sharing evidence that diversity is respected.

Create ways for students to express concerns. Peers often are the most likely group to know in advance about potential school violence. Effective schools create ways for students safely to report concerns about dangerous situations, as well as ways to protect students who report potential violence. Schools should be places where students and adults are safe, especially when sharing information about a potentially dangerous or harmful situation.

Help students to freely express feelings. Most professionals agree that children need to believe they are safe when expressing needs, fears, and concerns to school staff. Students who do not have experience freely expressing themselves to caring adults are more likely to engage in inappropriate social behaviors.

Have systems for addressing suspected abuse or neglect. Peers and teachers are often the first to notice signs of interpersonal struggles and the potential for seriously violent acts. Effective schools have systems in place to support students in situations that require assistance beyond the classroom. When building such systems, it is critical to ensure that they appropriately reflect local, state, and federal guidelines, so central office personnel should be involved in developing them.

Offer extended-day programs. Many effective schools use before- and afterschool programs in their efforts to address and reduce violence. These efforts must be well supervised, and they should offer a variety of personal and interpersonal supports, such as counseling, tutoring, and mentoring, as well as cultural arts activities, community service experiences, clubs, supervised and focused access to technology, and help with homework.

Promote citizenship and character. School professionals must help students become good citizens, as well achieve important academic and social behavior goals. They are expected to teach and represent the civic values set forth in our Constitution and Bill of Rights (e.g., patriotism; freedom of religion, speech, and the press; equal protection, nondiscrimination; and due process/fairness). They should also encourage and promote shared values of local communities, such as honesty, kindness, responsibility, and respect for others, as well as work in partnership with parents, helping them to be the effective educators of their children.

Identify problems and assess progress. School personnel must openly and objectively examine circumstances that are potentially dangerous for students and staff and situations where members of the school community are threatened or intimidated. Safe and effective schools continually assess progress by identifying problems and collecting information about progress toward solutions. They also share this information with students, families, and the community at large.

Provide support for transition to adult life and the workplace. Older students often need help planning for the future and developing life skills that will support and encourage success. Teachers and other school personnel should provide community service opportunities, work-study programs, apprenticeships, and other experiences that help connect students to caring adults in the community. Many believe that such relationships help in developing a sense of hope and security for the future.

As we have indicated throughout this book, much can be done to prevent the development of behavior problems, especially those seen as precursors to the kinds of antisocial, aggressive responses associated with school violence and other serious concerns, through effective, research-based practices. Further, as Dwyer et al. (1998) suggested, an important step is to learn the early warning signs of a child who is troubled so that effective interventions can be provided.

Early Warning Signs

In many cases, children exhibit aggressive behavior early in life, and if not provided support, will continue a progressive developmental pattern toward severe aggression or violence (Smith, Graber, & Daunic, 2009). In contrast, researchers point out that when children have a positive, meaningful connection to an adult—whether it be at home, in school, or in the community—the potential for violence is reduced significantly (Hughes, Cavell, & Jackson, 1999). As Dwyer et al. (1998) suggested, none of the "early warning signs" alone is sufficient for predicting who will be violent or aggressive in school. Therefore, it is inappropriate—and potentially harmful—to use the early warning signs as a checklist against which to match individual children. Rather, the following early warning signs (not equally significant and not presented in order of seriousness) are offered only as an aid in making decisions about who may need help.

Social withdrawal. Gradual or complete withdrawal from interpersonal relationships can be an important indication that a student is troubled and needing support. This is especially true when the withdrawal results from feelings of depression, rejection, persecution, unworthiness, or lack of self-confidence.

Feelings of isolation. While many children who are isolated and friendless are not violent, research has shown that others with similar experiences and feelings are sometimes troubled or withdrawn, or they may have other problems that reduce the development of positive social relationships. Researchers have also shown that in some cases, feelings of isolation and friendlessness are associated with children who exhibit aggressive and violent behavior.

Excessive feelings of rejection. In the course of development, many young people experience rejection and isolation from their families and peers. Many factors are responsible for how they react, but without support, some are at risk of expressing their feelings in negative, possibly violent, ways. The potential for inappropriate reactions is heightened when students find themselves associating with others who are rejected and who express violent tendencies.

Victimized by violence. Individuals who experience abuse or violent acts are more likely to be violent in their personal or interpersonal relationships than their peers. Signs of victimization may be evident in what happens in the community, at school, or at home.

Feelings of persecution. Individuals who are picked on, humiliated, bullied, ridiculed, or made fun of may initially become withdrawn. Without support, some may turn to violence as a way to deal with deal with how they are being treated.

Low affiliation with school. Lack of interest and low achievement can be caused by many factors and result in different behaviors inside and outside of school. For some, frustration, lack of self-worth, and ridicule—sometimes associated with school failure—result in aggression and acting out.

Violence in writings and drawings. Some students prefer to express their thoughts, feelings, or planned actions nonverbally. Although most of this written expression is harmless, some of it may signal the potential for violence. School professionals with expertise and experience working with different kinds of emotional and personal responses should be part of decision-making teams in all schools.

Uncontrolled anger. Anger is a common response to frustration and disappointment. When anger is the response to minor problems, it may become a source of subsequent personal or interpersonal violent acts.

Hitting, intimidating, and bullying behaviors. Although pushing, shoving, and minor physical aggression are common and accepted parts of interactions for some, chronic hitting and bullying of others, especially at an early age, may be signs of more serious violent behavior. Effective schools have early identification and intervention programs in place to prevent aggressive behavior from escalating.

Patterns of discipline problems. Chronic behavior and disciplinary problems, both in school and at home, sometimes signal that an individual's needs are not being met. Acting-out and aggressive behaviors may result in increasing levels of violating norms and rules, defying authority, and disengaging from school.

Patterns of violent and aggressive behavior. Children and youth who have a history of aggression or violence are likely to continue unproductive behaviors unless provided with support and counseling. Those who show an early pattern of antisocial behavior frequently and across multiple settings are particularly at risk for future difficulty. Similarly, students who engage in overt behaviors—such as bullying, generalized aggression, and defiance—and covert behaviors—such as stealing, vandalism, lying, cheating, and fire setting—also are at risk for more serious problems.

Intolerance for differences and prejudicial attitudes. Although all children have likes and dislikes, an intense prejudice toward others based on race, ethnicity, religion, language, gender, sexual orientation, ability, or physical appearance, when coupled with other factors, may lead to assaults against those perceived to be different. Membership in hate groups or the willingness to victimize individuals with disabilities or health problems should also be treated as early warning signs of violence.

Drug and alcohol use. Most school codes of conduct address possession and use of controlled substances as major violations. Apart from being illegal, drug and alcohol use reduce self-control and expose individuals to violence, either as providers, victims, or both. Effective schools address these serious offenses early and consistently.

Affiliation with gangs. Gangs typically promote antisocial values and behaviors and acts of violence that cause fear and stress among school personnel and students. Individuals who participate in gangs adopt antisocial values and act in violent or aggressive ways. Gang-related violence and turf battles tied to the use of drugs sometimes are transferred into the school environment.

Inappropriate use of firearms. Individuals who have uncontrolled access to firearms may present an increased risk for violence and may have a higher probability of becoming victims. Families should reduce inappropriate use by restricting, monitoring, and supervising their children's access to firearms and other weapons. Children who have a history of aggression, impulsiveness, or other emotional problems should not have access to firearms and other weapons.

Serious threats of violence. Idle threats are a common response to frustration. Alternatively, a reliable indicator that an individual is likely to commit a dangerous act toward themselves or others is a detailed and specific threat to use violence. Effective schools are ready to take steps to understand the nature of these threats and to prevent them from being carried out.

SUSTAINING EFFECTIVE PREVENTION PRACTICES

In the early 1990s, the U.S. Department of Education identified strategic targets focused on prevention through the improvement of school and community environments in support of *all* students' emotional or behavioral needs. Rather than being control oriented, classrooms and schools were to be places where students learn the social and academic skills they need to succeed (Dwyer & Osher, 2000; Osher & Hanley, 1996). Thus, the principles and strategies we have emphasized throughout this book were on the national agenda more than a decade ago. With the best of intentions, however, school administrators may initiate new programs without adequately gathering teacher input or thoroughly examining the supports required for proper implementation. The urgency to respond to public insistence on making schools safe is a case in point. District and school administrators who are pressured to demonstrate how they are addressing the need for safe schools may adopt a schoolwide discipline or bullying-prevention program, social skills curriculum, or conflict resolution program without sufficiently addressing how teachers and other school professionals will balance their time for academic instruction and new initiatives.

While changing the environment of schools is a complex and multilayered task, as we have illustrated in this book, many effective strategies can be facilitated and sustained by adhering to guidelines that have emerged from the school change literature, particularly studies related to social-emotional and academic innovations (Elias, Zins, Graczyk, & Weissberg, 2003), similar to those mentioned in Chapter 6. Following these guidelines will go a long way toward ensuring that prevention programs are institutionalized and sustained:

- Enhance teacher buy-in by connecting suggested social-emotional, behavioral, and academic programs to the problems teachers face on a daily basis. In this way, prevention and intervention will be seen as "part of the solution" and not just extra responsibilities.
- Address the practical, systemic supports that increase the feasibility of sustaining school-based innovations, such as making teacher time available and rewarding teachers and other school personnel for positive involvement and support.
- Designate a "lead" teacher or counselor with the interest and authority to engage colleagues. Thus, certain individuals will be clearly responsible for tracking program progress and holding school staff accountable for day-to-day implementation.
- Conduct ongoing formal and informal ongoing training, including the involvement of acknowledged experts.
- Maintain high program visibility in the school and community through ongoing efforts to communicate with stakeholders and school personnel.

Reducing violence and preventing discipline problems in schools is not the responsibility of any one group or individual. District and building administrators need cooperation from a diverse group of stakeholders to identify, implement, and support effective interventions. Teachers need assistance and support so they can effectively teach students appropriate behaviors to replace inappropriate ones and, at the same time, teach academics. Along with social, emotional, and academic instruction, teachers need to monitor student learning and assist students in generalizing learned skills. Parents and caregivers need to be included as partners in making schools safe and ensuring that they are positive places to send their children. In short, reducing violence and preventing discipline problems in the service of positive development for all children requires a plan.

PUTTING IT ALL TOGETHER

Guidelines for building and sustaining effective prevention and intervention practice have been offered in several chapters in this book, particularly in Chapter 3 (Schoolwide Positive Behavior Support), and Zins, Bloodworth, Weissberg, and Walberg (2004) offered several additional guidelines that help summarize successful efforts in the prevention of problem behaviors and the sustainability of these efforts:

- Carefully plan prevention and intervention programs with a focus on social and emotional learning. Use a clear agenda, including resource allocation, implementation monitoring, and ongoing program evaluation.
- Use a team-based approach to identify, implement, and evaluate best practices. Include administrators, teachers, school psychologists, other support personnel, and parents.
- Understand theories of child development, learning, and prevention science and use research-validated practices.
- Think first about preventing problems behaviors. Teach a broad spectrum of social and emotional skills, model appropriate social behavior, help students develop positive and prosocial behaviors that promote responsibility and cooperation, assist students so that they value themselves and others, and provide plenty of positive feedback.
- Build a positive view of school for students through adult engagement and caring, interactive and cooperative classrooms, and schoolwide initiatives. Provide a continuum of behavioral support by increasing resources and services for students as behavior problems increase.
- Use data-based systems to guide decisions and coordinate student support services to achieve maximum program success. Make initial staff training and ongoing support an imperative.

Safe and effective schools implement schoolwide campaigns that establish high expectations and provide support for socially appropriate behavior. They reinforce positive behavior and enforce sanctions against aggressive behavior. All staff, parents, students, and community members are informed about problem behavior, what they can do to counteract it, and how they can reinforce and reward positive behavior. In turn, the entire school community makes a commitment to behave responsibly. Effective and safe schools develop and consistently enforce schoolwide rules that are clear, broad based, and fair. Representatives of the total educational community develop rules and disciplinary procedures collaboratively. These rules are communicated clearly to all parties—but most important, they are followed consistently by everyone. Safe and effective schools implement strategies like those described in this book.

REFERENCES

Dinkes, R., Cataldi, E. F., Kena, G., & Baum, K. (2006). *Indicators of school crime and safety: 2006* (NCES 2007-003/NCJ 214262). Washington, DC: U.S. Department of Education and U.S. Department of Justice.

Dwyer, K. P., & Osher, D. (2000). *Safeguarding our children: An action guide.* Washington, DC: U.S. Department of Education and U.S. Department of Justice, American Institutes of Research.

Dwyer, K. P., Osher, D., & Hoffman, C. C. (2000). Creating responsive schools: Contextualizing *Early Warning, Timely Response. Exceptional Children, 66,* 347–365.

Dwyer, K. P., Osher, D., & Warger, C. (1998). *Early warning, timely response: A guide to safe schools.* Washington, DC: U.S. Department of Education. Retrieved October 28, 2009, from http://cecp.air.org/guide/guide.pdf

Elias, M. J., Zins, J. E., Graczyk, P. A., & Weissberg, R. P. (2003). Implementation, sustainability, and scaling up of social-emotional and academic innovations in public schools. *School Psychology Review, 32*(3), 303–319.

Henry, S. (2000). What is school violence? An integrated definition. *Annals of the American Academy of Political and Social Science, 567,* 16–29.

Hinshaw, S. P., & Lee, S. S. (2003). Conduct and oppositional defiant disorders. In E. J. Mash & R. A. Barkley (Eds.), *Child psychopathology* (2nd ed., pp. 144–198). New York: Guilford Press.

Hughes, J. N., Cavell, T. A., & Jackson, T. (1999). Influence of the teacher-student relationship on childhood conduct problems: A prospective study. *Journal of Clinical Child Psychology, 28*(2), 173–184.

Office of Special Education and Rehabilitative Services (OSERS). (1998). *A guide to safe schools.* Retrieved October 28, 2008, from http://www.ed.gov/about/offices/list/osers/osep/gtss.html

Osher, D., & Hanley, T. V. (1996). Implications of the national agenda to improve results for children and youth with serious emotional disturbance. In R. J. Illback & C. M. Nelson (Eds.), *Emerging school-based approaches for children with emotional and behavioral problems: Research and practice in service integration* (pp. 7–36). Binghamton, NY: Haworth.

Smith, S. W., Graber, J., & Daunic, A. P. (2009). Cognitive-behavioral interventions for anger/aggression: Review of research and research-to-practice issues. In M. Mayer, R. Van Acker, J. Lochman, & F. Gresham (Eds.), *Cognitive-behavioral interventions for emotional and behavioral disorders: School-based practice* (pp. 111–142). New York: Guilford Press.

U.S. Department of Education. (1998). *Early warning, timely response: A guide for safe schools.* Washington, DC: Author. Retrieved October 28, 2009, from http://www.ed.gov/about/offices/list/osers/osep/gtss.htm

Vossekuil, B., Fein, R., Reddy, M., Borum, R., & Modzeleski, W. (2002). *The final report and findings of the Safe School Initiative: Implications for the prevention of school attacks in the United States.* Washington, DC: U.S. Department of Education, Office of Elementary and Secondary Education, Safe and Drug-Free Schools Program, and U.S. Secret Service, National Threat Assessment Center.

Zins, J. E., Bloodworth, M. R., Weissberg, R. P., & Walberg, H. J. (2004). The scientific base linking social and emotional learning to school success. In J. Zins, R. P. Weissberg, M. Wang, & H. J. Walberg (Eds.), *Building academic success on social and emotional learning: What the research says.* (pp. 3–22)New York: Teachers College Press.

Postscript

What We Know About the Relationship Between Achievement and Behavior

Administrators, teachers, researchers, and other professionals have a continuing interest in the relationship between social behavior and academic achievement. Most of the research on this relationship started with early epidemiological work documenting rates of problem behaviors in young children. For example, in seminal work known as the Isle of Wight studies, parents rated children identified as scoring poorly on a psychological test battery as squirmy, disobedient, and unable to settle, and teachers rated them as solitary, having poor concentration, having speech difficulties, or often engaged in bullying (Rutter, Tizard, & Whitmore, 1970). Other researchers have contrasted achievement and behavior characteristics and outcomes for different groups of individuals, often involving "normal" and "clinical" distinctions. Over time, researchers have consistently reported correlations between academic failure and behavior problems as early as first grade and between antisocial behavior and achievement problems later in life. The general and continuing interest in documenting both behavior and achievement problems reported by teachers, parents, and young people themselves is evidenced in recent cross-cultural studies by Rescorla and colleagues (see Rescorla, Achenbach, Ginzburg, et al., 2007; Rescorla, Achenbach, Ivanova, et al., 2007a, 2007b).

The findings from this large body of research support the belief that interventions that prevent or reduce problem behaviors and promote social skill development are likely to improve academic achievement. They also support the belief that interventions that promote achievement are likely to improve problem behaviors. Prevention science, Response-to-Intervention, and other large-scale practices are grounded in this belief. From this perspective, children enter school with behaviors that restrict the quantity and quality of instruction that they receive or respond to, and they become academic casualties because no one is teaching them appropriate academic or behavior skills. Or they enter school with limited academic skills, do not receive or respond to appropriate or effective instruction for any of a number of reasons, fall behind, and develop patterns of problem behavior that further restrict the likelihood of success in school.

The ability to read depends heavily on learning to use letters and their associated sounds to identify large numbers of words. Until those words are consistently read accurately growth of accepted and expected fluent literacy skills will be slowed. Likewise, the ability to behave depends heavily on learning to follow critical rules and procedures, Until those rules and procedures are consistently followed, growth of expected and accepted behavior skills will be slowed. Problems beget problems, and as the cycle of failure spins even more strongly, the problems become more intractable. Thus, the path is clear: What we know about the observed relationships between achievement and behavior makes sense and demands, directs, and promises dividends from change.

At the schoolwide level, this means focusing on teaching social skills with the same willfulness, intensity, and scrutiny given to teaching academic skills. We have tools to identify children likely headed for early reading failure. We know that direct teaching of key literacy skills (e.g., alphabet knowledge, phonological awareness, fluency, vocabulary, and comprehension) improves reading. We know that direct teaching of other academic skills (e.g., counting, writing, speaking) improves other academic skills. We know that direct teaching of social skills (e.g., learning rules and following procedures, controlling anger) improves behavior. We know that effective instruction increases the amount of time students are actively engaged, which, in turn, increases achievement and decreases problem behavior. In this context, effective school, classroom, and individual systems of support enhance efforts to prevent academic achievement and social behavior problems by

- ensuring that academic *and* behavior instruction are part of every child's educational program.
- documenting that academic *and* behavior interventions are implemented with fidelity before measuring outcomes and assigning worth to them or blaming children for not achieving them.
- documenting the extent to which achievement and behavior outcomes occur in meaningful, important, and powerful ways.

In using what we currently know about the relationship between achievement and behavior, clearly "the greatest promise comes from the integration of preventive [achievement] and behavior support systems" (McIntosh, 2005a, p. 90). Widespread evidence is available for the practice of implementing schoolwide academic and behavioral systems to reduce incidences of academic and behavioral challenges (cf. McIntosh, 2005b; McIntosh, Chard, Boland, & Horner, 2006). Alternatively, progress on studying the relationship between achievement and behavior can be enhanced with research that extends what is known about designing and implementing highly efficient and practical interventions. These interventions should target all children, especially those at continued risk for serious achievement and behavior problems, despite living and learning in academically and behaviorally rich instructional environments.

Behavior and achievement are related. This truth is limited if accepted as evidence that poor achievement causes poor behavior, poor behavior causes poor achievement, good achievement causes good behavior, and/or good behavior causes good achievement. For even if these conclusions are correct, the direction for change points to improved instruction of a global rather than particular nature. Achievement and behavior are related; more importantly, what happens in achievement happens again in achievement, and what happens in behavior happens again in behavior. This truth is prescriptive if accepted as evidence that poor achievement and poor behavior are consequences of incomplete, inadequate, or ineffective instruction. Again, the direction for change points to improved teaching of a global and preventive rather than particular and prescriptive nature.

We know that large numbers of children fail to profit from the educational menu of experiences provided in schools. We know that systematic academic instruction and support improve achievement. We know that systematic behavior instruction and support improve behavior. We know that establishing reading and behavior skills *early* is predictive of later success in school. The trick at the school level is to determine if it is happening for all areas of academic achievement and social behavior and, if not, ensuring that it does. The trick at the level of the child who is evading this level of intensive attention to improve achievement in academics and behavior is to identify the antecedents and consequences of failure and manipulate changes that will enable the child to benefit from the high-quality instruction. Empirical evidence indicates that doing less leads to academic failure. The encouraging message from recent scholarship, however, is that effective tools for combining behavioral and academic supports are now available to prevent and ameliorate academic failure and problem behavior.

The road ahead is clear.

- Provide high-quality academic and behavior instruction for all children and regularly verify that it is happening with fidelity. The best medicine in the world will not produce desired effects if the patient does not take it. The best tools in the world do not help if nobody uses them properly. Evidence exists that implementing universal, schoolwide academic and behavior support systems reduces behavior and academic challenges, but more research is needed to convince educators to engage actively and relentlessly in evidence-based prevention.
- Provide focused and direct instruction in natural classrooms and groups, verify fidelity of implementation, and continuously monitor progress when frequent and direct measurements suggest that academic and social problems exist. The promise of prevention practice and Response-to-Intervention as salvation for the rising numbers of children requiring special education and the failure of prior practices to solve the problem is grounded in the belief that this can and will happen and make a difference. However, research is needed to convince educators that the dream is a reality and the promise is an effective practice.
- Continuously monitor progress and make appropriate adaptations as needed. Effective teaching is iterative, with every behavior of a learner serving as a basis for supportive or corrective subsequent action.

The road is clear, even though the page of history documenting the effects of taking it remains unwritten. In the end, the value of what has been shown about the relationship between achievement and behavior is prescriptive: We need to know the effects of implementing high-quality instruction on achievement *and* behavior, and continuing to do one without the other is moving in the wrong direction.

REFERENCES

McIntosh, K. (2005a). *Academic, behavioral, and functional predictors of chronic problem behavior in elementary grades.* Unpublished doctoral dissertation, University of Oregon, Eugene.

McIntosh, K. (2005b). *Academic, behavioral, and functional predictors of chronic problem behavior in elementary grades* (Research brief). Eugene, OR: Research Center on School-Wide Positive Behavior Support.

McIntosh, K., Chard, D. J., Boland, J. B., & Horner, R. H. (2006). Demonstration of combined efforts in school-wide academic and behavioral systems and incidence of reading and behavior challenges in early elementary grades. *Journal of Positive Behavior Interventions, 8,* 146–154.

Rescorla, L. A., Achenbach, T. M., Ginzburg, S., Ivanova, M. Y., Dumenci, L., Almqvist, F., et al. (2007). Consistency of teacher-reported problems for students in 21 countries. *School Psychology Review, 36,* 91–110.

Rescorla, L. A., Achenbach, T. M., Ivanova, M. Y., Dumenci, L., Almqvist, F., Bilenberg, N., et al. (2007a). Behavior and emotional problems reported by parents of children ages 6 to 16 in 31 societies. *Journal of Emotional and Behavioral Disorders, 15,* 130–142.

Rescorla, L. A., Achenbach, T. M., Ivanova, M. Y., Dumenci, L., Almqvist, F., Bilenberg, N., et al. (2007b). Epidemiological comparisons of problems and positive qualities reported by adolescents in 24 countries. *Journal of Consulting and Clinical Psychology, 75,* 351–358.

Rutter, M., Tizard, J., & Whitmore, K. (Eds.). (1970). *Education, health, and behaviour.* London: Longmans.

Index

Accommodation, 116, 188
Accountability:
  continuous evaluation and, 202
  high-stakes testing and, 14
  outcomes-based assessment and, 197
  problem-solving approach and, 21
  See also Assessment procedures; Prevention
    program evaluation; Progress monitoring
Action plans:
  annual action-planning documents, 204
  behavioral remediation and, 189
  Schoolwide Positive Behavior Support and, 42–43
  teacher observation and, 136–137
Administrative commitment:
  conflict resolution education programs and,
    117–118, 122
  prevention programs and, 5
  professional development needs assessment and, 7
Adolescents:
  maturation effects and, 177, 209
  peer conflict and, 116
  See also Child development; Youth violence
Aggressive behaviors:
  behavioral excesses and deficits and, 72
  cognitive-behavioral approaches and, 56
  multicomponent interventions and, 96–99, 97 (figure)
  physical aggression, 213
  RECESS program and, 89–90
  school violence/infractions and, 33–34, 218
  Second Step curriculum and, 76
  self-management/self-regulation strategies and,
    90–93, 91–92 (figures)
  See also Antisocial behaviors; Problem behaviors
Anger management training, 5, 40, 54, 117
  cognitive-behavioral approaches and, 56
  problem-solving steps and, 59–65
  Second Step curriculum and, 76
Antisocial behaviors, 71, 72
  deviancy training and, 100
  high status positions and, 72
  multicomponent interventions and, 96–99, 97 (figure)
  prosocial behavior, resources for, 110–111
  Second Step curriculum and, 76
  self-management/self-regulation strategies and,
    90–93, 91–92 (figures)
  See also Behavioral improvement; Conflict
    resolution education (CRE) programs; School
    violence prevention; Youth violence
Applied behaviorism, 169
Assessment procedures:
  benchmark assessments, 6, 7–8
  curriculum-based/norm-referenced tests, 197
  direct behavior ratings, 197
  End-of-Grade assessments, 46, 204
  formative and summative assessment, 197

functional assessment/analysis, 10, 145
functional behavior assessment, 41, 205
self-assessment, 177
social skills and, 81–83
Tier III intervention, selection of, 7
universal screening, 7
  See also Prevention program evaluation; Response
    to Intervention (RTI)
ASSIST program, 75–76, 77
At-risk students:
  early prevention efforts and, 169–170, 170 (figure)
  preventive interventions for, 5
  targeted group support and, 40
Aversive interventions, 35

Behavior contracts, 139
Behavior Education Program (BEP), 139, 141, 144
Behavior intervention plans (BIPs), 144–145, 147,
  147–148 (table), 150, 151 (figure)
Behavior and Reading Improvement Center (BRIC), 196
Behavior-academic achievement link, 8–10, 223–225
Behavioral disorders (BD):
  distress symptoms and, 177
  early warning signs and, 217–219
  parent perspective on, 19
  prevention strategies for, 214–216
  social skills training for, 81–82, 87–88
  See also Emotional and Behavioral disorders (EBD);
    Emotional disorders; Inappropriate
    behaviors; Parent-teacher partnerships;
    Problem behaviors; School connections
Behavioral entrapment, 74, 84, 86, 93, 95
Behavioral improvement:
  academic performance and, 8–10, 223–225
  contemporary management interventions and, 4
  effective schoolwide efforts and, 219–220
  functional assessment/analysis and, 10, 145
  resources for, 110–111
  rules/compliance, teaching of:
  systematic behavior instruction/support and, 9, 225
  See also Conflict resolution education (CRE)
    programs; Preschool behavior support;
    Prevention programs; Reinforcement systems;
    Schoolwide Positive Behavior Support
    (SWPBS) systems
Best practices:
  competence of school professionals, 161–162
  evidence-based education practices, 13
  multiple levels of intervention services, 5
  prevention science and, 4, 5
  Response to Intervention and, 7–8
Booster lessons, 65, 66 (figure)
Building Self-Esteem curriculum, 76
Bully-Proofing Your School, 76
Bullying behaviors, 76, 89, 113, 114, 120, 121, 218

Bullying Prevention Coordinating Committee, 121
Bullying prevention programs, 115–116
  adult supervision/monitoring and, 121
  bullying, definition of, 120
  comprehensive violence prevention programming
    and, 126
  Olweus Bullying Prevention Program, 121, 128
  schoolwide context of, 121–122
  Steps to Respect program, 129
  sustained implementation, elements in, 122–129
  See also Conflict resolution education (CRE) programs

CHAMPS system, 135
Changing criterion designs, 206
Check & Connect model, 98–99, 139
  progress monitoring and, 139
  See also Prevention program evaluation
Chicago Longitudinal Study (CLS), 169
Child Behavior Checklist, 98, 175
Child development:
  accommodation, challenge/support and, 116
  inappropriate behaviors, developmental processes
    and, 14–16, 17–18 (table)
  maturation effects and, 177, 209
  social competence skills and, 72–74, 73 (table)
  social-emotional competence and, 15, 16, 28
  supportive emotional experiences and, 16
  See also HighScope Perry Preschool Project;
    Preschool behavior support
Child Parent Centers, 169
Child/family services, 155, 167–169
CIPP evaluation model, 202
Classroom environment, 7, 9, 10
  Schoolwide Positive Behavior Support and, 36
  self-regulatory behaviors and, 16
  supportive/nurturing preschool classrooms, 20, 24, 26
  See also Classroom interventions; Classroom
    management; Culturally responsive teaching
Classroom interventions, 133–134
  CHAMPS system and, 135
  effective classroom management/organization and,
    134–136, 135–136 (table)
  Response to Intervention and, 134
  teacher observation, action planning and, 136–137
  See also Behavioral improvement; Bullying
    prevention programs; Conflict resolution
    education (CRE) programs; Peer mediation;
    Response to Intervention (RTI); Social skills
    instruction; Tier II interventions
Classroom management:
  behavioral expectations and, 37
  contemporary practices in, 4
  culturally responsive classroom management, 188–189
  effective management/organization, 134–136,
    135–136 (table)